Paddling
Northern California

A Guide to the Region's Greatest Paddling Adventures

Third Edition

Charlie Pike

T0352066

FALCONGUIDES

GUILFORD, CONNECTICUT

FALCONGUIDES®

An imprint of The Rowman & Littlefield Publishing Group, Inc.
4501 Forbes Blvd., Ste. 200
Lanham, MD 20706
www.rowman.com
Falcon and FalconGuides are registered trademarks and Make Adventure Your Story is a trademark of The Rowman & Littlefield Publishing Group, Inc.

Distributed by NATIONAL BOOK NETWORK

Copyright © 2019 The Rowman & Littlefield Publishing Group, Inc.

Photos by author unless otherwise noted
Maps by The Rowman & Littlefield Publishing Group, Inc.

All rights reserved. No part of this book may be reproduced in any form or by any electronic or mechanical means, including information storage and retrieval systems, without written permission from the publisher, except by a reviewer who may quote passages in a review.

British Library Cataloguing in Publication Information available

Library of Congress Cataloging-in-Publication Data

Names: Pike, Charles W., author.
Title: Paddling Northern California : a guide to the region's greatest paddling adventures / Charlie Pike.
Description: Third Edition. | Guilford, Connecticut : FalconGuides, [2019] | "Distributed by NATIONAL BOOK NETWORK"—T.p. verso. | Includes bibliographical references and index. |
Identifiers: LCCN 2019003694 (print) | LCCN 2019009638 (ebook) | ISBN 9781493043590 (e-book) | ISBN 9781493043583 | ISBN 9781493043583 (paperback : alk. paper) | ISBN 9781493043590 (ebook)
Subjects: LCSH: Canoes and canoeing—California, Northern—Guidebooks. | Kayaking—California, Northern—Guidebooks. | Sea kayaking—California, Northern—Guidebooks. | Rafting (Sports)—California, Northern—Guidebooks. | Camping—California, Northern—Guidebooks. | California, Northern—Guidebooks.
Classification: LCC GV776.C2 (ebook) | LCC GV776.C2 P55 2019 (print) | DDC 797.12209794—dc23
LC record available at https://lccn.loc.gov/2019003694

∞™ The paper used in this publication meets the minimum requirements of American National Standard for Information Sciences—Permanence of Paper for Printed Library Materials, ANSI/NISO Z39.48-1992.

The author and The Rowman & Littlefield Publishing Group, Inc. assume no liability for accidents happening to, or injuries sustained by, readers who engage in the activities described in this book.

Contents

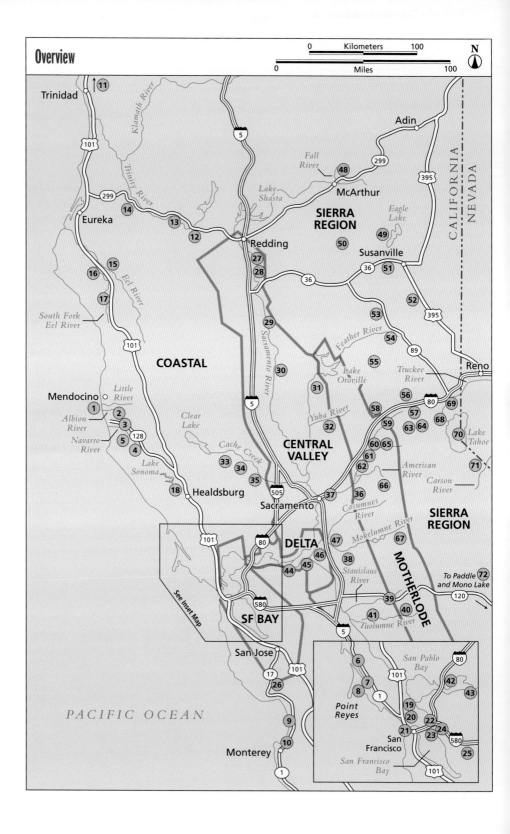

Preface

Many changes have occurred since *Paddling Northern California* was first published in 2001. Eight printings later, the third edition provides an update to describe many of the finest rivers, lakes, estuaries, and coastal waters of Northern California.

Many individual paddlers, outfitting shops, paddling clubs, and resource management agencies have contributed updated information for this edition.

This printed edition of *Paddling Northern California* provides information and resources seldom found on internet sites. In *Paddling Northern California* you can find:

- Detailed descriptions to water access;

- Desirable flow ranges for rivers;

- Contact information for land management agencies and information sources;

- Appropriate tide references and stream flow gauges;

- Best seasons to enjoy the waterways;

- Level of paddling difficulty;

- Sources for detailed maps; and

- Suitability of various watercraft.

This edition addresses a variety of changes. Of course there are physical changes of access points, structures, and lands along the waterways. Hydropower project relicensing affects the quantity and timing of stream flows. Land management changes public access. Invasive species now threaten inland waters. Technology changes help us, such as Dreamflow.com, with near-real-time flow information, Google Earth's satellite images, Global Positioning System (GPS) coordinates, and internet sources. The paddling public continues to evolve. Stand-up paddleboards are now popular on waterways both smooth and turbulent. Many folks use sit-on-tops for fishing—and because they are easy to board.

The criteria for including waterways in *Paddling Northern California* continue to be:

- Places of exceptional beauty

- Tours suggested by the paddling community

- Wild and scenic rivers, described in twelve chapters

- Waterways where attractive environmental improvements are being made

- Minimal conflict from large, fast motorboats. (San Francisco Bay and Lake Tahoe are exceptions because they are too outstanding to ignore.)

This third edition has substantial improvements:

- Two new chapters have been added to describe the wild and scenic Smith River, in California's northwesternmost county, and Delta Meadows, adjacent to the historic town of Locke between Lodi and Sacramento.

- Thirty-three miles of waterways have been added, for a total 902 miles of California paddling enjoyment. These waterways flow through thirty-one California counties ranging from the Oregon border to east of Yosemite.

- The chapters have been rearranged into six regions relating to different geographical and paddling environments.

- New color images enhance the look of the new edition.

- GPS coordinates are provided for access locations and other important sites.

- Maps have been revised using on-site inspections, National Geographic TOPO, Google Earth, and National Oceanic and Atmospheric Association (NOAA) navigational charts.

- Appendixes have been updated to help the reader find information about weather, sea conditions, flow gauges, places, land management agencies, and paddling organizations.

Hopefully my efforts to update this Falcon Guide have produced an attractive, valuable, and long-lasting reference that can be enjoyed by the public and guide paddlers as well as promote environmental awareness and be an information source for professional resource managers.

Happy Paddling!
Charlie Pike

Acknowledgments

Many people helped make every edition of this book possible. In addition to those who helped me create the earlier editions, many others have contributed more recently. Obviously paddling partners and members of canoeing and kayaking clubs deserve thanks for sharing their experiences. Retailers and outfitters provided guidance on equipment and support of the paddling community. Resource managers of national forests and parks, state parks, the Bureau of Land Management (BLM), and local and county facilities deserve recognition and appreciation for making their resources available to the public and providing information about specific waterways. Local, state, and national environmental organizations deserve our appreciation and support for the work they do to maintain the quality and availability of our experience on the water. To all of these I extend my sincere thanks. At the risk of omitting names (my apologies), they include:

Barbara Bitner; Bay Area Sea Kayakers; Bryant Burkhardt; Carol Kreuger; Steven Krystek of the Mono Basin Scenic Area Visitor Center; Cass Schrock and staff of Monterey Bay Kayaks; paddling partners Charles Ferris, Deb Gesler, and Jeanette Turvill; Dan Arbuckle of Headwaters Kayak Shop & Boathouse; Dan Efseaff; Davide Sartoni of Gold Country Paddlers; Elin Ljung, Geoffrey McQuilkin, Arya Degenhardt, and Rose Catron of the Mono Lake Committee; Eric See of the California Department of Water Resources; Erica Brenzovich of the Plumas National Forest; Gena Bentall of Sea Otter Savvy; Guy Hedges of the Sierra Outdoor Center; Jan Dooley of Six Rivers Canoe Club; Jackie House, Jeff and Terri Bedford of Sacramento Sea Kayakers; Jennifer Santos of Yolo County; Kathy Bunton of Delta Kayak Adventures; Keith Miller of California Canoe and Kayak; Kelsey Machen of USACE Lake Sonoma; Lawrence Ames and Pardee Bardwell of the BLM Ukiah Field Office; Lisa Herron of Lake Tahoe Basin Management Unit, USDA Forest Service; Marc Musgrove and Ed Rosenboom of Loma Prieta Paddlers; Nathan Houx of the City of Modesto; Pat Graham of the California Department of Fish and Wildlife in Suisun City; Meg Gonzalez and Patrick Koepele of the Tuolumne River Trust; Patrick Maloney and Jason Carkeel of Turlock Irrigation District; Paul Gilker of "Tidelog"; Paul Redd; Penny Wells of Bay Area Sea Kayakers (BASK); POST Canoe Club, including Kit Hewitt and Don Jarrell; Rick Doty shuttle service; Robin Schrock of the Trinity River Restoration Program; Sacramento Sea Kayakers; Sam Brown; Toby Wells of the City of Ceres; Todd Ehret of NOAA's Center for Operational Oceanographic Products and Services; and Tom Hoffman of the Heritage Oak Winery.

We miss the *Paddlers News Bulletin* editors and contributors, who provided trip reports for so many years identifying changes in river access and stream conditions.

Thanks to the folks at Globe Pequot who organized the material and made it publishable.

My wife, AJ, looks forward to the completed book. Special thanks and love to her for her bountiful support.

Beautiful Caspar Cove on the Mendocino Coast

A great blue heron looks over the Trinity National Wild and Scenic River.

Introduction

Lay of the Land

California is a large place of diverse climates and landforms. The 902 miles of waterways described in this guide are scattered over thirty-one counties that cover 53,400 square miles. To relate the waterways with the landforms and climates, the waterway descriptions are divided into six regions: Coastal, Coastal Mountains, San Francisco Bay Area, Central Valley, Sacramento–San Joaquin Delta, and Sierra.

Coastal Region

The Coastal Region refers to the immediate coast along the Pacific Ocean. The water temperatures stay 55°F to 60°F year-round. Winter weather ranges from mild temperatures with light winds to stormy periods with heavy wind and rain for days at a time. Snow and subfreezing temperatures are rare. Summer weather is typically cool (60s) with foggy mornings and northwesterly winds building in the afternoon. Summer rains are rare. To escape summer fog, go a few miles inland, where the sun is often shining. In general, spring and autumn weather is best for paddling along the coast.

Coastal Mountains

The rugged Coastal Mountains of northwestern California separates the Pacific Ocean from the Central Valley. Formed by the collision of the North American and Pacific Plates, the Coast Range enfolds the San Andreas Fault, which can easily be seen at waterways such as Tomales Bay. Coastal mountains collect heavy winter rainfall that swells the rivers into flood stage. Snow covers the higher areas for most of the winter and spring. Summer weather is comfortable, with warm sunny days and cool evenings. Summer rain is infrequent, and the flows in most of the undammed rivers quickly dwindle to non-paddling levels.

San Francisco Bay Area

San Francisco Bay surges with the rhythm of both tides and California's major rivers. Before Europeans arrived, the 50-mile-long bay mixed river water from the Central Valley with the Pacific Ocean to form one of the nation's most productive estuaries. San Francisco Bay offers great paddling. Protected from Pacific Ocean swells, the bay has great scenery with hundreds of miles of waterways to enjoy. The nearby reservoirs are great places to learn and practice paddling. The weather is moderate year-round, with summer winds and morning fog blowing through the Golden Gate. The same winds that delight sailors and windsurfers will challenge sea kayakers. You must plan for it. As a complement to this guide, the San Francisco Bay Area Water Trail (sfbay watertrail.org) helps you plan your adventures by identifying scores of access points for varieties of watercraft.

Central Valley

The Central Valley is flat. It was once a shallow sea, more than 400 miles long and about 50 miles wide, bounded by the Coast Range on the west and the Sierra Nevada on the east. Most rivers draining from the Sierra Nevada and Coast Ranges flow onto the Central Valley floor to join with the Sacramento River north of the Delta or the San Joaquin River south of the Delta. Dams and reservoirs affect flows on most Central Valley rivers. Reservoir releases sustain summer flows. Winter floods may raise Central Valley rivers to unsafe levels for weeks at a time.

Central Valley winter weather is cool and often foggy or rainy. Summer days become hot, with temperatures frequently exceeding 90°F. In the northern Sacramento Valley, 100-degree days are frequent. Summer evening temperatures often remain above 80°F near Red Bluff and Redding. Closer to the Delta, temperatures are moderated by ocean breezes and marine fog.

The Delta

The Sacramento–San Joaquin Delta is a 1,100-square-mile funnel capturing all the rivers flowing from the Central Valley through a vast marshland and a gap in the Coast Range to reach the San Francisco Bay and the Pacific Ocean. The 700 miles of Delta waterways are at sea level, subject to tidal variations.

Delta weather is a product of cool Pacific air flowing through the flat Delta lands into the Central Valley. Winter days, with the exception of storms or fog, are often mild with light breezes. Summer heat in the Central Valley sucks cool air through the Delta, producing strong winds and cool temperatures.

Prior to the Europeans' arrival, fresh and salt water mixed in the Delta to support one of North America's most environmentally productive estuaries. Beginning with the California gold rush and continuing into the twenty-first century, dramatic changes occurred in the Delta that continue to be the center of economic, environmental, and political controversy. Thirteen hundred miles of levees were built to convert the rich organic marsh soils into farmland. Levees confined waterways to narrow channels. Annual floods were reduced. Huge pumps pulled precious water from rivers for distribution to farms and at least half of California's population. The resulting environmental effects include loss of habitat for migratory birds from Alaska, Canada, and Siberia; dramatic decline in anadromous fisheries; and invasive flora and fauna that disrupt food production chains for native species.

Massive state and federal efforts attempt to restore the damaged ecosystems while continuing to export water to thirsty regions of California. The results will likely evolve for a long time to come.

Sierra Region

Nearer the California-Oregon border, the rugged Klamath Mountains are the meeting place of the Coast Range, Cascade Range, and the Sierra Nevada. Mount Shasta and Lassen Peak are the most distinctive Cascade volcanic cones in California. Until the 1980 eruption of Mount St. Helens in Washington, Mount Lassen was the most recently active volcano in the continental United States. The Modoc Plateau in northeastern California is a broad area of lava flows and small volcanic cones extending into eastern Oregon and Washington. In winter these northern mountains experience a cold continental climate with ample snow and subfreezing temperatures. Summer weather moderates, with warm days and cool nights.

The Sierra Nevada is a fault-block mountain range whose eastern slopes are steep and dry, while deep, river-cut canyons incise the western slopes. Winter snows normally pile 15 to 20 feet deep, making Sierra lakes and rivers inaccessible. Spring snowmelt swells the canyon and foothill rivers with some of the state's best clear, cold whitewater. Since Sierra rivers are mostly dam controlled, boatable releases persist through summer and sometimes into autumn.

Sierra summer weather is delightful. Daytime temperatures are often in the 70s, and skies are usually clear except for some late-summer thunderstorms. At the lower-elevation foothills, known as the "Mother Lode," temperatures climb to 90°F and higher. Most of the rivers flow to the west, and paddlers usually encounter westerly afternoon winds.

Scales of Paddling Difficulty

Paddling difficulty is based on two scales. The International Scale of River Difficulty applies to rivers. The Sea Conditions Rating System applies to marine waters and large lakes. The scales run from Class I to Class VI—the higher the class number, the greater the difficulty. Generally, rapids get more difficult as flow levels increase. Sea conditions and large lakes grow more difficult with high winds, large surf, distance from shore, and rocky shorelines. Boating along any waterway becomes more hazardous in cold water. Calm waterways with little difficulty are referred to as "flatwater."

INTERNATIONAL SCALE OF RIVER DIFFICULTY

(Updated in 1998 by the American Whitewater Affiliation. Reprinted with permission by American Whitewater, americanwhitewater.org.)

Class I: Easy. Fast-moving water with riffles and small waves. Few obstructions, all obvious and easily missed with little training. Risk to swimmers is slight; self-rescue is easy.

Class II: Novice. Straightforward rapids with wide, clear channels that are evident without scouting. Occasional maneuvering may be required, but rocks and medium-size waves are easily missed by trained paddlers. Swimmers are seldom injured, and group assistance, while helpful, is seldom needed. Rapids at the upper end of this difficulty range are designated "Class II+."

Class III: Intermediate. Rapids with moderate, irregular waves that may be difficult to avoid and can swamp an open canoe. Complex maneuvers in fast current and good boat control in tight passages or around ledges are often required. Large waves or strainers may be present but are easily avoided. Strong eddies and powerful current effects can be found, particularly on large-volume rivers. Scouting is advisable for inexperienced parties. Injuries while swimming are rare; self-rescue is usually easy, but group assistance may be required to avoid long swims. Rapids at the lower or upper end of this difficulty range are designated "Class III-" or "Class III+," respectively.

Class IV: Advanced. Intense, powerful-but-predictable rapids requiring precise boat handling in turbulent water. Depending on the character of the river, it may feature large, unavoidable waves and holes or constricted passages demanding fast maneuvers under pressure. A fast, reliable eddy turn may be needed to initiate maneuvers, scout rapids, or rest. Rapids may require "must" moves above dangerous hazards. Scouting may be necessary the first time down. Risk of injury to swimmers is moderate to high, and water conditions may make self-rescue difficult. Group assistance for rescue is often essential but requires practiced skills. A strong Eskimo roll is highly recommended. Rapids at the lower or upper end of this difficulty range are designated "Class IV-" or "Class IV+," respectively.

Note: Only three runs described in this guide have this level of difficulty.

Class V: Expert. Extremely long, obstructed, or very violent rapids that expose a paddler to added risk. Drops may contain large, unavoidable waves and holes or steep, congested chutes with complex, demanding routes. Rapids may continue for long distances between pools, demanding a high level of fitness. What eddies exist may be small, turbulent, or difficult to reach. At the high end of the scale, several of these factors may be combined. Scouting is recommended but may be difficult. Swims are dangerous, and rescue is often difficult even for experts. A very reliable Eskimo roll, proper equipment, extensive experience, and practiced rescue skills are essential. Because of the large range of difficulty that exists beyond Class IV, Class V is an open-ended, multiple-level scale designated by Class 5.0, 5.1, 5.2, etc. Each of these levels is an order of magnitude more difficult than the last. Example: Increasing difficulty from Class 5.0 to Class 5.1 is a similar order of magnitude as increasing from Class IV to Class 5.0.

Note: No streams of this difficulty are included in this guide.

Class VI: Extreme and Exploratory. These runs have almost never been attempted and often exemplify the extremes of difficulty, unpredictability, and danger. The consequences of errors are very severe, and rescue may be impossible. For teams of experts only, at favorable water levels, after close personal inspection and taking all precautions. After a Class VI rapid has been run many times, its rating may be changed to an appropriate Class 5.x rating.

Note: No streams of this difficulty are included in this guide.

Sea Conditions Rating System (SCRS)

Conceptually similar to the American Whitewater Affiliation's International Scale of River Difficulty, the Sea Conditions Rating System was developed by Eric Soares and Michael Powers of the Tsunami Rangers to gauge the hazards of coastal paddling. This guidebook uses SCRS to indicate the difficulty class of coastal waterways and large lakes. (Originally published in *Extreme Sea Kayaking* by Eric Soares and Michael Powers, 1999. Reprinted with permission.)

Factor	Computation Method	Maximum Points	Score
1–Water Temperature	1 point for each degree below 72°F	40	_____
2–Wind Speed	1 point per mph of wind speed	50+	_____
3–Wave Height	2 points per vertical wave foot	40+	_____
4–Swim Distance	1 point per 100 meters	20	_____
5–Breaking Waves	30 points if waves are breaking	30	_____
6–Rock Garden	20 points if rocks are present	20	_____
7–Sea Cave	20 points if entering sea caves	20	_____
8–Night	20 points if it is night	20	_____
9–Fog	Up to 20 points if fog is dense	20	_____
10–Miscellaneous	10 points or more for other danger	10+	_____
		TOTAL POINTS =	_____
	Divide total points by 20 to obtain CLASS LEVEL =		_____

Because wind is such an important factor in rating sea conditions for SCRS, the following Beaufort scale is provided to help make wind speed estimates.

Beaufort Force #	Wind Speed mph	Wind Term	Sea Surface Conditions
1	1–3	light air	Slightest ripples
2	4–7	light breeze	Small wavelets, no breaking, wind felt on face
3	8–12	gentle breeze	Large wavelets, crests begin to break, scattered whitecaps
4	13–18	moderate breeze	Small waves 1–4 feet, numerous whitecaps, hinders paddling progress
5	19–24	fresh breeze	Moderate waves 4–8 feet, many whitecaps, some spray, difficult conditions for skilled kayakers only
6	25–31	strong breeze	Larger waves 8–13 feet, whitecaps everywhere, more spray, small craft advisories, paddlers should be on shore
7	32–38	moderate gale	Waves 13–19 feet, white foam from breaking waves begins to be blown in streaks

Scoring Directions

Assess the conditions using instruments or conservative estimates, and rate each of the ten factors. Add up the scores and divide the sum by 20.

Score	Class	Skill Level
Up to 1.9	Class I	Easy to moderate difficulty, danger, and skills required.
2.0 to 2.9	Class II	Intermediate difficulty, danger, and skills required.
3.0 to 3.9	Class III	Advanced difficulty, danger, and skills required (e.g., a reliable roll and self-rescue a must).
4.0 to 4.9	Class IV	Extreme conditions, advanced techniques are required, loss of life possible in a mishap.
5.0 to 5.9	Class V	Very extreme, life-threatening conditions suitable only for a team of experts.
6.0+	Class VI	Nearly impossible conditions, loss of life probable in a mishap.

Skill Level

Related directly to the American Whitewater Affiliation and SCRS scales of paddling difficulty, skill levels are based largely on difficulty and perceived hazard. Add an extra level of difficulty if the waterway is remote or the weather or water temperature is extremely cold. The different levels of paddling skill are an approximation, based on the following parameters:

Beginner: Knows the basic strokes and can handle craft competently in smooth water. Knows how to bring a boat to shore safely in fast current, can negotiate sharp turns in fast current, can avoid strainers and other obstacles, and understands the difficulties of the stream to be floated. A beginner is not a person who is picking up a paddle for the first time. Those folks should get some practice on a lake or with an experienced paddler before taking their first trip. Streams with many obstacles or streams used for teaching whitewater skills are noted "beginners with whitewater experience."

Intermediate: Knows basic strokes and uses them effectively. Can read water well, can negotiate fairly difficult rapids with confidence, and knows how to safely catch an eddy. Won't panic, and knows what to do in the event of an upset. Can come to shore quickly to inspect dangerous spots and knows when to portage. The tandem paddler knows how to coordinate strokes between bow and stern and can paddle at either end.

Expert: Has mastered all strokes and uses them instinctively. Confident of ability, even in very difficult situations. Skillful in heavy water or complex rapids. Knows when a rapid is not runnable and has a deep respect for all safety precautions.

Planning Your Trip

Deciding where you want to go and when you want to be there depends a lot on what you would like to do. If your trip involves staying at or accessing waterways at

California state parks, call the park before you go. State park budget problems have caused changeable operating schedules.

Maps and Navigation

Maps are basic tools to help you decide where to paddle; how to get there, find the put-in and takeout, locate the desired campsites or hazards, and estimate how long the route will take to paddle; and help you locate your position when on the water. A second tool is a compass to show direction. The third tool is a clock to help determine time on the water and distance traveled. GPS devices and smartphone apps have combined the tools of map, compass, and timepiece where reception is available.

Many of the trips described in this guide can be completed in a day or less. So if you can find the put-in and takeout, why bring a navigation device?

If you are paddling a river, you can follow the channel—right? Consider some friends who put in late on a difficult unfamiliar whitewater run. Darkness fell while they were still on the water. Wisely, they beached their boats. Not knowing their location, they hiked up the 1,000-foot canyon and eventually found roads and a traveler who gave them a ride to friends waiting at the takeout—at 4 a.m. The friends had already notified the sheriff's office that a rescue might be needed for injured or lost companions. Oh, how maps and cell phones would have helped that situation!

Another situation, on flatwater with winding sloughs, such as the Delta: Landmarks are few, and there are no road signs. You need a map and compass on your deck to track your progress. If you become separated from the group, how do you get to the takeout?

Good planning can make your trip a little easier, such as bringing "wheelies" to transport your gear to the water.

A kayak compass is a basic tool showing in what direction your boat is heading.

Another summer day you explore beautiful Drakes Estero. Fog moves in as a thick wet blanket, and only the water under your boat is visible. The estero has several long fingers and lots of mudflats. Time for some navigation aids!

Yes, GPS devices can really help. So can smartphones if you've loaded the appropriate maps and apps and know how to use them. Both devices need charged batteries, and the electronics need protection from water.

Compasses have two forms: (1) the type used on land, which locates magnetic north and then you determine your direction; and (2) the type commonly mounted on sea kayaks that shows which way the boat is pointed (which is why I like the one I can mount on my deck).

Both compass types point to magnetic north—for Northern California, currently magnetic north is approximately14 degrees east of true north.

Three types of maps are easy to obtain: satellite images, navigation charts, and topographical (topo) maps. They provide different kinds of information.

Satellite images (e.g., Google Earth) are a wonderful tool as long as the user is aware of the constraints. The best resolution can show a large beach towel, a kayak, or an automobile at some instant in time. Images of the United States are frequently less than a year old. In a well-lit unshaded canyon, whitewater shows up clearly, but the rocks and logs that cause the turbulence may be a mystery. Some images have clouds or poor lighting obscuring the place of interest. Elevation is shown one point at a time. Water depth is unknown. Where available, "street views" may offer confirming information. Historical images may reveal features not shown in the current image; examples: high or low tides over mudflats, wave patterns produced by prevailing winds, or rivers in dry and flood stages.

Topographic maps are useful for inland rivers and lakes. Topo maps identify land features, elevation, rivers, and some man-made objects, such as roads, bridges, railroads, and structures. For many years the USGS was the major developer of topographic maps. Although many topos have not been updated in a decade or more, they still show much useful data for the backcountry. Formerly available at sporting goods shops, they are now published in electronic format on CDs or downloadable from the internet. The user is responsible for printing hard copy or transferring waypoints to a GPS device.

NOAA navigation charts provide a wealth of information for folks paddling marine waterways, such as the Delta, San Francisco Bay, or Tomales Bay. The "Rules of the Road" state that as master of your vessel, you are responsible for being knowledgeable of the chart for your location. The charts are produced and distributed by NOAA's Office of Coast Survey. These charts are legally required for navigation by commercial vessels and include lots of frequently updated information, such as water depth at low tide, buoy locations, navigation channels, wrecks, rocks, other obstacles, channels, sloughs, bays, estuaries, islands, and coastal landforms useful to watercraft. NOAA makes available "BookletCharts" for small boats. These up-to-date charts are free, are reduced scale, have complete information, and can be printed at home on 8.5 × 11-inch paper. The charts may be downloaded from charts.noaa.gov/Interactive Catalog/nrnc.shtml#mapTabs-1

If you like to make notes on your maps as you travel, consider tracing the map to Mylar. Mylar doesn't shred when wet, and pencil writes well on it.

For more detailed guidance about navigation, David Burch's book *Fundamentals of Kayak Navigation* explains a variety of techniques to find your position and plot a course.

For paddling in the San Francisco Bay, consult the BASK Trip Planner online at bask.org/trip_planner/. It offers graphics and tables regarding tides, currents, distances, current weather, put-ins, and destinations. Also look at the San Francisco Bay Area Water Trail (sfbaywatertrail.org) for access locations. The wise paddler utilizes all this information to plan the tour.

Weather, Tides, and Stream Flows

Before you leave on your trip, get up-to-date weather and water level information. Unexpected fog, strong winds, high waves, and tides can dramatically change your ocean paddling experience. Likewise, cold weather, snow, or unexpected flows can ruin a river trip.

Some coastal areas are navigable only at certain tide and current conditions. Some streams are runnable only within a desirable flow range. Real-time and almost-real-time flow data is available online at dreamflows.com. Currents in San Francisco Bay are published with some tide tables. Paddling clubs and retail stores may offer classes in interpreting the tables.

Appendix A lists websites related to marine buoys, marine weather, and stream gauges pertinent to waterways described in this guide.

Historic hydrographs indicate when desirable flows are likely to occur on uncontrolled streams. Flows from many reservoirs are regulated with new water release schedules, such as the Trinity (see appendix A) and the Tuolumne (see chapter 40). Dreamflows.com provides detailed flow charts for the most recent seven-day, thirty-day, and five-year periods using USGS and California Department of Water Resources data. Where appropriate, a picture of a stream's average annual ups and downs, as measured in cubic feet per second (cfs), is included with trip descriptions. Hydrographs show the size of a river (the greater the flow, the larger the stream) and the times when water flows are usually greatest or least. When seeking real-time flows on the internet, use the gauge name shown in the "Flow gauge" heading for a particular site.

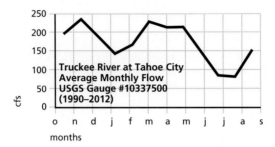

This historic hydrograph shows high water from winter storms, spring snowmelt, followed by summer reservoir releases diminishing in early autumn.

Safety on the Water and Paddling Etiquette

In California, county sheriffs coordinate search and rescue with appropriate land management agencies. If you need help, call 911 and ask for search and rescue. Before your trip, create a paddling plan and share it with others so they know where you are going, when you expect to return, and where to call if you do not return as expected.

"Rules of the Road"

Keep in mind that kayaks and similar small craft are difficult to see from large vessels and are often undetected by radar. Even if a kayak is observed by larger, faster vessels or a tug with a large tow, the larger ships require substantial time to change course. Such course changes may be restricted by designated navigation channels, especially in San Francisco Bay or the Delta. If it sees you, the larger vessel may toot its very loud horn.

For navigable waterways, the US Coast Guard publishes "Navigation Rules Online" (navcen.uscg.gov/?pageName=navRulesContent). These rules apply to hand-powered craft as well as large vessels. Basically they require all craft to be attentive, know the rules, and act to avoid collisions. David Burch's book *Fundamentals of Kayak Navigation* explains the rules as they apply to kayaks. Another reference is "Rules of the Road" by Craig Jungers, printed in the February 2009 issue of *Sea Kayaker* magazine.

As master of your vessel, you in the kayak are responsible for knowing the "Rules of the Road." You are responsible for keeping a proper lookout by sight and sound for making a full appraisal of the situation and of the risk of collision. You should know what actions are appropriate for the conditions, including the types of vessels being encountered. Even if your kayak is unlikely to do much damage to another craft in a collision, your actions could be interpreted by people on another vessel so that they take action that might cause damage, and you might face substantial fines if you are not adhering to the "Rules of the Road."

Below are some of the rules (abbreviated) that David Burch points out in his book. (Material on the rules of kayak navigation is adapted from *Fundamentals of Kayak Navigation: Master the Traditional Skills and the Latest Technologies*, fourth edition, by David Burch. The book is part of FalconGuides' "How to Paddle" series.)

- Rule 2b, Responsibility: "All vessels approaching you should take into account the limitation of your vessel."

- Rule 6a, Safe Speed: "All vessels approaching you should travel at a safe speed, meaning slow enough that they maintain full control and could avoid a collision in the prevailing conditions of weather and traffic."

- Rule 7a, Risk of Collision: "All vessels approaching you should continually assess whether there is a risk of collision. If doubt exists they must assume that there is a risk of collision and act accordingly." In actuality, they might give a long blast of the horn as a warning or five short blasts if danger is imminent.

- Rule 8, Action to Avoid Collision: "A vessel approaching you with a risk of collision should maneuver early enough to stay at a 'safe distance' when passing by using whenever possible a prominent course alteration that you can detect, as opposed to a series of small course and speed changes."

- Rule 13a & c, Overtaking: "Any vessel approaching you from behind (from within a cone, 67.5 degrees either side of your centerline) must stay well clear of you as it passes."

- Rule 16, Action by Give-way Vessel: "When a vessel is overtaking you, it should take early and prominent action to keep well clear of you when passing."

- Rule 17, Action by Stand-on Vessel: "When you do have right-of-way (meaning, for kayaks, when you are being passed by another vessel), you should maintain course and speed until the other vessel has passed you."

- Rule 9a, b, d, Narrow Channels: "Whenever it is safe to do so, you should transit narrow channels as close to the right-hand side as possible. . . . You are not allowed to impede vessels that can only navigate safely in certain parts of a channel or approaches to the channel (fairways)."

- Rule 10j, Traffic Lanes: "You must not impede any vessel following a designated traffic lane; this means ships and other large vessels, since small craft, both power and sail, also are discouraged by the Coast Guard from traversing the lanes just as much as kayaks are."

NOAA navigation charts depict the location of navigation channels. An interesting website showing the real-time movements of vessels in San Francisco Bay is boatingsf.com/ships-on-SF-bay/central-san-francisco-bay. Note how fast the ferries and cargo ships move and where the ferries go.

Paddling Safety Code

The American Whitewater Affiliation includes the following in its paddling safety code:

- Be a competent swimmer with the ability to handle yourself underwater.
- Wear a snugly fitting vest-type life preserver.
- Wear a solid, correctly fitted helmet when upsets are likely.
- Do not boat out of control. Be able to stop or reach the shore before reaching danger.
- Whitewater rivers contain many hazards: high water, cold, strainers, broaching, dams, weirs, ledges, reversals, holes, and hydraulics. These hazards may change.
- Boating alone is discouraged. The recommended minimum party is three people or two craft.
- Have a frank knowledge of your boating ability, and don't attempt rivers or rapids that lie beyond that ability. When in doubt, stop and scout. If you are still in doubt? Portage.
- Be practiced in self-rescue.
- Be trained in rescue skills, CPR, and first aid. Carry a first-aid kit. Know how to avoid poison oak and rattlesnakes. Be prepared to deal with these hazards.
- Carry equipment needed for unexpected emergencies, including good footwear for walking out. Approach remote rivers through isolated wilderness with caution, since aid is difficult or impossible to obtain in case of an accident.
- Be prepared for extremes in weather. Know about the dangers of hypothermia and how to deal with it. When air and water temperature add up to 120 degrees or less, hypothermia is a high risk. Wear a wet suit or dry suit for protection from cold water and cold weather.
- Know early signs and symptoms of heat exhaustion and dehydration in hot weather. Remember that certain medications can complicate these types of environmental injuries.
- Allow the craft ahead of you to pass through the rapid before you enter it. This will avoid a double disaster if the leading boat blocks the channel.

Minimum Impact Camping

(Adapted from Leave No Trace, BLM Minimum Impact Boating and Camping, and the California Department of Boating and Waterways. Reprinted with permission of the Bureau of Land Management—Idaho.)

Plan Ahead and Prepare

Public campgrounds and facilities often have special rules designed to protect both natural resources and the public. Learn about the regulations governing the sites you plan to visit. Summer camping in California is very popular, and you need reservations for developed campgrounds. For most state parks contact ReserveAmerica (ReserveAmerica.com). For forest service campgrounds contact the National Recreation Reservation Service (recreation.gov).

Camp on Durable Surfaces

Minimize your impact and preserve the wild nature of the rivers by using established campsites. Camp on sand or gravel bars to avoid trampling vegetation. Avoid the fragile green riparian areas along the riverbanks. Cooking areas should be set up in as durable a site as possible; sand or rocks are good places. Avoid cutting new trails. Stay on trails that are already established. Locate your shelter so that rainwater will drain away naturally, avoiding the need to dig a ditch around your tent or sleeping bag.

Water

Bring your own drinking water or be ready to boil, filter, and treat all drinking, cooking, and dishwashing water collected from available water sources. As in most of the world, pathogens now infect California's surface waters.

Trash

Pack out what you pack in, including food items such as fruit peels that attract wildlife. Keep trash bags handy in your camp area or watercraft. Never sink cans or bottles in the water. Pack the bags and all materials, including ashes, out with you.

Dishwater

Use biodegradable soap for your dishwashing and bathing needs. Food bits left in camp are a magnet for biting insects. Bring along a strainer or piece of screen to filter bits of food from dishwater. Scatter the strained water into vegetation at least 200 feet away from camp and the river; or dig a hole in the sand above the high-water line, strain your dishwater into it, and cover the hole when you finish. Be sure to bathe well away from the waterway.

Fire

Be careful of extreme fire hazards that develop in summer and autumn. Consider using a fuel stove; they are clean, easy to use, and cause no permanent impacts. Minimize impacts from campfires by using a fire pan elevated off the ground to prevent scorching. Carry a grill so no rocks will be blackened for a fire pit. Use dead and down fuel wood for your fire. If cooking with charcoal, take excess charcoal with you when you leave. Remove and pack out unburned contents of the fire, including ash.

Carry Out Solid Human Waste

At camp, set up your toilet facilities in a location screened from view and at least 100 feet from the water. Use sealable containers large enough to accommodate the entire party for the length of the trip. Pack out all toilet paper and hygiene products. (Massive wildfires have been caused by carelessly burning toilet paper.) If you are unable to transport human waste, dig a hole at least 6 inches deep and 150 feet above the high-water mark for this purpose. Put wastewater from cooking in the same hole, and cover it.

Private Property

Although rivers are public waterways, always respect private property and obey posted No Trespassing signs.

Hot Springs

Natural hot springs often support protected plants and animals. Federal and state laws prohibit digging, damming, or otherwise altering the natural flow or appearance of hot springs.

Archaeological Sites

An archaeological artifact may have been in place for hundreds of years. A rock may have lain in place for millions. Allow others a sense of discovery by leaving plants, rocks, archaeological artifacts, and all other objects of beauty or interest as you find them. Collecting, destroying, or disturbing artifacts and historic objects is prohibited by federal law.

Controlling Invasive Species

Invasive species are organisms (plants, animals, or microbes) from other parts of the world that spread to California through human interaction. Once in our wetlands and waterways, they displace native species, invade the food chain, disrupt the ecological balance of water bodies, and cause drastic economic damage by clogging water intake structures for water supplies and industrial cooling equipment.

There are many invasive species. You can obtain an excellent poster illustrating aquatic invasive species from the California Department of Fish and Wildlife online at nrm.dfg.ca.gov/FileHandler.ashx?DocumentID=78036&inline. Those of greatest concern include quagga and zebra mussels and New Zealand mud snails. The following is excerpted from California Department of Fish and Wildlife publications:

> *Invasive dreissenid mussels, commonly known as quagga and zebra mussels, first became a concern to California in 2007, and in early 2008 zebra mussels were discovered in Northern California. They reproduce quickly and in large numbers. The establishment in California waters could result in environmental and economic disaster.*
>
> *Environmentally, the concern is that they upset the food chain by consuming phytoplankton that other species need to survive. As filter feeders they consume microscopic plants and animals that form the base of the food web. The result could be a shift in native species and a disruption of the ecological balance of entire bodies of water.*

The economic impact in California can be tremendous. The mussels can colonize on hulls, engines, and steering components of boats and other recreation equipment. Their massive colonies can block water intake and threaten municipal water supply, agricultural irrigation and power plant operations. Infestations in the Great Lakes cost the power industry $3 billion in the 1990s.

To control the spread of these mussels, boats of all types are being inspected as they move from one water body to another. Car-top boats such as kayaks and canoes are also inspected. Boaters should check their boat, trailer, and vehicle every time a boat is taken out of the water. The following guidelines are from California Fish and Wildlife to help prevent the spread of quagga and zebra mussels:

- Remove plants, animals, and mud from gear, boat, trailer, and vehicle before you leave the area.

- Clean your gear before entering and leaving the recreation area.

- Drain bilge, ballast, wells, and buckets before you leave the area. Dry equipment before launching into another body of water.

- Dispose of unwanted bait in the trash.

- Wait before launching into different freshwaters. Waiting periods can vary— check with your local water body enforcement agency.

Anglers and boaters should be aware that the New Zealand mud snail has invaded California. It is a very small species that can interrupt freshwater ecosystems, including trout streams. People visiting these habitats should clean their gear carefully. If possible, freeze or completely dry any wet gear.

The Elkhorn Slough Foundation provides the following list of how you can prevent the spread of invasive species:

- Never dump aquarium contents into natural waterways or drainages that feed into them.

- When possible, clean boats and trailers before moving them between different areas (in particular, before bringing a badly fouled boat from a highly invaded area such as San Francisco Bay to a relatively pristine area such as Monterey Bay).

Canoes, kayaks, rafts, and other flotation devices should be cleaned, drained, and dry before moving boats from one water body to another.

- Never bring any plants or animals home from travels abroad.

- Clean hiking boots, camping gear, and muddy car tires before and after excursions.

- When hiking, be careful not to disturb natural terrestrial areas; when diving, take care not to disturb natural aquatic areas.

- Use native or at least noninvasive ornamental plants in landscaping, and encourage nurseries to stop stocking highly invasive nonnative plants.

- Do not attempt to eradicate aquatic invaders yourself (fragmentation of algal species during removal attempts may increase spread).

Wild and Scenic Rivers Protection

In 1969 Congress passed the National Wild and Scenic Rivers Act. The act declared that certain rivers that possess extraordinary scenic, recreational, fishery, or wildlife values shall be preserved in their free-flowing state, together with their immediate environments, for the benefit and enjoyment of the people. The State of California has created its own Wild and Scenic Rivers system. The following rivers described in this guidebook contain segments designated as "Wild and Scenic":

- Albion—California, chapter 3

- American River (Lower)—national and California designation, chapter 37

- American River, North Fork—national and California designation, chapter 59

- Cache Creek—California designation, chapter 33

- Carson River, East Fork—California designation, chapter 71

- Eel River System—national and California designation, chapters 15, 16, and 17

- Feather River, Middle Fork—national designation, chapter 54

- Trinity River System—national and California designation, chapters 12, 13, and 14

- Tuolumne River—national designation upstream of described waterway, chapters 40 and 41

Waterways selected for the National Wild and Scenic Rivers were designated "wild," "scenic," or "recreational." Different reaches of the same river may have different designations.

"Wild" rivers are those rivers or segments of rivers that are free of impoundments (dams) and generally inaccessible except by trail, with watersheds or shorelines essentially primitive and water unpolluted.

"Scenic" rivers are those rivers or segments of rivers that are free of impoundments, with shorelines or watersheds still largely primitive and shorelines largely undeveloped but accessible in places by roads.

"Recreational" rivers are those rivers or segments of rivers that are readily accessible by road or railroad, that may have some development along their shorelines, and that may have undergone some impoundment or diversion in the past.

People who enjoy rivers and would like to continue paddling with future generations should encourage Congress and the state legislature to add more streams to the protected Wild and Scenic Rivers status. Do it soon. There are already more than 1,300 dams in California. Support your local, state, and national conservation groups, such as Friends of the River, Save the American River Association, Tuolumne River Trust, and American Rivers to achieve these goals.

Marine Mammal Protection Act

Ocean and marine estuaries offer close encounters with marine wildlife. In popular paddling areas, such as Point Reyes, Monterey Bay, Mendocino, and Elkhorn Slough, you are probably not the first or last paddler to visit that day. In places where paddling opportunities and wildlife habitat overlap, wildlife may experience many disturbances to their natural behaviors every day. The cumulative effects can be harmful.

In the past, hunting severely reduced the population of many of these species. To protect the remaining populations and restore their numbers, Congress enacted the Marine Mammal Protection Act. The act makes it illegal to kill, hunt, injure, or harass marine mammals. The protected marine animals include dolphins, porpoises, whales, seals, sea lions, sea otters, polar bears, manatees, dugongs, and walruses. Harassment is defined as human activity having the potential to disturb a marine mammal in the wild by causing disruption of behavioral patterns, including but not limited to migration, breathing, nursing, breeding, feeding, or sheltering. An example of harassment is paddling to a group of harbor seals resting onshore and causing them to exhibit nervous alarm postures, such as lifting their heads or sitting up, or causing them to panic and flee into the water. Another form of harassment might be paddling toward the path of a swimming sea otter so that the otter changes course away from you. Continual disruption of these animals depletes their vital energy stores, may cause abandonment of young, and may cause abandonment of important habitat.

The Point Reyes National Seashore advises, "Harbor seals are extremely sensitive to human disturbance. Harbor seals and other pinnipeds need to 'haul out' for several hours every day to rest. Give them a berth of at least 300 feet when the seals are on land and 50 feet in the water. Never handle seal pups found anywhere." Some outfitters recommend staying a minimum of five lengths of your paddle craft from sea lions and sea otters. The National Marine Fisheries Service requires a minimum of 10 yards between whales and boats. Sometimes wildlife will initiate an approach. Do your best to discourage direct encounters, particularly animals climbing onto your kayak. The Elkhorn Slough Foundation recommends that people avoid sudden changes in course and speed. The Bay Area Sea Kayakers (BASK) have posted the following recommended etiquette ("PADDLE") on their website (bask.org/enviro/viewing.html) to help protect seals, birds, whales, and other creatures. "PADDLE" is adapted from "Seals and Sea Kayaks" by Winston Shaw, director, Coastal Maine Bald Eagle Project, published in the spring 1991 edition of *Sea Kayaker* magazine (reprinted with permission).

Pass Afar. *Maintain a distance so that animals do not feel threatened. Where trails and channels permit, stay at least 300 feet away (approximately the length of a football field) from seals, birds, and other wildlife. It is preferable to paddle at high tide in places like Bolinas Lagoon, because birds feed and seals haul out to rest on the mudflats.*

Approach Parallel. *Maintain a parallel course to the animal distribution. This is believed to be less threatening than a direct approach toward the animal. Pass at a constant speed. Do not slow down, speed up, or swing closer to seals or birds.*

Discrete Viewing. *Restrain your impulse to get closer: If you get too close, wildlife will leave. If you cause wildlife to become active to escape your approach, you have caused them to waste vital energy important for their survival. As you pass, do not engage in any "stalking" activity or attempt to approach animals undetected. Resist the temptation to take "selfies" with wildlife! Smartphones are not a good tool for wildlife photography. If you wish to observe wildlife behavior, use binoculars or a camera with a 500mm or longer lens.*

Defer Immediately. *"If they are looking at you, you're too close!" If seals or sea otters begin lifting their heads, or birds begin moving away or flapping their wings, retreat from the area. If seals stretch their necks or chests higher in the air, back off immediately. If seals start to move toward the water or enter the water, immediately leave the area to avoid prolonged stress on the animals. Back-paddle away from wildlife instead of turning your boat around.*

Leave Alone. *Do not handle or attempt to "rescue" seal pups that you believe are abandoned or injured. Mother and pup will usually reunite on their own. If you are concerned about a marine mammal, call the Marine Mammal Center at (415) 289-7325. They will notify the appropriate agency or respond directly.*

Explain Effects. *Tell other paddlers and small boaters how they can help protect wildlife.*

How to Use This Guide

This book describes a variety of the state's finest lakes, streams, and coastal waterways for the beginning and intermediate paddler. Included are waterways known for wonderful scenery, good fishing, calm relaxation, historical importance, practice spots close to home, remote overnight trips, whitewater to thrill and test the skill of experienced boaters, and marine wildlife.

Each trip description highlights the waterway attributes needed to select and plan a trip. *Paddling Northern California* divides longer waterways into several trips based on character, access, and difficulty. For example, the flatwater sections are separated from the whitewater sections on some rivers. Each chapter begins with an "at a glance" section, capsulized bits of information to help determine if the entire waterway description is of interest to you. Different headings are included or excluded for different trips, depending on the nature of the paddling (ocean, lake, or river). The information includes:

Length: One-way distance of the route in miles. For lakes, this category will be **Size** and provide the length and width of the lake and sometimes shoreline and acreage.

Average paddling time: The time it takes to paddle the route at an average pace. Generally it is based on a paddling speed of 2 to 3 mph plus rest breaks. Plan to travel more slowly if your group is large or inexperienced, or if there are difficult rapids to scout or portage, adverse tides, or winds.

Elevation: The elevation (in feet) of the put-in for high-mountain sites.

Difficulty: The general type of skills appropriate for the waterway. For instance, the level of whitewater skills or the ability to perform a self-rescue if capsize occurs on large lakes or ocean waters in rough conditions.

Rapids: If rapids exist, this indicates the whitewater class and relative frequency of rapids.

Marine weather: Radio channels or telephone numbers for marine weather advisories are specific to that location. Offshore buoy locations report sea swell and wave conditions. Fog, wind, building ocean swells, and high surf can dramatically alter the safety of your trip. Check the weather that day before you set out. See appendix A for a list of radio frequencies and websites providing NOAA weather forecasts.

Average gradient: The steepness of the streambed calculated as vertical feet per stream mile.

Tide references: Tides dramatically influence marine waters. This book provides the primary tide table location and corrections for each marine-influenced chapter. For California, high and low tides range from 6 to 7 feet, alternating on cycles that last a little more than 6 hours and change daily. When extreme high tides (flood tides) and extreme low tides (minus tides) follow each other, strong currents are induced in estuaries and channels. To make paddling easier and to avoid getting stuck on

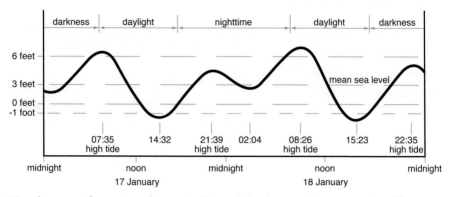

Sample Tide Chart for West Coast

Note the uneven fluctuations of successive tides and the changes with successive days. This particular pattern often occurs when the moon is full or new.

mudflats, plan your trip to go upstream with an incoming tide and return with an outgoing tide. Make wide channel crossings at slack tide (get "current tables") so you don't get swept away. When planning your trip, obtain daily tide tables, readily available from many sport fishing shops, marine boating suppliers, and on the internet.

Annual tide tables predict the times and heights of high and low tide for many primary locations such as San Francisco, Arena Cove, Monterey, and Port Chicago. Tide corrections tell the length of time that high or low tides occur before (-) or after (+) the tide at specific primary locations. Apply the tide corrections to the tide tables.

Optimal flow: "Optimal flow" is an inexact term. This range targets canoes, kayaks, and inflatable kayaks. Large rafts are suited for higher flows. At the very least, optimal flow indicates a level with enough water to float over most obstructions. Anglers may prefer lower flows, when fish are concentrated in pools. On the other hand, exuberant whitewater paddlers may seek higher water levels, when rapids are turbulent and more difficult. The upper limit indicated in these descriptions is the level at which most paddlers consider the river higher than ordinary and requires higher skills than suggested here. Be advised that all rivers are hazardous during high spring runoff and flood stages.

Flow gauge: The stream flow measurement station relevant to the river reach. Appendix A lists the IDs for the stations and also lists websites (e.g., dreamflows.com and waterdata.usgs.gov/ca/nwis/sw) providing recent flow data.

Water source: Indicates whether the stream flow results from rain runoff or snowmelt or is controlled by reservoirs.

Best season: Time of year when favorable conditions exist to make the trip. On some streams, rainfall or snowmelt dictates favorable conditions. On other waterways, wind, temperature, or fog may be a greater influence.

Land status: Indicates the general land ownership along the banks as private (no trespassing) or public, such as parks, national forests, or BLM lands.

Fees: Indicates if money is required to access the waterway.

Maps: Lists detailed maps depicting the waterway. These may include USGS topographic maps, national forest maps, NOAA navigation charts, or local maps. Appendix A provides contact information for these sources. Map illustrations in this book are designed for trip planning to give you a general idea of the water route; they are not meant to be navigational aids. They show only a few of the rapids or navigational concerns.

Craft: Type of watercraft most frequently used or encountered on this waterway.

Contacts: The names, phone numbers, and websites of organizations or agencies that may provide more specific information or answer questions. More complete information may be listed in appendix B.

Special considerations: Any unusual factors you may encounter that require your attention, planning, or special equipment. You can pay attention before you paddle or pay later when you are delayed or need emergency rescue and/or medical care.

Put-in/Takeout Information: Provides directions for legal approaches to waterways. Some are improved with launch ramps, paved parking, and restrooms. Others are informal sites with roadside parking and streambanks suitable only for hand-carried craft. Most require use fees.

Shuttle: The one-way driving distance and driving time to travel from the put-in to the takeout. For river trips, the most common way to regroup your vehicle and boat at the end of the trip is to run a shuttle: Put a vehicle at the takeout, and then return to the put-in with your gear. Alternative shuttle methods are bicycling, jogging, hiring a commercial shuttle driver, catching a ride with a commercial outfitter shuttle, or using a bus service available for paddlers on some rivers. Remember the vehicle keys!

Overview: Describes general features or background information.

The Paddling: Describes some of the features, challenges, or attractions that may be encountered while paddling.

Map Legend

Municipal

≡(80)≡ Interstate

≡(50)≡ US Highway

≡(267)≡ State Road

≡[CR 318]≡ Local/County Road

= = = = Unpaved/Forest Road

├──┼──┤ Railroad

─ ─ ·· ─ ─ State Boundary

──▲── Park/Recreation Area

Trails

------ Trail

Water Features

Body of Water

Marsh

River/Creek

------ Water Trail

▲ Put-in/Access

// Rapid

≋ Waterfall

Symbols

✈ Airport

||||||| Boardwalk

≋ Boat Launch

⌣ Bridge

▲ Campground

! Gate

❓ Information Station

🗼 Lighthouse

10 Mileage Marker

■ Point of Interest/Trailhead

⤫ Pass

🅿 Parking

▲ Peak/Elevation

🅰 Picnic Area

Ranger Station

🚻 Restroom

○ Town

Land Features

Lava Bed

Coastal Region

These waterways are directly connected to the Pacific Ocean, with the tides and winds the ocean creates. Whales, sea otters, seals, sea lions, and an abundance of seabirds inhabit these waters. The combination of wind, waves, and critters make this a wonderfully exhilarating region to experience.

An escapist's dream, this floating cottage harmonizes perfectly with the beautiful Albion River near Mendocino (chapter 3).

1 Mendocino Coast

Formerly a logging area, today Mendocino is a vacation location with art galleries, shops, and inns. The coast is a sea kayaking kaleidoscope of rock gardens, sea caves, and open ocean. The Marine Mammal Protection Act applies.

Length: Up to 5 miles per segment
Average paddling time: 2 to 4 hours
Difficulty: SCRS III to V, rock gardens, and open ocean; intermediate to advanced skills required
Marine weather: (707) 443-7062; www.wrh.noaa.gov/eka/. For sea conditions and wave heights, see NOAA Point Arena buoy #46014.
Tide reference: Arena Cove: High tides: +7 minutes; low tides: +1 minute
Best season: Spring, summer, and autumn
Land status: Mixed private and public
Fees: Required at launch sites
Maps: USGS Albion, Mendocino; NOAA navigation charts 18626 and 18628
Craft: Sea kayaks
Contacts: Mendocino Coast Chamber of Commerce for lodging and dining: mendocinocoast.com. Caspar Beach RV Park & Campground: (707) 964-3306; casparbeachrvpark.com. Caspar Headlands State Beach, Van

Damme State Park, Russian Gulch State Park: (707) 937-5804; parks.ca.gov. Albion River Campground and Marina: (707) 937-0606; albionrivercampground.com. Kayak Mendocino: (707) 813-7117; kayakmendocino.com.

Special considerations: The California Department of Boating and Waterways advises that this "coastline offers a variety of weather hazards—storms, dense fog, heavy surf, and very often rough seas." Pacific Ocean water temperatures in the Mendocino area seldom rise above 55°F, even in summer. Rock gardens, surf, occasional rogue waves, and caves add hazards (see the "Safety on the Water and Paddling Etiquette" section in this guide). Even in the calmest of weather, rogue waves may quickly disrupt your paddling pleasure. Sea kayakers venturing into these waters should paddle in teams and be able to perform self-rescues.

Put-in/Takeout Information

Caspar Beach (N39 21.604' / W123 49.031'): From Fort Bragg follow CA 1 until you cross Caspar Creek. From the bridge turn west and go 0.7 mile to the beach and RV campground. From Mendocino turn off at the Russian Gulch State Park exit sign, then immediately turn right, following Point Cabrillo Drive north 2.5 miles to Caspar Beach. The nearest restrooms are 0.5 mile away in the Caspar Beach RV Campground, which limits use of their restrooms to customers. Caspar Headlands State Reserve includes the south promontory of the cove. No fee for parking at the beach across from campground.

Russian Gulch State Park (N39 19.744' / W123 48.257'): Exit CA 1 at the Russian Gulch State Park, about 1.8 miles north of Mendocino, and head toward the sea. Turn left to the park kiosk, go down the hill, and turn right toward the beach. Fee area.

Mendocino Bay (N39 18.134' / W123 47.260'): Launching or landing from Mendocino Bay through surf can be difficult and hazardous, especially during ebb tides. Immediately south of Mendocino, CA 1 crosses the Big River. From the north end of the bridge, turn east to the broad parking area and gravel launch ramp. There are restrooms just past the gate to the logging road/hiking trail.

Van Damme State Park (N39 16.408' / W123 47.448'): Beachside parking and launching on CA 1 is 2.5 miles south of Mendocino. At the entrance to the park with its campgrounds, the cove is a favorite dive spot for abalone fishing. No fee required. Beach has restrooms.

Albion River Campground (N39 13.595' / W123 45.957') is under the CA 1 bridge, 6 miles south of Mendocino and 3.5 miles north of the junction of CA 1 and CA 128. Turn east from CA 1, 50 feet north of the Albion bridge. Descend steeply into the campground below the bridge, between the river and Albion Cove. Pay the campground fee for access to a boat ramp or to launch from a protected beach under the bridge. Alternatively, at the bottom of the hill follow the road upstream 0.5 mile to Schooners Landing marina and campground (N39 3.9' / W123 45.5').

Shuttle: Albion to Van Damme, 5 miles (15 minutes); Van Damme to Mendocino, 2.5 miles (10 minutes); Mendocino to Russian Gulch, 2.5 miles (10 minutes); Russian Gulch to Caspar, 2.7 miles (10 minutes)

Overview

Weather and sea conditions permitting, this is a spectacular area to paddle. Spring has wildflowers. Summer gives a cool respite from inland heat, and autumn offers warmer days with less chance of fog. Filmmakers have used the scenic coast, state parks, and community of Mendocino. Tourists visit this New England–style town with its rock-bound shoreline, clean air, windswept seas, and forested mainland.

Accommodations are numerous and popular. Van Damme, Russian Gulch, and MacKerricher State Parks provide nearby camping. Several excellent hotels and restaurants serve coastal visitors between Albion and Fort Bragg. Make summer reservations in advance. Commercial outfitters provide kayak tours from Van Damme Beach.

The rocky coast, sea stacks, and sea caves are exciting to explore. It is necessary to paddle with experienced teams, wear helmets, be dressed for immersion, and paddle during calm weather conditions. Check National Weather Service broadcasts from Eureka. If the sea conditions are unfavorable, then explore the neighboring Albion or Big Rivers described in chapters 3 and 2, respectively.

Since prevailing summer winds blow from the northwest, it is usually easiest to paddle from north to south so that the wind and swells help your passage. Your time to paddle from place to place can vary greatly depending on sea conditions and how much exploring you do.

The following tale by Aldine Garman provides a vivid picture of changeable sea conditions (From *Mendocino County Remembered—An Oral History*, volume 1, by

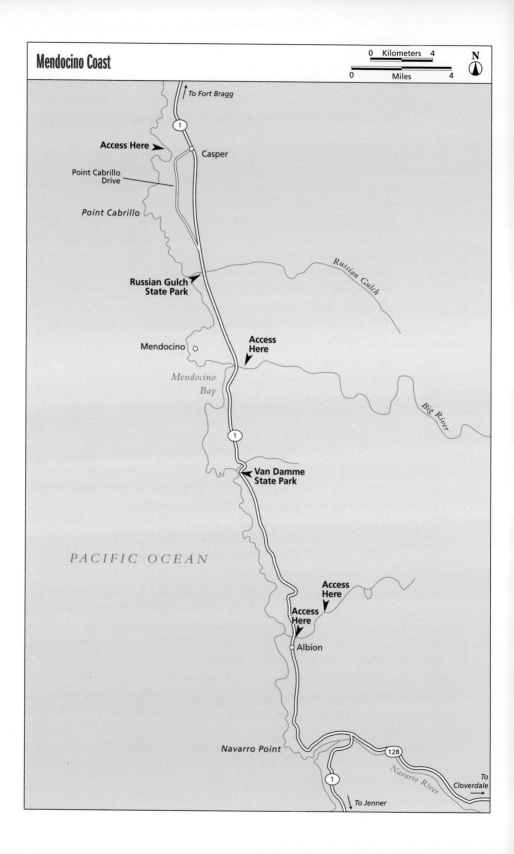

Mendocino Coast

0 Kilometers 4

0 Miles 4

N

To Fort Bragg

1

Access Here

Casper

Point Cabrillo
Drive

Point Cabrillo

Russian Gulch

Russian Gulch
State Park

Mendocino

Access
Here

Mendocino
Bay

Big River

1

PACIFIC OCEAN

Van Damme
State Park

Access
Here

Access
Here

Albion

Navarro Point

128

Navarro River

To
Cloverdale

1

To Jenner

Bruce Levene et al., Mendocino County, CA: The Mendocino County Historical Society, 1976. Used by permission.)

> *Three vessels were in Mendocino Harbor being loaded with lumber on a pleasant sunny day. Suddenly, big rollers came in, breaking from point to point across the harbor. The first heavy roller dashed two of these little vessels against the rocks. The surge carried one wrecked vessel across the harbor to the mouth of a big blowhole. When it first hit the mouth of the blowhole, the main mast was broken "like a pipestem." The receding wave carried it back to the same place where it had been and the boat righted itself. A second big wave came and carried the boat again to the same blowhole. This time all the superstructure was carried away. Six sailors had dived into the sea, hoping that they could either swim or be saved by the men dashing from the lumberyard down to the beach. One young man started to jump overboard, but he held onto the deck and just froze there. He just could not let go. Then a third wave came and carried it into the blowhole. It was never heard from since.*

The Paddling

Albion to Van Damme

Length: 4.5 miles

Average paddling time: 2 to 4 hours

At Albion, you have a choice of launching into the Albion River or carrying your craft across the beach at the campground and launching directly into the bay. The river current and volume of boat traffic under the high trestle bridge may influence your decision.

Because the Albion River provides a protected marina, commercial and charter boats frequent the serpentine channel in and out of Albion Cove. If you stay to the rocky north side, you should miss the traffic.

If skills, equipment, and sea conditions permit, you can probably visit the narrow channels, arches, and caves that connect with the north side of Albion Head. Farther north, the ocean has carved arches and sea caves into this coast. Some caves have multiple openings. A few tunnel into sunlit chambers with miniature beaches surrounded by cliffs. These are sinkholes. Other caves twist dangerously in the dark while echoing the ocean surge.

Several large sea stacks or small islands mark the approach to Van Damme Beach. Look for the hills descending to the creek at the parking lot and campground.

Paddlers explore sea caves along the Mendocino Coast.

Van Damme to Mendocino

Length: 3.5 miles

Average paddling time: 2 to 4 hours

Beachside parking is available immediately beside CA 1 opposite the entrance to Van Damme State Park. The carry to the generally low-surf beach is only 50 yards. If you do not have a boat, Kayak Mendocino leads guided tours.

The north side of the cove is often relatively calm. Towering sea stacks, shore cliffs, and clear tidal pools perk your enthusiasm. Sometimes seals swim up to investigate you. One passage leads to another, each teasing you with how far it goes. Eventually rocks and ledges block your way. Then the choice is to retreat a short distance and punch through the surf or retreat to the cove and paddle seaward to round the northerly headlands.

Note the buoy that marks the entrance to the cove. If you are traveling in a southerly direction, the buoy locates the passage to the beach. Avoid the deepwater reefs and waves that break in the outer cove. If fog rolls in, the buoy and beach will be difficult to find without negotiating the breakers.

Spectacular headlands and shoreline continue to Mendocino Bay. Its broad opening is unmistakable. You can paddle through the kelp beds with some work, but beware of the rock gardens when the surf is breaking nearby.

Aim for the CA 1 bridge in the northeast corner of the bay. The bridge marks the Big River and the beach takeout. The surf here is usually significantly bigger than the surf at Van Damme. Plan your arrival for an incoming tide to make the short upriver paddle easier. Another choice is to continue to Russian Gulch.

Mendocino to Russian Gulch

Length: 3.5 miles
Average paddling time: 2 to 4 hours

The Big River put-in is calm water. Paddling seaward, you soon encounter the surf at the river's mouth bar. You can examine the situation from the shore at the Mendocino Bay end of the put-in. Take care not be swept through the surf, especially at ebb tides.

The north side of the bay is under the cliffs of Mendocino Headlands State Park. At lower tides a sandy beach extends along part of this shore. Do not sit too close to the cliffs, since rockfall is common.

Paddling westward, you can look up at the tourists exploring the headlands and marveling at the roar and bellow of the sea caves below. Some of these caverns are very large, with several openings. During calmer conditions, sea kayakers paddle through them.

These caves connect with a series of rock channels, arches, and other caves that provide an inside passage to the west of Agate Beach. From there it is a brief paddle to the rock gardens approaching Russian Gulch.

You'll recognize Russian Gulch by the arched concrete bridge high over the creek. Land at the beach under the bridge.

Russian Gulch to Caspar

Length: 4 miles
Average paddling time: 2 to 3 hours

Russian Gulch State Park offers a protected beach, beachside parking, a port-a-potty, and sometimes a cold freshwater shower to rinse the salt from your body and gear. Coin-operated hot showers get lots of use in the campground.

The narrow mouth of Russian Gulch gradually opens to a wider cove. A small sea cave on the north side is easy to reach and explore.

Round the rocky headland and head northwest. If the ocean conditions are worse than you expected, you can retreat to the cove. If conditions are gentle, you may be comfortable exploring passages between the rocks and looking for arches and more caves.

If conditions let you stay inside, a series of channels, arches, and sea caves may be accessible that provide an inside passage to Caspar Anchorage. Don't be surprised if you encounter sea lions expressing their territorial presence over the narrow passageways.

If you go outside, the view of the coast is great, with the sight of the rock-studded shoreline leading to Cabrillo Lighthouse. Going over acres of floating kelp is like

Exploring sea stacks near Van Damme Beach

paddling over inflated bicycle tubes. You may seek corridors between the floating mats. Reefs near the southern approach to Caspar Anchorage warrant a detour seaward before heading into the cove.

Wide Caspar Cove is delightfully well protected from the prevailing summer winds. Look for the beach at the southeast end. As you approach the shore, you can usually choose between a calm-water or surf landing. Caspar is an uncrowded and pleasant place to practice surfing.

As you enjoy the quiet cove and beautiful Caspar, think of how it seemed when George He landed here in 1854. He came from China in a sampan about 8 feet high and 30 feet long. He and his crew rowed and sailed for eighteen months, living on an eight months' supply of rice, dried fish, and vegetables. Of seven sampans that set out to look for gold, two reached California—one in Monterey, the other in Caspar. Then they walked to Mendocino. (Information from *Mendocino County Remembered—An Oral History* by Bruce Levene et al., The Mendocino County Historical Society, Mendocino County, California, 1976.)

2 Big River

This easy paddle is just south of Mendocino. The Big River starts as a tidal estuary that turns into a placid, intimate stream bordered by North Coast forests. The Marine Mammal Protection Act applies.

Length: 8 miles
Average paddling time: 4 to 6 hours
Difficulty: Flatwater; beginner skills
Marine weather: 162.550 MHz; www.wrh.noaa
.gov/eka/marine
Tide reference: Arena Cove: High tides: +7 minutes; low tides: 0 minute
Best season: Spring and autumn
Land status: Private
Fees: None
Maps: USGS Mendocino, Mathison Peak; NOAA navigation chart 18628, Albion to Caspar

Craft: Canoes, kayaks, paddleboards, inflatables on the river
Contacts: Mendocino Coast Chamber of Commerce: mendocinocoast.com. Catch a Canoe & Bicycles Too: (707) 937-0273; catch acanoe.com. Skunk Train: (707) 964-6371; skunktrain.com (between Willets and Fort Bragg).
Special considerations: Consult tide tables to go with the flow and avoid being left high and dry.

Put-in/Takeout Information

Immediately south of Mendocino, CA 1 crosses the Big River. From the north end of the bridge, turn east to the broad parking area and gravel launch ramp (N39 18.134' / W123 47.260'). A locked gate blocks entry to a public hiking trail that follows the river.
Shuttle: None

Overview

The town of Mendocino and the Mendocino Bay area have long been retreats for artists and tourists. Earlier, this was the home of loggers and Native Americans. As you cruise the Big River, picture the river when lumber mills lined the lower river, logs floated downriver to the mills, and coastal lumber schooners waited in Mendocino Bay. The river has visually recovered from many of those activities.

Native Americans from interior valleys and mountains visited the mouth of the Big River for one or two weeks in summer. They gathered such sea delights as abalone, mussels, clams, and fish.

The Paddling

The Big River can be paddled year-round. However, during much of the summer, strong afternoon winds blow upstream from the ocean. The winds make the return paddle difficult. Spring and autumn are favored paddling seasons; then the Big River is a delight to paddle upstream during slack water or an incoming tide.

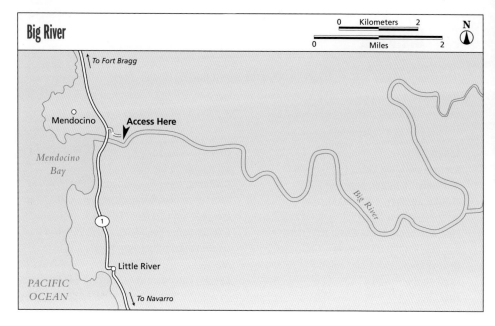

The put-in is easy. If you have your own boat, use the broad, unpaved parking lot just upstream of the CA 1 bridge on the Mendocino side of the river. Rental watercraft are available on the opposite side of the river, almost underneath the bridge.

For 3 miles the river is a wide estuary with a flat shoreline leading to hills that rise 500 feet. Paddling is easy, with occasional mudflats supporting kelp-like aquatic growth. Pilings along the broad banks are historic remnants from lumber mills. Ducks, geese, and other birds are plentiful, and sea lions sometimes enjoy lunch in the estuary.

Beyond 3 miles, the hills form steep banks down to the river, and the trees grow to the water's edge. Gradually, bigleaf maple, tanoak, and fir replace the alder. As the tidal influx slackens, the clearer water reveals a sandy river bottom. Farther upstream, gravel replaces sand, but large rocks are absent. Were the rocks removed in the days when they floated logs to the mills?

Occasional large stumps and logs lie buried in the river bottom. Note the pontoon craft bearing winches tied to the riverbank. Some sunken redwood stumps, abandoned years ago, are now highly prized for their color and grain. New treasure seekers use the pontoon craft to recover these prizes.

Comfortable lunch spots are few due to thick vegetation and steep banks. On one outing with an incoming tide, we found our cramped sandbar shrinking about our feet. An alternative is to tie the boats along the north bank and then climb through the brush to a narrow dirt road that follows the river.

From miles 3 to 8 the river becomes intimate as it carves lazy loops through growing forested hills. How far you can travel depends on how much water is in the river and your ambition. Eventually the banks close to less than 20 feet apart and tidal signs vanish. Summer flows become too thin to float the boats. Just remember that an ebbing tide can leave you with shallow water and a tough return trip.

3 Albion River

When steep waves or high winds make sea paddling uninviting, the Wild and Scenic Albion River is a calm alternative. The river is a beautiful escape along a gentle coastal stream snuggled between lush fir hillsides. The Marine Mammal Protection Act applies.

Length: 5 miles

Average paddling time: 4 to 5 hours

Difficulty: Flatwater; beginner skills

Marine weather: 162.400 MHz; www.wrh.noaa.gov/eka/marine

Tide reference: Arena Cove: high tides: +7 minutes; low tides: 0 minute

Best season: Spring and autumn

Land status: Private

Fees: Day-use fee

Maps: USGS Elk, Albion; NOAA navigation BookletChart 18626, page 13, Albion to Caspar

Craft: Canoes, kayaks, paddleboards, inflatable kayaks

Contacts: Albion River Campground & Marina: (707) 937-0606; albionrivercampground.com. Mendocino Coast Chamber of Commerce: (707) 961-6300; mendocinocoast.com.

Special considerations: Give right-of-way to occasional large fishing boats near the boat ramps and in Albion Cove. Consult tide tables to go with the flow and avoid being left high and dry.

Put-in/Takeout Information

Albion River Campground (N39 13.595' / W123 45.957') is under the CA 1 bridge, 6 miles south of Mendocino and 3.5 miles north of the junction of CA 1 and CA 128. Turn east from CA 1, 50 feet north of the Albion bridge. Descend steeply into the campground below the bridge, between the river and Albion Cove. A boat ramp is available for a fee, or you can park close to the water under the bridge and carry your boat to the channel. Alternatively, at the bottom of the hill, follow the road upstream 0.5 mile to Schooners Landing marina and campground (N39 3.9' / W123 45.5').

Shuttle: None

Overview

From the CA 1 bridge, the view upstream into the hills entices one to trace the Albion River. Access is easy from the wide Albion Flat under the bridge. The privately operated campground has hot showers, a small marina for fishing boats, a boat ramp, and a sandy beach facing seaward to Albion Cove. A use fee is charged.

Summer mornings are often foggy. During summer afternoons, strong winds blow upstream from the ocean and make downstream paddling difficult. Spring and autumn have brighter, calmer days.

Exploring the ocean waters of Albion Cove can be enticing but requires negotiating the fast water in the narrow channel under the south end of the bridge. (See chapter 1: Mendocino Coast, about paddling Albion Cove.)

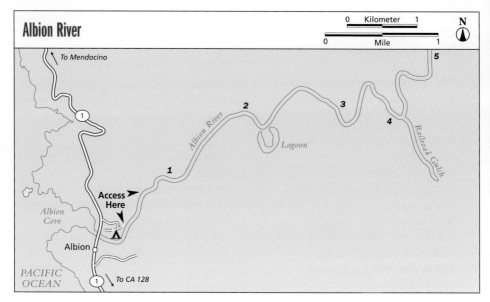

Albion River

0 ... Kilometer ... 1

0 ... Mile ... 1

N

To Mendocino

5

1

Albion River

2

3

4

Lagoon

1

Railroad Gulch

Access Here

Albion Cove

Albion

PACIFIC OCEAN

1

To CA 128

The Paddling

The campground's boat ramp is an easy put-in. Large fishing boats heading for the ocean also use it, so clear the narrow channel by the ramp soon after launching.

The Albion River is smooth, without rocks, and easy to paddle upstream with slack water or an incoming tide. At low tides, shallow mud bars can slow the inattentive paddler. A second small commercial marina and boat ramp is found about 0.25 mile upstream. The marina is quickly left behind, and the dense fir forest comes down to the water.

Several curious features characterize the Albion. About 1.25 miles from the bridge, a house on the south bank is all that remains of a floating assemblage of boats and floats once occupied by Dan (a colorful local character) and his dogs. Along the north bank, a narrow woods road is intermittently visible. Occasionally, low marshy grasses extend from the hillsides to the water. The Albion gently flows through a forested scene reminiscent of British Columbia.

A charming floating cottage heralds the entrance to the lagoon at 2.3 miles. The cottage is an escapist's dream, complete with fishing, forests, peace, and solitude. Please respect it as private property. Behind the cottage, a breach through an old levee provides entrance to the lagoon. Once a pond for storing logs, this picturesque crescent encloses a small, steep island. Over the years, sediment has filled much of the lagoon bottom with soft mud, making shore landings difficult.

Upstream, more float houses provide private vantage points to enjoy the marvelously beautiful setting. Along the channel, old weather-sculpted gray pilings recall past days of logging by rail. Soon the river becomes narrower, and snags lie in the channel to block passage at low water. The depth of the water and your energy level determine how far upstream you will navigate. Just remember that an ebbing tide can leave you with shallow water and a slow return trip.

4 Navarro River

The Navarro offers a wonderful wilderness canoe run through redwood forests during the rainy season. At nearly 20 miles, this paddle is long enough for overnight camping.

Length: 19.4 miles

Average paddling time: 7 to 10 hours, often paddled in two days

Difficulty: Fast, narrow channels and obstacles; Class II whitewater skills required

Rapids: Numerous Class I and Class II rapids with trees, brush, and rocks

Average gradient: 8 feet per mile

Optimal flow: 400 to 1,000 cfs

Flow gauge: Navarro #11468000

Water source: Storm water runoff

Best season: Winter and early spring during receding storm flows

Land status: Private

Fees: Required at parks

Maps: USGS Elk, Navarro, Cold Spring, Philo

Craft: Open canoes, kayaks, inflatables

Contacts: Hendy Woods State Park: (707) 937-5804; parks.ca.gov. Navarro River Water Trail Assessment: navarroriver.org.

Special considerations: Between Hendy Woods and Dimmick Campground, the steep canyon slopes are prone to landslides during prolonged winter rainstorms. The landslides regularly contribute rocks and trees to the river, creating new rapids and snag hazards. Brush lines many parts of the river. Occasionally landslides create temporary dams across the river. Avoid paddling the river when flows are rising. Telephone the rangers at Hendy Woods State Park to ask if recent storms have caused unusual changes in the river.

Put-in/Takeout Information

Hendy Woods State Park upstream of Philo-Greenwood Road bridge is the put-in. Hendy Woods State Park (N39 4.457' / W123 27.975') is in the Anderson Valley. From Boonville follow CA 128 for 8 miles to the Philo-Greenwood Road. Turn left. The park is 0.5 mile south on Philo-Greenwood Road. A trail through trees leads 200-plus yards from the day-use area parking lot. Fee area.

Dimmick Memorial Redwoods, a former campground, repeatedly damaged by floods and without drinking water (N39 9.412' / W123 38.299'), is located on CA 128, 8 miles east of CA 1 and 14 miles west of Hendy Woods State Park. The site is immediately above the confluence of the North Fork and the main stem of the Navarro. Limited roadside parking and a lengthy carry leads to the water.

CA 128 road mile marker 3.66 (N39 10.691' / W123 41.563'): Roadside parking is close to a 100-yard-long trail leading to a deep pool that is a local summer swimming spot. At CA 128 road mile marker 4.0, a roadside turnout named Hollow Log is closer to the river.

Shuttle: Hendy Woods to Dimmick: 14 miles (20 minutes); Dimmick to CA 128 mile marker 3.66: 4 miles (10 minutes)

Overview

The Navarro River Resource Center and Anderson Valley Land Trust promote efforts to preserve the environmental health of the Navarro River watershed. From the orchards and vineyards of the Anderson Valley, the Navarro River courses through remote, privately owned, richly forested canyons to the North Fork confluence at the former Paul Dimmick Campground site. Navarro River Redwoods State Park protects the rest of the river corridor to the ocean. Steelhead fishing is popular in the autumn.

Only the tidal section is boatable after the rainy season, which usually ends by mid-spring. If the winter has been wet and storms persist, the river may be runnable into late April. At 300 cfs, expect to walk your boat through the shallows. At lower flows, maneuvering around the brush becomes more difficult.

Rich riverside forests effectively screen from view the timber harvesting that continues on the slopes above. During the late 1800s, a railroad paralleled the river, lumber mills dotted the estuary, and lumber schooners loaded cargo in the estuary.

When the river is runnable, Hendy Woods State Park and the Paul Dimmick site are apt to be damp and cool. Summer weather at the campgrounds is warmer and less foggy than the seacoast. Hendy Woods contains a year-round campground and a grove of magnificent redwood trees.

Repeatedly flooded by winter storms, Dimmick Campground needs repair and has been closed.

Winter high flows topple trees into the Navarro, which requires caution and sometimes portages.

The Paddling

The parking lot at the Hendy Woods State Park picnic area is close to the river channel but screened by brush. During the past decade, the water has meandered 100-plus yards farther away. Fast-flowing water soon requires adroit paddling skills to avoid the steep-cut left bank. Apple orchards line the right bank. A mile downstream, the high concrete bridge for the Philo-Greenwood Road crosses the river.

Beyond the bridge 1.5 miles, the river leaves Anderson Valley and enters the remote canyon. For the first few miles the river drops 17 feet per mile. Steep slopes rise 800 feet to Greenwood Ridge. Although a new generation of redwood trees and Douglas fir have regrown, tributary names such as Skid Gulch and Floodgate Creek reflect times when lumbermen denuded the hills and floated or hauled the logs to mills along the river estuary. Obscure remnants of old logging roads and railroads still parallel the river.

The most difficult obstacles are brush and fallen trees in the channel. Their location changes from year to year, and the paddler must stay alert. One example of the caution required is found about 2 miles below the bridge. When we floated it, dense brush lined both sides of the narrow channel, and a tree lay diagonally across the river. Two canoes in our party capsized. Some paddlers lined their gear-laden boats past this section.

During major floods, large landslides contribute huge amounts of gravel, rocks, and debris to the river channel. During one winter storm, a landslide blocked the river, creating a 2-mile-long lake. What remains are shallow, Class II rocky rapids that will change with the passing years. At 300 cfs, we walked our canoes through the shallows.

Campsites are where you find them. Since the banks are very steep and wooded, most campsites are on gravel bars. The higher the river, the fewer the campsites. A large landslide on the left identifies what was once a picturesque campsite 7 miles below Hendy Woods. Landmarks here were house-size boulders at the slide's bottom, a deep pool, and a rapid as the river turns sharply right. A steep tributary on the left had formed a large gravel bar flat enough for camping. Three more miles downstream, another reliable campsite is the peninsula at Cape Horn.

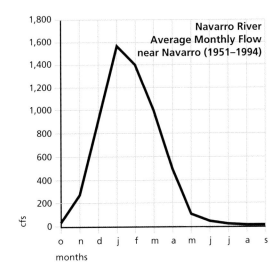

Between these campsites, a tremendous old redwood stump lies in the river. Guidebook author Dick Schwind reported the stump here in the 1970s. Other fallen trees and stumps provide obstacles to paddlers all the way to the takeout.

Navarro River & Navarro River Estuary

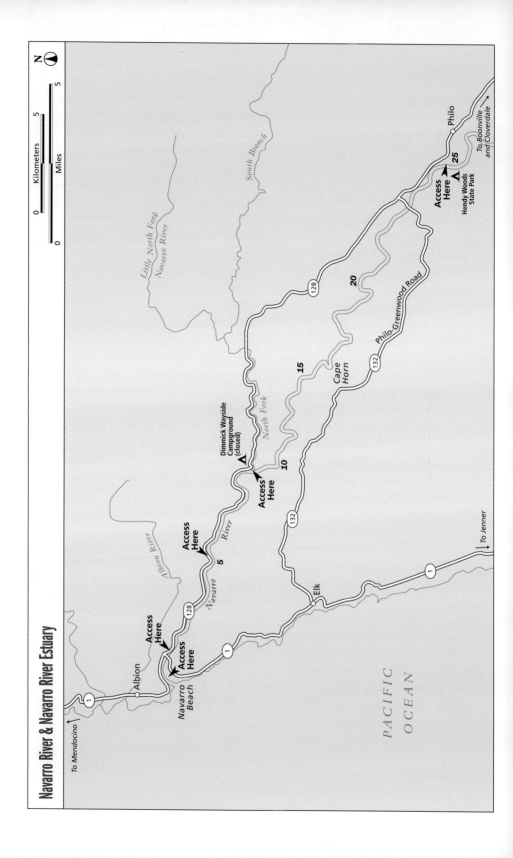

The scenic Navarro River changes with every turn, from easy paddling to fallen trees. Even experienced paddlers should pay attention.

The most popular takeout is the former Paul Dimmick Campground, where the wide North Fork joins the Navarro. No other tributary this large joins the river. Dimmick is on river right immediately downstream of the North Fork. Climb the slope and carry 200 yards to the road. At higher flows the current in the Navarro is fast. Be sure to be able to recognize the takeout by looking at it carefully when you do the shuttle.

The river continues this character for another 4.4 miles, which you can paddle in about 2 hours. CA 128 closely follows the right bank. Groves of redwoods sometimes block the sight and sound of the traffic. It is well worth landing to walk among these redwood groves. Large second-growth trees circle the stumps of their ancestors. The root systems of the original redwood sent sprouts to form clones of the original tree. Mud stains high on the tree trunks mark flood heights that at one time even covered the highway.

The stream gradient steepens to 8 feet per mile between the North Fork confluence and the gauging station. Below river mile 5, the tidal influence becomes noticeable. Views expand as the channel width doubles. A cable stretched high above the river marks the flow gauging station. The staging markers may be visible in the sand along the right bank.

There's a short takeout 4.5 miles past Dimmick. It occurs just upstream of where the river bends to the left and the road clings to the right bank (CA 128 mile marker 4.0).

If you continue downstream, a majestic stand of second-growth redwoods quickly separates the river from the road. Screened from the road by the forest giants, the wonderful deep pool and sandy beach (locally known as the "Iron Bridge site") offer another takeout at one of the nicest spots below Dimmick.

5 Navarro River Estuary

The Navarro River broadens in the estuary as it approaches the beach. This place hosts lots of birds on the water and marine life on the beach. If the summer winds are not blowing, enjoy a gentle float between the beach and the redwoods. Downstream of CA 1, the river is designated a State Marine Protected Area.

(See map on page 38.)
Length: Up to 5 miles
Average paddling time: 2 to 4 hours
Difficulty: Tidal flatwater; beginner skills
Tide reference: Arena Cove: High tides: +7 minutes; low tides: +1 minute
Best season: Year-round except during floods
Land status: Private and public at beach
Fees: Required at state park

Maps: USGS Albion, Elk; NOAA BookletChart 18626, page 18; Navarro River Redwoods State Park brochure
Craft: Open canoes, kayaks, dories, sea kayaks
Contacts: Navarro River Redwoods State Park: (707) 937-5804; parks.ca.gov; camping: 10 sites (first-come, first-served). Navarro-by-the-Sea Center: navarro-by-the-sea-center.org.
Special considerations: For much of the year, and especially at high winter flows, the river surges directly into the Pacific surf.

Put-in/Takeout Information

Navarro River Redwoods Beach (N39 11.453' / W123 45.568') has lots of parking in a spectacular setting. At the south end of the CA 1 bridge, turn west and go 0.7 mile along the south side of the river to the beach. Floating over sandbars is easier than slogging through silty sand, so use this location only at higher tides.

Navarro Estuary (N39 11.762' / W123 44.642'): From the CA 1 bridge, go upstream on CA 128 for less than 0.2 mile. A long, wide shoulder is next to a crude, unpaved boat ramp. The site is useful to hand-launch boats. The bank is only 5 feet high, and the water level rises and falls with the tides.

CA 128 mile marker 3.66 (N39 10.691' / W123 41.563'): Roadside parking is close to a 100-yard-long trail leading to a deep pool that is a local summer swimming spot. At CA 128 mile marker 4.0, a roadside turnout named Hollow Log is closer to the river. From here downstream, the tidal influence allows summer paddling.
Shuttle (optional): 1 mile (5 minutes) along estuary; 4 miles (7 minutes from CA 128 marker 3.66)

Overview

Navarro River Redwoods State Park protects the river corridor between the former Paul Dimmick Campground and the ocean. Steelhead fishing is popular in the autumn. Only the tidal section is normally boatable after early spring. The Anderson Valley Land Trust has proposed the creation of a Navarro River Water Trail.

In the late 1800s, railroads paralleled the river and lumber mills dotted the estuary. To keep the mouth of the river open for lumber schooners, seamen built a breakwater from the big pointed rock (Pinnacle Rock) to the bluff. Today the beach provides campsites and a great place to watch whales and seals.

Navarro Beach has a small, no-frills campground, no drinking water, and offers a smorgasbord of natural delights. One May evening I looked over the high tide to see a huge dorsal fin less than 25 yards away. It charged the beach through the surf and then slid back to deeper water. Again it rushed toward the beach, paused just beyond the wave break, and then ebbed to the sea. The next morning, twenty seals had hauled out onto the sand near the mouth. A park ranger told me that gray whales and calves also frequented the cove during much of the winter and spring.

The Paddling

Like other tidal waters, the easiest way to explore this waterway is to go upstream with the incoming tide, then follow the ebb downstream. Depending on recent rainstorms, the mouth may close with sand, minimizing tidal influence and current. The channel is wider, slower, and deeper than the upper reaches. If the wind is strong, paddle from the estuary upstream as far as CA 128 mile marker 3.66 or 4.0.

The mile of estuary between the beach and the CA 1 bridge is more than 100 yards wide. Steep hillsides form the north bank, and a broad terrace lines the south bank.

Upstream of the bridge, CA 128's presence along the north bank does not seem to deter the wildlife. I have listened to loons on the river, paddled next to seals, and gazed up at ospreys. The channel narrows dramatically. Two miles from the bridge, redwoods occupy the river terraces.

A very different activity existed one hundred years ago. Lumber mills lined the river, and schooners sailed in from the ocean. Now only Captain Fletcher's Inn (recently used by the Navarro-by-the-Sea Center) remains from that era on the road to Navarro Beach.

6 Estero Americano

Estero Americano starts as a rural smooth-water creek bordered by pastures and then leads to a wide estero alive with birdlife. Nearing the ocean, high hills look down at a beach with thundering surf. Since 2010 the downstream 1.5 miles of the estero has been designated a State Marine Recreational Management Area. Please respect the private property that borders the entire length of the estero. The Marine Mammal Protection Act applies.

Length: 5.8 miles

Average paddling time: 2 to 6 hours

Difficulty: Flatwater estuary; beginner skills

Tide reference: San Francisco: High tides: -12 minutes; low tides: +20 minutes

Optimal flow: Medium to high tides

Best season: Autumn through spring

Land status: Private

Fees: None

Maps: USGS Valley Ford, Bodega Head; NOAA navigation chart 18643, Tomales Bay & Bodega

Craft: Canoes, kayaks, inflatables

Contacts: Marin County Watersheds: marinwatersheds.org/estero_americano.html

Special considerations: Getting stuck in the wrong channel at low water can cause a serious delay in your trip. At the ocean beach, land so that the current will not pull you into the surf. Summer often brings fog and upstream winds.

Put-in/Takeout Information

From CA 1 at Valley Ford, turn south onto Valley Ford Estero–Franklin School Road. Go about 1 mile, cross the bridge, and turn left onto Marsh Road. A paved lane by the bridge usually allows parking for about six cars and an easy put-in (N38 18.573' / W122 56.150'). The nearest toilet facilities are in the community of Valley Ford.

Shuttle: None

Overview

Americano Creek offers a delightful smorgasbord of paddling environments, from rolling hills to a steep, fjord-like mouth; from a narrow creek to a wide estero; from warm sun to cold fog and wind.

Estero Americano State Marine Recreational Management Area is one of twenty-two marine protected areas adopted by the California Department of Fish and Wildlife. The north-central coast's new marine protected areas were designed by local divers, anglers, conservationists, and scientists to preserve sensitive sea life and habitats while enhancing recreation, study, and education opportunities. Estero Americano SMRMA includes the waters below the mean high tide line within Estero Americano and extends about 1.5 miles inland. As of December 2012, no fishing is permitted in this area.

Estero Americano emerges from the pastoral Marin Hills into a series of wide bays as it winds to the ocean.

Private lands border both sides of the estero, and livestock graze on the hills, which turn wonderfully green in winter. In their season, migratory waterfowl, shorebirds, eagles, and red-tailed hawks dwell here. Duck hunters seasonally enjoy hunting the waterfowl along this scenic treasure.

A local winter paddling event is a fun race called the Cow Patty Pageant. Kayakers splash from the bridge to the beach and then return.

The broad, sandy beach at the mouth of the estero provides a great view extending from Bodega Head to Tomales Point. On the ocean side the surf pounds against huge rocks and headlands. A lonesome house on the northern headland overlooks the beach and the ocean. Informal beach camping is enjoyable when the wind is mild. No facilities exist here, and campers should carry out all waste.

Summer days regularly bring in low clouds, cold fog, and winds strong enough to test any paddler's will. Late autumn, winter, and spring months offer sunny days warm enough to allow you to remove layers down to T-shirts. Courtesy suggests that you do not undress in view of the neighbors' homes or the highway.

The Paddling

Water levels and currents in the estero are subject to storms and tides. During the early winter, high winter surf re-forms the sandbar blocking the estero's mouth and the water level rises. Then Estero Americano forms 0.5-mile-wide lagoons, similar to Elkhorn Slough or Drakes Estero. Paddling is a delight. You can explore the enlarged shoreline, enjoy soaring eagles, and watch the abundant waterfowl.

If winter rains flood the valley, the estero overflows the sandbar and washes a new channel. If Mother Nature has not cooperated, and if the water covers too much of their roads and pastures, local farmers bulldoze the channel. Then the estero becomes subject to the ebb and flow of the tides and it is time to consult your tide book.

At the put-in, pasture lands border the well-defined channel that is only two boat lengths wide. The channel quickly turns north in a long loop that returns 0.2 mile from the starting point. Your first view depends on the water level. You may look

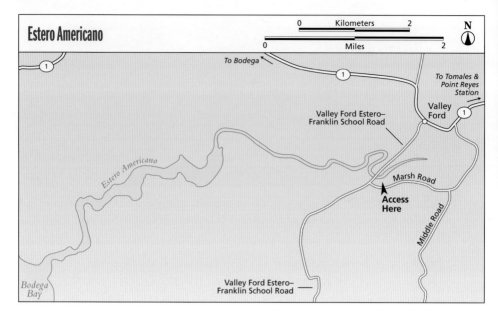

Estero Americano

Kilometers 2
Miles 2
N

To Bodega
1
To Tomales & Point Reyes Station

Valley Ford
1

Valley Ford Estero–Franklin School Road

Marsh Road

Access Here

Middle Road

Estero Americano

Bodega Bay

Valley Ford Estero–Franklin School Road

above the scene in full view of your paddling partners; float at eye level with the grass, catching only glimpses of paddle blades; or descend into the channel, isolated from all except the cows and the channel ahead.

Where the channel turns west again, the estero widens, your view expands, and some bay trees mark the south hillside.

Three miles from the bridge, the estero widens into the first broad bay. At low tides this is as far as you can easily paddle, since the wide bays divide into shallow channels. If you choose the wrong channel, the water turns to deep, sticky mud that you have to push or wade through—a very unpleasant and exhausting experience. At high tides, or if the estero mouth is blocked, the water backs up to form wide bays and pools that are havens for waterfowl. Bring your favorite field guide to help identify the various birds.

When the water is high, the lagoons expand and submerge adjacent pastures. The widest lagoons have barbwire fences extending from the north shore to the channel. Beware of them, particularly if paddling at twilight.

Two miles from the mouth, the estero briefly narrows again. Farm buildings and a few houses look down from the 500-foot-high ridge to the north. The lower water-side bluffs offer pleasant viewpoints. Around the next turn, another wide bay opens.

The west end of this bay narrows like a fjord between 500- and 600-foot-high ridges. Observers have reported golden eagles soaring on the Pacific winds over the ridges. The estero turns south for 0.5 mile before turning west to the beach.

Land along the beach where changing currents will not pull you or your boat into the surf. Then enjoy the surfside view from the other side of the dune. Since the surf usually dumps directly onto the beach, this is not a good launching site to venture into Bodega Bay. At the south end of the beach, a rocky outcrop provides a campfire site and some shelter from westerly winds.

7 Tomales Bay

Point Reyes National Seashore borders this 12-mile-long bay sitting atop the San Andreas Fault. Easy access, surf-free beaches, boat-in camping, marine wildlife, and a pastoral setting make these paddles especially attractive. The Marine Mammal Protection Act applies.

Size: 15 miles long, 0.5 to 1.2 miles wide
Average paddling time: 2 to 5 hours
Difficulty: Open water; beginner to intermediate skills required
Marine weather: 162.50 MHz; www.wrh.noaa.gov/mtr
Tide reference: Golden Gate–Tomales Bay entrance: High tides: -12 minutes; low tides: +20 minutes; Inverness: high tides: +29 minutes; low tides: +1 hour, 8 minutes; Marshall: high tides: +38 minutes; low tides: +1 hour, 16 minutes
Best season: Year-round
Land status: East shore and Inverness are private; outer west shore is state park and national seashore.
Fees: Required for camping and state parks
Maps: USGS Inverness, Tomales, Point Reyes NE; NOAA BookletChart 18643, pages 9, 10, 14 & 19, Tomales; Point Reyes National Seashore
Craft: Canoes, sea kayaks, sailboats, motorboats
Contacts: Point Reyes National Seashore: (415) 464-5100, ext. 2; nps.gov/pore. Point

Reyes camping reservations: (877) 444-6777. Tomales Bay State Park, Millerton Park, and Heart's Desire Beach: (415) 669-1140; parks.ca.gov. Coastal Traveler: coastaltraveler.com (for tourist information). Tomales Bay Resort: (415) 669-1369; tomalesbayresort.com. Lawson's Landing: (707) 878-2443; lawsonslanding.com. Blue Waters Kayaking: (415) 669-2600; bluewaterskayaking.com.

Special considerations: Although Inverness Ridge protects most of the bay from Pacific swells, the mouth of Tomales Bay is exposed to wind and sometimes breaking surf. Waves break on the rocky coast and across the extensive shallows off Dillon Beach. During ebb tides, the current exiting Tomales Bay may be strong enough to carry boaters into this broad surf zone. Tomales Bay water is cold, and even summer weather deserves protective clothing. Prevailing northwesterly winds may make paddling toward the mouth of the bay difficult. Thick fog sometimes reduces visibility and makes navigation difficult. Check marine weather forecasts for fog and wind before starting out.

Put-in/Takeout Information

Millerton Point (N38 6.512' / W122 50.692') at Tomales Bay State Park's Alan Sieroty Beach lies on the east shore 4.3 miles north of Point Reyes Station. Look for the eucalyptus grove at Millerton Point. Carry your boat 100 yards to a sheltered beach at medium to high tides. This day-use park is a fee area with toilet.

Miller County Park / Nick's Cove (N38 11.996' / W122 55.281') on CA 1 is 13 miles north of Point Reyes Station and 4 miles south of Tomales. This Marin County park charges a daily fee (bring paper money or plastic for the machine) and permits overnight parking.

Lawson's Landing (N38 13.912' / W122 58.087'): From CA 1 in Tomales, go west on Dillon Beach Road for 4 miles to Dillon Beach. Lawson's Landing is at the end of the county road south of Dillon Beach in the RV park. Lawson's charges launch and camping fees.

Heart's Desire Beach (N38 7.915' / W122 53.622') lies on the west shore, 4 miles north of Inverness on Pierce Point Road. This very popular day-use area in Tomales Bay State Park has restrooms and drinking water but charges fees to park and launch at the beach. Only credit or debit cards accepted for payment.

Inverness—Blue Waters Kayaking (N38 6.458' / W122 51.782') is immediately adjacent to the water at Chicken Ranch Beach on Sir Francis Drake Boulevard, 1 mile north of Inverness and a few yards north of the Tomales Bay Resort. Total distance from CA 1 is 4.6 miles.

White House Pool (N38 3.741' / W122 49.006') is located on Sir Francis Drake Boulevard 0.7 mile west of Point Reyes Station.

Shuttle (optional): One-way time, less than 1 hour from White House Pool to Heart's Desire or Nick's Cove.

Overview

Beautiful Tomales Bay is a great place to take the family and introduce newcomers to sea kayaking. Close to the San Francisco Bay Area, Point Reyes is a popular retreat for beach walking, clamming, picnicking, and boating. The bucolic setting, small villages, and recreation opportunities were preserved from wanton development when Congress established the Point Reyes National Seashore (PRNS) in 1962.

Called an "Island in Time," Point Reyes is a tectonic island separated from the California coast by the San Andreas Rift Zone. Tomales Bay sits atop the rift zone.

Paul Revere's grandson visited Point Reyes in 1846. He reported hundreds of elk, many wild horses, mountain lions, antelope, wolves, coyotes, black grouse, crested partridges, geese, blue cranes, wild pigeons, and turkeys. Today, tule elk have been restored to the Point Reyes peninsula. Tomales Bay is now part of the Gulf of the Farallones National Marine Sanctuary.

Ten miles of the western shore are public lands managed by the Tomales Bay State Park and the PRNS. The eastern shore is privately owned.

PRNS permits boat-in camping on beaches north of Indian Beach. Camping regulations require that all waste, including human waste, must be packed out. Campers must obtain camp permits and fire permits in advance. Carry water, or be prepared to treat any water from park streams. Collecting driftwood for fires is prohibited on Tomales Bay, so bring your own fuel (but not oak, madrone, or tanoak, to reduce the spread of sudden oak death infestation). Build fires below the high-tide line.

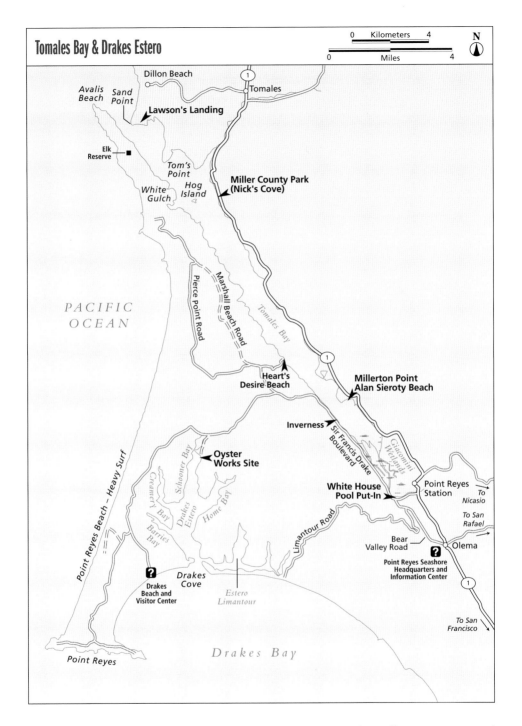

Tomales Bay & Drakes Estero

0   Kilometers   4

0   Miles   4

N

Dillon Beach

Avalis Beach *Sand Point*

1

Tomales

Lawson's Landing

Elk Reserve

Tom's Point

White Gulch

Hog Island

Miller County Park (Nick's Cove)

PACIFIC OCEAN

Pierce Point Road

Marshall Beach Road

Tomales Bay

1

Heart's Desire Beach

Millerton Point Alan Sieroty Beach

Inverness

Sir Francis Drake Boulevard

Giacomini Wetlands

Oyster Works Site

Schooner Bay

Creamery Bay

Drakes Estero

Home Bay

Barries Bay

White House Pool Put-In

Point Reyes Station

To Nicasio

To San Rafael

Limantour Road

Point Reyes Beach – Heavy Surf

Bear Valley Road

Olema

Point Reyes Seashore Headquarters and Information Center

1

Drakes Cove

Drakes Beach and Visitor Center

Estero Limantour

To San Francisco

Point Reyes

Drakes Bay

Point Reyes Station, Inverness, and Olema have several excellent restaurants and good motels. The region has fine bed-and-breakfast accommodations for those wanting a more pampered life. Kayaking outfitters lead trips to Tomales Bay.

Paddling Distances and Times

Starting Point	End Point	One-way Paddling Distance	Approximate One-way Paddling Times
Millerton Point	Inverness	0.7 mile	30 minutes
Inverness	Heart's Desire Beach	2.8 miles	1 hour
Heart's Desire	Millerton Point	3.7 miles	1.5-2 hours
Nick's Cove	Lawson's Landing	4.0 miles	2 hours
Nick's Cove	Avalis Beach	4.0 miles	2 hours
White House Pool	Giacomini Wetlands	1.5 miles	45 minutes

Note: Paddling times will double or triple with adverse winds or tides.

Paddlers can reach Tomales Bay from a half dozen points scattered along its 15-mile length. Paddling across the narrow bay is easy. In summer the wind predictably blows from the northwest and increases in the afternoon. Use the wind and tide to your advantage by paddling northward in the morning and then returning with the flood tide and the wind at your back.

The south end of the bay is shallow and interesting to explore from Inverness or Millerton Point at high tides. Many birds inhabit the area, and harmless rays and leopard sharks swim in the shallows.

Lagunitas Creek is a sheltered paddle that offers a chance to view the Giacomini Wetland Restoration Project in progress. At the extreme south end of Tomales Bay, the creek flows from Point Reyes Station, turns north at White House Pools, and then flows through tidal marshes toward the bay. For decades the levee on the east side excluded seawater from a former marsh that was transformed into a pasture. To restore marshland ecology, the National Park Service breached the levee in 2008 to allow seawater into the pasture. Tideland vegetation, birds, and marine organisms can now be seen there. Tour operators only paddle here when the tide is 3 feet and higher. Return to the put-in to complete your paddle. If the tide is still high enough to float you past the mudflats, continue north to Millerton Point or Inverness.

On the east shore is the Marconi Conference Center, site of the 1913 trans-Pacific Marconi wireless station. If you stay at the center, plan to kayak Tomales Bay. Other historic sites include schooner landing wharves at Lairds Landing, Pierce's Wharf, and Paper Mill Creek.

Paddling northward from Inverness, 8 miles of the west shore has a beach in almost every cove. Teachers, Shell, Heart's Desire, and Indian Beaches are located in Tomales Bay State Park. Land at Indian Beach to see a Miwok Indian lodge replica, like those that used to exist along Tomales Bay.

Also on the west shore, Kilkenny, Marshall, Tomales, White Gulch, Blue Gum, and Avalis Beaches have space above high tides suitable for camping. Low tides expose narrower sandy areas suitable for lunch stops.

At higher tides, paddlers can explore the restored Giacomini Wetlands at the south end of Tomales Bay.

Tule elk roam the hills once used for cattle grazing. North of Pelican Point, look for antlered elk bulls on the skyline. At White Gulch we saw more than fifty elk. The elk cropped the grassy flat behind Avalis Beach like a park. PRNS advises that camping should be only at the north or south end of Avalis Beach.

To protect wildlife, PRNS has instituted wildlife protection closures: Pelican Point, the east side of Hog Island, and Duck Island are closed all year. South Blue Gum Beach (between green buoys #1 and #3) is closed March 1 through June 30 to provide a safe haul-out for harbor seals during pupping season.

PRNS advises, "Harbor seals are extremely sensitive to human disturbance. Harbor seals and other pinnipeds need to haul out for several hours every day to rest. Stay away 100 meters (300 feet) from whales, seals, and sea lions." Never handle seal pups found anywhere.

PRNS notes that from 2000 to 2016, great white sharks attacked four people in the Point Reyes area. Such rare events are most likely to happen at seal haul-out areas, such as Tomales Bay north of Tom's Point.

From Miller County Park (Nick's Cove), it is an easy 0.75-mile paddle to Hog and Duck Islands. Both sprout a grove of trees above the high-tide lines. Look, but do not land.

Continuing westward, a white cliff marks the cove at White Gulch and a nearby beach. The easiest paddle northward is along the west shore, where the water is deeper and more sheltered from the wind. Pleasant but narrow sandy beaches line the coast.

Avalis Beach provides fine camping at the north end of Tomales Bay, close to the Pacific Ocean.

For an exhilarating adventure, ride the morning ebb out toward Avalis Beach. Other beaches line the route to match your personal comfort with the wind, waves, and current. Remember that only rocks line the coast north of Avalis Beach, and the narrow channel at Sand Point accelerates the current out to sea. Avoid the shallows and surf on the Dillon Beach side. In the afternoon, ride the flood into the bay and surf the waves with the wind at your back.

From Sand Point and Tom's Point, the shortest route is not always the quickest. The water south of both points is very shallow and the tide channels convoluted. Commercial metal shellfish cages line the shallow bottom to scrape your boat bottom between Tom's Point, Walker Creek, and Hog Island. Floating the main channel toward Hog Island is faster and easier.

For windy days with a high tide, explore the sheltered lower reaches of Walker Creek, paddling between Nick's Cove and the access near Camp Tomales along CA 1.

8 Drakes Estero

Point Reyes National Seashore surrounds this protected multi-fingered bay that is a wildlife watcher's dream. The Marine Mammal Protection Act applies.

(See map on page 47.)
Length: 3.4 to 8.0 miles round-trip
Average paddling time: 2 to 4 hours
Difficulty: SCRS I to II; beginner skills
Marine weather: 162.50 MHz; www.wrh.noaa.gov/mtr
Tide reference: San Francisco: Point Reyes high tides: -51 minutes; low tides: -31 minutes (Because of the narrow opening, the tides inside Drakes Estero can be hours out of phase with the Point Reyes tides.)
Best season: July 1 through Feb 28 each year; Port Reyes National Seashore (PRNS) regulations
Land status: Mixed private and national seashore
Fees: None
Maps: USGS Drakes Bay; NOAA navigation charts 18647 and 18643; Point Reyes National Seashore
Craft: Open canoes, sea kayaks

Contacts: Point Reyes National Seashore: (415) 464-5100, ext. 2; nps.gov/pore. Point Reyes camping reservations: (877) 444-6777. Coastal Traveler: coastaltraveler.com (for tourist information).
Special considerations: During ebb tides, beware that the current exiting Drakes Estero may be strong enough to carry boaters into the surf zone at the narrow entrance. Prevailing northwesterly winds may make paddling back to Schooner Bay difficult. Point Reyes water is cold, and the weather is often cool enough to require warm jackets, even in summer. Since much of Drakes Estero is very shallow, avoid being stranded on the expansive mudflats at low tides. Tides higher than 3 feet are desirable. Thick fog (Point Reyes Lighthouse has the reputation of being the foggiest place in North America) may reduce visibility dramatically and make navigation difficult. Check marine weather forecasts for fog and wind before starting out.

Put-in/Takeout Information

Oyster works site (N38 4.917' / W122 55.947'): From CA 1 take Bear Valley Road or Sir Francis Drake Boulevard to Inverness. Continue on Sir Francis Drake, up the hill, and toward the lighthouse. Go 2.8 miles past the junction with the Pierce Point Road and look for a narrow road on the left, signed "Drakes Estero." Park adjacent to the beach, near the toilet.

Limantour Beach (N38 1.724' / W122 52.965') is seldom used because of extensive mudflats if you miss the high tide. From CA 1 take Bear Valley Road west 2 miles to Limantour Road. Go up the hill, enjoy the view, and end at beachside parking. You can either carry to open water on Limantour Estero or, if you have the skills, try a surf launch into Drake's Bay. The mouth of Drakes Estero is almost 3 miles west of Limantour Beach.
Shuttle: None

Overview

Miwok Indians once occupied Drakes Estero. They used boats made of bundled rushes to navigate the calmer waters. In 1579 English navigator Sir Francis Drake stopped for a month to clean the bottom of his ship, the *Golden Hinde*. Drake's crew complained of the cold and foggy days. The next visitor was Sebastian Rodriguez Cermeno, en route to Acapulco from the Philippines. Heavy winds drove him to seek shelter at Drakes Bay on November 6, 1595, and later destroyed the ship. Cermeno and his remaining crew safely sailed the ship's small launch to Acapulco. Hoping to recover the wreck, explorer Don Sebastián Vizcaíno arrived on January 6, 1603, the day of the Three Holy Kings. Vizcaíno named the place "Puerto de Los Reyes" and the cape "Punta de Los Reyes" in honor of the three kings of Cologne.

During the 1800s, schooners landed at Creamery, Schooner, and Home Bays to transport the highly prized Point Reyes butter and pork to San Francisco. The agricultural era faded with the threat of residential development and creation of the PRNS to preserve the peninsula for the public.

Other than a bathroom, the closest public facilities to Drakes Estero are at the Bear Valley Visitor Center or the Ken Patrick Visitor Center at Drakes Beach.

Wildlife abounds here. The park service reports that Drakes Estero offers the best birding opportunities during the autumn migration and winter layover. You can see the largest harbor seal breeding colony in Point Reyes (and 20 percent of California's mainland harbor seal population) at Drakes Estero. To protect the seal population, Drakes Estero is closed to boaters for the seal pupping season, March 1 to June 30. PRNS management advises, "Harbor seals are extremely sensitive to human disturbance. Harbor seals and other pinnipeds need to haul out for several hours every day to rest. Give them a berth of at least 300 feet when the seals are on land and 50 feet in the water."

Elephant seals spend winter months on the extreme western beaches of Drakes Bay to give birth and breed. Docents with telescopes are sometimes available near the Point Reyes Lifeboat Station.

PRNS permits no camping within Drakes Estero.

The Paddling

	Paddling Distances	Average Paddling Time
Oyster Works to mouth of Home Bay	1.7 miles	30 minutes–1 hour
Home Bay mouth to Drakes Cove	2.2 miles	45 minutes–1.5 hours
Drakes Cove to Drakes Head	1.4 miles	30 minutes–1 hour
Oyster Works to Bull Point	1.7 miles	30 minutes–1 hour
Bull Point to Creamery Bay landing	0.7 mile	15 minutes–0.5 hour

Note: Paddling times will double or triple with adverse winds or tides.

Paddlers rest beside the monument to Sir Francis Drake, who cleaned the hull of the Golden Hinde *here in 1579. The nearby hill offers great views of the estero and approaching weather.*

Start at the oyster works site with high tide so that you have ample depth in the estero, can float out with the ebb, and can return with the incoming tide. Note the high white cliffs south of the put-in in Schooner Bay. They are good landmarks when you return.

Note: The oyster racks were removed in 2016 as part of the Phillip Burton Marine Wilderness restoration.

From Schooner Bay you have the choice of heading south to Home Bay or west to the landing on Creamery Bay.

An old schooner landing sits at the seaward end of Home Bay. At low tide, scores of gulls, cormorants, egrets, and American white pelicans may inhabit the sandbar. Large rafts of the pelicans float in Home Bay. Most of the north end is very shallow. The large grove of overgrown Christmas trees is reputed to host several owls.

Contrasting sharply with the surrounding brown hills, the dark green pines make a distinctive landmark.

Paddle south across Home Bay to the low bluffs on the east side of the estero. Hikers often frequent the Sunset Beach Trail paralleling this shoreline. Paddle close to the shore until it turns eastward and becomes mudflats.

Expect to encounter harmless bat rays and leopard sharks in the shallows. Rays may suddenly splash their "wings" if surprised. Look for the ends of their wings moving like two parallel dorsal fins. To find paddling depth in the shallows, look for long sea grass. It likes deeper water than the algae that cover mud only a few inches deep.

The low-water route to Drakes Cove continues southwest to the far side of the estero. Then follow the steep bluffs seaward.

Drakes Cove is one of the few sandy beaches in Drakes Estero. Below the bluff just inside the estero is the cove where historians believe Sir Francis Drake landed the *Golden Hinde* for repairs. A large post and plaque commemorate the 1579 event.

A nearby grove of pines is home to egrets, great blue herons, and ravens in their respective breeding seasons. Near the pines is a dirt road and trail leading to the hilltop. On clear days, a spectacular view extends from Bolinas, along the PRNS surf line, to the distant ends of Schooner and Limantour Bays. The hilltop is also a good place to make a reality check on the weather and tides.

If fog is absent and the tide is not ebbing, you might paddle eastward from Drakes Cove to Estero Limantour. En route you will encounter waves that penetrate the mouth of the estero. Nearby sandbars are favorite places for seals to haul out. Some seals may surface near you for inspection. Soon Limantour Spit protects the estero from waves, and it is an easy paddle to the wind-protected beach at Drakes Head.

If you have timed the tour right, the incoming tide will assist your return paddle.

Much of the estero shoreline is muddy or covered with seaweed that the high tide floods. An exception is the landing site in Creamery Bay. Nearby bluffs protect the beach from the wind. The site has concrete pilings, footprints of wildlife visitors, and a small marsh.

Bring a map or a Google Earth image showing the location of the major mudflats. At low tide, paddle the channels between them. Along the cliffs, the water is usually deep enough for paddling.

9 Elkhorn Slough

Paddling calm water in the Elkhorn Slough offers an unforgettable opportunity to view marine wildlife. For extra appreciation of Elkhorn Slough, visit the Monterey Bay Aquarium and the Elkhorn Slough National Estuarine Research Reserve Visitor Center. The Marine Mammal Protection Act applies.

Length: Up to 5 miles each way
Average paddling time: 3 to 7 hours
Difficulty: Flatwater estuary; beginner skills
Marine weather: www.wrh.noaa.gov/mtr
Tide reference: Monterey: Elkhorn Slough, CA 1 bridge, high tides: +3 minutes; low tides: -2 minutes; Kirby Park, high tides: +26 minutes; low tides: +8 minutes
Best season: Year-round; winter for best birding
Land status: Private and public
Fees: Required at launch ramps

Maps: USGS Moss Landing, Prunedale; NOAA navigation chart 18685, Monterey Bay; Elkhorn Slough Foundation
Craft: Canoes, kayaks
Contacts: Monterey Bay Kayaks: (831) 373-5357; montereybaykayaks.com. Sea Otter Savvy: seaottersavvy.org. Elkhorn Slough Foundation: (831) 728-5939; elkhornslough.org.
Special considerations: Fishing and pleasure boats ply Moss Landing Harbor. Strong ebb tides can sweep unwary paddlers into the CA 1 pilings or carry you into the open ocean. Afternoon winds can make paddling difficult.

Put-in/Takeout Information

Moss Landing Harbor District launch ramp (N36 48.749' / W121 47.189') is on the west side of CA 1, just north of the Elkhorn Slough bridge and the huge power plant and next to the Monterey Bay Kayak shop. MBK rents boats and leads tours of Elkhorn Slough. There is a parking fee for ramp users.

Kirby Park (N36 50.415' / W121 44.614') has parking, toilet, boat ramp, and dock at the east end of the slough. From CA 1 northbound, turn east onto Dolan Road at the Moss Landing Power Plant. After 3.5 miles turn left at Elkhorn Road and then go 4.5 curvy miles (pass the Elkhorn Slough National Estuarine Research Reserve Visitor Center) to Kirby Park. Look for a sign on the left. Call MBK before you head out to make sure Kirby Park is open.

From CA 1 southbound, turn east at Salinas Road and go 1.4 miles to Werner Road. Turn right onto Werner, then right again (south) on Elkhorn Road, and then bear right once more to stay on Elkhorn Road. Go about 2.4 miles, paralleling the slough, to Kirby Park. From US 101, go west on CA 156 toward Castroville. Turn north onto Castroville Road, bear right (east) onto Dolan Road; then turn left (north) at Elkhorn Road and go about 4.5 curvy miles to Kirby Park. *Caution:* Car break-ins have been reported at Kirby Park.

Shuttle (optional): From Moss Landing to Kirby Park is 8 miles (about 20 minutes)

Overview

Expect to spend lots of time enjoying the marine and avian wildlife at one of the largest salt marshes between San Francisco and Morro Bay. Rolling hills with coastal oak and Monterey pine overlook tidal creeks and salt marshes in this outstanding Monterey Bay wetland with more than 300 bird species inhabiting the mudflats, marshes, and uplands surrounding the slough. Some formerly endangered or threatened species have recovered enough to be delisted.

Sea Otter Savvy reports that sea otters have been in Moss Landing for decades, but the population back in the upper waters of Elkhorn Slough has grown over the last fifteen years or so. On average, there are currently about one hundred sea otters in the harbor and slough. This protected habitat may be especially important to sea otters now that the mortality from great white shark bites has skyrocketed.

Moss Landing State Wildlife Area borders 3 miles of the slough along the north and west sides. East of the power generating plant, the National Estuarine Research Reserve (NERR) manages 1,700 acres on the south and east shores. Elkhorn Slough is one of only three such reserves in California. Plan to explore the visitor center at 1700 Elkhorn Road.

Plan your trip to take advantage of the winds and currents. Strong afternoon winds blowing inland from Monterey Bay can make the paddle to Moss Landing difficult. Please help protect all plant and animal life in the slough. East of the railroad tracks, the Elkhorn Slough Reserve and connected waterways are off-limits. Posted areas on the west side are closed to boaters. The NERR allows no camping or fires. Landing sites and toilets can only be found at Kirby Park and the Moss Landing put-in. The state permits seasonal waterfowl hunting in the main waterway and Moss Landing Wildlife Area.

Ask the folks at Monterey Bay Kayaks to recommend nearby restaurants in Moss Landing. That harbor town sits at the mouth of the slough. A prominent whaling center in the nineteenth and early twentieth centuries, the marinas now are home to hundreds of pleasure boats, commercial fishing vessels, and two marine research institutes.

The Paddling

Consult your tide tables to plan this trip. The slough's tides can give you a free ride back to your launch site, leave you stranded on a mudflat, or even wash you out to sea. Start at Moss Landing Harbor with an incoming tide, or start at Kirby Park when the tide is high. With favorable wind and tides, you can float the entire distance from Kirby Park to Moss Landing. Otherwise, start and end at the same place.

When entering or leaving Moss Landing Harbor, observe the "Rules of the Road." Stay to the extreme right side of the channel or in the shallow areas. Remember that canoes and kayaks are hard for large boats to see and avoid.

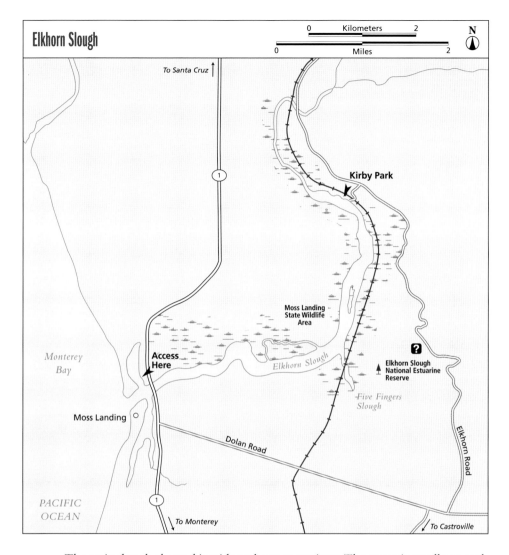

Elkhorn Slough

0 Kilometers 2
0 Miles 2

N

To Santa Cruz

Kirby Park

Moss Landing
State Wildlife
Area

Access
Here

Monterey
Bay

Elkhorn Slough

Elkhorn Slough
National Estuarine
Reserve

Five Fingers
Slough

Moss Landing

Dolan Road

Elkhorn Road

PACIFIC
OCEAN

To Monterey

To Castroville

The main slough channel is wide and easy to navigate. The water is usually smooth and so turbid that the bottom is impossible to see even when the water is only a few inches deep. Don't be surprised if you go aground on a mud bar in the middle of the channel. One clue to a mud bar is the harbor seals hauled out midstream.

One mile from the CA 1 bridge, the slough bends to the north. Seals often haul out on the north side, so keep your distance. The south bank is often home to a lineup of pelicans.

Sea otters have returned to the slough during the past two decades. Take care not to disturb them.

Rubis Creek forms a loop on the north side of the main channel. At higher tides, the tidal creeks offer close-up views of marsh birds, crabs, and other mud bank–dwelling critters. Birds, sea otters, and fish prey on these invertebrates, so they are an

Gena Bentall, SeaOtterSavvy

important part of the food web. The many sinuous turns test your maneuvering ability and get more difficult as the tide ebbs. If you get stranded at low water, you may have to wait for the next high tide to get out. The gluey goo under the pickleweed is too soft to support a person, and the salt marsh is sensitive to trampling.

A wide mouth under a shaded oak hillside proclaims the east end of the Rubis Creek loop. Look across the broad expanse of water to the east. You can probably see the visitor center far up the hillside.

Five Fingers Slough open to the south. Paddle only as far as the railroad trestle. Returning to the main slough, you can paddle another 2 miles to Kirby Park. Marshland, with attendant birdlife, borders both sides. Near the shallows look for the dorsal fins of smooth hound and leopard sharks or the wing tips of bat rays slicing the water. The two islands splitting the distance are closed to visitors.

Start your return to Moss Landing by early afternoon. Especially in summer, the northwest winds build into a stiff headwind by late afternoon. It may be the hardest paddling you do all day.

The CA 1 bridge pilings are one of the few potential hazards to careless paddlers. The hazard occurs only when the tidal current is strong or the wind strongly opposes the current. Keep your boat in line with the current through the bridge. Then head to the north side and the launch area. Take care not to be swept through the narrow harbor mouth into the swells of open Monterey Bay. Paddling upstream is difficult, and many large boats use that passage. The sandy beaches outside the harbor require a surf landing.

10 Monterey Bay–Cannery Row

A beginning kayaker's delight offers seaside views of Cannery Row as you paddle among sea otters, seals, whales, and sea lions. The Marine Mammal Protection Act applies.

Length: 2 miles each way
Average paddling time: 1 to 3 hours
Difficulty: SCRS I to III; beginner to intermediate skills required
Marine weather: 162.45 MHz; www.wrh.noaa.gov/mtr. For sea conditions and offshore wave heights, see NOAA Monterey buoy #46042.
Tide reference: Monterey: High tides: 0 minute; low tides: 0 minute
Best season: Year-round
Land status: Mixed public and private
Fees: Required for parking
Maps: USGS Monterey, Seaside; NOAA navigation chart 18685, Monterey Bay
Craft: Sea kayaks
Contacts: Monterey Bay Kayaks: (831) 373-5357; montereybaykayaks.com. Sea Otter Savvy: seaottersavvy.org. Monterey Bay Area

State Parks: parks.ca.gov. State parks camping reservations: (800) 444-7275; Reserve America.com. Monterey Bay Aquarium: (831) 648-4800; montereybayaquarium.org.
Special considerations: Large powerboats frequent Monterey Harbor. Although the Monterey Peninsula protects this coast from Pacific swells, the peninsula seaward of Lovers Point and especially beyond Point Pinos is exposed to the full waves, winds, and force of the Pacific Ocean. Since Monterey Bay water seldom warms above 55°F, even summer weather warrants a wet suit or dry suit in case of an upset. Strong northerly winds increase the size of the shore break at the put-in/takeout. Thick fog sometimes reduces visibility and makes navigation difficult. Check marine weather forecasts for fog and wind before starting out.

Put-in/Takeout Information

Monterey Beach State Park (N36 36.061' / W121 53.273'), adjacent to the Municipal Wharf: Follow Del Monte Avenue into Monterey and pass the Sloat Avenue traffic signal. With El Estero Park on the left and the beach on the right, turn into the parking area on the right. The friendly folks at Monterey Bay Kayaks have a place to change, shower, and wash your boat. Metered parking.

Fisherman's Wharf (N36 36.124' / W121 53.468') is at the next stoplight west of Monterey Beach. Look for the parking signs. Turn right toward the parking lot and Municipal Wharf, then left toward the marina. The free boat ramp is beside the harbor master's building. Monterey enforces metered parking 24 hours a day. Beware of motorized and sail craft in the marina.

Coast Guard Pier ramp (N36 36.547' / W121 53.660'): Continue west toward Cannery Row and go through the tunnel. Immediately after the tunnel is the Coast Guard Pier on the right. Adjacent to the jetty is a free boat ramp into the harbor. If you do not like the boat ramp, and if the surf is calm, sandy San Carlos Beach lies just past the jetty. It avoids the harbor traffic and is right next to the kelp beds. Like the other places in Monterey, the city meters parking.

Shuttle: None

Overview

As you paddle along the scenic Monterey Peninsula, try to envision the coastline as it used to be: first when Sebastián Vizcaíno discovered it in 1602; later as the backwater capital of Alta California (1775–1846); and then in Steinbeck's day as a bustling sardine-fishing center. Today the tourist mecca of Monterey Bay is the nation's largest marine sanctuary, and the Pacific Grove State Marine Gardens Fish Refuge protects the shoreside waters north of Pacific Grove. Together they provide a protected habitat that is rich in marine life.

Tour the Monterey Bay Aquarium before you paddle the bay. The aquarium's marvelously detailed exhibits will greatly add to your appreciation of the critters you meet and see on the water.

Today's 2,000-plus California sea otters have all bred from a colony of fewer than fifty animals that survived near Big Sur. During the 1700s and 1800s, fur traders hunted sea otters for their rich pelts, with as many as one million hairs per square inch.

Paddlers should enjoy viewing sea otters from a distance. Gena Bentall

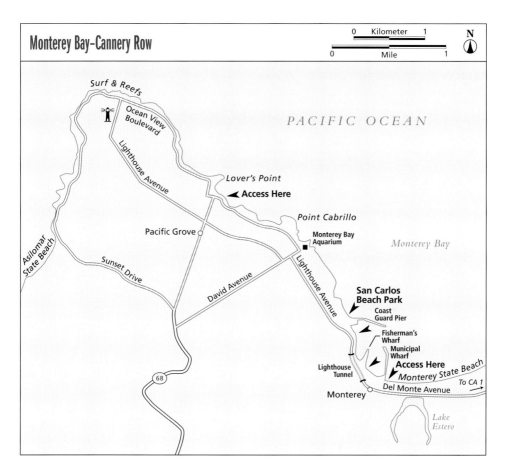

0   Kilometer   1

0   Mile   1

N

Surf & Reefs

Ocean View Boulevard

PACIFIC OCEAN

Lighthouse Avenue

Lover's Point
◄ **Access Here**

Point Cabrillo

Pacific Grove

Monterey Bay Aquarium

Monterey Bay

Asilomar State Beach

Sunset Drive

David Avenue

Lighthouse Avenue

San Carlos Beach Park

Coast Guard Pier

Fisherman's Wharf

Municipal Wharf

Access Here

68

Lighthouse Tunnel

Monterey State Beach

To CA 1

Del Monte Avenue

Monterey

Lake Estero

The Paddling

The Municipal Wharf and Monterey Harbor protect this broad section of Monterey State Beach from wave action. Launching from the beach also avoids the busy harbor lanes. Added luxuries are available at the adjacent facilities of Monterey Bay Kayaks.

Paddle toward the end of the Municipal Wharf, taking care where commercial fishing boats unload their catch. Large sea lions bark loudly from under this commercial wharf. Some bolder ones may swim close to your boat and usually dive under it.

Toward the ocean from the Municipal Wharf is the end of the Coast Guard Pier and breakwater. When they are not visiting warmer waters in breeding seasons, hundreds of male California sea lions congregate on the rocks. Sea lions have large front flippers that they use to lift themselves. Stay out of the way of the many large boats using the entrance to the harbor.

Inside the harbor, a concrete seawall protects the marina. At low tides the wall offers a display of sea stars, barnacles, and small sponges. Harbor seals and sea otters bask on the rocks and kelp beds between Fisherman's Wharf and the Coast Guard Pier.

Outside the breakwater, head toward the bulky gray Monterey Bay Aquarium. The route takes you through the kelp beds frequented by sea otters. When not swimming, they look like pairs of brown bumps floating amid the kelp. The otters wrap themselves and their young in kelp to stay stationary and use rocks to break shellfish held on their chest. Remember to keep your distance from sea otters and other marine mammals. (See the introduction regarding the Marine Mammal Protection Act.)

Few easy landing sites lie beyond Point Cabrillo except a small surfers' beach next to Lovers Point. Beyond, rocks and reefs line the shore where the surf breaks constantly. Pacific swells crash directly on Asilomar Beach.

Even a return to the harbor can be exciting. On a January tour, three gray whales surfaced within 50 yards of us just outside the breakwater. That was a great day!

11 Smith River

This northernmost Wild and Scenic River in California is famous for its sparkling clear waters, majestic coastal redwoods, and trophy-size salmon. Paddling runs on the North, Middle, and South Forks of the Smith are much more difficult and not included here. (Description contributed by Paul Redd.)

Length: 18 miles
Average paddling time: 4 to 6 hours
Difficulty: Class II whitewater skills
Rapids: Numerous Class I and II rapids; strainers/wood visible and easily avoided
Average gradient: 9 feet per mile
Optimum flow: 1,500 to 2,500 cfs
Flow gauge: Smith River at Jedediah Smith Redwoods State Park
Water source: Free-flowing wet season runoff
Best season: Winter through early summer, with spring providing more desirable weather
Land status: Private and state park
Fees: Required for some access

Maps: USGS Crescent City, Hiouchi; Jedediah Smith Redwoods State Park brochure
Craft: Canoes, kayaks, paddleboards, inflatable kayaks, rafts, drift boat dories
Contacts: Jedediah Smith Redwoods State Park: (707) 465-7335; parks.ca.gov. Camping: reservecalifornia.com. Shuttle services by Brad Camden: (707) 457-3365.
Special considerations: The Smith River drainage gets lots of rain: 5–8 feet or more per year. Winter rains quickly raise flows by thousands of cfs. Consider the weather forecast, and paddle when flows are diminishing.

Put-in/Takeout Information

Forks Boat Ramp (N41 47.957' / W124 3.288'): From US 101 go east on US 199 past Jedediah Smith Redwoods State Park and Hiouchi (about 7 miles) to the bridge onto South Fork Road. Go 0.25 mile from bridge to Forks Access Road, which leads to a paved parking area, toilets, and a boat ramp with gravel bar on river left, 0.4 mile upstream from the South Fork Smith River confluence.

Jedediah Smith Redwoods State Park (N41 48.147' / W124 5.099'): From US 101 go east on US 199 to the park. Pay the entry fee then follow signs to the picnic area. Carry over the gravel bar to water.

A ramp is also available at the campground (N41 47.596' / W124 5.194').

Templeman Grove (N41 49.025' / W124 5.551'): From US 199 turn north on North Bank Road. Go 1.25 miles to a side road and gravel bar on river right.

Walker Road access (N41 48.693' / W124 6.521'): From US 199 west of the Jedediah Smith park entrance and 1.5 miles west of the North Bank Road intersection, turn north into the Simpson Reed Redwood Grove. Follow the rough road 0.7 mile toward the river; turn right where the road forks to a gravel bar on river left (N124 6.521' / W124 6.429'). Walking through the redwood groves here is an experience you will long remember.

Ruby Van Deventer County Park (N41 51.128' / W124 7.250'): Located on North Bank Road, 3 miles north of Templeman Grove. From Crescent City, it's faster to go north on US 101 to North Bank Road and turn right. Continue 2.6 miles to the park. Paved parking area, campsites, toilets, huge gravel bar. Memorize this take-out by the houses across the river.

Fred D. Haight Drive launch ramp (N41 53.433' / W124 8.880'): From US 101, go 0.1 mile north of North Bank Road; turn left (west) onto Fred Haight Drive. Go 0.7 mile and turn left into two large vacant areas; go toward the river to the boat ramp. No facilities.

Ship A Shore (N41 56.643' / W124 11.911') is a motel/RV park and restaurant with a boat ramp at the river mouth at the Pacific Ocean. From North Bank Road and the Smith River bridge, go toward Oregon 6.5 miles on US 101 to Ship A Shore. Turn left and follow Chinook Street 0.25 mile to the ramp. May be filled during winter fishing season.

Shuttle: Service by Brad Camden of Gasquet, California: (707) 457-3365; brad camden@earthlink.net. Forks to Ruby Van Deventer County Park: 7 miles (about 15 minutes); Ruby Van Deventer County Park to Ship A Shore: 9 miles (about 25 minutes).

Overview

This chapter describes the only Class II and tidal sections on the Smith River. The Smith River is a favorite whitewater mecca for many paddlers.

Located at the extreme northwest corner of California, almost in Oregon, the Smith River is remote from the population areas of California and Oregon. Take your time and savor this area with the splendors of huge old-growth coastal redwood forests now preserved in Redwood National and State Parks. Take time to visit Stout Grove and the Simpson-Reed Groves. Contact a rafting company for a wilder run on the North or South Fork. Visit the spectacular shoreline in Crescent City, Patrick Point Vista, or Brookings, Oregon.

Pacific storms dump an average annual rainfall of 5 to 8 feet on the watershed. Stream flows quickly rise, sometimes 10,000 cfs in a day. Following winter storms, the water clears to a memorable emerald green, with even the bottoms of the deepest pools visible.

The best Class II paddling is from the Forks access to Ruby Van Deventer Park.

The Paddling

Forks to Ruby Van Deventer Park

Length: 9 miles
Average paddling time: 3 to 4 hours
Difficulty: Class II whitewater
Rapids: Numerous Class I and Class II rapids

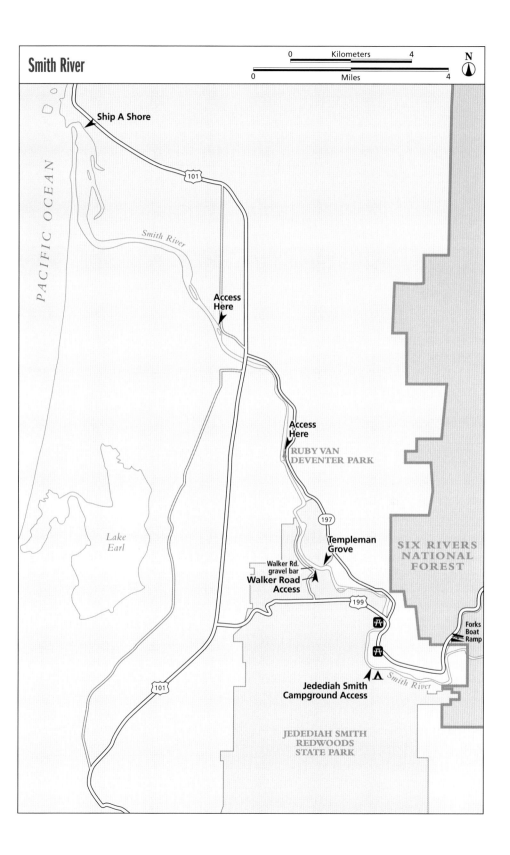

Paddlers enjoy the emerald-clear water near Jedediah Smith Redwoods State Park. PAUL REDD

Average gradient: 10 feet per mile

The winter rainy season and cold water here usually dictate wet suits or dry suits.

The Forks Access run starts with a Class II- rapid right after the put-in. Spend some time in the gorgeous rock-walled confluence with the South Fork area. This point of land and two rivers is an iconic spot found on postcards and calendars. It's nearly sacred ground for Smith River lovers. Watch for otters here and elsewhere along the river.

After the confluence, there are several Class I+ and II- rapids. The river is wide, and channels are clearly visible. Any strainers in the flow are usually visible in advance. In some places the current is continuous. You will see a covered bridge at mile 0.8 over a side creek on river left. This is the road to the amazing Stout Grove.

At mile 2.1 you enter Jedediah Smith Redwoods State Park. The redwood forests on both sides become thick and towering. A large gravel bar on river right fronts the campground. On river left is Stout Grove with fabulous, enormous old-growth redwood trees. At mile 2.5 a summer footbridge is erected every year connecting the campground area with Stout Grove. The campground boat ramp is visible on the right at mile 2.6. At mile 3.2 a gravel bar on river right marks the beginning of perhaps the longest stretch of continuous fast current and a Class II wave train along the left bank. Upsets here could result in longer swims, especially when flows exceed 2,500 cfs. The 0.3-mile-long wave train ends near the day-use area of Jedediah Smith Redwoods State Park on river right. This could be used for a short takeout or a put-in.

Downstream, the beauty continues unabated, with easy rapids and lush landscapes. Go under the US 199 bridge at mile 3.9, then paddle around an interesting island on the left at mile 4.6. At mile 5.8 is a notable Class II- rapid that splits the current around a rock island, followed by a hard left turn that is visible from the Walker Road gravel bar. Run either side of the island, but the left is easier. Immediately downstream, the Walker Road access is at mile 6.0 on river left, denoted by a steep, sandy bank. This is a good takeout for a shorter day, or if afternoon wind is forecast.

After Walker Road, the river opens up a bit. There are still Class I+ rapids, but there is also more flatwater and paddling required. At mile 7.8 there is an easy riffle if you go straight or a Class II- path through the rocks on the right. State park lands are replaced by homes and private property from here. In the afternoon, strong gusty winds can occur, which can make the paddling difficult.

The Ruby Van Deventer County Park takeout at mile 9.0 is most easily spotted by noting the distinctive homes/decks directly across from the gravel bar when you leave your vehicle there.

Ruby Van Deventer Park to Ship A Shore

Length: 9 miles
Rapids: A few gravel bars
Difficulty: Class I whitewater to flat tide water
Tide reference: Same as Crescent City

In the 3.3 miles between Ruby Van Deventer Park and the Fred Haight Drive launch ramp, there are a few gravel bar riffles before the river flattens out and widens. A mile

A fun rapid awaits paddlers just below the put-in. PAUL REDD

River otters can be seen near the South Fork confluence. PAUL REDD

downstream of the US 101 bridge, the concrete Fred Haight Drive ramp is on river right. Barefoot Brad, the shuttle driver, says you can paddle past here to the coast and have dinner! Subject to tides and winds, the river meanders through flat farmlands to the ocean. The best reason to float this reach is for salmon fishing. Bring your fishing rod and rain gear!

Coastal Mountains

The rugged Coast Mountains of northwestern California collect heavy winter rainfall that swells the rivers and supports magnificent forests of redwood and Douglas fir. Snowmelt from higher peaks prolongs the spring flows. While the water lasts, these rivers offer a variety of paddling experiences, from challenging whitewater to smooth family outings.

Spring brings fine weather and modest flows to make the mighty Eel River enjoyable (chapter 15).

12 Trinity River–Lewiston to Junction City

Reliable flows, pretty mountain scenery, easy access, and gravel bar rapids attract paddlers to this Trinity River reach. It is famed for its fly fishing. The Trinity River Restoration Program continues to mechanically modify streambeds to improve the fishery habitat along this National Wild and Scenic River.

Length: 33 miles
Elevation: 1,800 feet
Average paddling time: 4 to 7 hours per segment
Difficulty: Advanced beginner with fast-water experience negotiating brush and rocks
Rapids: Class I to Class II whitewater
Average gradient: 12 feet per mile
Optimal flow: 450 to 1,000 cfs
Flow gauges: Lewiston or Douglas City
Water source: Clair Engle and Lewiston Lakes
Best season: Summer and early autumn
Land status: Mixed private and public
Fees: Required at some sites
Maps: USGS Lewiston, Weaverville, Junction City; BLM Wild and Scenic Trinity River Public Access; Shasta-Trinity National Forest

Craft: Whitewater canoes, kayaks, inflatables, rafts
Contacts: BLM Redding Field Office: (530) 224-2100; blm.gov/ca. Shasta Trinity National Forest–Weaverville Ranger District: (530) 623-2121; fs.usda.gov/main/stnf. Trinity River Restoration Program (TRRP): trrp.net. Trinity County Chamber of Commerce: trinitycounty.com.
Special considerations: Brush along the streambanks and fallen trees are the primary concerns to the paddler. Flow schedules from Lewiston Dam change annually depending on winter precipitation. Flows may be higher than the release schedule due to contributions from tributary runoff. Channels may move from year to year due to streambed restoration. (See flow release graph and discussion in appendix A, page 331.)

Put-in/Takeout Information

Lewiston weir (N40 43.188' / W122 48.204'): At the north bank of the Trinity Dam Boulevard bridge, turn upstream to a gravel area just below the weir and next to the gauging station. Trinity Dam Boulevard exits north from CA 299 about 27 miles west of Redding.

Old Lewiston bridge (N40 42.477' / W122 48.519') connects Deadwood Road in Lewiston with Rush Creek Road along the north bank. The large gravel bar access is at the north end of the one-lane bridge. Trailers are OK, but there are no toilets.

Rush Creek (N40 43.284' / W122 50.076'): From Trinity Dam Boulevard, cross the Trinity River bridge, then turn west onto Rush Creek Road. The graded gravel parking area is about 2.1 miles from the Trinity Dam Boulevard bridge. A toilet is available.

Bucktail Hole fishing access (N40 42.263' / W122 50.780'): From CA 299 go north on Old Lewiston Road for 3 miles to Browns Mountain Road. Turn onto Browns Mountain Road for 0.25 mile. BLM access has a paved road, a toilet, and

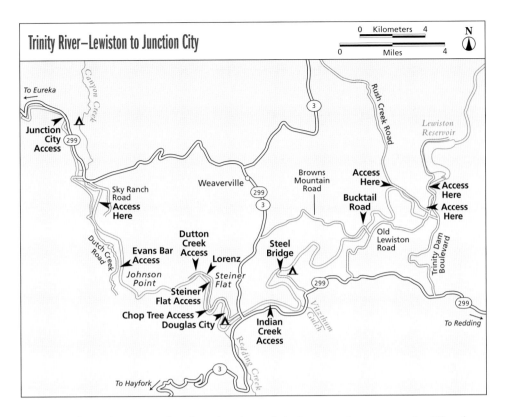

0   Kilometers   4

0   Miles   4

N

To Eureka

Canyon Creek

Junction City Access (299)

Sky Ranch Road Access Here

Weaverville (299) (3)

Browns Mountain Road

Access Here

Bucktail Road

Rush Creek Road

Lewiston Reservoir

Access Here

Access Here

Old Lewiston Road

Trinity Dam Boulevard

Dutch Creek Road

Evans Bar Access

Dutton Creek Access

Lorenz

Johnson Point

Steiner Flat

Steiner Flat Access

Chop Tree Access

Douglas City

Steel Bridge

(299)

Indian Creek Access

Weaver Creek

(299)

To Redding

Redding Creek

(3)

To Hayfork

---

space for trailers. Here the clear river is small, intimate, and very attractive. The channel meanders into a cliff 0.25 mile upstream.

Steel Bridge Day-Use Area (N40 40.462' / W122 55.176'): From CA 299 turn onto Steel Bridge Road about 3 miles east of Douglas City. Go about 2 miles to the end of the road. The day-use area provides riverside parking with easy put-in suitable for trailers next to the old bridge abutment. A toilet is available. Upstream within walking distance is Steel Bridge Campground. Fee-area campground is open mid-May until weather forces closure.

Indian Creek (N40 39.459' / W122 54.837') is adjacent to CA 299 about 1.4 miles east of the Douglas City junction with CA 3. The gravel parking area is OK for trailers.

Entrance to Douglas City Campground and day-use area (N40 38.916' / W122 57.190') is on Steiner Flat Road, 0.5 mile downstream of Douglas City and CA 299. This fee area is open mid-May through October.

Chop Tree Access (N40 39.282' / W122 57.785') is public land. Flag the site if taking out there. Steiner Flat (N40 39.636' / W122 57.944') is public land with primitive designated campsites and a toilet off Steiner Flat Road, 2.1 miles beyond the Douglas City Campground on Steiner Flat Road. There may be a BLM sign to this fee area, which is open year-round, weather permitting.

Lorenz Access (N40 39.820' / W122 57.952') is a BLM access with ample parking, easy launch, and a toilet. A big log pile on a mid-river gravel bar marks the takeout.

Dutton Creek Access (N40 40.498' / W122 58.251') is a BLM river access site at the junction of Dutton Creek and Steiner Flat Roads near a one-lane bridge about 3.8 miles from Douglas City. There is ample parking nearby but no toilet.

Evans Bar (N40 40.689' / W123 1.725') is a remote gravel bar on a straight stretch of the river where it heads north about 1.4 miles downstream of Johnson Point. To get there by road, take Dutch Creek Road from CA 299 near Junction City. Follow Dutch Creek Road 4 miles. Turn left onto Evans Bar Road and go about 0.75 mile to accessible gravel bars.

Sky Ranch (N40 43.433' / W123 2.934'): Where CA 299 rejoins the Trinity River west of Oregon Summit and east of Junction City, turn south onto Sky Ranch Road. Immediately look for the gravel roads leading to the river. Flag trees to mark the takeout between the bushes.

Dutch Creek Road at CA 299 (N40 43.719' / W123 3.633') is adjacent to a huge gravel bar but may be private property.

Junction City access (N40 44.789' / W123 3.927') is across CA 299 from Junction City Campground, about 1 mile west of the Canyon Creek bridge. A gravel road 50 feet east of the campground entrance leads to a large gravel bar with ample parking. This access has a history of car break-ins. The fee campground may be safer and provides potable water, toilets, tables, and campsites from mid-May to November 30, weather permitting.

Shuttle: Lewiston to Steel Bridge Campground: 15 miles (30 minutes); Steel Bridge Campground to Douglas City Campground: 6 miles (20 minutes); Douglas City Campground to Junction City Campground: 17 miles (30 minutes)

Overview

Near the fishing resort town of Lewiston, the Trinity River emerges clear and cold from Trinity and Lewiston Lakes into a mountain valley. Soon the valley narrows and the Trinity looks like other famous fly-fishing streams from an Orvis catalog. Below Douglas City, the river changes to a broad canyon surrounded by mountains. Boating difficulty remains consistent, with Class I and II rapids, gravel bars, brush hazards, and fallen trees.

Trinity County has an abundance of camping places. Steel Bridge, Douglas City, and Junction City Campgrounds are on the river. Downstream of Steiner Flat, you can choose your own unimproved site on public land, but please respect private property.

When the Trinity River Division of the Central Valley Project was completed in 1960, the Bureau of Reclamation diverted up to 90 percent of the Trinity's water to the Central Valley. The result was a devastating decline in the steelhead and salmon fisheries. With major flood flows subdued by reservoirs, the streambed changed. Trinity Lake captured gravel from the mountains. Sediment accumulated in the gravel bars instead of being washed higher onto the riverbanks. Brush emerged and stayed on the gravel bars without storm flows to uproot it.

Decades of studies have sought solutions to these problems. The Trinity River Restoration Program (TRRP) implements solutions with gravel bar restoration, channel modification, riparian vegetation management, and high flow releases. (See the "Stream Flows, Reservoir Inflows, and Releases" section of appendix A for a description of Trinity River typical flows.) Each spring a specific flow schedule is developed for the year and posted on the TRRP website. The maximum flow releases may be more than 6,000 cfs from early May to early July.

Spring and early-summer releases (over 6,000 cfs) may be too high for some paddling. Late-summer and early-autumn releases extend the boating season. Fish habitat improvements add cobbles and remove brush. Paddlers should expect changes to the river channels, requiring extra alertness. The increased pulses of water will be most noticeable along the approximately 40 miles between Lewiston and Big Bar. In odd-numbered years (e.g., 2021, 2023), releases are made in late August or early September for the Native American Boat Dance Flows. Boat Dance Flows typically reach 2,000 to 3,000 cfs. Flow manipulation lasts about a week for ramping up, holding at the high flow for a day or two, then ramping back down again to summer base flow.

The Paddling

Lewiston to Steel Bridge Day-Use Area

Length: 12 miles

Average paddling time: 4 to 6 hours

The put-in at the weir is only 1 mile below the Lewiston dam and fish hatchery. The cold water dumps over the weir into a brief eddy that exits into a brief rapid above and below the Trinity Dam Boulevard bridge. The narrow channel and frequent riffles require your attention. The splashy riffles continue over the spawning gravels near Lewiston.

Downstream 0.8 mile is the restored, one-lane Lewiston bridge, originally built in 1903. The north end of the bridge has a great put-in. Between Lewiston and the Rush Creek access, the Trinity is a drift boater's dream. These 2.1 miles mix calm water and riffles, great for paddling and fly fishing. The Rush Creek access is on river right, at the bottom of the hill where the river and road diverge.

The mouth of Rush Creek forms the next riffle as the river turns south again to the private river crossing between Salt Flat and Goose Ranch. This area has several large gravel bars, riffles, and brush. In the next 2 miles the river follows a long U-turn to the northwest into a steep bank. Then the narrow channel turns south to the Browns Mountain Road bridge with its parking area, fishing access, and takeout. It is all readily visible from the river.

Below the bridge 0.1 mile is an abrupt right turn into a local fishing hole. Browns Mountain Road parallels the right bank for 1.1 miles before climbing up Trinity

Lewiston's general store reflects the Trinity River region's past, dating back to gold mining in 1850.

House Gulch. Half a mile downstream the river braids, with snags and a long island supporting Bridge Road. Houses and summer camps are scattered along the banks between Grass Valley Creek, Poker Bar, and Limekiln Gulch.

Below Poker Bar, starting near Limekiln and China Gulches, the BLM manages the land for the next 2 miles to Steel Bridge Campground. Approaching Steel Bridge Campground, the channel splits around a gravel bar. The campground is on the left bank and is screened by trees. Downstream 0.25 mile, the day-use area takeout is easy to spot on river left where large concrete bridge abutments are on both sides of the river.

Steel Bridge Campground to Douglas City Campground

Length: 6.3 miles

Average paddling time: 2 to 4 hours

Put-ins are easy at the Steel Bridge day-use area. The Trinity runs swiftly over a gravel-lined bed through this area. Tall trees shade much of the river's width and help keep the clear water cold. At many river bends, trees have fallen into the river, creating hazards. About 1.5 miles below the put-in, the channel next to Steel Bridge Road has been choked by trees, so the right channel may be clearer. A short distance beyond this point, some large midstream rocks are easy to paddle around at low flows but can provide turbulent, swirling currents at high flows. This section of the Trinity reminded me of Vermont because of its clear water, green hills, and small houses scattered along the left bank. Some houses have wide lawns next to their own fly-fishing paradise.

Below Vitzthum Gulch, CA 299 joins the river. A small gravel bar on the left bank presents a lunch spot away from the houses, out of sight of the highway and on public land. Soon you approach the Indian Creek access on river left.

Approaching the CA 299 bridge at Douglas City, a series of islands and shallow channels have been created on river right. The left bank below the bridge is the site of Reading Bar, named for Major Reading, who discovered gold here.

A trailer park on the right bank signals your approach to a rapid with a little more spice, perhaps Class II. As the river starts a long U-turn, it bends abruptly to the west. Gravel piles line the right bank. In river center there is a large rock, and sometimes logs.

Continuing to curve north, the river encounters another riffle marked by bedrock rising from the right bank. In the late 1990s the rapid was a mild chute at 450 cfs, but years earlier it was a more difficult challenge.

Fifty yards below the rapid is the takeout at the BLM's Douglas City Campground. The picnic area and parking are on river right.

Douglas City Campground to Junction City

Length: 14.5 miles

Average paddling time: 4 to 7 hours

The takeout for the previous run is the put-in for this run. Here the river begins to change character. The channel has cut deeper into the canyon, and bedrock layers begin to appear. Other folks visit this very scenic section to fish or pan for gold. Most of the land between Douglas City Campground and Steiner Flat is public land managed by the BLM.

From Douglas City Campground the river turns west and then south. Several exposed ledges appear on river left. Although the river seems remote from civilization, Steiner Flat Road unobtrusively hugs the right slope. Above the road, steep forested slopes drop down from high ridges.

Gravel bar rapids occur less frequently on this stretch, with deeper cut channels between rocks and high-cut banks taking their place. Fallen trees are still a challenge to avoid. Some rapids above Steiner Flat are more technical than the rapids above Douglas City.

When we floated this stretch, two capsizes occurred at a simple-looking rapid that directed water from a gravel bar into a cut left bank. A fallen tree along the left bank and a stump in the fast water demanded careful boat control, which not everyone displayed. Be careful through here.

Near Steiner Flat, several houses are visible, including some that look new and well appointed. This remote community at the end of Steiner Flat Road is neatly nestled into the canyon above the Wild and Scenic Trinity River.

Look for another bouncy Class II rapid; then, at 0.75 mile below Dutton Creek, a gravel bar provides a welcome campsite. An old steel structure once emerged from the gravel that earlier was in a channel. These changes, plus debris high in the neighboring trees, evidence the magnitude of past floods. From here to Junction City the river is less difficult and you can make faster time. Wide gravel bars, suitable for camping, alternate from one side of the river to the other. The ridges are still steep and high but are more set back from the river.

Near Johnson Point, a large landslide—a remnant of hydraulic mining—scars a steep hillside on river left. Soon the river makes two sharp turns. Between the turns a gravel bar sends the flow into a high-cut bank on river right. Beware of nasty snags.

Starting near Johnson Point, the land ownership is a mixture of private, USDA Forest Service, and BLM all the way to CA 299. Since the gravel and sand flats look ripe for camping, check with the Weaverville Ranger Station. Seemingly incongruous among the long gravel and cobble bars is a huge house with spacious lawns about 1.5 miles below Johnson Point and opposite the Evans Bar river access.

At Bell Gulch the river turns northeast to expose the first water-level views of the 8,000-foot Trinity Alps, almost 20 miles away. A few more riffles, easy rapids, and avoidable snags speckle the river as it flows in a valley once exploited by hydraulic mining and gold dredges. From a canoeist's view, emerging trees and brush hint that the scars are beginning to heal.

Two roads, set well back from the river, parallel the last few miles: Sky Ranch Road on the east side and Dutch Creek Road on the west. Both join CA 299 in Junction City. CA 299 rejoins the Trinity River near Oregon Creek. About 4 miles up the creek, hillsides exposed by the famous La Grange hydraulic gold mine are slowly healing.

The next obvious landmark is the Dutch Creek Road bridge and, 0.5 mile afterward, the mouth of Canyon Creek, with high gravel mounds. During spring and early summer, Canyon Creek contributes a lot of snowmelt from the Trinity Alps to the river.

Through this section, the river flows immediately next to CA 299. The Trinity then swings south and forms a large loop away from the highway. The gravel bar inside this loop (river right) is the takeout. If you paddled next to CA 299 again, you went too far. Go back upstream to the gravel bar.

13 Trinity River–Junction City to Cedar Flat

This mountain river in deep canyons is popular for its exciting whitewater action and lots of easy access. Commercial whitewater outfitters offer rafting trips on this Wild and Scenic River.

Length: 23 miles
Average paddling time: 2 to 6 hours per segment
Difficulty: Intermediate to advanced whitewater skills required
Rapids: Class II, III, and IV whitewater
Average gradient: 16 feet per mile
Optimal flow: 400 to 1,500 cfs
Flow gauge: Burnt Ranch or Douglas City
Water source: Snowmelt plus releases from Lewiston Lake
Best season: Spring through early autumn
Land status: Mixed private and public
Fees: Required at most sites

Maps: USGS Junction City, Dedrick, Helena, Del Loma; Shasta-Trinity National Forest; BLM Wild and Scenic Trinity River Public Access
Craft: Whitewater canoes, kayaks, inflatables, rafts
Contacts: Shasta Trinity National Forest–Weaverville Ranger District: (530) 623-2121; fs.usda.gov/main/stnf. Trinity River Restoration Program (TRRP): trrp.net. Trinity County Chamber of Commerce: trinitycounty.com. Bigfoot Rafting Company shuttle service: (530) 629-2263; bigfootrafting.com.
Special considerations: Several rapids are severe enough to warrant scouting and, at some flows, portaging. Be prepared for high water and very cold snowmelt in spring.

Put-in/Takeout Information

The Junction City access (N40 44.789' / W123 3.927') is across CA 299 from Junction City Campground, about 1 mile west of the Canyon Creek bridge. A gravel road 50 feet east of the campground entrance leads to a large gravel bar with ample parking. This access has a history of car break-ins. The fee campground provides potable water, toilets, tables, and campsites from mid-May to November 30, weather permitting.

Bagdad River access (N40 46.252' / W123 7.536'): Adjacent to CA 299 on river right, just upstream of the North Fork bridge and Helena Road; paved road, parking, and toilets. Fee area.

Pigeon Point Campground (N40 46.037' / W123 7.952'): CA 299 mile marker 36.5. Paved road and toilets; heavily used in summer by rafters. Fee area.

Big Flat (N40 44.454' / W123 13.049'): CA 299 mile marker 30.4. Paved road, paved parking, and toilet. Fee area.

Skunk Point (N40 44.219' / W123 14.072'): Group campground with paved road, paved parking, and toilet. Fee area.

Whites Bar River access (N40 45.339' / W123 17.043'): CA 299 mile marker 26.5.

French Bar River access (N40 46.558' / W123 18.607'): CA 299 mile marker 23.61. Marked by a retaining wall down to the river made of native rock and concrete; gravel road to parking area, wide gravel bar, two picturesque rocks in the river. Easy put-in and takeout.

Del Loma access (N40 46.526' / W123 19.5278'): CA 299 mile marker 22.4. Dirt road to river, sandy beach, and gravel bar for an easy put-in and takeout.

Hayden Flat (N4047.036' / W123 20.677'): CA 299 mile marker 20.57, across from Hayden Flat Campground. Camping and toilets. Fee area. Steep paved footpath at downstream end of site leads to the river.

Cedar Flat access (N40 47.414' / W123 26.340'): At the CA 299 bridge (14 miles east of Salyer). Provides a takeout with parking and restroom.

Shuttle: Junction City to Pigeon Point: 5.3 miles (10 minutes); Pigeon Point to Big Flat: 6 miles (10 minutes); Big Flat to Hayden Campground: 10 miles (20 minutes); Hayden Campground to Cedar Flat: 6 miles (10 minutes)

Overview

The Wild and Scenic Trinity River provides whitewater excitement for boaters with prior whitewater experience. The steep whitewater on the Pigeon Point to Big Flat Run is a favorite commercial run for outfitters using rafts and inflatable kayaks. Most of the rapids have pools at the bottom. Downstream reaches are popular for training and overnight runs. Many larger rapids are visible from the road for easy scouting.

Throughout the reach, CA 299 parallels the north side of the river, with many access points on national forest lands. You can camp along the river. Most folks stay at established campgrounds and take day trips.

Be careful with fire—during the past decade there have been several large wildfires in the region.

During May, stream flows may be considerably increased by releases from Lewiston Reservoir. During odd-numbered years, Lewiston releases of 2,000 to 3,000 cfs are made in late August or early September for the Native American Boat Dance Flows. (See chapter 12 for details.)

The Paddling

Junction City to Pigeon Point

Length: 6.1 miles
Average paddling time: 2 to 4 hours
Difficulty: Class I to Class II whitewater; advanced beginner with whitewater experience

The Junction City put-in is the same as the takeout for the Douglas City reach. The river starts swiftly as it heads into a left turn along the road. For the next 2.5 miles, wide gravel bars, remnants of gold-dredging days, alternate along the banks. By late summer the wide riffles become shallow between deeper pools.

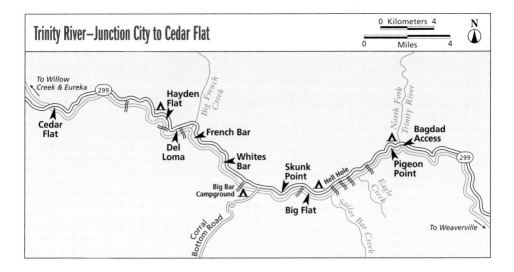

Below Coopers Bar the river turns west again, leaves the dredge tailings behind, and enters a much narrower channel. Downstream 1.5 miles, a steeper riffle drops you into the North Fork Trinity River confluence in sight of the bridge. This major tributary contributes high flows during spring runoff.

Bagdad access is immediately upstream of the North Fork bridge. Alternatively, busy Pigeon Point access is 0.5 mile downstream. You can see this popular access on river right with a campground in the trees beyond. Land quickly—the river runs fast here.

Pigeon Point to Big Flat

Length: 5.5 miles

Average paddling time: 3 to 5 hours

Difficulty: Class III to IV whitewater; intermediate to expert whitewater skills required

Average gradient: 21 feet per mile

From Pigeon Point, the canyon becomes prettier. Enjoy the scenery when you can, because exciting whitewater will soon take all your attention. If you are not ready to navigate steep, complicated, rock-filled rapids that are dangerous to swim, then enjoy this stretch of river from the road. There are plenty of milder rapids in downstream reaches.

The Trinity runs fast at the put-in, and you can quickly sense that the river is getting steeper. Bedrock instead of gravel creates the rapids. Ledges drop down to the water, and steep banks guard both sides. At first some short riffles alternate with calmer sections. Then, about 1.2 miles from Pigeon Point, there is a significant drop, soon followed by more brisk rapids. Approaching Eagle Creek (2 miles from Pigeon Point), you will encounter a significant steep drop, quickly followed by two more spicy rapids.

Hell Hole Falls excites many paddlers on the popular Pigeon Point Run.

Hell Hole rapid (N40 44.655' / W123 10.617') was once known as Malcolm's Delight. From a broad pool, the channel turns to the right, with shallow rocks on the right and bedrock ledges on the left. This Class III or IV rapid (depending on water level) runs to the left, goes over a couple of ledges, then drops vertically into a pool. Choose your route with care; some rocks are close to the surface at summer flows. Easy to scout from either bank, the easier portage is on the right.

Below Hell Hole, an easier section contains a couple of larger rocks before and in the middle of a riffle. The fun is not over yet. Almost at the confluence with Sailor Bar Creek is Sailor Rapid, once known as Triple Drop. A half mile beyond that is Pin Ball, an extended rapid with rocks in the middle, lots of choices to make, and splashy waves. Pin Ball demands respect and good paddle strokes to enjoy the pool at the bottom.

Opposite the Fishtale Inn is the long and complicated Fishtale rapid, Class III. In the river just beyond are some big boulders for a slalom course that at high water can make bouncy rapids with strong hydraulics. Gigantic boulders in the river and a huge rock outcropping on river right mark the Big Flat river access. The takeout is about 100 yards from the paved road, toilets, and parking.

Big Flat or Skunk Point to Hayden Flat

Length: 10.5 miles

Average paddling time: 3 to 6 hours (This stretch is sometimes combined with the Hayden Flat to Cedar Flat reach for a two-day trip.)

Difficulty: Class II whitewater; intermediate whitewater skills required

Average gradient: 16 feet per mile

This section is much easier than the Pigeon Point run. Just out of sight of the put-in is a rapid that has waves and requires maneuvering, followed by 0.7 mile of calm stretch. Then the river turns right with a rocky gravel bar and trees on the right. Some folks avoid this rapid by starting at Skunk Point group campground. The river below stays slow, with a few big rocks.

The Corral Bottom Road bridge connects to Big Bar Campground on the south side of the river. On the north side is the Big Bar Ranger Station. The banks are high and steep, offering poor river access. Enjoy the rocky rapid as you leave Big Bar. Below Denny Creek 0.5 mile are some more rocky rapids with bouncy waves at the bottom. After another 0.25 mile, a gravel bar rapid narrows the river, with big boulders in the channel and on both sides.

Where the road climbs higher above the river, look for the Whites Bar river access. Named Little Prairie, this pretty section of river has rapids scattered frequently along the next 1.3 miles. At 0.1 mile below Rock Bar Creek is a long rapid with big rocks in the center, some big waves, and holes. The Trinity turns north and then east as it approaches French Bar and the French Bar river access. Across from the access is a tunnel gold miners dug to divert the river through the promontory. French Bar is an easy put-in and takeout.

More rapids are found both upstream and downstream of Big French Creek. A rocky rapid and then a long flat section come just upstream of the Del Loma access road. The area has several sandy beaches and swimming holes where the river sweeps in a long arc from southwest to northeast. Expect some more rapids near the tiny community of Del Loma.

The highway and river rejoin here and turn southwest again, eventually coming to the picturesque Hayden Flat river access. The campground is across CA 299 from the river.

Hayden Flat to Cedar Flat

Length: 7 miles

Average paddling time: 3 to 5 hours

Difficulty: Class II to III whitewater; intermediate whitewater skills required

Visit the rocks above the river in the evening or early morning. You will treat yourself to a wonderful, peaceful view of the river. However, the pace soon changes to rapids alternating with pools. Below Little Swede Creek is a rock garden with a modest drop. At Schneider's Bar, a ledge extends diagonally across the river with hard-to-see slots and some boulders. This rapid has been dubbed "Picket Fence."

On the highway side, steep rocks lead up from the river. The south side has small, sandy flats for camping. The highway is far enough above the river to be out of mind. One mile below Schneider's Bar, the river takes two quick turns, first south then west. The Sandy Bar river access is the broad gravel bar at the second turn. There are riffles about the bar.

Approaching Don Juan Point, the rapids continue. A ledge extends upstream into the pool and starts a nontrivial rapid that includes a pour-over, a snaggle tooth, and waves that could swamp an open boat. Flows above 500 cfs may cover more of the rocks and make passage easier. This is a bouncy ride for inflatables and rafters wearing helmets. It is a test of skills for canoeists in open boats.

Just around the sharp bend of Don Juan Point is the final Class III rapid of the run. A mile downstream is the stream flow gauge known as Trinity River near Burnt Ranch. Downstream 700 feet, the CA 299 bridge crosses the Trinity at Cedar Flat.

Take out on the right just upstream of the Cedar Flat bridge. In past years a sign at the takeout read "Caution: Extremely Difficult Rapids. Experts Only 1.5 Miles below This Point." This sign refers to the Class V Burnt Ranch Gorge, which is beyond the scope of this guidebook.

14 Trinity River–Hawkins Bar to Willow Creek

This Trinity River reach has forgiving rapids that subside into fast water in richly forested canyons. This is a designated Wild and Scenic River.

Length: 15 miles
Average paddling time: 2 to 5 hours per segment
Difficulty: Beginners with whitewater experience and skills
Rapids: Class II whitewater
Average gradient: 12 feet per mile
Optimum flow: 700 to 2,000 cfs
Flow gauges: Burnt Ranch, Cedar Flat, and Hoopa
Water source: Snowmelt in spring; Lewiston releases and South Fork Trinity River flows in summer
Best season: Spring and summer

Land status: Mixed private and national forest
Fees: Required at some sites
Maps: USGS Hennessey Peak, Salyer, Willow Creek; Six Rivers National Forest
Craft: Whitewater canoes, kayaks, inflatables, rafts
Contacts: Six Rivers National Forest–Lower Trinity Ranger District: (530) 629-2118. Trinity River Restoration Program (TRRP): trrp.net. Trinity County Chamber of Commerce: trinitycounty .com. Bigfoot Rafting Company shuttle service: (530) 629-2263; bigfootrafting.com.
Special considerations: The Trinity has the typical hazards of whitewater streams.

Put-in/Takeout Information

Hawkins Bar (N40 52.389' / W123 31.669'): Turn north from CA 299 at a national forest sign that reads "River Access," 0.1 mile west of the Denny Road intersection. The gravel river access road heads downstream to a large gravel bar with a toilet, parking, and a 75-yard walk over cobbles to the water.

Sayler Bridge (N40 53.562' / W123 35.115'): Turn north from CA 299 at the Sayler Store onto Sayler Loop Road. Cross the bridge then look on the upstream side for a footpath descending 175 yards and 100 vertical feet to the river. Limited parking along downstream side of the bridge. There have been security issues with cars here.

South Fork confluence (N40 53.364' / W123 35.975'): From CA 299 150 yards east of the bridge, an anglers' path leads 300 steep yards and over rocks down to the gravel bar. Limited road shoulder parking. May best be considered a bailout point.

Kimtu Bar day-use area (N40 56.853' / W123 36.862') and campground have a large gravel beach, easy access, picnic tables, and a partly paved road. From CA 299 entering Willow Creek, turn east on Country Club Road and follow it to Kimtu Road. Turn right onto Kimtu Road toward the recreation area and Kimtu Beach at the end. Driving distance is about 1.2 miles from CA 299. Toilet and fee area.

Big Rock access (N40 56.809' / W123 37.992') at Willow Creek is accessible from CA 96 only 0.4 mile north of the junction with CA 299. A paved road leads 0.2

mile behind a large gravel operation. Paved parking lot, ample parking, toilet, picnic tables, and launch ramp lead to the water and wide gravel bars.

Shuttle: Hawkins Bar to near Salyer: 6 miles (20 minutes); Salyer to Willow Creek: 8 miles (20 minutes)

Overview

A highway sign greets visitors: "Welcome to Willow Creek—River Fun in the Mountain Sun." You too will enjoy this river. These two canyons provide whitewater fun that changes into fast riffles in a much bigger, richly forested section below the South Fork confluence. Bring your fishing rod for that reach. With the highway several hundred feet above the water, the river seems remote.

Upstream of the South Fork confluence, flows depend on river restoration flows from Lewiston and snowmelt from the major tributaries between Junction City and Hawkins Bar. Late summer is the exception, when Lewiston releases of 450 cfs sustain the flows. Downstream of the South Fork Trinity River confluence, spring and early-summer flows are greatly augmented by the South Fork Trinity River.

Exceptions: During odd-numbered years, Lewiston releases of 2,000 to 3,000 cfs are made in late August or early September for the Native American Boat Dance Flows. (See chapter 12 for more details.)

The Paddling

Hawkins Bar to Salyer

Length: 7 miles
Average paddling time: 2 to 4 hours
Difficulty: Advanced beginner with whitewater experience
Rapids: Class II whitewater
Optimal flow: 700 to 2,000 cfs (Burnt Ranch gauge station)

The paddling starts with fast, rocky water, and you get to use your whitewater skills in a hurry. A mile below the put-in, the river turns north into a 2-mile-long horseshoe bend. Trinity Village is spread on the gentler slopes where the bend begins. The water slows into long pools between rapids.

Past some houses on the left, the river turns west into a rocky rapid. Even at 500 cfs, some rapids have large enough waves that open whitewater canoes will need to bail. Fortunately, pools follow most rapids. Another horseshoe turn brings you to a promontory with a secluded beach on river left. A steep path leads from here to the highway. In the next 1.5 miles, the river flows under two bridges without access to CA 299.

To take out at Sayler, land on the gravel bar just upstream of the bridge on river right. A steep narrow path leads to the road at the bridge.

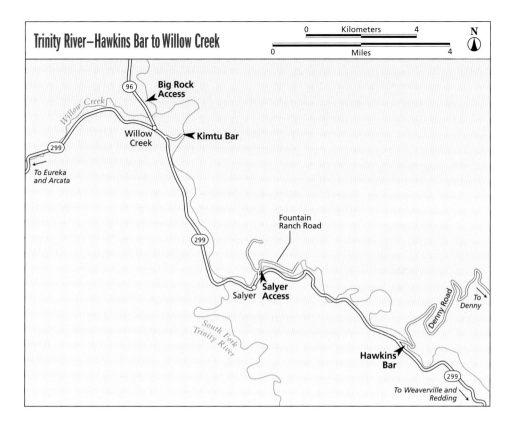

Big Rock
Access

Willow
Creek

Kimtu Bar

To Eureka
and Arcata

Fountain
Ranch Road

Salyer
Access

Salyer

South Fork
Trinity River

To
Denny

Hawkins
Bar

To Weaverville and
Redding

Salyer to Willow Creek

Length: 8 to 9 miles
Average paddling time: 2 to 5 hours
Difficulty: Beginner with whitewater experience
Rapids: Class II whitewater
Optimal flow: 1,200 to 2,000 cfs (Hoopa gauge)

From Salyer the Trinity continues with few riffles 1 mile to the South Fork Trinity River confluence. Between Salyer and the South Fork, the gravel bars broaden.

From under a high bridge, the South Fork Trinity River substantially adds to the flows in the main channel. Near the confluence, the channel widens markedly with large, flat-topped gravel bars. At higher flows, water courses over many gravel bars, making the river easier to float. A few houses at the confluence are close to water level, but most buildings are much higher above flood level. CA 299 parallels the river 100 to 200 feet up the west side of the canyon. On the east side, Campbell Ridge Road follows the canyon for much of the distance between the South Fork confluence and Willow Creek.

Kimtu Bar access is in a calm horseshoe bend on river left. Opposite Kimtu, a small canyon road comes plainly into view. This popular day-use area has a wide gravel bar and a rich conifer forest on river left.

An open canoeist enjoys some fast whitewater near Hawkins Bar.

Below Kimtu Bar, the river flows west under the Country Club Road bridge about 0.5 mile above the Big Rock Trinity River access. The river turns right at the Willow Creek confluence amid large gravel bars. Look for the large gravel piles on the left, indicating the takeout location. Follow the channel downstream, and then work your way through the gravel bars to the boat ramp at the Big Rock Trinity River access.

15 Eel River–Alderpoint to McCann

This National Wild and Scenic River is a delight for canoe camping. Springtime trips are a joy. The hillsides are green, the water is translucent, the luscious-looking pools are swimmable, and the paddling is relaxing.

Length: 25 miles
Average paddling time: 3 leisurely days
Difficulty: Class: I+; fast-moving water skills required
Average gradient: 5 feet per mile
Optimal flow: 1,000 to 4,000 cfs
Flow gauge: Fort Seward
Water source: Rainy season runoff
Best season: Spring
Land status: Private
Fees: None

Maps: USGS Alderpoint, Fort Seward, Garberville, Myers Flat, Blocksberg, Weott; Six Rivers National Forest
Craft: Whitewater canoes, kayaks, inflatable kayaks, rafts, dories
Contacts: Shuttle services (Rick Doty): (707) 926-5444. Humboldt Redwoods State Park: (707) 946-2263; humboldtredwoods.org.
Special considerations: During rainy season, flows can rise dramatically in a short time. Strong upstream winds may battle boaters.

Put-in/Takeout Information

Private property borders the Eel River and includes the roads leading to river gravel bars. Property owners have placed locked gates at access points (e.g., Eel Rock) because of rowdy behavior, littering, and fire hazards exhibited by some river users. To placate the property owners, do not camp or start campfires at the access points. To avoid potential vandalism, leave your vehicle with a local shuttle driver or in a public location.

All roads approaching the river are narrow, mountainous, and slow. There are no quick routes to anywhere. The river sometimes washes out the last 100 yards leading down to the gravel bars, so expect to use four-wheel-drive vehicles or hand-carry gear. Gravel bars are sometimes too soft to support vehicles.

Alderpoint (N40 10.031' / W123 36.127'): From US 101 at Garberville, exit to Redwood Highway north; turn right (east) onto Alderpoint Road. Follow the mountainous Alderpoint Road with great views of the Coast Range for 21 miles to the town of Alderpoint. Follow Alderpoint Road as it turns east then south past the high bridge. Go upstream on River Road about 0.5 mile to a small water tank. Descend steeply to the old railroad bed; go downstream as far as you dare.

Fort Seward (N40 13.479' / W123 38.359'): Go to Alderpoint, cross the bridge, and follow paved Alderpoint Road about 9 miles over the mountain to the junction with Fort Seward Road. Turn left (west); go about 0.25 mile to an unmarked, unpaved pullout that leads 0.15 mile to a large gravel bar on river right.

Eel Rock (N40 17.126' / W123 43.839'): Because of undesirable behavior by some river bar users, the gate is now locked.

Whitlow (N40 18.830' / W123 48.136') is seldom used because of limited parking and a steep path to the river. From US 101 take exit 656 at Myers Flat to Avenue of the Giants south toward Hidden Springs Campground. Follow Avenue of the Giants 1.8 miles and then turn

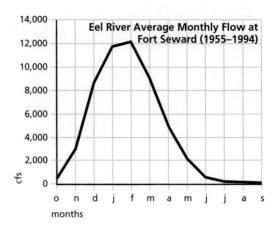

onto Elk Creek Road. Go east to the junction of Dyerville Loop and Whitlow Roads. Go down Whitlow Road to the flat called Whitlow/Sequoia. Where the road flattens and turns right, look for a parking space. A foot trail follows the railroad downstream to a trestle and then turns downhill to the mouth of Sonoma Creek. Carry distance is about 0.25 mile. To find this takeout from the river, look for the creek on river left and the two hillside houses on river right.

McCann (N40 19.610' / W123 50.195'): From US 101 take exit 663 to Avenue of the Giants; drive through Founders Grove on Dyerville Loop Road. Follow the narrow road approximately 7.5 miles to the low, long concrete bridge across the river. Park on the north side (river right).

Shuttle: Alderpoint to McCann: 45 miles (1 hour, 30 minutes) via US 101; Fort Seward to McCann: 55 miles (1 hour, 45 minutes) via Alderpoint and US 101

Overview

Draining 3,680 square miles of the remote Coast Range of northwestern California, the Eel is a big river in a 2,000-foot-deep canyon. Expansive views open to the forested western slopes and the grass-covered ridges to the east. Some ridges descend as cliffs directly to the water. The channel is more than 100 yards wide. Huge rock outcroppings dot the shores and river channel. Sometimes the wildlife will come to you. We saw fresh bear tracks emerging from the river when we floated this stretch. Gravel bars seem to be everywhere. Some even have nice sandy campsites. One school group enjoyed this river run for twenty consecutive years.

The untamed Eel is a river of extreme flows. Winter flows average more than 13,000 cfs, and floods max out at 560,000 cfs. Late-summer flows dwindle to 55 cfs or less. Very flashy, Eel River flows sometimes jump 10,000 cfs in a day. High-water marks on the cliffs and trees are 20 feet above desirable paddling stages. At high water, the river extends from bank to bank in a wide, powerful torrent. Rain is always a possibility. The paddlers' trick is to be there in spring, when the river is dropping and the weather is dry.

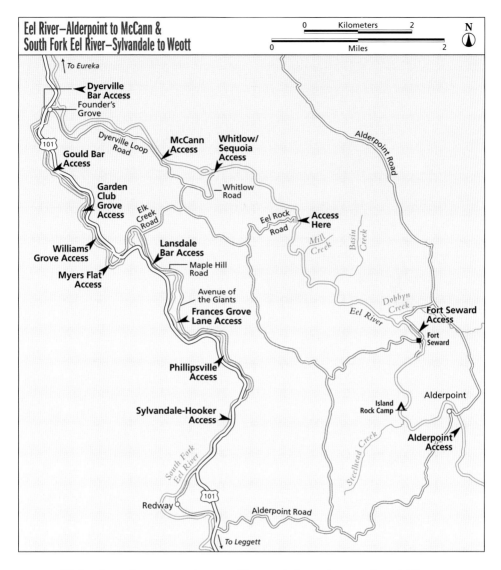

Kilometers

Miles

N

To Eureka

Dyerville
Bar Access

Founder's
Grove

Dyerville Loop
Road

McCann
Access

Whitlow/
Sequoia
Access

Alderpoint Road

101

Gould Bar
Access

Garden
Club
Grove
Access

Elk
Creek
Road

Whitlow
Road

Eel Rock
Road

Access
Here

Mill
Creek

Basin
Creek

Williams
Grove Access

Lansdale
Bar Access

Myers Flat
Access

Maple Hill
Road

Avenue of
the Giants

Frances Grove
Lane Access

Dobbyn
Creek

Eel River

Fort Seward
Access

Fort
Seward

Phillipsville
Access

Alderpoint

Island
Rock Camp

Sylvandale-Hooker
Access

Alderpoint
Access

South Fork
Eel River

Steelhead Creek

101

Redway

Alderpoint Road

To Leggett

High winter flows move the gravel bars and channels, sometimes hiding or exposing large rocks. It is never the same two years in a row.

As you traverse the length of the canyon, the remains of the Northwestern Pacific Railroad hide behind redwood trees, dart through tunnels, cross trestles, and lie under landslides. The former railroad is the only path attempted along the unstable terrain.

Start early and get off the river by midafternoon to avoid strong winds blowing up the canyon. Strong winds and low flows can result in dreary paddling and may be too strong for rafts to make downstream progress.

The Paddling

Since the shuttle can take 3 hours, bring some entertainment while you wait. Better yet, have the boats loaded and lunch ready for the shuttle crew before paddling begins.

Above 3,000 cfs the current is fast and makes for swift downstream progress. At that level, large rocks with sharp eddy lines may require some forceful paddling to avoid upsets. At 700 cfs the pace is slower, but it took us only 2 hours of steady paddling to go 7.25 miles.

Only 4.5 miles below Alderpoint, a trestle with concrete abutments crosses Steelhead Creek on river left. Steel rails scattered along the left bank and an old railroad tunnel announce the approach of Island Rock. Its big ledges offer wind protection and sandy campsites. Additional campsites are a short distance downstream.

This toddler, Jacob Verhaegh, grew up to become a junior national team member in whitewater canoe slalom.

Three miles beyond is Fort Seward. On the way, enjoy the midstream rock outcroppings with their inviting swimming holes. The Fort Seward access is on the river right about 1 mile downstream of the Fort Seward bridge.

Dobbyn Creek is a boisterous stream with a wide delta and giant rocks (N40 13.843' / W123 39.565') about 2 miles below the Fort Seward bridge. Some years this is a good camping site. We noted interesting tracks, perhaps bear. Of more interest is the rapid there—the gravel bar pushes the river to the left, directly into big midstream rocks. We paddled to the right.

Several huge rock peninsulas jut into the river, causing some interesting currents that vary with flow levels. At Yellow Jacket Buttes, the river turns north for 1 mile then west just beyond two big midstream rocks. Basin Creek is on the right with its pretty falls (N40 15.047' / W123 42.078') and popular campsites. Above the falls is a narrow ravine with a series of plunge pools.

At Mill Creek (N40 16.119' / W123 43.556') the river meets a ledge jutting 300 feet from the right bank. The ledge redirects the river to the opposite bank. Some paddlers avoid the shallow gravel bar on the left by maneuvering through the slalom course to the right of the big midstream rocks.

At low flows, practiced eyes can find routes over thinly covered gravel bars.

Downstream 1.5 miles, with the river running north, look for the rough road on the left bank that is the Eel Rock takeout. As of this writing, a locked gate bars public access.

Along the left bank, the railroad enters a tunnel at a huge jointed rock face that has split into the river.

A cable high above the river marks the approach to Whitlow. At the next bend, Sonoma Creek joins on the left. This is the Whitlow takeout. Two houses sit far across the Eel on the opposite shore. A trail leads 200 yards along the creek and up the bank to the old railroad bed.

Another 2.25 miles downstream is the McCann Road bridge takeout. This is much easier access than Whitlow. Expansive gravel bars line river right, with lots of space for taking out.

16 South Fork Eel River–Sylvandale to Weott

Flowing through Humboldt Redwoods State Park and followed by Avenue of the Giants, this Wild and Scenic River is lined with majestic redwood groves. This broad river flows between gravel bars with easy paddling that invites early-season boating.

(See map on page 89.)
Length: 24 miles
Average paddling time: From a few hours to 3 days
Difficulty: Beginner to intermediate moving-water skills required
Rapids: Class I to Class II whitewater
Average gradient: 6 feet per mile
Optimal flow: 900 to 2,500 cfs
Flow gauge: Miranda
Water source: Rainy season runoff
Best season: Spring
Land status: Mixed private and public

Fees: Required for access
Maps: USGS Garberville, Miranda, Myers Flat, Weott; Humboldt Redwoods State Park
Craft: Canoes, kayaks, inflatable kayaks, rafts, dories
Contacts: Humboldt Redwoods State Park: (707) 946-2263; humboldtredwoods.org. Giant Redwoods RV & Camp: (707) 943-9999; giantredwoodsrv.com.
Special considerations: During rainy season, flows can rise dramatically in a short time. Dress for cool weather and cold water. Several rapids require fast-water skills.

Put-in/Takeout Information

Sylvandale-Hooker Road (N40 10.837' / W123 46.787'): Take exit 645 from US 101 to Avenue of the Giants. Where Avenue of the Giants meets Hooker Road, follow the dirt road north to gravel bar access about 0.25 mile upstream of the US 101 bridge.

Phillipsville (N40 12.443' / W123 47.394'): From Avenue of the Giants in Phillipsville, follow Phillipsville Road as it loops west to the river. Access is at river mile 21.

Maple Hill Road bridge (N40 13.103' / W123 48.931'): Take exit 630 from US 101 to Maple Hill Road. Cross the bridge to a large pullout and gravel road to the river on river right.

Frances Grove Lane (N40 13.534' / W123 49.316') is a side road from Avenue of the Giants between Maple Hills Road and Miranda. Gate may be closed.

Lansdale Bar (N40 16.150' / W123 51.037') can be reached from a side road from Avenue of the Giants, 0.7 mile south of Elk Creek Road at river mile 13.5.

Myers Flat (N40 15.714' / W123 52.723'): US 101 and Avenue of the Giants intersect here. Next to the general store, take Myers Avenue west to the Giant Redwoods RV & Camp. A footpath leads 50 yards to a gravel bar. This is a fee area with toilets, parking, picnic tables, and camping.

Williams Grove (N40 16.555' / W123 53.339'): One mile north of Myers Flat, turn from Avenue of the Giants into Williams Grove. Go toward the river. Access is at river mile 8.1.

Garden Club Grove (N40 17.504' / W123 54.111'): From Avenue of the Giants 2.3 miles north of Myers Flat, turn into the Garden Club Grove Picnic Area. Access is at river mile 6.5. Gate may be locked during the wet season.

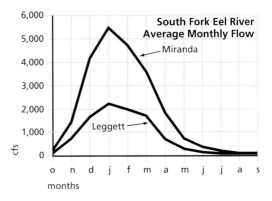

Gould Bar (N40 18.961' / W123 55.351'): Exit US 101 at Weott; go west to Avenue of the Giants. Turn south on Avenue of the Giants for 0.5 mile to a side road leading toward the river. Access is at river mile 3.0. Gate may be locked during the wet season.

Leatherwood Bar (N40 21.336' / W123 55.294'): Dyerville Road, Avenue of the Giants, and US 101 come together at the South Fork Eel River confluence with the main Eel River. From Dyerville Road, next to the Dyerville overlook, a side road slopes down to the river near the US 101 bridge. Access is at river mile 0.4.

Shuttle: Driving distances are slightly shorter than river distances. Speeds along Avenue of the Giants are 20 to 30 mph.

Overview

Humboldt Redwoods State Park contains most of the lower portions of the South Fork Eel River. Magnificent redwood groves, with some trees thousands of years old, border this National Wild and Scenic River. Much of the channel is wide, with immense gravel bars. These would be ripe for camping except that they are in the state park, where camping and campfires are limited to designated campgrounds. Fishing is popular for wild salmon and steelhead. Some years, park rangers or docents lead canoe trips in spring. Take time to hike the short Rockefeller Loop trail at the mouth of Bull Creek.

Without reservoirs, the flows rise with the rains in winter and dwindle in summer. Winter flows average more than 5,500 cfs; late summer flows dwindle to 60 cfs or less. Flow volumes at Miranda are usually 2.5 to 3.5 times greater than flows at Leggett. Winter and spring water levels are more desirable when the water clears after storms. Anybody taking a trip on the Eel should be ready for rain.

River access is generally easy from the many facilities in the park and the riverside communities. US 101 follows the west bank, and the scenic Avenue of the Giants parallels the right bank.

Rainy season camping may be available at Humboldt Redwoods State Park, Richardson Grove State Park, Benbow Lake State Recreation Area, and several private campgrounds.

Wind can be a serious nuisance to Eel River paddlers. When the weather warms up inland, the fog comes to the coast. Then the prevailing northwest winds blow up the river canyons from the cool coast to the warm interior. Start early in the day, as the winds strengthen later in the afternoon. Since inflatable boats perform poorly in strong wind, use hard-shell craft here.

The Paddling

Only 0.25 mile below the Hooker Road put-in, US 101 crosses the river again. The bridge is also the site of the USGS gauge known as South Fork Eel River at Miranda.

After 2 miles the broad river terrace of Phillipsville appears on river right. Access is on river right.

Sliding quickly through broad gravel bars, the river turns west as it approaches the Fish Creek confluence on river right. Then the hills close in as the river again turns northward to Miranda.

Approaching Miranda, you pass under the Maple Hill Road bridge and the channel widens into giant gravel bars. These continue to the Jensen Grove at Dry Creek.

The riverside land downstream is mostly in Humboldt Redwoods State Park. Enjoy the views of the redwoods that the park preserves. Better yet, take the time to walk slowly through these forest giants. You will long remember that experience.

After passing Dry Creek, the riverbed braids before again narrowing where US 101 cuts away from the river across the base of Eagle Point. The absence of vehicle noise is welcome. Look for additional riffles as the river rounds the horseshoe bend. Twists and turns provide an isolated feeling between the 200-foot-high slopes, beaches, and redwood forests. They also protect you from much of the upstream wind.

The next landmark is the US 101 bridge near Myers Flat. This is the last bridge before the bridges at the main Eel confluence. Myers Flat has an access site. The next access site is at Williams Grove, 2 miles downstream. Look for the summer road crossing there.

Additional summer bridges cross the river at Garden Club Grove, Robinson Creek, and Bull Creek (Federation Grove). These are underwater at boatable flows and may cause some bouncy riffles. They also mark the access points.

Redwood trees line the South Fork of the Eel River. This tree in the Founders Grove eclipses the size of a pickup truck.

The final takeout on the South Fork Eel is Leatherwood Bar at the last US 101 bridge. Takeout is on the right.

17 South Fork Eel River–Leggett to Redway

This National Wild and Scenic River boasts salmon and steelhead fishing, magnificent redwood groves, and fine paddling. California State Parks has a series of campgrounds adjacent to the river along the Avenue of the Giants.

Length: 24 miles
Average paddling time: 3 to 6 hours per segment
Difficulty: Intermediate whitewater skills required
Rapids: Class I to Class III whitewater
Average gradient: 8 to 16 feet per mile
Optimal flow: 500 to 1,000 cfs
Flow gauge: Leggett
Water source: Rainy season runoff
Best season: Spring
Land status: Public parks and private lands
Fees: Required in parks

Maps: USGS Leggett, Noble Butte, Piercy, Garberville
Craft: Whitewater canoes, kayaks, rafts, dories
Contacts: Humboldt Redwoods State Park: (707) 946-2263; parks.ca.gov; humboldt redwoods.org. Richardson Grove State Park: (707) 247-3318. Benbow State Recreation Area: (707) 923-3238. Benbow Inn: (707) 923-2124; benbowinn.com. Standish-Hickey SRA: (707) 925-6482. Smithe Redwoods State Natural Reserve: (707) 247-3318.
Special considerations: During rainy season, flows can rise dramatically in a short time. Several low-water bridges require portages.

Put-in/Takeout Information

Leggett (N39 52.304' / W123 42.979'): Where CA 1 meets US 101, a gravel road runs north from a wide gravel area. Follow the increasingly steep, unpaved road down to a gravel bar. Four-wheel drive is recommended to come back up the hill.

Standish-Hickey State Recreation Area (N39 52.584' / W123 43.979') is 1.5 miles north of Leggett on US 101. The gate to the steep paved road to the river is closed during the rainy season, so carry 0.4 mile to the river.

Smithe Redwoods State Natural Reserve (N39 53.893' / W123 45.089'): Four miles north of Leggett, turn into the reserve from US 101.

Reynolds Wayside (N39 57.077' / W123 46.734'): Take exit 625 off US 101 to CA 271 North. Follow CA 271 about 0.75 mile. Look for a gravel road going left (under US 101) 0.3 mile to the river and a big gravel bar.

Richardson Grove State Park (N40 1.200' / W123 47.397') is near US 101, 7 miles south of Garberville.

Benbow Park (N40 3.977' / W123 47.403'): Exit US 101 at Benbow. Go west to Benbow Picnic Area with its restrooms, paved parking, and grassy lawns.

Tooby Park (N40 5.356' / W123 47.863'): From US 101, exit at Garberville onto Redwood Drive. Turn west onto Sproul Creek Road, going under US 101 and then bending south. Follow to the junction of Kimtu Road and Tooby Park next to the Sproul Creek Road bridge.

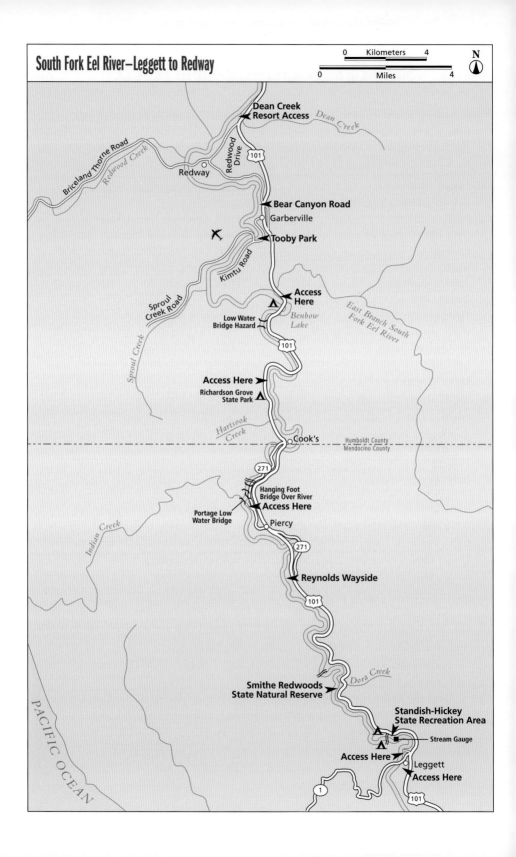

South Fork Eel River–Leggett to Redway

Bear Canyon Road near Garberville (N40 6.434' / W123 47.810'): From Garberville go north on Redwood Drive, cross US 101, and pass Alderpoint Road. From Redwood Drive turn left onto Bear Canyon Road, past the Pacific Gas & Electric service center, and bear right down the steep, paved road to the gravel bar under the high bridge.

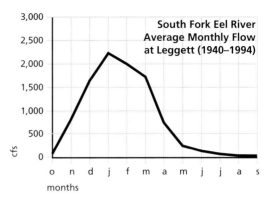

Dean Creek Resort (N40 8.475' / W123 48.625'): From US 101, exit onto Redwood Drive north of Garberville. Go south on Redwood Drive 0.2 mile to the resort. This commercial RV park and campground affords easy access to the river.

Shuttle: Leggett to Piercy: 10 miles (20 minutes); Piercy to Benbow: 10 miles (15 minutes); Benbow to Garberville/Redway: 6 miles (15 minutes)

Overview

The South Fork Eel River is designated a National Wild and Scenic River. Free-flowing waters, wild salmon and steelhead, magnificent redwood groves, and fine boating are prime attractions. Following the rains, many small waterfalls appear along the river.

Without reservoirs, the flows rise with the winter rains and shrink in summer. Winter flows average more than 2,000 cfs; late-summer flows dwindle to 55 cfs or less. The water level is more desirable a few days after storms, when the water clears. Anyone planning a trip on the Eel should be ready for rain.

This reach is the southern entry to the majestic stands of redwood trees preserved in state parks along the Avenue of the Giants.

As the watershed was subjected to road building and timber harvesting, salmon populations in the South Fork Eel River declined drastically. The 1930s fish counts at Benbow showed that approximately 20,000 chinook salmon and 15,000 to 17,000 coho salmon annually returned to the river. Recent estimates suggest that severely reduced numbers of adult coho salmon return to the watershed. The National Marine Fisheries Service has listed the chinook salmon, coho salmon, and steelhead as threatened species under the Endangered Species Act. Federal, state, and local groups are working to restore fish habitat.

When the South Fork Eel is running clear, the water is an inviting, translucent blue-green hue. Under those conditions, steelhead fishing is popular, producing fish from 8 to 16 pounds. Other fish recorded in the river include chinook salmon, coho salmon, coastal cutthroat trout, chum salmon, green sturgeon, Pacific lamprey, and American shad.

Rainy season camping is available at Humboldt Redwoods State Park, Standish-Hickey State Recreation Area, Richardson Grove State Park, Benbow State Recreation Area, and several private campgrounds.

Below Leggett, the river has cut a deep, narrow canyon. Many landslides line the river. Since winter flows scour the riverbed, little vegetation survives in the channel, and only an occasional stump or log remains.

The Paddling

Leggett to Reynolds Wayside

Length: 11 miles
Average paddling time: 4 to 5 hours
Difficulty: Class II to Class III whitewater
Optimal flow: 500 to 750 cfs

Standish-Hickey State Recreation Area campgrounds are convenient to this portion of the South Fork Eel. From Leggett or Standish-Hickey, put into this beautiful river lined with forests in a narrow canyon rising to expansive ridges.

At Leggett the river is pool and run. It changes to a Class II rocky rapid at the summer road crossing in Standish-Hickey State Recreation Area.

As the river cuts deeper into the canyon, the walls become more impressive. Rocky rapids become the norm. You can view much of the river from US 101. Paddling an open canoe, we carried one rapid with a large hole at the bottom. A tall, black tree trunk on the right bank marks it. You can easily see the tree and rapid from US 101 at mile marker 95.

Smithe Redwoods State Natural Reserve provides another put-in and takeout only 3 miles below Standish-Hickey. The Smithe access is on the upstream side of Dora Creek.

At 400 cfs, several rapids are so shallow that you might walk your canoe. One narrow, more difficult rapid includes brush, a log on the right bank, another log mid-channel, shallow rocks guarding a favorable route, and current washing into a boulder. Higher flows make the river bouncier, sometimes more technical, and more enjoyable in a good whitewater boat.

Reynolds Wayside to Benbow

Length: 14 miles
Average paddling time: 4 to 6 hours
Difficulty: Class I to Class III whitewater

This reach starts busily and has major hazards.

Two miles above Piercy, the river makes a hairpin turn under two US 101 bridges. The wider canyon affords longer views of green hillsides and wildflowers. The geology also changes into interesting sandstone and siltstone strata.

Much of the South Fork Eel River is visible from US 101.

Some paddlers avoid this reach with its low-water bridges and more severe rapids. Below Piercy, at Dimmick Road near Indian Creek, is a low-water bridge that may collect trees and form a hazard requiring a portage. Just downstream, a hanging footbridge crosses above the river. Rounding the bend toward US 101 is a rocky chute—Class III at higher flows. The next 1 mile relaxes a bit. As the river veers away from US 101, you encounter several shallow rapids.

Passing a few houses once known as "Cook's," the river swings east under bridges for CA 271 and US 101. A terrace topped with redwoods sits on the left above the easy channel. Gravel bars and a rock quarry border the left side. As you round the long loop toward the highway, rocky ledges border the right side.

Below Hartsook Creek, Richardson Grove State Park borders both sides of the river. The impressive trees here include the ninth-tallest coastal redwood. The park includes campgrounds, hiking trails through the redwoods, and river access across broad gravel bars.

US 101 crosses the river twice more. Between the US 101 crossings is a low-water bridge known to collect trees to form a severe hazard. If you run this section, approach with great caution and portage. The second crossing is close to the upstream end of Benbow Park. The picnic area and river access are on river right.

Benbow to Redway

Length: 11 miles
Average paddling time: 3 to 5 hours
Difficulty: Class I to Class II whitewater

Benbow dam and lake are no more. The dam was removed and the river channel restored in 2017. The historic Benbow Inn still provides accommodations. Next to the inn, the East Branch adds significant flows.

Beyond the East Branch the river sweeps in a wide loop away from the highways and settlements. This section is one of the prettiest parts of the river above Redway. Rich forests cover the slopes. Sproul Creek, with good habitat conditions, is an important coho salmon spawning stream.

As you slide over easy gravel bar riffles, the current carries you quickly. Only an occasional rock or stump demands much maneuvering.

After running due north, the river turns abruptly east, then north again. Kimtu Road parallels the right bank. Sproul Creek Road and the Garberville Airport parallel the left bank. Downstream of the airport, the Sproul Creek Road bridge marks the Tooby Park takeout. Land at the bridge on river right.

Downstream 2.3 miles, the bridge at Bear Canyon Road and adjacent gravel bar form a put-in and takeout between Garberville and Redway.

Flows as low as 400 cfs at Leggett (or 1,000 cfs at Miranda) will suffice near Redway, but more water is better. At 400 cfs, sharp-eyed paddlers can find the deeper channels around gravel bars with little scraping and no carry. There are only a couple of rocks and stumps adjacent to the banks.

At this flow, the current moves steadily for an easy Class I paddle. The scenery is appealing, although Redwood Drive is perched 100 feet above the right bank and many Redway cottages are tucked under the trees. A loon sang to us from the river before diving and disappearing. Deep pools and some smooth, moss-covered rocky ledges drop into the water. Rope swings show the popularity of some pools for summer swimming. In contrast, the wide, brush-free gravel bars suggest the bed-scouring capacity of winter storm flows. The lush riverside foliage includes redwood, alder, Douglas fir, and laurel trees.

Next to Redwood Creek, the Briceland-Thorne bridge crosses the river. It marks the upstream portion of Humboldt Redwoods State Park. Two miles downstream is the takeout at Dean Creek Resort on the right bank.

18 Lake Sonoma

Picture a narrow-fingered lake featuring fine fishing, several low-speed zones, and boat-in camping in the heart of wine country. Winter and early spring are the most attractive seasons for paddlers for wildlife watching and avoiding warm-season powerboats.

Size: 7 miles of lake with restricted speeds, 0.1 to 0.5 mile wide
Average paddling time: 2 hours to several days
Difficulty: Flatwater lake; beginner
Best season: Winter, spring, and autumn
Land status: Public
Fees: Required to launch
Maps: USGS Warm Springs Dam, Cloverdale; US Army Corps of Engineers, Lake Sonoma; Fish-n-Map Company, Lake Sonoma

Craft: Canoes, kayaks, sailboats, motorboats
Contacts: US Army Corps of Engineers: (707) 431-4533; spn.usace.army.mil/Missions/Recreation/Lake-Sonoma. National Recreation Reservation Service: (877) 444-6777; recreation.gov (camping reservations).
Special considerations: Outside the restricted speed zones, waterskiing and fast motorboats are popular. Underwater dead trees commonly reach to the water surface along the narrow lake fingers.

Put-in/Takeout Information

Yorty Creek Recreation Area (N38 46.356' / W123 4.329') has a wide, sandy swimming beach, picnic pavilions, and a launch ramp for car-top boats. From US 101 exit 518 in Cloverdale, go west to South Redwood Highway. Go north (right) 0.1 mile then turn right onto Treadway Drive. Go to the end at Foothill Boulevard and turn right. Go 0.4 mile then turn left (west) on Hot Springs Road (aka Shady Lane), well-marked with signs to Yorty Creek. Follow Hot Springs Road for 4.5 narrow (five steep hairpin turns) miles to the recreation area. Enjoy the sight of the magnificent old oaks profiled along the ridge leading down to the lake.

Lake Sonoma Marina (N38 42.446' / W123 1.141') is designed for powerboats. To avoid water-skiers, visit during the cool seasons. From Healdsburg take Dry Creek Road and turn left onto Skaggs Springs Road. Go 1.8 miles uphill and turn left onto Stewart Point–Skaggs Springs Road. Go 0.7 mile and then turn right onto Marina Drive. Go downhill to the marina and boat ramps.

Launch ramp off Rockpile Road (N38 42.986' / W123 1.083'): From Skaggs Springs Road continue straight onto Rockpile Road (instead of turning left onto Stewart Point–Skaggs Springs Road). Cross the bridge and immediately turn into the parking area and launch ramp. Distance from launch ramp to parking area is approximately 0.25 mile.
Shuttle: None

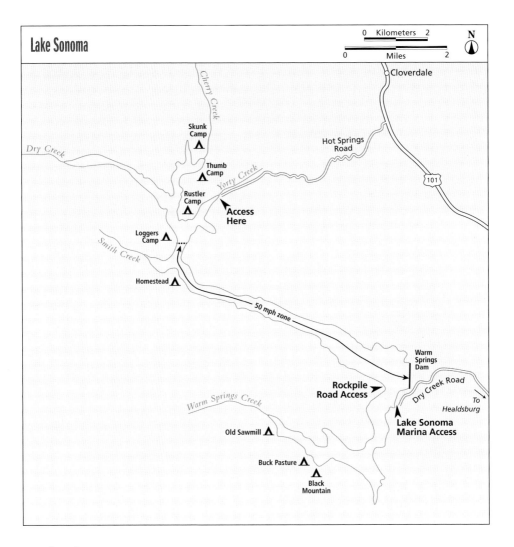

Overview

Warm Springs Dam impounds the canyons of Dry, Warm Springs, Yorty, and Cherry Creeks to form 2,700-acre Lake Sonoma. These narrow fingers have no-ski and 5-mile-per-hour zones desirable for paddle craft. Avoid the southern portions during waterskiing seasons. Cool seasons offer good paddling, fishing, green hillsides, and birding when there are fewer water-skiers.

Thirty-nine boat-in campsites are situated along the lake's low-speed reaches. Amenities include picnic tables, fire pits, chemical toilets, and tent pads, but bring your own drinking water and reserve your campsite in advance.

Nearby ridgetops rise 800 feet above the lake surface. Summers can be hot. If not rainy, winter days are often clear here when the lowlands are foggy.

The limbs of a drowned tree seem to be reaching for this paddler.

Submerged trees still stand in the upper reaches of the lake to provide habitat for fish. As a result, the lake holds largemouth bass, trout, Sacramento perch, channel catfish, and sunfish.

The US Army Corps of Engineers normally lowers winter lake levels to provide storage space for flood control.

Yorty Creek Arm

Length: Up to 12 miles round-trip

Average paddling time: 2 to 6 hours plus camping

Yorty Creek boat ramp provides an easy put-in for canoes and kayaks. In summer, water warm enough for swimming adds to the attraction. An easy 0.8-mile paddle brings you to the Brush Creek and Dry Creek fingers. From here it is fun to explore and fish the different reaches.

Hillside Rustler Camp (eight sites) is at the confluence of the Yorty and Brush Creek fingers. Rustler is the closest camp to the put-in. Brush Creek finger is short. Dry Creek finger extends 3 miles to the north and west. The 0.5-mile-broad confluence with Cherry Creek is most apt to be affected by blowing winds.

Cherry Creek finger stretches 2 miles around a long horseshoe bend to Thumb Camp (ten sites) and Skunk Camp (twelve sites), which are in "no-wake" zones. Powerboaters also use these camps. At the northernmost arc of the horseshoe bend, a cool, narrow, tree-shrouded ravine invites exploration until fallen trees block your paddling.

Warm Springs Creek Arm

Length: Up to 10 miles round-trip

Average paddling time: 3 to 5 hours plus camping

From the marina, head south and west. After 1 mile, the no-wake zone ends and the lake broadens into the waterskiing area. Continue west toward the narrowing Warm Springs Arm and into the intimate no-wake zone, which extends almost 2 miles to the confluence of Rancheria and Warm Springs Creeks. In the canyon, old trees emerge from the water, craggy cliffs loom above, and madrone, giant manzanita, and fern-draped oaks cloak the slopes. Vineyards can be spotted along the ridge crest.

Black Mountain (five sites), Old Sawmill (nine sites), and Buck Pasture (thirteen sites) boat-in camp areas are scattered along the south shore of this no-wake zone.

The arm leads to the confluence of Warm Springs Creek and the smaller Rancheria Creek. Both have steep-sloped canyons. We were able to paddle up Warm Springs Creek for 0.5 mile and enjoy lunch on the old roadbed.

Green hills and solitude greet wintertime paddlers.

San Francisco Bay Region

Fifty miles long and surrounded by high hills, San Francisco Bay is reputed to be one of the finest harbors of the world. The rivers of the Central Valley flow through the bay to form a huge estuary on the way to the Pacific Ocean. The spectacularly scenic bay offers world-class boating from the exciting Golden Gate to calm estuaries.

Paddlers enjoy a glorious day viewing Alcatraz and the San Francisco skyline.

19 Marin–China Camp Shoreline

Bordered by oak-studded hillsides, this bird-filled marshland opens to the broad expanse of San Pablo Bay and the San Francisco Bay National Estuarine Research Preserve. The Marine Mammal Protection Act applies.

Length: 4.25 miles to China Camp; 5 miles to McNears Beach

Average paddling time: 3 to 4 hours

Difficulty: Open water, SCRS I to III; beginner with experience to intermediate skills

Marine weather: 162.40 MHz; www.wrh.noaa.gov/mtr

Tide reference: San Francisco: Gallinas Creek high tides: +1 hour, 18 minutes; low tides: +1 hour, 25 minutes. Point San Pedro high tides: +1 hour; low tides: +1 hour

Best season: Year-round

Land status: Private and state park

Fees: Required at parks

Maps: USGS Petaluma Point, Novato, San Quentin; NOAA BookletChart 18654, pages 16 & 17

Craft: Canoes, sea kayaks, sailboats, motorboats

Contacts: China Camp State Park: (415) 456-0766; parks.ca.gov; camping at China Camp: (800) 444-7275; parks.ca.gov. McInnis Park: marincounty.org/depts/pk/divisions/parks/mcinnis-park. McNears Beach: marincounty.org/depts/pk/divisions/parks/mcnears-beach. San Francisco Bay Area Water Trail: sfbaywatertrail.org.

Special considerations: Summertime winds, particularly in the afternoon, blow away from the shore. Some powerboats share the channel to Gallinas Creek. When they occur, northerly winds blow across a wide fetch of San Pablo Bay, creating large waves. As the tide ebbs, stay in the Gallinas Creek channel to avoid being stranded on the mudflats.

Put-in/Takeout Information

John F. McInnis County Park (N38 1.094' / W122 31.397'): From US 101, exit at Lucas Valley Road and then turn east onto Smith Ranch Road. Go 0.7 mile to McInnis County Park. Cross the railroad tracks, pass under the park entrance arch, and turn right into a small parking lot. A small dock provides easy canoe and kayak access to the slough. If you passed all the sports fields and approached the golf course, you went too far.

Bullhead Flat (N38 0.220' / W122 28.031'): From US 101, exit at North San Pedro Road and follow the "China Camp State Park" signs about 4.75 miles to the Bullhead Flat parking area. Fee area.

China Camp Beach (N38 0.057' / W122 27.697'): Follow North San Pedro Road another 0.25 mile to China Camp Village. Turn left down the hill to parking. Fee area.

McNears Beach (N37 59.504' / W122 27.072'): Continue past China Camp Village on San Pedro Road another 0.6 mile to the park entrance at Cantera Way. Pay the day-use fee and follow the road to the beach parking area. OK for hand-launch boats. The 500-foot-long fishing pier is a major landmark. San Francisco Bay Area Water Trail access point.

Shuttle: 8.4 miles (20 minutes)

Overview

Popular McInnis County Park provides a great beginning or end for a paddling tour of the marshlands of southwestern San Pablo Bay. The nearby hills of China Camp State Park offer scenic protection from the summer winds blowing in from the Golden Gate. At the end of the peninsula, the old fishing village of China Camp was once the site where hundreds of Chinese established a shrimp fishing village. The shrimp fishing activities have ceased.

Back Ranch Meadows Campground, in the state park, offers walk-in campsites in the nearby hills. The trails are popular with mountain bike enthusiasts. Reservations are recommended on weekends and during the summer.

The Paddling

For favorable tides, start at high tide at McInnis Park and ride the ebb to China Camp, or start at China Camp with an incoming tide and ride the flood to McInnis.

At McInnis Park's small boat dock, Gallinas Slough is barely two kayak lengths wide. The bank on the park side is solid, but across the channel an expanse of marsh grasses extends to the south. Easy to paddle with the tide, the park is quickly left behind. Bright white egrets frequently catch the eye. Some seem almost tame, allowing paddlers to come within two boat lengths before taking flight. Less-showy great blue herons stalk among the grasses.

The much wider South Fork joins the tide 0.6 mile from the put-in. This area is the Santa Venetia Marsh Preserve. Wharves extend from the south bank from some long-established homes. Some utility lines stretch overhead. An osprey rewarded our visual search of the marsh.

The marsh extends on both sides of the channel as broad San Pablo Bay comes into view. The breezes from the bay may feel gentle, but look to the open water for the sight of whitecaps. Their presence may signal that you need to make a choice: a wet, difficult paddle; a return to the launch point; or a shortened tour, with a takeout at Bullhead Flat. Invariably, the winds will get stronger as you continue toward China Camp.

The edge of the bay has three visual zones: 10 miles of open water to the north, the 0.5-mile-wide swath of marsh grasses to the south shore, and the 1,000-foot-high, oak-covered hills of China Camp State Park.

About 2.5 miles from McInnis Park, small hills emerge above the marsh. Turtleback Hill, Jake's Island, Bullet Hill, and Chicken Coop Hill are all within the state park. Just offshore are duck blinds, most frequently occupied by gulls and egrets. You can paddle right into the blinds. Other blinds lie hundreds of yards out in the shallow

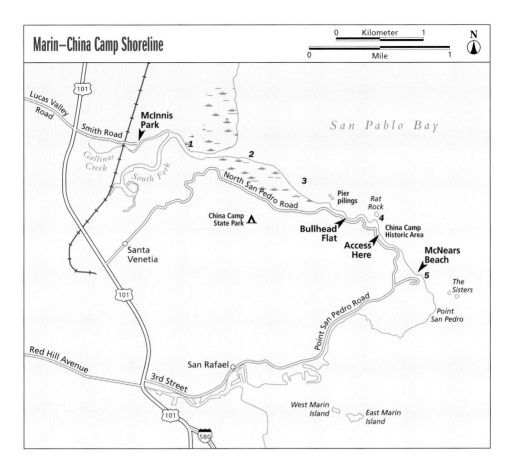

0   Kilometer   1

0   Mile   1

N

San Pablo Bay

McInnis Park

Lucas Valley Road

101

Smith Road

Gallinas Creek

South Fork

1

2

3

North San Pedro Road

Pier pilings

Rat Rock

China Camp State Park

Bullhead Flat

Access Here

China Camp Historic Area

McNears Beach

5

The Sisters

Santa Venetia

101

Point San Pedro Road

Point San Pedro

Red Hill Avenue

San Rafael

3rd Street

101

580

West Marin Island

East Marin Island

bay. Old pier pilings, called dolphins, remain at Buckeye Point. A few yards to the west is a narrow, sheltered beach suitable for lunch if the tide is not too high.

Rounding Buckeye Point, the wind begins to exert its full force in your face. It may be hard work to paddle an open canoe, although comfortable for sea kayaks. The boat ramp at Bullhead Flat provides a takeout and put-in for a shorter trip. Continuing eastward, Rat Rock lies 80 yards from China Camp Point. Naked on the bottom and bushy on top, this small island offers fishing and tide-pooling at a low tide.

Another 300 yards beyond are the sandy beach and pier of China Camp Village. At low tides the bottom may be soft. Hopefully the historic fishing pier and Quan Brothers snack shop will remain open on weekends. A small museum describes the history of the Chinese fishermen at China Camp. Old fishing boats may await inspection. The facilities are supported entirely by Friends of China Camp. Restrooms and drinking water are also available.

McNears Beach is another 0.75 mile southeast of China Camp Village. It can be a pleasant paddle with great views of the Point Pinole Regional Shoreline across the bay. A popular beach with a 500-foot-long pier marks McNears. Land at the north end of the beach.

20 Marin–San Pablo Strait to Raccoon Strait

More spectacular San Francisco Bay scenery and exciting waters await the paddler exploring the coast and islands along the bay side of Marin County. Enjoy the somewhat quieter water from Point San Pedro to Paradise Beach, or turn the corner at Bluff Point to enter Raccoon Strait. It will be a day to remember! The Marine Mammal Protection Act applies.

Length: 4 to 15 miles
Average paddling time: 2 to 6 hours
Difficulty: Open windy waters, SCRS II to III; self-rescue skills required
Marine weather: 162.40 MHz; www.wrh.noaa.gov/mtr
Tide reference: San Francisco: Gallinas Creek high tides: +1 hour, 18 minutes; low tides: +1 hour, 25 minutes. Angel Island east-side high tides: +16 minutes; low tides: +20 minutes.
Best season: Year-round
Land status: Mostly private
Fees: Required at parks
Maps: USGS San Quentin, San Francisco North; NOAA BookletChart 18654, page 17; 18649, pages 5, 9 & 10

Craft: Canoes, sea kayaks, sailboats, motorboats
Contacts: McNears Beach and Paradise Beach Park: (415) 473-6405; marincounty.org/depts/pk/divisions/parks. Loch Lomond Marina: (415) 454-7228; lochlomondmarina.com. San Francisco Bay Area Water Trail: sfbaywatertrail.org. Marin Islands: fws.gov/refuge/marin_islands.
Special considerations: Be alert for high-speed ferries serving Marin communities. Study the tide and current tables. Raccoon Strait has strong currents. Strong winds and steep waves may challenge your abilities.

Put-in/Takeout Information

McNears Beach (N37 59.504' / W122 27.072'): From US 101 in San Rafael, exit at Central San Rafael and go east on Second Street. That street merges with Third Street, which becomes Point San Pedro Road. Follow Point San Pedro Road to a right turn at Cantera Way. Follow Cantera to the park entrance and the beach parking area. The 500-foot-long fishing pier is a major landmark. Fee area.

Paradise Beach Park (N37 53.626' / W122 27.409'): From US 101 in Mill Valley, exit at East Blithedale Avenue/Tiburon Boulevard. Go east on Tiburon Boulevard, and turn at Trestle Glen Boulevard. Turn right at Paradise Drive and follow the curvy road to the park entrance on the left.

Loch Lomond Marina (N37 58.375' / W122 29.052'): From US 101 in San Rafael, exit at Central San Rafael and go east on Second Street. That street merges with Third Street, which becomes Point San Pedro Road. Go about 2.25 miles from US 101 and turn right into Loch Lomond Marina. A launch ramp exists at the west end; a dirt beach at the extreme east end offers closer parking. Fee area.

Jean & John Starkweather Shoreline Park (N37 56.666' / W122 28.823') is located at the west end of I-580 at the Richmond–San Rafael bridge. Look for the fishing pier. If driving eastbound, exit at San Quentin, turn left under the freeway, and then go straight into the parking area. If westbound, take the first exit (San Quentin) at end of bridge. Immediately turn right into the park with its launch ramp and toilet.

Ramillard Shoreline (N37 56.550' / W122 30.076') is on Sir Francis Drake Boulevard east, where there is a small parking area and a 500-foot carry. It is a bailout location on public land.

East Fort Baker—Horseshoe Bay (N37 50.029' / W122 28.458') can be a launching point for trips into the bay or around the Marin Headlands. Immediately outside the breakwater are some of the wildest sea conditions on the West Coast. Steep waves, strong winds, and fast, swirling currents are the norm. Check your tide tables and weather before you paddle here. Adding to the confusion are many pleasure craft and large oceangoing vessels transiting the Golden Gate.

Shuttle: McNears Beach to Starkweather ramp: 7.75 miles (20 minutes); Starkweather ramp to Paradise Beach: 9.5 miles (25 minutes); McNears Beach to Horseshoe Bay: 16 miles (40 minutes); Starkweather ramp to Horseshoe Bay: 11.5 miles (30 minutes)

Overview

This route has been a favorite paddle of the Sacramento Sea Kayakers. Some folks start at the Petaluma River and cross 10 miles of San Pablo Bay. Others join the pod at China Camp or McNears Beach for the more interesting part of the tour. Careful attention is paid to tide tables to identify a day when paddlers can ride on strong ebb currents. Be ready for weather and sea changes. The eastern Marin shores tend to be warmer—why else would one name a cove "paradise"? Going south, the winds from the Golden Gate increase and the waters get much lumpier.

The Paddling

Note: The distances are not all cumulative. Horseshoe Bay and Schoonmaker Point are alternative end points.

Sample Paddling Distances

McNears to Starkweather (Richmond–San Raphael bridge)	4.2 miles
Starkweather to Paradise	4.5 miles
Paradise to Schoonmaker Point	5 miles
Paradise to Horseshoe Bay	6 miles

Heading 0.5 mile southeast from McNears Beach, the first notable features are The Sisters, two small rocky islets on the north side of San Pablo Strait. Strong currents

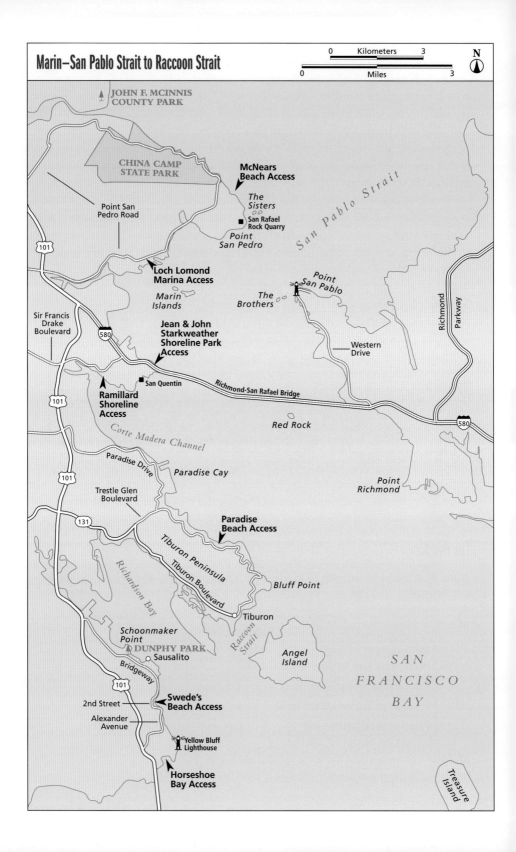

Marin–San Pablo Strait to Raccoon Strait

0   Kilometers   3

0   Miles   3

N

JOHN F. MCINNIS
COUNTY PARK

CHINA CAMP
STATE PARK

McNears
Beach Access

The
Sisters

San Rafael
Rock Quarry

Point San
Pedro Road

Point
San Pedro

San Pablo Strait

101

Loch Lomond
Marina Access

Marin
Islands

Point
San Pablo

The
Brothers

Richmond
Parkway

Sir Francis
Drake
Boulevard

580

Jean & John
Starkweather
Shoreline Park
Access

Western
Drive

101

Ramillard
Shoreline
Access

San Quentin

Richmond–San Rafael Bridge

580

Corte Madera Channel

Red Rock

Paradise Drive

Paradise Cay

Point
Richmond

101

Trestle Glen
Boulevard

131

Paradise
Beach Access

Tiburon Peninsula

Tiburon Boulevard

Richardson Bay

Bluff Point

Tiburon

Schoonmaker
Point

Raccoon Strait

DUNPHY PARK

Sausalito

Angel
Island

SAN

Bridgeway

FRANCISCO

101

BAY

2nd Street

Swede's
Beach Access

Alexander
Avenue

Yellow Bluff
Lighthouse

Horseshoe
Bay Access

Treasure Island

and waves will cause some interesting eddy lines and wave reflections as the narrow strait accelerates the tidal flows to and from the bay.

Onshore at Point San Pedro is the huge San Rafael Rock Quarry with its loading docks. The hundred-year-old operation is able to load rock and gravel for barge transport to Northern California levee and construction sites.

East and West Marin Islands lie 1.5 miles to the southwest. The islands with the surrounding submerged wetlands are now the Marin Islands National Wildlife Refuge, part of the San Francisco Bay National Wildlife Refuge complex. According to the Fish and Wildlife Service, West Marin Island supports the largest heron and egret rookery in the San Francisco Bay Area. The birds are so large that their snowy-white plumage can be seen on some Google Earth images. What was once a private vacation home remains on East Marin Island. The refuge is closed to the public without special permit.

Loch Lomond Marina has a launch ramp and dirt beach 0.8 mile northwest of the islands.

Richmond–San Rafael bridge dominates the skyline to the south. Close to the west end, Starkweather Shoreline Park provides a launch ramp for easy put-in and takeout. As you pass under the bridge, notorious San Quentin Prison is the next landmark.

Just south of the prison is the Corte Madera Channel, with high-speed ferry traffic. NOAA charts show only 1 to 2 feet of water over the mudflats at low tide. It gets deeper as you head toward Paradise.

Paradise Cay extends 0.25 mile into the bay. Many of the homes here have their own boat dock. Their boats may come in handy if global warming raises sea levels much.

Heading southeast another 1.25 miles along the Tiburon Peninsula, you arrive at the park and fishing pier of Paradise Cove. The cove is a "banana belt" that is sometimes used by pleasure craft as an overnight anchorage. Consider the takeout here carefully. The winds from "the Gate" may increase substantially when you round Bluff Point into Raccoon Strait. Paradise Cove is the last takeout before Richardson Bay unless you head for Angel Island. **Reminder:** The ferry from Angel Island to Tiburon does not take kayaks! And the winds get stronger crossing Richardson Bay.

(See chapter 21 for descriptions of waters around Angel Island, Richardson Bay, and Horseshoe Bay.)

21 Marin–Angel Island

This world-class sea kayak tour enjoys great views and spectacular sailing waters, and also visits some really expensive real estate and the largest island in San Francisco Bay. The Marine Mammal Protection Act applies.

Length: 5.6 to 10 miles from Sausalito
Average paddling time: 4 to 7 hours
Difficulty: Open, windy waters with strong currents, SCRS II to III; self-rescue skills required in rough water
Marine weather: 162.4 MHz; www.wrh.noaa.gov/mtr
Tide reference: San Francisco: High tides: +10 minutes; low tides: +21 minutes
Best season: Year-round
Land status: Private and public
Fees: Yes
Maps: USGS San Francisco North, San Quentin, San Rafael; NOAA BookletChart 18649, pages 9 & 10
Craft: Sea kayaks

Contacts: San Francisco Bay Area Water Trail: sfbaywatertrail.org. Angel Island State Park: (415) 435-1915; parks.ca.gov. Angel Island Ferry: angelislandferry.com. Fort Baker–Horseshoe Bay–Golden Gate National Recreation Area: nps.gov/goga/planyourvisit/fort-baker.htm. Sea Trek: (415) 332-8494; seatrek.com.

Special considerations: Sausalito is a busy nexus of marinas and pleasure craft. Beware of the considerable marine traffic, and adhere to the navigation "Rules of the Road." Raccoon Strait has strong currents and is a deepwater channel sometimes used by oceangoing cargo ships. Study the tide and current tables. Strong winds and steep waves may challenge your abilities along the San Francisco and Golden Gate sides of Angel Island.

Put-in/Takeout Information

Schoonmaker Point Beach and Marina (N37 51.821' / W122 29.371'): From US 101 exit south, looking for the "Bay Model" signs. At the light, turn left onto Liberty Ship Way and follow it all the way to Schoonmaker Marina and beach next to Sea Trek. Unload at the sandy beach, and then find a legal parking space. This is a protected starting point for cruising Richardson Bay.

Swede's Beach (N37 50.883' / W122 28.797') is at the bay end of Valley Street in Sausalito. Steep stairs descend the 30-plus feet to the sand beach. Since there is minimal on-street parking and no restrooms, this site is best used as a bailout shore on a rough day.

East Fort Baker—Horseshoe Bay (N37 50.029' / W122 28.458') can be a launching point for trips into the bay or around the Marin Headlands. Immediately outside the breakwater are some of the wildest sea conditions on the West Coast. Steep waves, strong winds, and fast, swirling currents are the norm. Check your tide tables and weather before you paddle here. Adding to the confusion are many pleasure craft and large oceangoing vessels transiting the Golden Gate.

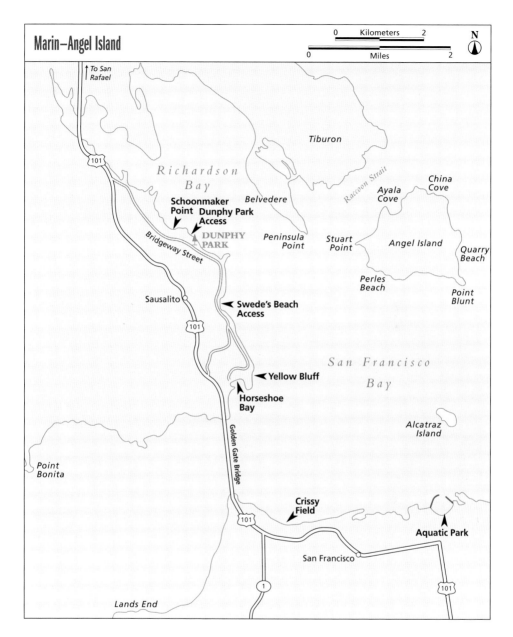

0   Kilometers   2

0   Miles   2

N

To San
Rafael

101

*Richardson
Bay*

Tiburon

Raccoon Strait

China
Cove

Ayala
Cove

Schoonmaker
Point Dunphy Park
Access

Belvedere

DUNPHY
PARK

Bridgeway Street

*Peninsula
Point*

Stuart
Point

Angel Island

Quarry
Beach

Sausalito

Swede's Beach
Access

Perles
Beach

Point
Blunt

*San Francisco
Bay*

Yellow Bluff

Horseshoe
Bay

Alcatraz
Island

Golden Gate Bridge

Point
Bonita

101

Crissy
Field

101

Aquatic Park

San Francisco

Lands End

1

101

Dunphy Park (N37 51.733' / W122 29.223'). In Sausalito, from Bridgeway turn east onto Napa Street to parking lots. Carry 50 yards to launch ramp.
Shuttle: None

Overview

The largest island in San Francisco Bay, Angel Island State Park has a rich history that includes Spanish ranchers, US Army bases, "the Ellis Island of the West Coast,"

Paddlers from Sacramento Sea Kayakers enjoy a calm moment outside Horseshoe Bay near the Golden Gate Bridge. JONATHON SPRINGER

and Nike missile sites. World travelers visit by ferryboat from San Francisco, Vallejo, and Tiburon. Many paths and fire roads allow hiking and bicycle exploration of the beaches, historic barracks, and summit of 752-foot-high Mount Caroline Livermore.

Raccoon Strait and the east side of the island are usually protected from wind and waves. The west and south shores are exposed and rocky.

Angel Island State Park has several walk-in campgrounds, including one for kayakers. In contrast, the new Cavallo Point resort at Fort Baker offers luxury accommodations.

The Paddling

Consider the wind and current in planning this tour. Slack tide is best. A flood tide makes it easier to get to the island, and an ebb tide eases the return trip. The current that accompanies exceptionally high or minus tides may be stronger than your paddling ability. If the prevailing westerly wind is strong, the paddling will be wetter and more tiring if you decide to circumnavigate the island.

Most folks put in at Dunphy Park (Schoonmaker Point) or Horseshoe Bay in Sausalito, cross through the pleasure-boat traffic on Richardson Bay, then round Peninsula Point to Tiburon. From Tiburon paddle 0.6 mile across busy Raccoon Strait to Angel Island. Sheltered Ayala Cove is the busy landing for ferryboats and is an anchorage for pleasure craft staying overnight. Continue clockwise for more sheltered and quieter beaches at China Cove or Quarry Beach (0.7 mile and 1.9 miles, respectively, from Ayala Cove).

If you choose to continue paddling from Quarry Beach past Point Blunt, you will encounter all the force of wind and waves the bay offers that day. The rocky shoreline to Perles Beach and Stuart Point (2.6 miles from Quarry Beach) offers little shelter. You will also experience one of the greatest views in the world—the Golden Gate and San Francisco. Calm or windy, it is an exhilarating tour. *Note:* The ferry from Angel Island to Tiburon does not take kayaks.

On the Sausalito shore, Swede's Beach offers a bailout point for paddlers wishing to avoid the turbulence of Yellow Bluff. Unfortunately, the only access is steep stairs to Valley Street.

Yellow Bluff (N37 50.191' / W122 28.312') is a 90-foot cliff about 0.5 mile east of the entrance to Horseshoe Bay. The rocky point creates a strong eddy line and steep waves when fast ebb currents exit Richardson and San Francisco Bays. Yellow Bluff is a play spot for kayakers honing their rough-water skills.

22 East Bay–Richmond to Emeryville

This is an exhilarating paddle against a backdrop of the three Bay bridges, Alcatraz, and the East Bay Hills. The Marine Mammal Protection Act applies.

Length: 6 miles each way
Average paddling time: 3 to 4 hours
Difficulty: Open windy waters, SCRS I to II; beginner to intermediate skills required
Marine weather: 162.4 MHz; www.wrh.noaa.gov/mtr
Tide reference: San Francisco: High tides: +21 minutes; low tides: +38 minutes
Best season: Year-round
Land status: Mixed private and public
Fees: Required for parking
Maps: USGS Oakland West, Richmond; NOAA BookletChart 18649, pages 6, 7, 10 & 11

Craft: Sea kayaks, sailboats, powerboats
Contacts: San Francisco Bay Area Water Trail sfbaywatertrail.org. Bay Area Sea Kayakers (BASK): bask.org. Brooks Island: (888) 327-2757; ebparks.org/parks/brooks_island. McLaughlin Eastshore State Park: ebparks.org/parks/eastshore.
Special considerations: Strong summer winds push the cold San Francisco Bay waves into a steep chop. Powerboats ply the channels leading to the marinas. Beware of powerboats, fast-moving sailboarders, and kiteboarders.

Put-in/Takeout Information

Vincent Park, Richmond (N37 54.471' / W122 21.028'): From I-580 between the Richmond Bay Bridge and I-80, exit Marina Bay Parkway south. Go about 1 mile and bear right on Peninsula Drive around the housing development to the park. The park has parking, toilets, and a 50-yard carry to a sand beach. San Francisco Bay Area Water Trail access point.

Berkeley Marina North Basin launch ramp (N37 52.115' / W122 19.062'): From I-80 exit University Avenue, go west 0.3 mile and turn right onto Marina Boulevard. Follow Marina north 0.4 mile; turn west on Spinnaker Way and continue to the third parking entrance, with large launch ramps.

Berkeley small craft launch (N37 51.796' / W122 18.739') is on the south side of University Avenue west of I-80. Bear left past Marina Boulevard, and then take the first left into a dirt parking lot. Launch from the low dock marked with the "Small Craft Launching Docks" sign. No toilets.

Point Emery (N37 51.064' / W122 18.010'): This sand-and-mud beach was once popular for "free-form" sculpture. Find the Frontage Road immediately adjacent to the shore between University Avenue, Berkeley, and Powell Street, Emeryville. Marked parking spaces indicate the shore access.

Emeryville Marina (N37 50.288' / W122 18.799'): From I-80, exit at Powell (if westbound, follow the frontage road to Powell). Go west on Powell past the Watergate Buildings to the marina. The marina has a popular public launching ramp, toilets, and

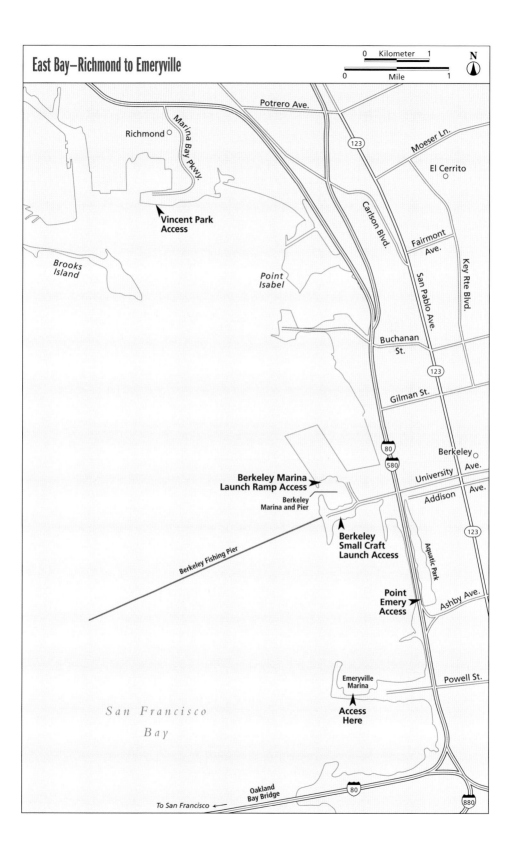

East Bay—Richmond to Emeryville

0   Kilometer   1

0   Mile   1

N

Potrero Ave.

Richmond ○

Marina Bay Pkwy.

Moeser Ln.

123

El Cerrito ○

Carlson Blvd.

Fairmont Ave.

Vincent Park Access

San Pablo Ave.

Key Rte Blvd.

Brooks Island

Point Isabel

Buchanan St.

123

Gilman St.

80

580

Berkeley ○

Berkeley Marina Launch Ramp Access

Berkeley Marina and Pier

University   Ave.

Addison   Ave.

Berkeley Small Craft Launch Access

123

Berkeley Fishing Pier

Aquatic Park

Point Emery Access

Ashby Ave.

Powell St.

Emeryville Marina

Access Here

San Francisco Bay

Oakland Bay Bridge

80

880

To San Francisco ←

paved parking. Alternatively, go to the extreme north end of the marina. Inside the breakwater is a shallow launching place within easy carrying distance of parking and toilets. San Francisco Bay Area Water Trail access point.

Shuttle (optional): Richmond to Berkeley, 7.5 miles (20 minutes); Berkeley to Emeryville, 3.5 miles (15 minutes)

Overview

During recent decades, the shoreline has become dedicated to public access parklands, including Eastshore State Park, Point Isabel, and Brooks Island. The Eastbay shoreline is popular because of its proximity to Berkeley and the Bay Area population of eight million people. Prime attractions include views of San Francisco, the Golden Gate Bridge, and the Oakland Bay Bridge, especially when lighted at night. Invigorating winds that blow through the Golden Gate add to the experience.

Weather-wise, summer days are often windy under low clouds blowing from the Golden Gate to the Berkeley Hills. Spring and autumn yield some of the sunniest days. Except on stormy days, winter winds are milder.

The Paddling

You can paddle in either direction, set up a shuttle, or return to the starting point. Basically the wind will blow from the Golden Gate, creating significant wind waves. Low tides expose mudflats into the bay. In deeper water, large powerboats move fast and have the right-of-way. No matter where you start, you will experience an exhilarating setting.

Emeryville Marina is busy with large and small yachts and charter fishing craft. Launch from the floating low dock next to the launch ramp. Since the channel leading into the marina is narrow and the adjacent water is shallow at low tides, clear the channel as quickly as possible to allow powerboats to pass. Once outside the marina, the view of the San Francisco–Oakland Bay Bridge is awesome. If the summer wind machine is working, paddling in the waves will be a great workout.

A shallow reef lies between Emeryville and Berkeley. Minus tides expose it, and some adventurous paddlers have picnicked there. Expect to detour around it.

The Berkeley fishing pier once extended 2.5 miles to the San Francisco county line. A 0.5-mile section remains open to public use. If you choose to go under the pier, beware of fishing lines from above. On shore are restaurants, with customers admiring your courage and abilities. Put on a good show for them as you surf the wind waves.

Shorebird Park is south of the restaurants and pier. Avoid the riprap shoreline, then turn north to reach quieter water and the beach takeout. Keep an eye out for the many fast-moving sailboarders and sailboats nearby.

The Berkeley Marina entrance is north of the pier and guarded by a breakwater. After entering the marina, head north to the launch ramp.

Only 0.6 mile from Richmond is Brooks Island, a tempting place to visit. The north and east sides are a combined 1.5 miles. A 1-mile-long breakwater extends from the west end. The 370-acre island preserve is home to eighteen bird species and a caretaker. Access is permitted only by reservation from the East Bay Regional Parks District. Kayak tours to the island can be arranged.

23 East Bay–San Leandro Bay and Alameda Island

Protected from the full force of San Francisco Bay's wind and waves, this shallow estuary and wildlife refuge is an escape from the industrial East Bay. The Martin Luther King Jr. Regional Shoreline encompasses the bay and includes the Tidewater Boating Center, Arrowhead Marsh observation tower, and the MLK launch ramp. The Marine Mammal Protection Act applies.

Length: 3 to 5 miles

Average paddling time: 2 to 4 hours

Difficulty: SCRS I, flatwater estuary; beginner skills required

Marine weather: 162.4 MHz; www.wrh.noaa .gov/mtr

Tide reference: Golden Gate: High tides: +42 minutes; low tides: +52 minutes

Best season: Year-round

Land status: Mostly private

Fees: Required for launching

Maps: USGS San Leandro, Oakland East; NOAA BookletChart 18649, page 15

Craft: Sea kayaks

Contacts: Tidewater Boating Center and Martin Luther King Jr. Regional Shoreline: (888) 327-2757; ebparks.org/parks/martinlking. San Francisco Bay Area Water Trail: sfbaywatertrail .org. Bay Area Sea Kayakers (BASK): bask.org. Crown Memorial State Beach: ebparks.org/ parks/crown_beach.

Special considerations: Cold water traditional to San Francisco Bay, strong winds, oceango-ing ships, the presence of powerboats, and the wide expanse of mudflats that emerge at low water in San Leandro Bay and near Alameda Island. The water is unfit for swimming.

Put-in/Takeout Information

Tidewater Boating Center (N37 45.678' / W122 13.386') is located in an industrial area on the Oakland Estuary at 4675 Tidewater Avenue. From I-880 or I-580, exit to High Street south. From I-880 go about 0.25 mile, then turn left onto Tidewater Avenue (before the High Street bridge to Alameda). At 0.2 mile look for the "Tide-water Boating Center" sign and turn right into the Tidewater Boating Center drive-way. Facilities include a low float dock, staging and boat drop-off areas, boat rinsing hose, restrooms, picnic tables, barbecues, and drinking fountain. Boat wheels may be available to borrow (dock is 100 yards from parking area). Free parking. San Francisco Bay Area Water Trail access point.

Martin Luther King Jr. Regional Shoreline (N37 44.329' / W122 12.853'): From I-880 exit at Hegenberger Road and go west toward Oakland Airport. Turn right onto Doolittle Drive, which parallels the shoreline of San Leandro Bay. Go 1 mile and turn into the parking lot with a launch ramp. There's another parking area with a low dock 0.3 mile farther on Doolittle Drive.

Crown Memorial State Beach (N37 45.785' / W122 16.343'): From Oakland take the Webster Street tunnel to Alameda Island. Follow Webster, turn left onto Lincoln

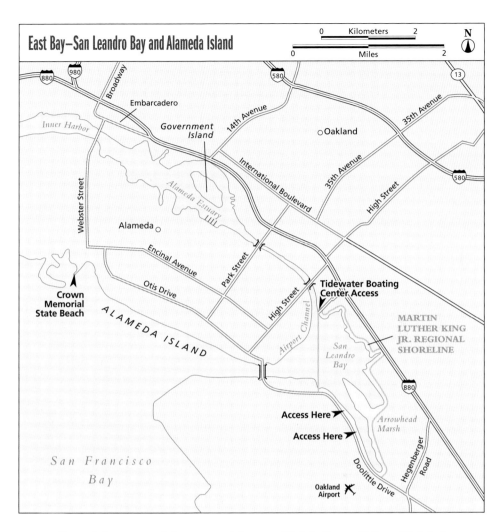

Kilometers 2

Miles

N

or Central Avenue, and then turn right onto Eighth Street. Follow Eighth Street to Crown Beach. The state beach has a sand beach, parking, and toilets. Fee area. San Francisco Bay Area Water Trail access point.

Shuttle (optional): Tidewater Center to Crown Memorial BEach: about 4 miles (15 minutes)

Overview

San Leandro Bay is a place of contrasts—an estuarine wildlife sanctuary bounded by the Oakland Alameda County Coliseum to the east and the Oakland International Airport to the west. East Bay Regional Parks District (EBRPD) manages the new Tidewater Boating Center as part of the Martin Luther King Jr. Regional Shoreline, a 1,220-acre park that helps protect a remnant of what was once an extensive marshland. Between Airport Channel and San Leandro Creek, 50-acre Arrowhead Marsh is part of the Western Hemisphere Shorebird Reserve Network. EBRPD offers a walking trail and observation tower.

Alameda Island is a city where many personnel from the Alameda Naval Air Station once resided. Crown Beach provides 2-plus miles of sandy shoreline facing San Francisco across San Francisco Bay. That shoreline is favored by sailboarders and sun lovers.

The Paddling

From the Tidewater Boating Center, you can paddle south a few hundred yards to shallow San Leandro Bay. Two-thirds of a mile wide, it splits around Arrowhead Marsh, San Leandro Creek to the east, and Airport Channel to the west, next to Doolittle Drive. Pay attention to the locations of the deeper channels to avoid getting stuck in the mud.

San Leandro Bay offers a quiet paddle with opportunities to see shorebirds and harbor seals and, if you are lucky, leopard sharks and bat rays. San Leandro Bay is a refuge, so be sure to keep a respectful distance from sensitive wildlife and habitat. You will be rewarded with the chance to observe natural wildlife behavior.

Motorized boats and personal watercraft are restricted.

When you have your fill of watching wildlife, you can head west under the drawbridge and bicycle bridge through the San Leandro Channel between Alameda and Bay Farm Islands. That will provide more challenging boating conditions on the open waters of San Francisco Bay.

Paddling along the Alameda shoreline provides great views of San Francisco and the San Francisco–Oakland Bay Bridge. Crown Memorial State Beach lines 2 miles of the Alameda shore. From the water you should be able to see the beach, with the buildings lining Shore Line Drive. Look for the place where Shore Line Drive and the buildings retreat from the water. Beach parking and your takeout are there.

24 Lafayette Reservoir

Nestled in the East Bay hills, this park is popular for paddling, fishing, picnicking, walking, and relaxing. The climate is comfortable year-round.

Size: Length 0.6 mile, width 0.7 mile; 2.6 miles of shoreline
Average paddling time: 1 to 2 hours
Difficulty: Flatwater lake; beginner skills
Best season: Year-round
Land status: Public
Fees: Park fees required

Map: USGS Briones Valley
Craft: Canoes, kayaks, other car-top boats
Contacts: East Bay Municipal Utility District: (925) 284-9669; ebmud.com/recreation/lafayette-reservoir
Special considerations: EBMUD prohibits swimming and standup paddleboards.

Put-in/Takeout Information

Lafayette Reservoir (N37 53.016' / W122 8.624'): From CA 24 exit to Acalanes Road south. Go east on Mount Diablo Boulevard for 0.8 mile to the park entrance. From the CA 24 Pleasant Hill Road exit, go south to Mount Diablo Boulevard and then west 2.5 miles to the park. Follow signs to the boat launch area. EBMUD charges day-use, invasive species boat inspection, and boat-launching fees. For people using public transit, the park is 1 mile from the Lafayette BART station.
Shuttle: None

Lafayette Reservoir is a pleasant place for peaceful paddling in the East Bay hills.

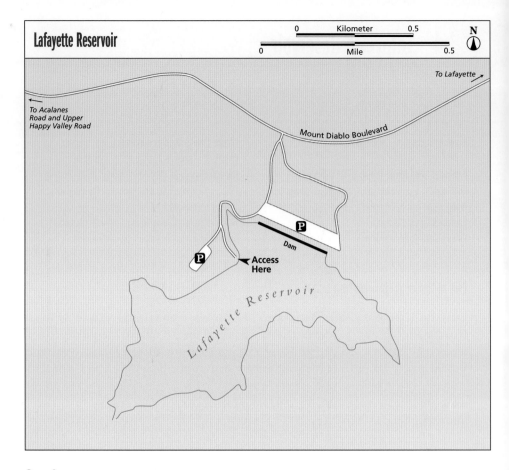

Overview

East Bay Municipal Utility District owns and operates this popular day-use area for jogging, fishing, boating, and picnicking. You can rent rowboats, pedal boats, and kayaks at the lake. Because the reservoir holds emergency drinking water supplies, EBMUD prohibits gasoline engines. Fees are charged for parking and boat launching.

The Paddling

Good facilities make this a favorite place for Bay Area paddling clubs to train new members. The road from the dam leads to the rental boat docks, concession building, and restrooms. Nearby is a small dock for launching canoes and other small, private boats. After unloading your gear, move your vehicle to the parking area on the dam or above the visitor center.

The surrounding hills climb 560 feet above the lake. Grasslands and a verdant mix of coastal trees disguise the proximity of urban development. Irregular in shape, the shoreline is long enough for the energetic paddler to get a good workout. Located between the ocean and the Central Valley, the climate is delightful year-round.

25 Lake Del Valle

Deep in a valley framed by oak-covered hills, Del Valle is like a lakeside resort only 10 miles south of Livermore. The park centerpiece is a lake 5 miles long with swimming, boat rentals, and all kinds of water-oriented recreation.

Size: 4.8 miles long, 0.25 mile wide; 14.6 miles of shoreline
Average paddling time: 1 to 4 hours
Difficulty: Flatwater lake; beginner skills
Best season: Year-round
Land status: Public
Fees: Park fees required
Maps: USGS Mendenhall Springs; East Bay Regional Parks (ebparks.org/parks/maps)
Craft: Canoes, kayaks, sail craft, fishing boats, standup paddleboards

Contacts: East Bay Regional Park District: (888) 327-2757, option 3, ext. 4524; ebparks .org/parks/del_valle
Special considerations: Lifeguards are available only at the posted swimming areas. Boat inspection for invasive species is required. During winter, lower water levels expose more obstacles. Watch out for fast-moving sailboarders.

Put-in/Takeout Information

Del Valle Regional Park (N37 35.177' / W121 42.151'): Exit I-580 at North Livermore Avenue in Livermore. Head south and proceed through town. Approximately 3.2 miles from I-580, Livermore Avenue becomes Tesla Road. After another 0.5 mile, turn right at Mines Road. Go about 3.5 miles and continue straight on Del Valle Road (Mines Road turns left). The park entrance is about 4 curvy miles ahead.
Shuttle: None

Overview

Operated by the East Bay Regional Park District, the 5,000-acre Del Valle Regional Park offers picnicking, camping, swimming, boating, boat rentals, hiking, and horseback riding. Trout are stocked in winter; catfish are stocked in summer. Bass, striped bass, and panfish yield excellent fishing. Wooded hills surrounding the lake rise to 2,000 feet. Constructed as part of the State Water Project, 700-acre Del Valle Reservoir stores water for the South Bay Aqueduct. EBRPD charges fees for day and overnight use.

The Paddling

Wide, sandy East Beach, with its ample parking, makes a great put-in. Excellent facilities make this a favorite place for Bay Area paddling clubs to train new members.

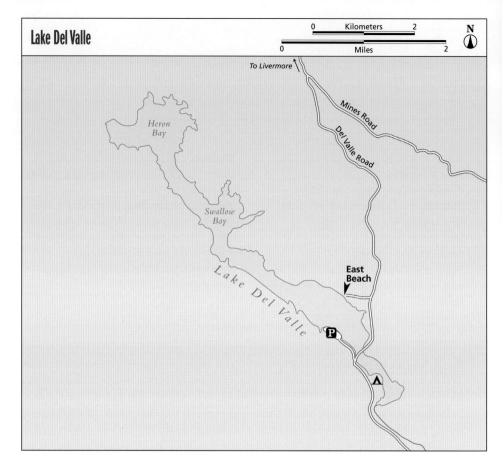

Long and skinny, the several coves are fun to explore. North of the ramp, swimming is permitted anywhere the park allows boats. South of the ramp, swimming is restricted to designated swim beaches. EBRPD rules restrict boats from the area near the dam and impose a 10-mile-per-hour speed limit.

Blustery summer afternoon winds blow from the northwest end of the lake. The winds that create good windsurfing also make for tough upwind paddling. Winter water levels drop enough to expose the bottom at the southeast end and along parts of the lake's east side.

26 Lexington Reservoir

Located in the Santa Cruz Mountains a short distance from Silicon Valley, this lake is popular for rowing, paddling, and fishing.

Size: 2.2 miles long, 0.2 mile wide; 7.2 miles of shoreline
Average paddling time: 1 to 3 hours
Difficulty: Flatwater lake; beginner skills
Best season: Year-round
Land status: Mixed public and private
Fees: Park and boat inspection fees required
Maps: USGS Los Gatos; Santa Clara County Parks
Craft: Canoes, kayaks, sailboats, fishing boats

Contacts: Santa Clara County Lexington Reservoir County Park: (408) 356-2729; sccgov .org/sites/parks/parkfinder. Boat inspections: (408) 355-2201.
Special considerations: The lake is open to boating daily mid-Apr to mid-Oct. Check with the park for changes in schedule. To stop the spread of quagga and zebra mussels, boats are inspected to make sure they are clean and totally dry.

Put-in/Takeout Information

Lexington Reservoir (N37 12.003' / W121 59.191'): From southbound CA 17, exit at Bear Creek Road, cross the highway, and reenter CA 17 northbound. Exit at Alma Bridge Road and go east on Alma Bridge Road 0.3 mile to the dam. Cross the dam to the launching area. From northbound CA 17, exit directly to Alma Bridge Road.
Shuttle: None

Overview

Santa Clara County manages the 960-acre Lexington Reservoir County Park. This day-use park is popular for hiking, fishing, boating, and picnicking. The lake is reported to support black bass, trout, bluegill, and crappie. The park limits water activities—from 8 a.m. to 30 minutes before sunset—and prohibits swimming and gasoline engines.

The lake sits astride the San Andreas Rift Zone surrounded by steep hills rising more than 1,000 feet above the water. These Santa Cruz Mountains support redwood forests, chaparral, grasslands, hardwoods, and mixed conifer habitats.

Summer days are comfortable, although fog often swirls atop the mountain ridges to the west. Bring a jacket and your wallet for the day-use and boat inspection fees. Open to nonmotorized boats only.

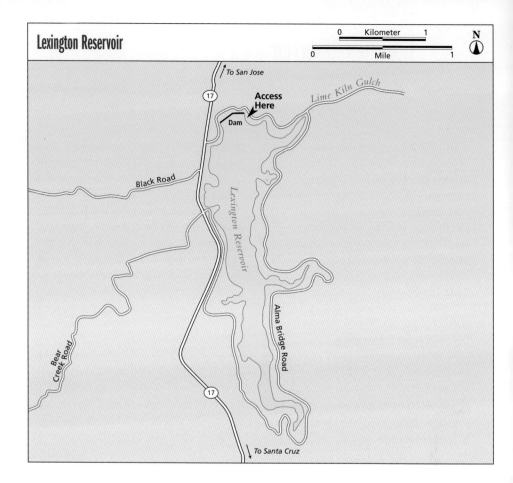

0   Kilometer   1

0   Mile   1

N

To San Jose

17

Access Here

Dam

Lime Kiln Gulch

Black Road

Lexington Reservoir

Alma Bridge Road

Bear Creek Road

17

To Santa Cruz

The Paddling

Proximity to the South Bay and public access make this a favorite place for South Bay paddling clubs and kayaking shops to train beginners. Several rowing clubs take advantage of the lake's straight 2-mile midline for rowing practice.

A few landing spots are scattered along the western (freeway) side of the lake, but the eastern shoreline tends to be very steep. Several short side canyons are interesting to explore at higher water levels.

Central Valley

The Central Valley comprises two major components: the Sacramento River Valley in the north and the San Joaquin River Valley in the south. The valley is the flat agricultural heart of California. Huge reservoirs lining the western slopes of the Sierra Nevada release water to the irrigation canals and tributaries of the Sacramento and San Joaquin Rivers. On its way to the Delta, some of this water can be enjoyed for paddling and fishing as described in the following chapters.

Large pleasure craft frequently spend summer days moored near the confluence of the American and Sacramento Rivers (chapter 37).

27 Sacramento River–Redding to Balls Ferry

With fast, dependable flows, the longest river in California is extremely popular for boating, fishing, and rafting as it flows through the expanse of the upper Sacramento Valley.

Length: 22 miles
Average paddling time: 5 to 7 hours
Difficulty: Fast water and waves; moving-water skills required
Rapids: Class I whitewater due to waves and currents
Average gradient: 6 feet per mile
Optimal flow: 5,000 to 12,000 cfs
Flow gauge: Bend Bridge
Water sources: Lake Shasta and the Trinity River through Keswick Reservoir
Best season: Spring through autumn
Land status: Private riverbanks and public gravel bars
Fees: None
Maps: USGS Redding, Enterprise, Cottonwood, Balls Ferry, Bend, Red Bluff East; BLM *Sacramento River Bend Area Guide*

Craft: Canoes, kayaks, dories, rafts, shallow-draft powerboats
Contacts: BLM Redding Field Office: (530) 224-2100; blm.gov/office/redding-field-office. Sacramento River National Wildlife Refuge: (530) 934-2801; fws.gov/refuge/sacramento. Shasta Cascade Wonderland Association: (530) 365-7500; shastacascade.com.
Special considerations: The Sacramento River—the longest river in California—deserves respect. The summer currents are strong, so stay with your boat in case of an upset. Eddies like the one below Tobiason Rapid are strong enough to thwart a swimmer getting to shore. Each year new snags and shifting shoals reshape the river channel. Avoid winter flood flows, as they often contain trees and other dangerous debris.

Put-in/Takeout Information

Turtle Bay Park (N40 35.444' / W122 22.999'): From I-5 in Redding, go west on CA 44, cross the Sacramento River bridge, then immediately exit at Sundial Bridge Drive to Turtle Park. Follow the sign to the boat ramps; take the first right turn and then turn left at the traffic island. Stay as close as possible to the river, which should lead to (1) a small grassy launch site for canoes, kayaks, and rafts; and (2) 200 yards upstream, behind the rodeo arena, a concrete boat ramp with dock.

South Bonnyview Road (N40 32.246' / W122 21.467'): South of Redding, take I-5 exit 675 onto South Bonnyview Road, go west across the river, and turn south at Indianwood Drive. The John Reginato River access has a paved boat ramp on the west side of the river and downstream of the bridge. A short slough separates the ramp from the river.

Anderson Riverside Park (N40 28.068' / W122 16.791'): Exit I-5 at Anderson. If southbound, exit onto North Street, turn east past I-5, then immediately turn south onto McMurray. Follow signs to Balls Ferry Road, and then turn east onto Balls Ferry Road. If northbound on I-5, exit at Balls Ferry Road east. Follow Balls Ferry

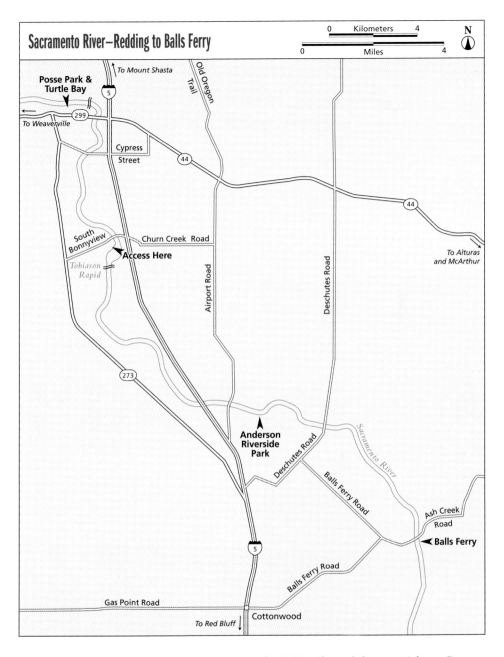

0   Kilometers   4

0   Miles   4

N

To Mount Shasta

Posse Park &
Turtle Bay

5

299

To Weaverville

Old Oregon Trail

Cypress
Street

44

44

To Alturas
and McArthur

South
Bonnyview

Churn Creek Road

Access Here

Tobiason
Rapid

Airport Road

Deschutes Road

273

Anderson
Riverside
Park

Deschutes Road

Sacramento River

Balls Ferry Road

Ash Creek
Road

Balls Ferry

5

Balls Ferry Road

Gas Point Road

Cottonwood

To Red Bluff

Road 0.5 mile, turn left onto Stingy Lane for 0.25 mile, and then go right on Rupert Road 0.7 mile to Anderson Riverside Park. On your left, close to the park entrance, are a parking lot and the boat ramp. Popular for community sports as well as river access, the park has flush toilets and a pay phone.

Balls Ferry (N40 25.033' / W122 11.575'): From I-5 at Cottonwood, take exit 664 (Gas Point Road). Go east 1 mile on Fourth Street to Balls Ferry Road. Take

Balls Ferry Road left (parallel to the railroad tracks) 3.5 miles to the intersection with Ash Creek Road. Follow Ash Creek Road 1.2 miles across the bridge to the access and boat ramp downstream of the bridge. Alternatively, from Anderson take the I-5 exit to Balls Ferry Road east, or take the Deschutes Road exit east 2 miles to where it intersects Balls Ferry Road and then turns southeast. Follow Balls Ferry Road 3 miles to Ash Creek Road and the bridge. A paved launch ramp and toilet are on river left, downstream of the bridge.

Shuttle: Turtle Bay Park to Balls Ferry: 20 miles (35 minutes)

Overview

The Sacramento River, 377 miles long, is fed by Lake Shasta and diversions from the Trinity River. Summer flows on the Sacramento often range from 8,000 to 12,000 cfs. Frequent riffles, standing waves, some choices of channel, and occasional submerged snags characterize the channel. Summer daytime temperatures in Redding are often above 100°F, and the nights may stay in the 80s, so bring sun protection and lots of drinking water.

Where the banks are low, a wide panorama reveals 14,179-foot Mount Shasta dominating the northern horizon, 10,457-foot Lassen Peak crowning the Sierras, and splendid views of the 7,000-foot Coast Range summits.

Many people share the Sacramento River. Dory fishermen row and motor the river during fishing season. Often friendly, they wave and greet paddlers. The Sacramento is also a great place for wildlife watching. On one trip, several great blue herons played follow the leader. Above Anderson, four river otters provided entertainment diving and splashing. Their slide down the riverbank was plainly visible. Overhead, an osprey greeted another osprey carrying a fish to its nest. Close to the right shore, a huge nest was perched on top of a utility pole. From September through May, the salmon repeat their spawning spectacle.

Sundial Bridge is a distinctive Redding landmark in Turtle Bay Park, where this river run begins.

Three brothers enjoy an autumn day salmon fishing near Redding.

The Paddling

At Turtle Bay Park, the long riffle immediately below the put-in requires some attention. Make an extended ferry toward the opposite bank to avoid shallow rocks. A short distance downstream, a submerged rock mid-river produces waves large enough to swamp a heavily loaded canoe.

Between Redding and Anderson, the river races at 4 or 5 mph down a 15-feet-per-mile gradient. Strong eddies and wave trains evidence the strength of 10,000 cfs flowing more than 100 yards wide. High bluffs line river left for the next 2 miles, then shrink to river level past the Cypress Street bridge. Impressive homes with large yards line the right bank—these must be cool, refreshing sites during the hot Redding summers. Farther downstream, many houses are set well back from the river's edge, and the opposite shore is low enough for the winter high water to flood the land and not the buildings. On a recent trip, we were pleased to see river otters playing near here.

Downstream of the golf course, the left bank of the river again rises to a high bluff with a large building and nearby driving range. Below the driving range, a large eddy swirls against the cliff and gravel bar on river right.

The South Bonnyview Road boat ramp is tucked against the right (downstream) side of the bridge. Just downstream, the river divides around a large island. Most of the river flows left to Tobiason Rapid, a series of bouncy, jumbled waves. The right channel around the island starts calmly, descends through a minor riffle, and then joins more smooth water. Where the two channels join, the main current slams into the lesser chute. Together they form a fast, oval-shaped eddy, more like a whirlpool. The resultant flow goes first toward midstream and then abruptly turns 90 degrees, flowing slightly downstream and closer to shore. About 15 yards from shore, water wells up from the bottom, forcing the current upstream and back into the jet. Paddlers who upset their boat can circle a long time in this mid-river merry-go-round.

Downstream, the riffles become easier and the waves smaller as the gradient eases to 6 feet per mile. A series of islands line the right side. The views expand to include the Coast Range. More homes with sumptuous yards border the river. It was a bucolic scene when we floated past, with little kids playing on the banks and teenage rafters exploring a huge snag stranded mid-river.

The Anderson Riverside Park boat ramp is on the right bank, downstream of the I-5 bridge. Below I-5, Airport Road crosses on a smaller bridge. On its girders are painted the words "Rafters take out ½ mile." After you pass more homes, the park comes into view just before the river sweeps left. Watch carefully between the trees for a narrow slough cut into the bank. The boat ramp is 20 yards up the slough. If you miss the ramp, the park extends downstream, but the bank is steep.

Below Anderson, the Sacramento winds around the islands upstream of Stillwater Creek, then passes under the Deschutes Road bridge. Cow Creek soon joins on the left. Large gravel bars spread along the right bank opposite a low-cut bank.

Balls Ferry fishing access ramp rises steeply up the left bank immediately downstream of the Ash Creek Road bridge. It should end a long and pleasant day.

For descriptions of the next reach, see Chapter 28.

28 Sacramento River–Balls Ferry to Red Bluff

Through this section, the Sacramento cuts deep into lava flows down Chinese Rapids and scenic Iron Canyon. It is one of the most interesting sections of the river.

Length: 33 miles

Average paddling time: 9 to 12 hours; often done over 2 days

Difficulty: Fast currents, waves, and strong eddies; beginning whitewater skills required

Rapids: Chinese Rapids, Class II whitewater

Average gradient: 3 feet per mile

Optimal flow: 6,000 to 12,000 cfs

Flow gauge: Bend Bridge

Water sources: Lake Shasta and the Trinity River through Keswick Reservoir

Best season: Spring, summer, and autumn

Land status: Private riverbanks and public gravel bars

Fees: Required at some sites

Maps: USGS Balls Ferry, Bend, Red Bluff East; BLM *Sacramento River Bend Area Guide*, Red Bluff

Craft: Canoes, kayaks, dories, rafts, shallow-draft powerboats

Contacts: BLM Redding Field Office: (530) 224-2100; blm.gov/office/redding-field-office. Sacramento River National Wildlife Refuge: (530) 934-2801; fws.gov/refuge/sacramento. Shasta Cascade Wonderland Association: (530) 365-7500; shastacascade.com. Tehama-Colusa Canal Authority: tccanal.com/fishpassage.htm.

Special considerations: The strong currents accelerate through bedrock rapids instead of the gravel bar variety upstream. Beware of large fish traps attached to the Red Bluff diversion dam. Even in summer, the water stays cold.

Put-in/Takeout Information

Balls Ferry (N 40 25.033' / W122 11.575'): From I-5 at Cottonwood, take exit 664 (Gas Point Road). Go east 1 mile on Fourth Street to Balls Ferry Road. Take Balls Ferry Road left (parallel to the railroad tracks) 3.5 miles to the intersection with Ash Creek Road. Follow Ash Creek Road 1.2 miles across the bridge to the access and boat ramp downstream of the bridge. Alternatively, from Anderson take the I-5 exit to Balls Ferry Road east, or take the Deschutes Road exit east 2 miles to where it intersects Balls Ferry Road and then turns southeast. Follow Balls Ferry Road 3 miles to Ash Creek Road and the bridge. A paved launch ramp and toilet are on river left, downstream of the bridge.

Historic Reading Island (N40 23.172' / W122 11.870') is 5.4 miles east of Cottonwood at the end of Adobe Road. Adobe Road meets Balls Ferry Road 0.5 mile east of the point where the road and railroad separate, 1.4 miles west of the Ash Creek Road junction. The concrete boat ramp is unusable to all but the most determined paddlers due to dense aquatic vegetation and shallow water in the slough leading to the river.

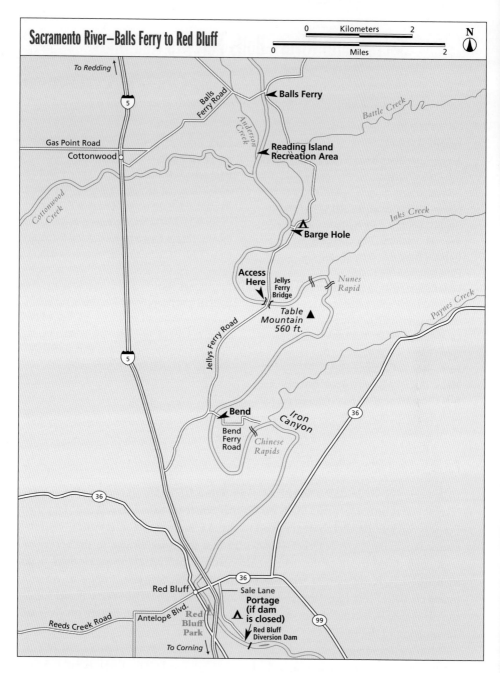

Barge Hole fishing access (N40 20.819' / W122 10.931') is at the mouth of Battle Creek. A well-used, unpaved, unmarked road leads to a large gravel bar and primitive ramp. From the Jellys Ferry bridge, continue another 2.4 miles along Jellys Ferry Road upstream until the road comes close to the river. Look for a dirt road toward the river, and expect to walk or use four-wheel drive on the gravel bars. No toilets.

Jellys Ferry bridge (N40 19.086' / W122 11.342'): From I-5 exit 653, follow Jellys Ferry Road 7.3 miles to the marked access. It is 4.5 miles north of the Bend Ferry Road junction. This BLM day-use area provides access for hand-launch and small trailered watercraft plus toilets.

Bend Ferry bridge (N40 15.821' / W122 13.345'): From I-5 exit 653, follow Jellys Ferry Road 2.7 miles to the Bend Ferry Road junction, then 0.3 mile to the bridge, paved parking, picnic tables, toilet, and launch ramp.

Red Bluff River Park (N40 10.343' / W122 13.691') used to be on the shores of Lake Red Bluff behind the Red Bluff diversion dam. Now the gates are open and the lake is gone. The park is on the west bank of the river. From the intersection of CA 36 and Main Street, go south on Main Street a few blocks. Turn left either onto Sycamore Street or directly into the park by the chamber of commerce building. The well-developed park provides day-use facilities. Carry across the lawns and gravel bar. Optionally, the launch ramp offers a shorter carry.

Lake Red Bluff Recreation Area (N40 9.231' / W122 11.923') is adjacent to the Red Bluff diversion dam on the east side of the Sacramento River. From I-5, take exit 649 and go east on CA 36. Turn right onto Sale Lane by the stoplight and fast-food places. Follow Sale Lane south 2.5 miles to the launch ramp downstream of the dam. This campground and park has toilets, water, parking, and launch fees.

Shuttle: Balls Ferry to Red Bluff diversion dam: 25 miles (40 minutes)

Overview

The deceptively calm surface cloaks the river's strength. The BLM manages miles of land between Balls Ferry and Red Bluff. Permitted activities include hiking, picnicking, camping, and wildlife watching. The Sacramento is famous for great salmon, steelhead, and trout fishing. Other local wildlife include river otters, ringtail cats, black-tailed deer, red-tailed hawks, ospreys, and bobcats.

What used to be the still waters of Lake Red Bluff are now a moving river channel. As of September 2011, the gates of the Red Bluff diversion dam remain open year-round. This status is in response to a federal court order to allow threatened and endangered salmon, steelhead, green sturgeon, and other fish species to migrate past the dam without disruption. The US Bureau of Reclamation and the Tehama-Colusa Canal Authority have built large fish screens and installed huge pumps to lift water from the river into the Tehama-Colusa and Corning Canals for delivery to farmers.

The Paddling

Fifty yards below the Balls Ferry boat ramp, a riffle stretches across the channel, stranding logs at the center. Beyond, the Sacramento River continues its fast flow in the wide, tree-lined channel. Two miles downstream, where the channel narrows a little, the Reading Island Recreation Area (a historic site) occupies the terrace along a cut right bank. This BLM site provides day-use facilities and group camping

Large fish traps are anchored from the Red Bluff diversion dam all year to sample the numbers of fish passing through the dam. Beware of these navigation impediments.

by permit. Hundreds of oaks have been planted to restore the once-dense riparian habitat. The best landing spot is at the downstream confluence with little Anderson Creek.

The land along the right bank between Reading Island and the mouth of Cottonwood Creek is a state wildlife area. Camping there is prohibited. Across the river is another gravel bar. The riverbank beyond the gravel bar is private land.

About 1.7 miles downstream from Battle Creek is a housing development on river right. Around the bend is a large gravel bar island reputedly owned by the state that might be used for camping.

Enjoy the view upstream where snowcapped, 14,179-foot Mount Shasta gleams 70 miles to the north. Below Cottonwood Creek, lava beds intermittently emerge to obscure the view. Two miles farther, Battle Creek joins the Sacramento from the slopes of Lassen Peak. In 1998 diversion dams were removed from Battle Creek to help restore salmon spawning. A mile below Battle Creek, the huge gravel bars of Barge Hole occupy river left. This BLM land is open to primitive access. Where the river again turns to the south, the BLM manages more land on river left.

Jellys Ferry bridge is the next put-in and takeout site. Look eastward to 10,457-foot Lassen Peak, about 35 miles away.

Below Jellys Ferry, the river landscape changes. First turning north and then south, the river has cut through the lava that composes Table Mountain. Sheer canyon walls, oak slopes, and riverside terraces replace farmlands. The speed and waves of Jellys Ferry Rapid add excitement to boating.

Inks Creek meets the canyon at the apex of the northerly turn. The area is interesting to explore. Below Inks Creek is Nunes Rapid and the "rock wall" rising to Table Mountain. Where the wall drops down to river level is a large gravel bar, Massacre Flat (N40 19.118' / W122 9.256'), where primitive camping is permitted.

As you pass Lookout Mountain, Bend Bridge comes into view. A good access ramp, parking, and restroom are on river left. At 4,400 cfs, expect some broad gravel bars and bouncy wave trains. As the channel loops to the east, then north around the flat farmlands of Bend, you can build your anticipation for Chinese Rapids and Iron Canyon.

As the channel bends northward, the mini-beaches between the rock outcroppings on the left are private lands, but river right is BLM land. The channel narrows as it approaches Chinese Rapids. The 0.5-mile-long rapid consists of haystacks in a generally clear channel that curves to the right in the bottom half, where you encounter strong eddy lines. Boulders, sand, and bedrock alternate along both banks. Just when you think you have reached the rapid's end, lava boulders block the channel's left half. The wide sluice on the right is clear and bouncy.

Paynes Creek, with its wetland reserve, enters on the left. Here impressive Iron Canyon begins. The river turns sharply south, and the sheer canyon walls rise 300 feet. After 2 miles the wall on river left turns to rolling hillsides and the river flows in an almost straight line to Red Bluff. Ida Adobe State Historic Park overlooks the river from the picturesque bluff just upstream of Dibble Creek.

Since autumn 2011, the gates of the Red Bluff diversion dam remain open, allowing the river and boats to pass without interruption. However, beware of the fish traps in the water at the dam. You can take out at the boat ramp below the dam on river left.

For descriptions of the next reach, see chapter 29.

29 Sacramento River—Red Bluff to Woodson Bridge

Swift currents, wide horizons, big gravel bars, and good fishing make this an attractive float trip through elements of the Sacramento River National Wildlife Refuge.

Length: 25 miles

Average paddling time: 6 to 8 hours

Difficulty: Fast currents and occasional snags; Class I paddling skills required

Average gradient: 3 feet per mile

Optimal flow: 5,000 to 12,000 cfs

Flow gauge: Vina-Woodson bridge

Water sources: Lake Shasta and the Trinity River diversion through Keswick Reservoir

Best season: Spring, summer, and autumn

Land status: Private riverbanks and public gravel bars

Fees: Required at some sites

Maps: USGS Red Bluff East, Gerber, Los Molinos, Vina; BLM Red Bluff CA; US Fish and Wildlife Service "Sacramento River National Wildlife Refuge Visitor Access/Use Maps"

Craft: Canoes, kayaks, dories, rafts, shallow-draft powerboats

Contacts: Woodson Bridge State Recreation Area: (530) 839-2112; parks.ca.gov; camping: www.reservecalifornia.com. Sycamore Grove Camping at Red Bluff diversion dam: recreation.gov. Sacramento River National Wildlife Refuge: (530) 934-2801; fws.gov/refuge/Sacramento_River. Shasta Cascade Wonderland Association: (530) 365-7500; shasta cascade.com.

Special considerations: The summer current is strong, so stay with your boat in case of an upset. Outboard motorboats frequently travel the deeper channels. Each year new snags and shifting shoals remake the river channel. Avoid winter flood flows, as they often contain floating trees and other debris.

Put-in/Takeout Information

Lake Red Bluff Recreation Area (N40 9.231' / W122 11.923') is adjacent the Red Bluff diversion dam on the east side of the Sacramento River. From I-5, take exit 649 and go east on CA 36. Turn right onto Sale Lane by the stoplight and fast-food places. Follow Sale Lane south 2.5 miles to the launch ramp and parking downstream of the diversion dam. This campground and park has toilets, water, parking, and launch fees.

Mill Creek access (N40 1.905' / W122 7.061'). From I-5, take exit 636 onto Gyle Road (CR A11) east. Go 5 miles, then A11 turns north into Fifth Street. Turn east on C Street toward the Sacramento River bridge. Cross the bridge, immediately turn left (north) under the railroad and bear right onto Tehama-Vina Road to the park entrance. Facilities include parking, launch ramp, and toilets.

East of the bridge, C Street is named Aramayo Way. One mile to the east, it connects with CA 99 north of Los Molinos.

Tehama County River Park (N39 54.588' / W122 5.443'): From I-5 at Corning, take exit 630 to South Avenue going east. Woodson Bridge State Recreation Area and Tehama County River Park are 6 miles east. Cross the Sacramento River bridge. The county park with the launch ramp is immediately downstream. Woodson Bridge

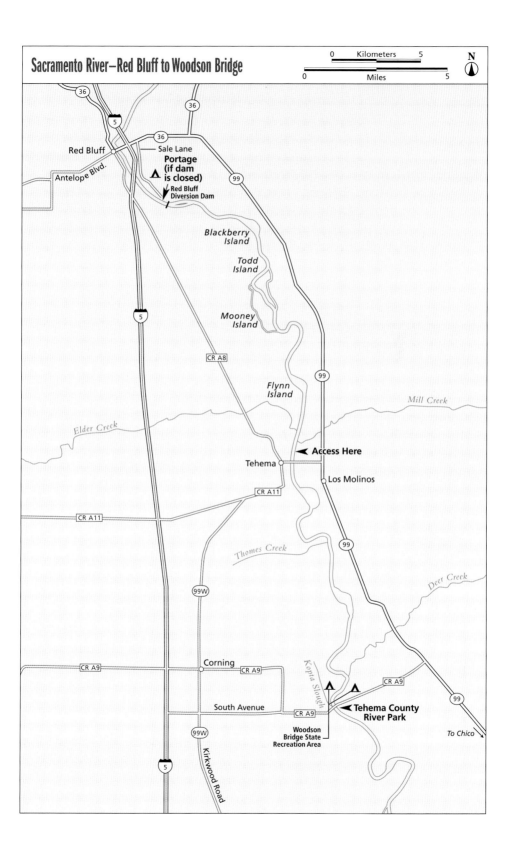

Sacramento River–Red Bluff to Woodson Bridge

Kilometers
0   5

Miles
0   5

N

36

5

36

36

Red Bluff — Sale Lane

Portage
(if dam
is closed)

Antelope Blvd.

Red Bluff
Diversion Dam

99

Blackberry
Island

Todd
Island

Mooney
Island

5

CR A8

Flynn
Island

99

Mill Creek

Elder Creek

◀ **Access Here**

Tehema

Los Molinos

CR A11

CR A11

Thomes Creek

99

Deer Creek

99W

CR A9

Corning

CR A9

99

Kopta Slough

CR A9

South Avenue

CR A9

◀ **Tehema County
River Park**

99W

Woodson
Bridge State
Recreation Area

To Chico

5

Kirkwood Road

State Recreation Area campground is on the north side of CR A9, opposite the county park. The bridge is 3 miles west of CA 99.

Shuttle: Red Bluff to Mill Creek: 15 miles (25 minutes); Mill Creek to Woodson Bridge: 13 miles (20 minutes)

Overview

Along this stretch of river, wide channels and low banks allow expansive views of Mount Shasta, the Trinity Alps, and Lassen Peak. Winter flows from the Sacramento's many tributaries move the channel frequently, creating new oxbows and cutoffs. A floatable channel one year may be a sandbar the next.

Twenty-eight units of the Sacramento National Wildlife Refuge protect and restore waterfowl and fish habitats along 75 river miles between Red Bluff and Princeton. Easy-to-see summer species include ospreys, turkey vultures, red-tailed hawks, and some bald eagles. Look for some of them perched on the tall cottonwood snags or oaks along the banks. The US Fish and Wildlife Service "Sacramento River National Wildlife Refuge Visitor Access/Use Maps" states: "Camping is allowed within the refuge only on gravel bars for up to 7 days during a 30-day period, but camping is prohibited on other refuge lands."

Woodson Bridge State Recreation Area is a 142-acre oak woodland park nestled along the Sacramento River. Kopta Slough provides access to boat-in campsites. Adjacent to the park is a 328-acre riparian forest preserve. This junglelike array of large valley oak, California black walnut, Oregon ash, black cottonwood, sycamore, and willow provide a winter home to bald eagles and summer nesting sites for yellow-billed cuckoos. Car-camp on the east side of the river, 0.5 mile from the Tehama County River Park launch ramp.

Summer daytime temperatures often exceed 100°F, with only mild cooling at night, so bring lots of drinking water.

The Paddling

Normal summer flows exceed 10,000 cfs and give a fast 4 mph ride. Riffles add excitement at the bottom end of many gravel bars, particularly near Blackberry Island, Craig Creek, and Sacramento Bar.

Blackberry Island (N40 8.327' / W122 8.577'), Todd Island (N40 6.870' / W122 8.162'), Mooney Island (N40 5.964' / W122 7.941'), and Flynn Island (N40 3.637' / W122 6.829') are national wildlife units with big gravel bars. Depending on the channel-carving whims of recent floods, you can probably explore the side sloughs around the oxbows and gravel bars. Satellite images and topographic maps show many old channels.

Wide turns interspersed with riffles continue to the mouth of the North Fork of Mill Creek on the left bank and Elder Creek on the right bank. Here orchards and houses line the bank, the channel straightens, and the Tehama bridges come into

Boats like this are often used to fish for salmon, steelhead, striped bass, sturgeon, and trout along the Sacramento River.

view. Upstream of the bridges, look for the Mill Creek boat ramp on the left bank just below the mouth of Mill Creek.

Two miles below the Tehama bridges, and upstream of Thomes Creek, the river makes a long horseshoe bend with several gravel bars. Then it straightens before 2 more miles of bends, gravel bars, and shallow riffles around Copeland Bar.

Where the river turns abruptly south, China and Deer Creeks join with the Sacramento. Theodora Kroeber's book *Ishi in Two Worlds* made Deer Creek famous. It is the true story of Ishi, the last Yahi Indian, who emerged from the wilderness in 1911.

When you round the bend you'll see Vina-Woodson bridge. Aquatic vegetation impedes paddling up Kopta Slough (river right) to the former boat-in campgrounds of Woodson Bridge State Recreation Area. The Tehama County River Park boat ramp is on the river-left bank.

For information about going downstream, see chapter 30.

30 Sacramento River–Woodson Bridge to Colusa

Popular for fishing, camping, and floating, this reach of the Sacramento River meanders through the heart of Northern California farmlands. The adjacent wildlife refuges are visited by 40 percent of the waterfowl in the Pacific Flyway.

Length: 74 miles

Average paddling time: 2 to 3 days

Difficulty: Fast currents and occasional snags; Class I paddling skills required

Average gradient: 2 feet per mile

Optimal flow: 5,000 to 12,000 cfs

Flow gauge: Woodson Bridge or Colusa

Water sources: Lake Shasta and the Trinity River diversion through Keswick Reservoir

Best season: Spring, summer, and autumn

Land status: Private riverbanks and public gravel bars

Fees: Required at some sites

Maps: USGS Vina, Foster Island, Nord, Ord Ferry, Llano Seco, Butte City, Glenn, Princeton, Sanborn Slough, Moulton Weir, Colusa, Meridian; US Fish and Wildlife Service "Sacramento River National Wildlife Refuge Visitor Access/ Use Maps"

Craft: Canoes, kayaks, dories, rafts, shallow-draft powerboats

Contacts: Woodson Bridge State Recreation Area: (530) 839-2112; www.parks.ca.gov; camping: (530) 839-2112; reservecalifornia .com. Sacramento River National Wildlife Refuge: (530) 934-2801; fws.gov/refuge/ sacramento river. Bidwell Sacramento River State Park: (530) 342-5185; parks.ca.gov. Colusa-Sacramento River State Recreation Area: (530) 329-9198; parks.ca.gov.

Special considerations: The hot summer days invite swimming, but be careful. The summer current is strong, so stay with your boat in case of an upset. Each year new snags and shifting shoals re-form the river channel. Avoid winter flood flows, as the cold water often contains floating trees and other debris.

Put-in/Takeout Information

Tehama County River Park (N39 54.588' / W122 5.443'): From I-5 at Corning, take exit 630 to South Avenue going east. Woodson Bridge State Recreation Area and Tehama County River Park are 6 miles east. Cross the Sacramento River bridge. The county park with the launch ramp is immediately downstream. Woodson Bridge State Recreation Area campground is on the north side of A9, opposite the county park. The bridge is 3 miles west of CA 99.

The Irvine Finch River access (N39 45.008' / W121 59.826') is 1 mile east of Hamilton City and about 8.9 miles west of Chico, on river right downstream of the CA 32 bridge over the Sacramento River. This fee site provides parking, toilets, water, and a launch ramp.

Pine Creek Landing (N39 44.715' / W121 57.961') is a state park launch site 0.25 mile up Pine Creek from the river. On River Road, it is 0.6 mile south of CA 32 and 2.3 miles east of Hamilton City. The site is a fee area with toilet and parking.

Scotty's Landing (N39 44.291' / W121 57.570') is a fee area with an RV park, party beach, launch ramp, and over-the-counter food and beverage sales. Located at the mouth of Pine Creek, it is on River Road, 0.8 mile south of CA 32 and 2.3 miles east of Hamilton City.

Sacramento River access at Pine Creek (N39 44.247' / W121 57.480') is located at the mouth of Pine Creek immediately adjacent to Scotty's Landing. The launch ramp being developed is OK for hand-carried boats. This is a fee area with picnic tables, parking, and toilet.

Glenn County Ord Bend Park (N39 37.808' / W121 59.707') is 0.6 mile east of the intersection of CA 45 and CR 32 in Ordbend. The parking area and concrete launch ramp are on the west bank, upstream of the CR 32 (Old Ferry Road) bridge. Fees for boat launching.

Butte City County Park (N39 27.870' / W121 59.539'): From the CA 162 bridge over the Sacramento River, follow CA 162 (Main Street) north about 0.5 mile to a left turn onto a paved road over the low levee into the park with day-use facilities, toilets, and a launch ramp. Since the slough is obscured from the river, be sure to inspect this takeout before you put in.

Princeton (N39 23.954' / W122 0.322'): From I-5, take exit 595 and follow Norman Road east about 10 miles to Princeton. Go south on CA 45 to the high school. Opposite State Street turn left (east) over the levee to several rough unpaved roads that lead 0.3 mile to the riverbank for hand-launching boats.

Colusa–Sacramento River State Recreation Area (N39 13.030' / W122 0.765'): In Colusa at the intersection of CA 20 and CA 45, take 10th Street north past Market and Main Streets into the park. Excellent facilities in this fee area with a concrete launch ramp constructed in 2018 where a narrow slough meets the Sacramento River.

Shuttle: Woodson Bridge to Colusa: 65 miles (1.5 hours)

Overview

Bring your fishing rod, sunhat, bird book, binoculars, and lots of water. The mix of easy water, pastoral lands, riparian vegetation, beaches, and gravel bars make this a favorite summer float trip. Summer days can be very hot, with only mild cooling at night. Many different kinds of watercraft use the river, and every spring hundreds of students from California State University in Chico ride their homemade "floats" near Chico landing. Several marinas sponsor fishing tournaments. Many shallow-draft powerboats ply the waters as the summer temperatures rise.

The winter flood flows contributed by the Sacramento's many tributaries move the channel frequently, creating new oxbows and cutoffs. Aerial images plainly show that a floatable channel one year may be a sandbar the next year. Deeply eroded banks topped by orchards with exposed irrigation pipes further evince the power of winter flows. In the entire reach, we saw only one set of rocks; they once served as riprap.

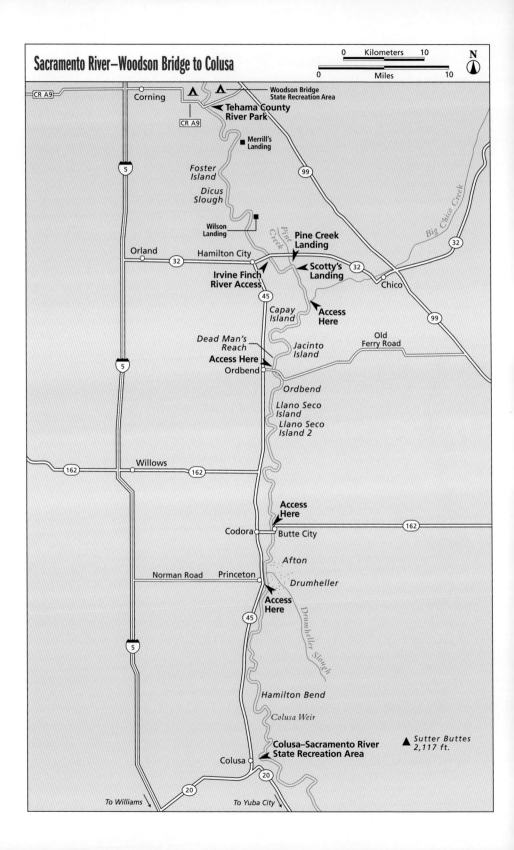

Sacramento River–Woodson Bridge to Colusa

0 Kilometers 10

0 Miles 10

N

CR A9

Corning

Woodson Bridge
State Recreation Area

Tehama County
River Park

CR A9

Merrill's
Landing

5

Foster
Island

99

Dicus
Slough

Big Chico Creek

Wilson
Landing

Pine Creek
Landing

32

Orland

32

Hamilton City

Irvine Finch
River Access

Scotty's
Landing

32

Chico

45

Capay
Island

Access
Here

99

Dead Man's
Reach

Access Here

Jacinto
Island

Old
Ferry Road

5

Ordbend

Ordbend

Llano Seco
Island

Llano Seco
Island 2

162

Willows

162

Access
Here

162

Codora

Butte City

Afton

Norman Road

Princeton

Drumheller

Access
Here

45

Drumheller Slough

5

Hamilton Bend

Colusa Weir

Sutter Buttes
2,117 ft.

Colusa–Sacramento River
State Recreation Area

Colusa

20

20

To Williams

To Yuba City

Woodson Bridge State Recreation Area facilities are described in the preceding chapter. The state park's 328-acre riparian forest preserve is part of the multiagency effort to preserve and restore riparian forests along the Sacramento River corridor. The US Fish and Wildlife Service reports: "This riparian community is one of the most important wildlife habitats in California and North America. Riparian habitats along the Sacramento River are critically important for various threatened species, fisheries, migratory birds, plants, and the natural system of the river itself. There has been an 85 percent reduction of riparian vegetation throughout the Sacramento Valley and foothills region. The relatively small amount of riparian woodlands that remain provides a strikingly disproportionate amount of habitat value for wildlife."

Glenn and Butte County farms grow large amounts of rice. Following the rice harvest in late summer and autumn, some farmers burn the residual stubble. The burning creates lots of smoke, and some of it blows close to the river.

The Paddling

At 10,000 cfs summer flow, the river continues the fast (4+ mph) current for 10 miles below Woodson Bridge. The pastoral setting invites floating, fishing, and birding. Look for osprey nests near Merrill's Landing and Foster Island, as well as an occasional bald eagle. Keep one eye on the river to avoid sandbars and snags. The reach is popular for Boy Scout canoe trips. Most of the powerboats they encounter are considerate of the canoes.

More signs of man-made activity are visible on this long stretch of river. One example is at the bottom end of Snaden Island. The right channel leads to the large screened intake for the Glenn Colusa Canal.

Near the Glenn-Tehama county line, the river velocity begins to slow noticeably. Five miles downstream, houses are visible along the left bank upstream of the CA 32 bridge. On the downstream side of the bridge, the Irvine Finch boat-launching ramp is tucked into the right bank. This ramp is a popular put-in for short floats to Big Chico Creek Beach.

A mile downstream, both banks form great beaches and gravel bars. The 2-mile-long double oxbow once known as Jenny Lind Bend has been cut through to 0.5 mile. Now Pine Creek Landing is 0.25 mile up Pine Creek instead of being riverfront property. Scotty's Landing, a focal point for powerboats, and the state-owned Sacramento River access are now at the confluence.

Land management around the Pine Creek confluence has changed to restore flood-prone agricultural land to riparian forest. It has become part of the Sacramento River National Wildlife Refuge. The Sacramento River Project focuses on the restoration and protection of habitats between Red Bluff and Colusa. Look for changes in the vegetation patterns and different wildlife in future decades.

Boy Scout troops enjoy overnight camping along the Sacramento River.

Units of the Sacramento National Wildlife Refuge that have gravel bars that may be suitable for camping include:

- Merrill's Landing (N39 52.614' / W122 3.903')
- Foster Island (N39 50.762' / W122 3.736')
- Dicus Slough (N39 49.995' / W122 3.940')
- Wilson Landing (N39 47.414' / W122 1.934')
- Capay Island (N39 41.705' / W121 56.644')
- Jacinto Island (N39 38.871' / W121 58.437')
- Dead Man's Reach (N39 38.719' / W121 59.307')
- Ordbend (N39 36.680' / W121 58.776')
- Llano Seco Island (N39 34.430' / W122 0.035')
- Llano Seco 2 (N39 33.534' / W121 59.562')
- Afton (N39 25.830' / W122 0.238')
- Drumheller North (N39 25.242' / W121 59.747')

Only a couple miles below Pine Creek are the wide beaches of Bidwell Sacramento River State Park and the old Chico Landing site. The large gravel bar at the mouth of Big Chico Creek is a popular launching and takeout spot for many rafters and personal watercraft. For the next several miles, clear early-summer days offer views of the distant snow-covered Cascade and Coast Mountains.

The next landing is the Glenn County Ord Bend Park at Ord Ferry Bridge. It lies at the head of a short, murky slough on river right and upstream of the CA 45 bridge. The day-use area has shade that is welcome on a hot day.

For 20 miles, backwater sloughs and old oxbow lakes reflect the river's geomorphology. The channel is straighter these days, but what will happen without the winding miles to dissipate the energy of flood flows?

The next set of large irrigation pumps is near Sidds Landing. At Sidds Landing, CA 45 is visible along the right bank atop the flood-control levee. The flood-control levees on river left begin 2 miles downstream. That levee is initially unnoticeable, since it is set back from the current channel. As you float along the river, note how the river carves its changing course within the 0.5- to 1-mile corridor between the levees.

Above Hartly Island, fly-fishing anglers line the long, sweeping gravel bar on river right in early summer. The ospreys must agree with the fishing prospects, since a pair nests in a snag a short distance downstream. When you spot the CA 162 bridge at Butte City, look on the left for the slough leading to the launching ramp. It is about 0.5 mile upstream from the bridge.

Between Packer Island and Princeton, you can see the first river views of the Sutter Buttes to the southeast. The 2,100-foot ancient volcanoes are landmarks for much of the southern Sacramento Valley. Soon afterward, on river right, tiny Princeton shows its rickety old cable ferry that was the last to carry vehicles across the Sacramento River. In contrast, a gigantic new pumping plant sprawls along the left bank.

Boggs Bend still supports some impressive-looking riparian forest. Three miles downstream, the low structure on the left bank, called Moulton Weir, permits some floodwaters to escape the river and flow to the Butte Sink.

Levees now redirect the river to a shorter course around Hamilton Bend. High flood flows sometimes leave high sandy beaches with pleasant views on river right. The next major flood-control structure is the Colusa Weir. Like the Moulton Weir, it is a low levee on the left bank that allows floodwater to escape the river to a flood bypass. The most visible feature is the bridge structure supporting River Road across the weir. The river's course may lead away from the weir, so it is sometimes unobtrusive.

Twin water towers mark the town of Colusa. Paddle toward them until you come to a narrow slough and new boat ramp on river right.

The river downstream of Colusa is less desirable for paddling because of increased motorboat traffic, levees that closely confine the river, little riparian vegetation, and few sand or gravel bars.

31   Feather River–Oroville to Wildlife Refuge

Reliable flows provide year-round easy paddling through the Oroville Wildlife Area.

Length: 9.5 miles from Bedrock Park to Oroville Wildlife Area
Average paddling time: 3 to 5 hours
Difficulty: Fast water with some obstacles; maneuvering skills required
Rapids: Class I whitewater; one Class II rapid
Average gradient: 5 feet per mile
Optimal flow: 1,500 to 4,000 cfs
Water source: Fish barrier dam at Oroville Reservoir plus Thermalito discharge
Flow gauge: Gridley
Best season: Year-round
Land status: Private in Oroville, public in wildlife refuge
Fees: Not at this writing

Maps: USGS Oroville, Palermo, Biggs; Oroville Wildlife Area; Department of Water Resources (DWR), South Oroville Recreation Area
Craft: Canoes, kayaks, inflatables, dories
Contacts: Oroville Area Chamber of Commerce: (530) 538-2542; orovillechamber.com. Oroville State Wildlife Area: (530) 538-2236; wildlife.ca.gov/Lands/Places-to-Visit/Oroville-WA. Department of Water Resources, Oroville Recreation Area: water.ca.gov/recreation/locations/oroville/maps. Feather River Fish Hatchery at Oroville: (530) 538-2222.
Special considerations: Releases above 5,000 cfs from Thermalito Afterbay require extreme caution, lining, or portaging to avoid the turbulent discharge.

Put-in/Takeout Information

Riverbend Park, Oroville (N39 30.294' / W121 34.678') is at the west end of Montgomery Street. Follow the parking areas downstream to the launch ramp. This is now the preferred put-in and alternative to Bedrock Park.

Bedrock Park, Oroville, river mile 66 (N39 30.724' / W121 34.168'): From CA 70 take any of the three Oroville exits (Pacific Heights Road, Oroville Dam Road, or Montgomery Street) and turn east until you intersect Feather River Boulevard. Turn north and follow Feather River Boulevard until it ends at Bedrock Park. Use the lower parking area and paved bicycle trail to reach the river below the lagoon.

Thermalito Afterbay outlet boat ramp, river mile 59 (N39 27.389' / W121 37.966'): From CA 70 go west 1.8 miles on Oroville Dam Road (CA 62) to Larkin Road. Turn south and follow Larkin Road until the Thermalito Afterbay is on your right. Before you get to the discharge canal, look to the left for a paved road (signed "Oroville Wildlife Area"). Follow the curve 0.3 mile to the unpaved launch area. Avoid using this put-in when the discharge is above 5,000 cfs—the current is so strong, it will carry a paddler directly into the powerful discharge turbulence.

Vance Avenue to Oroville Wildlife Area, river mile 57.8 (N39 26.261' / W121 38.335') is on the west side of the river. From Larkin Road, 1.8 miles south of the Thermalito Afterbay outlet, turn east onto Vance Avenue. Go past the pavement to the levee top, jog right 100 yards, and then bear left off the levee to river level. The unimproved site is suitable for trailer launch but is not marked from the river.

Oroville Wildlife Area, river mile 56.5 (N39 25.371' / W121 37.399'): From Bedrock Park go 7 miles south on CA 70. Past Golden Oaks mobile home park and opposite a large empty barn, turn west on a paved road with a large sign that reads "Oroville Wildlife Area." Go 1 mile to the high levee adjacent to the haul road where you see the river. Either turn left down the rough track to the gravel bar or continue upstream 50 yards to a low area near the culvert connecting the wildlife ponds with the river. Continuing upstream, the road leads to the levee opposite the Thermalito Afterbay outlet (N39 27.295' / W121 37.991'). This is a steep but possible takeout. The dirt road continues east to connect with Pacific Heights Road, which leads northeast and connects with CA 70. During floods, these roads may be impassable.

Palm Avenue to Oroville Wildlife Area, river mile 55.4 (N39 24.643' / W121 37.640'): From Larkin Road on the west side of the river, go 2.2 miles south of Vance Road, or 0.5 mile south of East Biggs Highway. Turn east onto Palm Avenue, go up on the levee, and continue east into the Oroville Wildlife Area. On top of the tailings, several dirt roads come together. Go north (upstream) 200 yards to an easy graded access to the river.

Shuttle: Bedrock to Oroville Wildlife Area: 8 miles (15 minutes); Bedrock Park to Palm Avenue: 12.3 miles (25 minutes)

Overview

Oroville Reservoir generates hydropower and stores water for the State Water Project (SWP). Below the Feather River Fish Hatchery, the once mighty Feather River glides tamed and cold through the heart of Oroville. Except during floods and pulse flows for fish, the SWP releases a flow of 600 to 800 cfs past the fish barrier dam into the Feather River channel. Downstream 7 miles, the bulk of the SWP water joins the river on its way to the Sacramento–San Joaquin Delta. From the Delta, the pumps and aqueducts transport SWP water to farms of the San Joaquin Valley, San Francisco Bay, the Central Coast, and Southern California.

The flood flows of the 2017 Oroville Dam spillway failure scoured the river channel. Gravel bars and brush will eventually return. Most of the low-flow stretch of river has only a few gravel bars and a couple of snags to challenge the paddler. Fly fishing for steelhead is very popular in the low-flow section between Oroville and Thermalito. The most serious paddling concern on this easy run is the outflow from Thermalito Afterbay, an off-stream reservoir connected by pumped storage facilities to the Oroville reservoir. Releases from the afterbay to the river cause severe turbulence across the entire channel when the outflow exceeds 5,000 cfs. High releases may occur any time of year. Below Thermalito, many powerboats ply the river when flows allow.

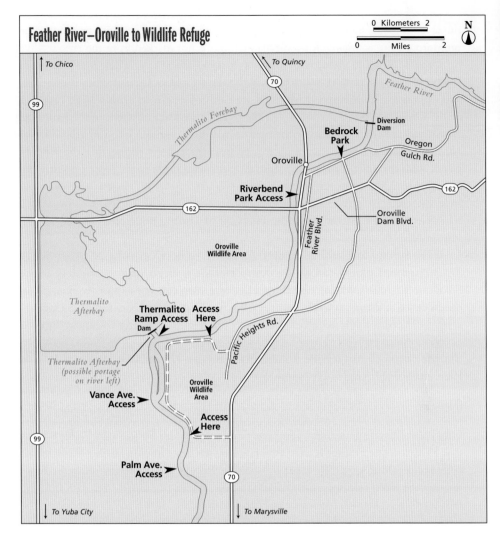

Feather River–Oroville to Wildlife Refuge

0 Kilometers 2

0 Miles 2

N

To Chico

To Quincy

70

99

Feather River

Thermalito Forebay

Diversion Dam

Bedrock Park

Oregon Gulch Rd.

Oroville

Riverbend Park Access

162

162

Oroville Dam Blvd.

Oroville Wildlife Area

Feather River Blvd.

Thermalito Afterbay

Thermalito Ramp Access

Access Here

Dam

Pacific Heights Rd.

Thermalito Afterbay (possible portage on river left)

Vance Ave. Access

Oroville Wildlife Area

Access Here

99

Palm Ave. Access

70

To Yuba City

To Marysville

The 8,000-acre Oroville Wildlife Area borders 10 miles of the Feather River. The area allows primitive camping, boating, fishing, swimming, and seasonal hunting. With a bird list of 178 species, the refuge is a favorite of birders.

The Paddling

Put in at the downstream end of Bedrock Park in Oroville. The river is smooth and wide, a good place for beginners and novices to practice their paddle strokes.

After flowing under the CA 70 bridge, the calm river swings south. The right bank rises 80 feet above the water. Homes adorn the right shore above the Oroville Dam Boulevard bridge. Riverbend Park, with a launch ramp, occupies the left bank. Downstream of the bridge you encounter the first fast water, almost a riffle. Fast flows continue 1 mile to another riffle favored by fly fishers. Just below, an RV park (with a boat ramp) occupies the left bank. Oroville Wildlife Area manages the opposite side, where the landscape is tall trees and dredge tailings from gold-mining and dam-building eras.

As the river turns west, you may spot the cranes of a gravel operation on the left. Soon some broken pilings and boulders cross the river. Take care to align your boat with the open channels. Several wide, shallow riffles and braided channels follow. One longer riffle has a reputation for changing from year to year. The river cuts abruptly left, with trees and brush lining the left side. In the steepest drop of the reach, the current charges 150 bouncy yards around a gravel bar, past some strong eddies, and into a steep bank. Pools at the bottom provide easy recovery from an upset, while the right bank offers a portage for the cautious or inexperienced.

After you pass the large, rotating fish trap, focus on the discharge from Thermalito Afterbay. You can see the outlet structure and flow from 0.5 mile away. At discharges above 5,000 cfs, swift, exploding waves sweep across the entire river channel. The flow divides, much of it running swiftly upstream along the high levee on river left. This action forms a huge eddy that returns to the turbulence along the right bank. If water covers the gravel bars and you can see lots of white from the outlet, stick closely to the left bank. Even next to the bank, the current is strong enough to make paddling difficult. You will not be the first to decide to line boats along the bank or portage along the levee top. If you can see exposed gravel bars on the left side, stay on the water and enjoy the ride.

If you carelessly floated to river right, swept by fast current toward the discharge, paddle furiously for the boat ramp on the right bank upstream of the discharge. You will be safe there even if you cannot easily join your friends on the other side of the river. That requires going far upstream and crossing the river.

Below Thermalito Afterbay the flows usually match the size of the wide river. Even where islands divide the channel, flows are deep enough for many motorboats during salmon season. The paddling is generally fast and easy, with only a couple of riffles below 2,000 cfs.

Bounded on both sides by the wildlife refuge, this is a great place for birding. On a recent winter trip, we spotted ospreys, bald eagles, red-tailed hawks, great American egrets, great blue herons, red-shouldered hawks, and myriad ducks.

After the river turns right, 2.5 miles below Thermalito, look for the takeout on river left. You can probably see through the trees to spot cars parked atop the high levee. Immediately upstream is a low spot with a small inlet and a culvert from wildlife ponds.

You can extend your paddle another 1 mile by continuing past the island and taking out on river right at Palm Avenue.

32 Yuba River

With summerlong flows, the Yuba is a clear and dependable float for novices. Rich in gold-mining history, the river scampers through immense dredge tailings of the Yuba gold fields.

Length: 17.9 miles
Average paddling time: 2 to 5 hours
Difficulty: Quick water and gravel bar riffles; fast-water experience and skills required
Rapids: Class I to Class II whitewater
Average gradient: 4 to 12 feet per mile
Optimum flow: 500 to 3,000 cfs
Flow gauge: Below Englebright Dam
Water source: Bullards Bar Reservoir discharges plus the South Fork Yuba River through Englebright Reservoir
Best season: Summer and autumn
Land status: Private and public
Fees: Possible county park fees

Maps: USGS Smartville, Browns Valley, Yuba City
Craft: Canoes, kayaks, rafts, sit-on-tops
Contacts: Yuba County Parks, Sycamore Ranch RV Park & Campground: (530) 749-5420; parks.yuba.org. South Yuba River Citizens League (SYRCL): (530) 265-5961; yubariver .org. Dreamflows: dreamflows.com.
Special considerations: Slopes of the tailings piles are unstable. If you try to climb them, rocks large and small will slide under your feet and bring you crashing down in a landslide. Daguerra Point Dam is a hazard to boaters at any flow. Portage the dam on river left.

Put-in/Takeout Information

Parks Bar Bridge (N39 13.257' / W121 20.035') is 18 miles east of Marysville on CA 20. When the large concrete bridge comes into view, look for the Parks Bar side road on the right. Follow it about 0.5 mile, past some houses and under the bridge, then bear right toward the water. No fees or toilet. *Note:* The gravel bar on the opposite end of the bridge requires four-wheel drive over loose cobbles.

Yuba County Hammon Grove Park (N39 13.808' / W121 23.950'): Adjacent to Sycamore Ranch, the park has picnic tables, a toilet at the entrance, and rattlesnake warnings. Go to the parking area overlooking the river, and carry 100 yards down a foot trail to river's edge.

Sycamore Ranch RV Park & Campground (N39 13.388' / W121 24.473') is located 14.4 miles east of Marysville at the Dry Creek confluence with the Yuba. The campground is between CA 20 and the river. Fee area.

Hallwood Boulevard (N39 11.017' / W121 30.655') is 7.4 miles east of Marysville on CA 20. Turn south 1.7 miles to the end of the road. Because this residential road is posted "No Parking," the neighbors advise that you find a shuttle driver rather than leave your vehicle here.

Riverfront Park (N39 8.299' / W121 36.169') is well developed, with many sports fields, picnic areas, paved parking, restrooms, and a paved launch ramp. In Marysville, turn west off CA 70 at the light onto Third or Fourth Street. Go 1 block and turn left (south) onto F Street. Follow F Street, and take the right fork up the levee on Biz Johnson Drive, which becomes 14th Street. Just before the highway bridge, turn left into the parking lot to the lagoon and launch ramp.

Yuba City boat ramp (N39 7.788' / W121 36.052') is on the west side of the Feather River downstream of the Twin Cities Memorial Bridge. If you used CA 20 to cross the Feather River, turn south onto Sutter Street. At the Memorial Bridge, Sutter Street becomes Second Street. If you used Marysville's Fifth Street to reach the Memorial Bridge, turn onto Second Street going south in Yuba City. Continue south (bear left) on Second Street until you see the large sign for the launch ramp and paved parking area.

Shuttle: Parks Bar to Dry Creek: 4 miles (10 minutes); Dry Creek to Hallwood Boulevard: 9 miles (15 minutes); Hallwood Boulevard to Marysville or Yuba City: 10 miles (15 minutes)

Overview

Above Daguerra Point Dam, the landscape is typical California foothills: oak trees and grasslands. Beautiful with wildflowers in spring, they toast to California brown in the hot summers. Contrasting with the foothills are the mile-wide Yuba River gold fields.

Gold dredging created mountains of rock along the Parks Bar section of the Yuba River.

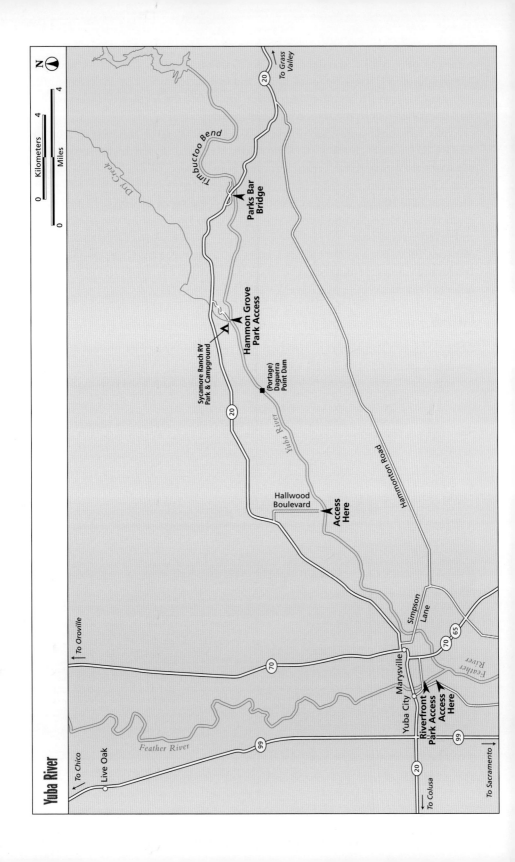

Yuba River

In years past, giant machines floated over the geologic river channel, dredging all the cobbles and gold down to bedrock. Mining companies kept the gold and left the endless rows of dredge tailings that line the river. Mining continues today near Parks Bar. The winter floods of 2017 washed and shifted the gravel bars.

Below Daguerra Point Dam, orchards, farms, and homes eventually border the river. High levees protect the city of Marysville. Wildlife watchers will enjoy this river. Striped bass, steelhead, and shad spawn in spring, and salmon return in autumn. Overhead, hawks and occasional ospreys soar, while turkey vultures and gulls line the banks. All wait for a fish dinner. A special treat in this part of the Central Valley is the annual migration of North American waterfowl. Hundreds of high-flying birds often fill late-afternoon autumn and winter skies as they return to the wildlife refuges and grain fields in the Sacramento Valley.

Sustained summer flows (dreamflows.com) are the result of two features. The Yuba County Water Agency delivers water for diversion at Daguerra Point Dam. YCWA also sells surplus water to other parts of the state. YCWA conveys water from New Bullards Bar, through Englebright Reservoir, and down the Yuba, Feather, and Sacramento Rivers to the Sacramento–San Joaquin Delta.

The Paddling

Parks Bar to Hallwood Boulevard

Length: 10.9 miles
Average paddling time: 3 to 6 hours
Difficulty: Class II whitewater; moving-water skills required
Average gradient: 12 feet per mile

For decades, the Sierra Club River Touring Section conducted training trips on this reach. The rocks along river right create some fun waves, jets, and eddies for practice. You need to sustain a strong ferry to cross the fast, wide channel. For more variety, go upstream, where the river charges between the rocky islands that once supported a bridge. Here the current is faster, the waves bouncier, and the eddies (particularly on river right) more placid than below. It takes some work to get there. Upstream 1 mile, near Timbuctoo Bend, is where some paddlers can explore the islands and riffles.

With an average gradient of 12 feet per mile, the trip downstream is a fast float. You can kick back and relax or work out in the splashy wave trains and distinct eddies below the riffles.

Unlike many other dam-controlled rivers, the Yuba has remarkably little brush. Two miles below Parks Bar, the river splits around gravel bars. You may hear the sounds of a gravel-mining operation to the north. The right channel has eroded the bank and left trees standing in fast water. You can avoid these obstacles by taking the other channel or executing a good eddy turn.

About 3.7 miles below Parks Bar are Hammond Grove Park and the Dry Creek confluence, both on river right. A small gravel bar and hillside footpath indicate the county park and close parking. Dry Creek is another 0.2 mile downstream. On the south bank are towering tailings piles. At lower river stages, Dry Creek may flow swiftly near the river. This condition requires some lifting over one or two gravel riffles. Continuing upstream, Dry Creek deepens and slows to provide 0.3 mile of paddling under a riparian forest canopy. Sycamore Ranch RV Park & Campground occupies the west bank of Dry Creek.

The channel stays close to the north bank most of the 1.8 miles from Dry Creek to Daguerra Point Dam (N39 12.455' / W121 26.658'). The dam funnels irrigation water into canals on both sides. Both ends of the dam support concrete fish ladders. From upstream, Daguerra Point Dam is difficult to see. Gravel has filled the 600-foot-wide river channel to the lip of the dam. Water pours directly over the top and down the rough dam face into a dangerous reversal below.

Portage on river left. One hundred yards downstream of the left diversion structure and 100 yards above Daguerra Dam, a quiet side channel offers easy paddling closer to the dam. From there, carry 0.25 mile up the dirt road to the hilltop oaks and then down to the base of the dam. A gravel bar parallels the dam to form a long pool for easy launching.

You can watch large salmon jumping below the dam during summer and autumn. In 2012 the National Marine Fisheries Service ordered the US Army Corps of Engineers, which owns the dam, to improve salmon passage by the dam. The same year, hydropower generation facilities were proposed. Time will tell if either action occurs or will change the portage.

Steel towers support power lines across the river 1.5 miles and 2 miles below the dam. Here the dredger tailings diminish, then disappear. Wide, flat gravel bars line the river. Beyond the gravel bars, the banks rise 20 to 40 feet to well-tended orchards.

Small power lines spanning the river mark the takeout. Supported by wood poles, the wires are directly in line with Hallwood Boulevard on the right bank. The end of the road, where you'll pick up your shuttle, is 200 yards across the flat gravel bar.

Hallwood Boulevard to Marysville

Length: 7 miles
Average paddling time: 2 to 5 hours
Difficulty: Class II riffles; fast-water skills required
Average gradient: 4 feet per mile

Below Hallwood Boulevard the river displays increasing evidence of recent human activity. Pumps extract water for the orchards lining the riverbanks. About 2 miles below Hallwood, broken concrete riprap slows erosion on the right bank. Soon the river braids and fallen trees lie in the left channel. When you see the large Yuba-Sutter Recycling Center buildings above the right bank, the channel braids and turns abruptly to the left. A gravel bar, some brush, and a midstream snag are obstacles to avoid.

Soon the river channel narrows dramatically between clay banks lined with trees. Sand and silt replace gravel on the river bottom. A sandy beach beside slower water occurs about 1 mile upstream of Simpson Lane. Simpson Lane is the first bridge as you approach Marysville. The steep south bank provides an unattractive emergency takeout.

As the river arcs southwest, the water funnels through some faster chutes with a few waves. If you dump over here, you can go to the left shore with the gravel bars and beaches of Shad Park. On the negative side, you will want a four-wheel-drive vehicle to negotiate the 300-plus yards of loose sand and gravel near the river.

Continuing downstream under the first railroad bridge, Shad Park continues on the left. The river swirls around old broken bridge abutments that trap debris to form a low dam. The clearest low-water channel may be on the far left. At higher water, the river rushes around the pilings, producing some fast chutes requiring good boat alignment. Past the CA 65/70 bridge, more old pilings and another railroad bridge dominate the last river mile.

As you approach the Feather River confluence, Riverfront Park occupies the right bank. A flock of white pelicans has been known to occupy a sandbar at the confluence. Unfortunately, the Riverfront Park shores here are 40 feet high and steep, so taking out is not practical. However, two takeout options remain. Paddle to the confluence, then upstream on the Feather River. Look across the Feather for the concrete boat ramp on the Yuba City side. Look up and down the river for motorboats and personal watercraft, then paddle for the ramp. That is the shorter and easier takeout route. The other option is the Marysville Riverfront Park launch ramp, 0.75 mile up the Feather River against the current. Paddling this stretch is character-building work at the end of a long float trip. A small lagoon, dock, and ramp are 20 yards from vehicle access.

33 Cache Creek–North Fork to Bear Creek

Rising in the Coastal Mountains, Cache Creek flows from Clear Lake and Indian Valley Reservoir into the Central Valley and the Yolo bypass. This upper reach provides a warm Class II stream in remote canyons with fine camping, big wildlife, and few people in the Cache Creek Wilderness Area. This is a California Wild and Scenic River.

Length: 19 miles
Average paddling time: About 8 hours, usually spread over 2 days
Difficulty: Class II whitewater; intermediate whitewater skills required
Rapids: Numerous Class II rapids
Average gradient: 18 feet per mile
Optimal flow: North Fork, at least 100 cfs; Cache Creek, at least 400 cfs
Flow gauge: Indian Valley release and Rumsey
Water source: Clear Lake and Indian Valley Reservoir
Best season: Spring, summer, and winter
Land status: Mixed Bureau of Land Management (BLM) and private, Yolo County
Fees: Fees at parks

Maps: USGS Lower Lake, Wilson Valley, Glascock Mountain; BLM Redbud Trail, Ridge Trail, Cache Creek South
Craft: Canoes, kayaks, inflatables, including small rafts
Contacts: Cache Creek Regional Park–Yolo County Parks Division: (530) 406-4880; yolo county.org. BLM Ukiah Field Office (regarding federal lands bordering Cache Creek): (707) 468-4000.
Special considerations: Because of the remote backcountry wilderness location, help is far off and you must be self-sufficient. The road to Buck Island has been blocked at CA 16. Cache Creek has the hazards of brush, strainers, and rocks, as well as some bears. Be extremely careful with fire—the wildfire hazard is extremely high all summer and autumn.

Put-in/Takeout Information

CA 20 bridge over the North Fork Cache Creek (N38 59.242' / W122 32.375'): The BLM has established a put-in and staging area with parking lot, information kiosk, and toilet. It is on the west side of the river, 200 yards below the bridge.

The Bear Creek confluence (N38 55.576' / W122 19.917') or the Yolo County Cache Creek parks along CA 16 in Rumsey Canyon. Fee areas.
Shuttle: 20 miles (35 minutes)

Overview

The clear water of the North Fork Cache Creek comes from Indian Valley Reservoir some 11 miles upstream. Yolo County Flood Control and Water Conservation District operates Indian Valley Reservoir and Clear Lake to provide irrigation flows of 200 to 600 cfs to Capay Valley farmers. The irrigation demand provides boating flows through the wilderness run, Rumsey Canyon, and Capay Valley. Without snowmelt, the water is relatively warm in spring and almost tepid in summer. This river reach is designated a California Wild and Scenic River.

Watch along the banks for impressive wildlife, such as bear, bobcat, or river otter. We saw bear scat and scratched trees near our camp, and another paddler saw the bear! The Department of Fish and Wildlife protects tule elk in the game preserves along the upper sections of Cache Creek. Overhead, we saw ospreys and a bald eagle pair soaring the canyon in summer. Several bald eagle pairs are regularly visible in winter months, when they feed on the carp in the creek.

The BLM manages Kennedy Flats, Wilson Valley, and most of the other lands bordering Cache Creek down to and including the Bear Creek confluence at CA 16. The New Cacheville property (2 miles upriver from Buck Island) is private, as is the property just upstream of Mad Mike Rapid.

The California Office of Environmental Health Hazard Assessment advises that fish in the Clear Lake and Cache Creek drainage may be contaminated with methyl mercury and may be hazardous for some people to eat in quantity.

Streamside campsites are plentiful, particularly in Wilson Valley and Kennedy Flats. The long Redbud Trail extends from the North Fork access, across the peninsula, then along Wilson Valley. Bring lots of drinking water during summer, as much as 1 gallon per person per day. Without local towns, highway traffic, or lights, the nighttime star watching is great.

Be really cautious with fire. The intensely hot summers dry everything to tinder, and the dry brush has the explosive energy of gasoline. Open fires are illegal during Cal Fire–declared fire season, usually starting in May or June. Then only stoves may be used outside designated campgrounds. Recent years have seen huge wildfires in the Cache Creek drainage, potentially resulting in increased sediment and snags in the river.

The Paddling

From the CA 20 bridge to the confluence with Cache Creek, the North Fork is 2.3 miles of narrow channel (two to three boat lengths wide) mixed with brush, sharp blind turns, and trees. These obstacles reflect the dramatic changes to many stream channels caused by periodic floods. The North Fork obstacles are all negotiable with a little time and care. Along the way, the shade opens up to reveal some walls of dark sedimentary rocks and sandy beaches. Note that 1 mile downstream from the put-in, the creek passes through 1 mile of private property

The main stem of Cache Creek is much wider, with fast-moving, smooth water between the many short Class II riffles. Some riffles have bouncy wave trains; others provide trees, strainers, or boulders for obstacles. Absent is the sharp river-bottom bedrock that dominates Rumsey Canyon.

Downstream 12.3 miles from the North Fork confluence, Buck Island is no longer accessible by long, rough dirt Yolo CR 40, which starts at the low-water bridge over Cache Creek in Rumsey Canyon. The two restrooms at Buck Island are infrequently

Cache Creek—North Fork to Bear Creek

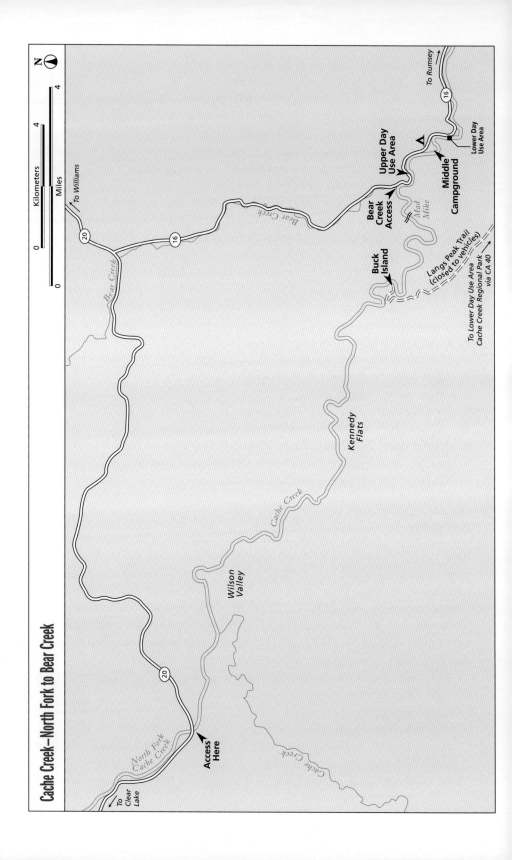

maintained, if they are still there, because of inaccessibility. Two miles below Buck Island, the creek makes a sinuous channel. When the channel turns northeast, look for 2,800-foot Cortina Ridge rising above nearby 1,800-foot Cache Creek Ridge. When you can see the high ridge, you are nearing Mad Mike Rapid.

A black-shale cliff abruptly turns the channel to the north. Opposite the cliff, a private hunting camp sits on a riverside flat. Immediately downstream is Mad Mike, by far the most difficult rapid on the run. Mad Mike drops about 20 feet in 200 narrow yards. At summer flows of 400 cfs to 1,000 cfs, the run is straightforward. Select an approach through the guard rocks at the beginning, and then avoid the major submerged boulder under the picturesque tree. At high winter flows, lots of water hurrying downhill causes strong hydraulics. Beware! A portage is available on the right bank. At the bottom a long, quiet pool leads to the Bear Creek confluence, 0.3 mile below.

Relax on the smooth water to Bear Creek, because that is where the Rumsey Canyon rapids begin. Here CA 16 joins the creek. Take out at any of the Yolo County parks along the river. (See chapter 34 for the Rumsey Canyon description.)

34 Cache Creek–Rumsey Canyon

A summer favorite, the warm shallow rapids and easy access of this stretch provide a great whitewater practice run. Rafting outfitters offer day paddles with two- or three-person rafts, which are very popular on weekends. This is a California Wild and Scenic River.

Length: 8.4 miles
Average paddling time: 3 to 4 hours
Difficulty: Beginner with fast-water experience to intermediate whitewater skills required
Rapids: Class II whitewater; one Class III rapid
Average gradient: 27 feet per mile
Optimal flow: 500 to 1,000 cfs
Flow gauge: Rumsey
Water source: Clear Lake and Indian Valley Reservoir
Best season: Spring, summer, and winter
Land status: Public, except private at Rumsey Bridge
Fees: Required at Yolo County Parks
Maps: USGS Rumsey, Glascock Mountain
Craft: Whitewater canoes, kayaks, small rafts

Contacts: Cache Creek Regional Park–Yolo County Parks Division: (530) 406-4880; yolocounty.org
Special considerations: A special hazard is the Yolo CR 40 low-water bridge at the Lower Cache Creek Park. The culverts under the bridge often contain debris that will trap a boat, raft, or swimmer. The preferred portage is on river left in summer. When high water flows over the bridge, a dangerous reversal forms here. Land well above the bridge on river right. Also note that Rumsey Canyon bedrock is notoriously sharp. Definitely wear a helmet. Rowboat Rapid (aka The Mother), just downstream of the CA 16 bridge, is much more difficult than the rest of the stream.

Put-in/Takeout Information

There are multiple access points. The Bear Creek confluence (N38 55.576' / W122 19.917') has limited road shoulder parking along CA 16 at the county line, 8.4 miles above Rumsey.

Cache Creek Regional Park Upper Site (N38 55.376' / W122 19.676'), adjacent to CA 16, has day-use parking 7.9 miles above Rumsey. Fee area.

Cache Creek Regional Park Middle Site campground (N38 54.998' / W122 19.048') offers day-use, overnight parking, and camping. Check with the park host to bring vehicles to the top of the road near the beach. The campground is 6.7 miles above Rumsey. Fee area.

Cache Creek Regional Park Lower Site (N38 54.508' / W122 18.714') is located 5.9 miles above Rumsey. CR 40 to the low-water bridge is barricaded and the bridge closed to vehicles. Foot access to the bridge is a 0.5-mile hike down the road.

CA 16 bridge (N38 54.608' / W122 16.750'), 3.7 miles above Rumsey, has limited road shoulder parking upstream of the bridge. You can walk to a good view of Rowboat Rapid from here. If you are not confident about running Rowboat, you might park a vehicle nearby.

After the excitement of Rowboat Rapid, rafters regroup on their way to the takeout.

Camp Haswell (N38 54.528' / W122 15.949') is a former Boy Scout camp on a large flat 3 miles above Rumsey. When the gate is closed, paddlers often park in the wide turnout adjacent to CA 16 and carry across the flat to the creek. This is now a better takeout option than the brush-choked gravel bar at Rumsey Bridge, and it avoids the small gravel dam downstream.

Rumsey Bridge (N38 53.449' / W122 14.286') is visible from CA 16 in the hamlet of Rumsey. Roadside access is east of the bridge and is limited to loading and unloading space. A signed path leads 75 yards down the riverbank to the overgrown gravel bar under the bridge. Property adjacent the bridge is private and posted "No Trespassing." Parking space may be available 0.25 mile away in Rumsey. Rumsey is about 21 miles northwest of Esparto.

Shuttle: Bear Creek to Rumsey Bridge: 7.5 miles (15 minutes)

Overview

Cache Creek has cut through 2,000 feet of inclined and bent sedimentary rock to form Rumsey Canyon. Unlike most rivers, where the ledges lie across the channel, in Rumsey Canyon the sharp edges of ledges parallel the streambed. The resulting bedrock rapids are well suited to boaters seeking a busy technical challenge to improve their skills. In the days before plastic boats, time was usually set aside for repairs after a Rumsey Canyon run. Shallow with frequent pools, the river is so forgiving that commercial outfitters send thousands of people down the river in two-person rafts. Other folks try inner tubes at the risk of injuring their fannies. You can see enough of the creek from the road to give you a good idea of the paddling.

Winter rains can quickly raise the flow to thousands of cfs that quickly subside. Irrigation releases from Clear Lake and Indian Valley Reservoir prolong summer flows. Without snowmelt, the water is almost tepid in summer. Visitors can see wildflower displays and green canyons during late winter and early spring.

Cache Creek access is good, with CA 16 closely paralleling the stream along the entire run. Much of the land is publicly owned. Yolo County Parks Division operates a large campground and two large picnic areas. Be aware that summer temperatures often exceed 100°F, and there is little shade.

Summer weekends see hundreds of small rafts on Cache Creek, clients of several commercial rafting outfitters.

The Paddling

Loosen up your body and mind on the riverbank, because the rapids start at the put-in. Cloudy water hides many submerged rocks. On river right, just below Bear Creek, the current pushes into a wall that has upset many a neophyte paddler. The shallow, rocky Class II rapids require continuous river reading.

Several rapids are obscured from the road. These include a robust pair upstream from the campground and a long drop that follows a left turn above the low-water bridge. Fortunately, a long, smooth run separates the rapid from the hazardous bridge, which must be portaged.

The CA 16 bridge marks the start of Rowboat Rapid. A Class III drop at the foot of a landslide, it is a steep rock garden at low flows. At about 700 cfs, the route is a dogleg turn to the right. At high water there are strong hydraulics. The action

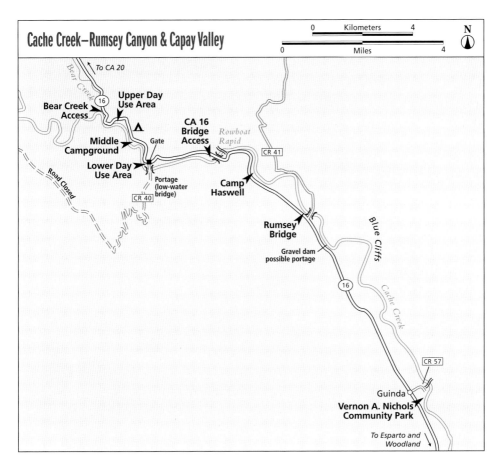

continues for another 100 yards before it slows. Scouting and portaging are difficult, since the left bank is the base of an eroding landslide and the right bank is covered by thick brush.

After Rowboat, the gradient slackens a little as it rounds a bend to the south. At the bend is a gravel bar on the right, followed by a larger gravel bar on the left. Obscured by brush and trees is a big flat area on the right called Camp Haswell, a favored takeout. Before starting the run, note how this area looks from the river, since thick brush obscures the view of the parking area. Maybe even "flag" your intended takeout location.

If you continue to Rumsey Bridge, you encounter more widely spaced rapids. Immediately below Camp Haswell, the right channel is no longer runnable. The wide main channel is rock-strewn at low water, but readily runnable at 700 cfs, with a bouncy wave train at the bottom. A gravel dam (N38 54.083' / W122 15.521') 0.6 mile downstream diverts water and blocks the channel. At some flows it may be carefully run.

Commercial rafting rescuers perch on a midstream rock in Rowboat Rapid to help novice rafters.

The landscape changes as the canyon begins to open into Capay Valley. Gravel bars and occasional brushy islands define the channel instead of the steep-walled canyon upstream. Channels around the islands end in rapids with wave trains bouncy enough to be fun—or flip the careless.

Rumsey Bridge is a large, double-span, concrete structure. The takeout is on the left side of the brush-overgrown gravel bar.

35 Cache Creek–Capay Valley

Released from the confines of Rumsey Canyon, this seldom-paddled reach meanders below the steep hills bordering the east side of Capay Valley. The valley is rich in almond and walnut orchards, and their blossoms are beautiful in late winter and early spring. Water destined for downstream farmers maintains summer flows.

(See map on page 169.)
Length: 7 miles
Average paddling time: 2 to 3 hours
Difficulty: Beginner with fast-water experience
Rapids: Class I+ whitewater
Average gradient: 13 feet per mile
Optimal flow: 550 to 1,000 cfs
Flow gauge: Rumsey
Water source: Clear Lake and Indian Valley Reservoir
Best season: Spring, summer, and winter
Land status: Private

Fees: Required at Nichols Park
Maps: USGS Rumsey, Guinda
Craft: Canoes, kayaks, rafts
Contacts: Cache Creek Regional Park–Yolo County Parks Division: (530) 406-4880; yolocounty.org
Special considerations: Trees have fallen into the river and may block the channel. Strong currents try to carry boaters into overhanging brush and trees. The most difficult whitewater rapid is plainly visible from the takeout at Yolo County's Nichols Park. Beware of rattlesnakes.

Put-in/Takeout Information

Rumsey Bridge (N38 53.449' / W122 14.286') is visible from CA 16 in the hamlet of Rumsey. Roadside access is east of the bridge and is limited to loading and unloading space. A path leads 75 yards down the riverbank to the overgrown gravel bar under the bridge. Property adjacent to the bridge is private and posted "No Trespassing." Parking space may be available 0.25 mile away in Rumsey. Rumsey is about 21 miles northwest of Esparto.

Vernon A. Nichols Community Park (N38 49.677' / W122 11.068') is 0.2 mile south of the Guinda Grocery store and the post office, east of CA 16 at the picnic sign. Go east on CR 57 for 0.4 mile to the bridge. The easiest takeout is under the bridge on river right. Carry boats up the gentle path 75 yards to the gated day-use area. Park vehicles on the upstream side of the road.
Shuttle: 5.5 miles (10 minutes)

Overview

The streambanks support a variety of orchards, vegetable farms, tamarisk islands, pampas grass, bamboo, and the usual cottonwoods, willows, and oaks. Great blue herons, egrets, ospreys, and other large birds are commonly visible near the water, while turkey vultures soar overhead. The gravel bars are wider here, but the land is private, so no camping is allowed.

The stream intersperses a mixture of Class I riffles, bushy islands, and cut banks between the quiet pools and runs. You can easily see the strongest eddy immediately upstream of the takeout at Guinda.

A sign at the Guinda takeout warns that rattlesnakes have been seen in the area.

The Paddling

From Rumsey Bridge, Cache Creek turns east to run at the base of high bluffs. Opposite the bluffs, tamarisk and willows fringe the gravel bars. Several Class I riffles are scattered along the way.

Returning to a more southerly course, the creek heads toward some Rumsey homes. The 1997 and 1998 floods severely eroded the Capay Valley orchards and changed the creek's course. To protect their property from more erosion, Rumsey landowners placed large rocks (riprap) on the right bank.

Upstream are great views of the Rumsey Canyon. Downstream, the creek swings east toward the Blue Cliffs. Rising 500 feet above the creek, these mud and soft rock cliffs dominate the river. Swallow nests are common. Great blue herons play hide-and-seek from shallows and snags on the opposite bank. A ravine through the cliffs is a landmark of a brisk riffle among rocks at the cliff base.

A quarter mile beyond the cliffs, a large metal barn sits on river right. About 0.5 mile below the barn, the river has reclaimed old channels. Floods act to braid river channels for 0.5 mile, with much of the water flowing left, depending on the flow volume.

About 1.5 miles upstream from Guinda on river left is a large slope with many landslides. Even in summer, the practiced eye can distinguish the potential landslides, suspended on the slope until the next wet season, when they will contribute rocks and gravel to the creek. Near the downstream end of the slope, the water abandons the right bank and swings toward the slope. In the middle of the fast riffles are several snags, which should be avoided. Their exact location will change each flood season, but others will take their place.

Depending on channel changes, the last bend above the Guinda bridge may offer some whitewater practice. Since the rapid is within sight of the takeout, it is a good place for novices to practice eddy turns and ferries.

36 Lake Natoma

Only 20 minutes from downtown Sacramento, this long, narrow lake is a great place to fish, learn to paddle and sail, watch wildlife, and relax. Classes and boat rentals are available at the Sacramento State Aquatic Center.

Size: 4.5 miles long, 0.15 mile wide; 11.0 miles of shoreline; surface area: 500 acres
Average paddling time: 2 to 6 hours
Difficulty: Flatwater lake; training beginners
Best season: Year-round
Land status: Public
Fees: Required at access points
Maps: USGS Folsom; Folsom Lake State Recreation Area brochure

Craft: Canoes, kayaks, sail craft, fishing boats, paddleboards, rowing shells, sit-on-tops
Contacts: Folsom Lake State Recreation Area: (916) 988-0205; parks.ca.gov. CSUS Aquatic Center: (916) 278-2842; sacstateaquatic center.com. Adventure Sports Rentals: (916) 622-0489; adventuresports.rentals
Special considerations: Nimbus Dam is well marked with buoys.

Put-in/Takeout Information

Sacramento State Aquatic Center (N38 38.060' / W121 13.203'): From US 50, exit north onto Hazel Avenue. At the stoplight before the bridge, turn east into the Aquatic Center (opposite Nimbus Fish Hatchery). This fee area rents boats and has toilets.

Nimbus Flat (N38 38.111' / W121 13.012'): From US 50, exit north on Hazel Avenue. Turn east just before the Aquatic Center entrance. This state park fee area provides picnic sites, restrooms, a beach, and a launch ramp.

Willow Creek access (N38 38.917' / W121 11.416') is about 0.3 mile northeast of US 50. From US 50, exit onto Folsom Boulevard and go northeast. Since Folsom Boulevard is a divided highway at this point, go north to Blue Ravine Road and come back about halfway toward US 50. This state park fee area has a gravel launch ramp and parking area.

Negro Bar (N38 40.787' / W121 11.025'): Turn south from Greenback Lane some 0.3 mile west of Auburn–Folsom Road. This state park fee area provides picnic sites, restrooms, a beach, and a launch ramp.

Shuttle (optional): Aquatic Center to Negro Bar: 6 miles (20 minutes); Aquatic Center to Willow Slough: 2.6 miles (10 minutes)

Overview

Only 20 minutes from downtown Sacramento, Lake Natoma is popular for canoeing, crew races, sailing, kayaking, and other aquatic sports. The area is steeped in California history.

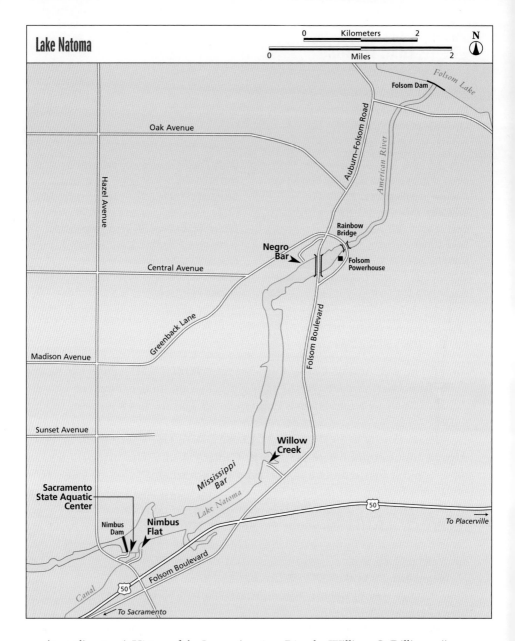

Kilometers

Miles

N

Folsom Lake

Folsom Dam

Oak Avenue

Auburn-Folsom Road

American River

Hazel Avenue

Rainbow
Bridge

Negro
Bar

Folsom
Powerhouse

Central Avenue

Greenback Lane

Folsom Boulevard

Madison Avenue

Sunset Avenue

Willow
Creek

Mississippi
Bar

Sacramento
State Aquatic
Center

Lake Natoma

50

To Placerville

Nimbus
Dam

Nimbus
Flat

Canal

50

Folsom Boulevard

To Sacramento

According to *A History of the Lower American River* by William C. Dillinger, "several hundred Negroes mined the bar adjacent the Folsom business district during 1849–50." Now named Negro Bar, this boat access, beach, and picnic site are part of Folsom Lake State Recreation Area.

Near Rainbow Bridge, Folsom Powerhouse was the source of the world's first long-distance (22 miles) transmission of electrical power in 1895. A September 1895 celebration dubbed a "Grand Electric Carnival" was a night parade of illuminated

Long, narrow Lake Natoma is popular for paddling and collegiate rowing.

floats mounted on electric streetcars rolling down Sacramento streets ablaze with electric lights. Lights visible for 50 miles outlined the capitol building.

Another historical feature, Folsom Prison, was the topic of a Johnny Cash song. In 1880 inmates built Folsom Prison from granite quarried on-site. Since the prison still tries to separate the public from the inmates, authorities prohibit paddling upstream of a cable and sign upstream of Rainbow Bridge.

Lake Natoma is part of the Folsom gold dredge fields, an area 10 miles long and up to 7 miles wide. The last dredge ceased operation in 1962. Even today, huge piles of dredge tailings are plainly visible.

Created in 1954 as part of the Central Valley Project, Lake Natoma links Folsom Lake with the American River and diverts water into the Folsom South Canal. Since water comes from the depths of Folsom Lake, Natoma's water temperature stays chilly all summer. At the west end of the lake, Sacramento State Aquatic Center rents equipment and offers classes in sailing, canoeing, and kayaking. The center is also a hub for rowing and outrigger canoeing clubs. Open to the public, the center operates seven days a week, year-round. Kayak rentals have recently been made available at Negro Bar, at the lake's east end.

The bicycle trail along the north shore of Lake Natoma links Beals Point on Folsom Lake to the American River Bike Trail and downtown Sacramento. A multi-purpose trail parallels Lake Natoma's south shore to complete an off-highway circuit around the lake.

The Paddling

One of the widest parts of the lake is directly across the water from the Aquatic Center. Here is cobble-studded Mississippi Bar, which extends almost 1 mile to the north and east. Before the gold rush, a fur trader set up business with the local Indians on a large sandbar. Later, many men exploited the rich gold deposits here. As late as 1900, two gold dredges operated here. Now the bicycle trail skirts the resultant tailings piles.

The Nimbus Dam end is the focal point of much aquatic activity, including crew races and sailing. If the Delta breeze blows, expect to see many sailboarders and Laser sailboats. At the opposite end of the lake, Negro Bar launch ramp sits almost under the Folsom Boulevard bridge. Adventure Sports rents kayaks and standup paddleboards here during summer. From here you can explore the islands along the Folsom shore or try your moving-water skills near Rainbow Bridge. With a fair current from Folsom Dam and some large rocks, you can learn eddy turns and cross-channel ferries in easy water.

Willow Creek access is on the south side between Folsom Powerhouse and Nimbus Dam. Egrets and herons have established rookeries adjacent to Willow Creek access and on the north lakeshore.

37 American River Parkway

Easy access, dependable flows, and natural surroundings attract more than 1 million people a year to the American River Parkway and to float the designated Wild and Scenic American River in the heart of the Sacramento metropolitan area.

Length: 23 miles
Average paddling time: 2 to 5 hours per segment
Difficulty: Mostly flatwater; suitable for beginner skills except for two rapids
Rapids: San Juan and Arden rapids both whitewater Class II
Average gradient: 2 to 5 feet per mile
Optimal flow: 1,500 to 5,000 cfs
Flow gauge: Nimbus Dam release
Water source: Folsom and Natoma Lakes
Best season: Year-round
Land status: Public between the levees
Fees: Sacramento County park fees required

Maps: USGS Sacramento West, Sacramento East, Carmichael, Citrus Heights, Folsom; American River Parkway Foundation; Sacramento County Parkway map
Craft: Canoes, kayaks, rafts, dories, paddleboards, small powerboats
Contacts: American River Parkway Foundation: (916) 486-2773; arpf.org. Sacramento County Parks: (916) 875-7275; regionalparks .saccounty.net.
Special considerations: Snags lie under the surface of this cold, strong river to catch the careless.

Put-in/Takeout Information

Note: All motor vehicle access points charge fees.

Sailor Bar (N38 38.061' / W121 14.033'), river right: From Sunrise Boulevard in Fair Oaks, go east 2 miles on Winding Way to Illinois Avenue and then south on Illinois to the park entrance.

Upper Sunrise (N38 38.139' / W121 15.839') and Lower Sunrise (N38 37.907' / W121 16.199'), river left in Rancho Cordova: From US 50, exit at Sunrise Boulevard and go north for 1.5 miles. Turn east onto South Bridge Street and pass the commercial raft rentals and shuttle buses. Where the road intersects in a T, turn east toward Upper Sunrise, or turn west to go under Sunrise Boulevard to Lower Sunrise by the Jim Jones footbridge.

Sacramento Bar (N38 38.004' / W121 16.368'), river right in Fair Oaks: From Sunrise Boulevard go west 0.1 mile on Fair Oaks Boulevard and then south at Pennsylvania Avenue. Go slowly through the residential neighborhood downhill to the river.

El Manto (N38 37.479' / W121 17.538'), river left: From Sunrise Boulevard go west 0.9 mile on Coloma Road to El Manto Drive. Follow El Manto north to the marked river access. This is upstream of San Juan Rapid.

Rossmoor Bar (N38 37.462' / W121 18.067'), river left: From Sunrise Boulevard go west 1.5 miles on Coloma Road to Rossmoor Drive. Follow Rossmoor into the park. This is downstream of San Juan Rapid.

Ancil Hoffman Park (N38 36.661' / W121 18.553'), river right: From Fair Oaks Boulevard opposite El Camino Avenue, turn west onto Van Alstine Avenue. Follow Van Alstine to California Avenue and turn north. Follow California for 2 blocks and then turn east on Tarshes Drive into the park. Park in the lot at the upstream end of the giant picnic area, and carry 400 yards to the river.

River Bend Park (formerly Goethe Park) (N38 35.731' / W121 19.807'), river left: From Folsom Boulevard go 1.2 miles west of Coloma Road; turn north onto Rod Beaudry Road and continue 0.7 mile into the park. Bear left at the intersection for the closest parking to the river. Look at the river to orient yourself to the footbridge and the takeout. When available, use the shuttle buses to the Sunrise put-in.

Harrington Way (N38 34.826' / W121 20.463'), river right: From Fair Oaks Boulevard in Carmichael, go east on Arden Way and then turn south onto Kingsford Drive, which becomes Harrington Way and leads to riverside parking.

Gristmill Dam (N38 34.711' / W121 20.516'), river left: From Folsom Boulevard in Rancho Cordova, 0.8 mile west of Bradshaw Road, turn north onto Mira Del Rio Drive and follow it about 0.8 mile to the river access.

Watt Avenue (N38 33.972' / W121 22.995'), river left: From Watt Avenue, exit onto La Riviera Drive. The access is 50 yards east of the Watt Avenue bridge.

Howe Avenue at La Riviera Drive (N38 33.585' / W121 24.336'), river left: From Howe Avenue, exit onto La Riviera Drive. The access is 100 yards east of the Howe Avenue bridge.

Tiscornia Park (N38 35.867' / W121 30.428') is on river left at the Sacramento River confluence. From I-5, exit onto Richards Boulevard and then go west. Almost immediately turn north onto Jibboom Street. Pay at the entrance kiosk, but do not cross the bridge. Instead turn right to the parking area. Launch from the beach.

Discovery Park (N38 36.065' / W121 30.517') is on river right at the confluence with the Sacramento River. From I-5, exit onto Richards Boulevard and then go west. Almost immediately turn north onto Jibboom Street. Pay at the entrance kiosk, cross the steel bridge, and then turn west toward the launch ramps.

Shuttle: Sunrise to River Bend Park: 6.5 miles (20 minutes); River Bend Park to Howe Avenue: 7.5 miles (15 minutes); Howe Avenue to Tiscornia Park: 9 miles (20 minutes)

Overview

Since the California gold rush, the American River has been a focal point for navigation, commercial, and recreation activity. Now a recreational river in the National Wild and Scenic River System, the American River Parkway winds through the urban heart of Sacramento. With the urging of the Save the American River Association, Sacramento has acquired a wide riparian corridor protected from development.

American River Parkway

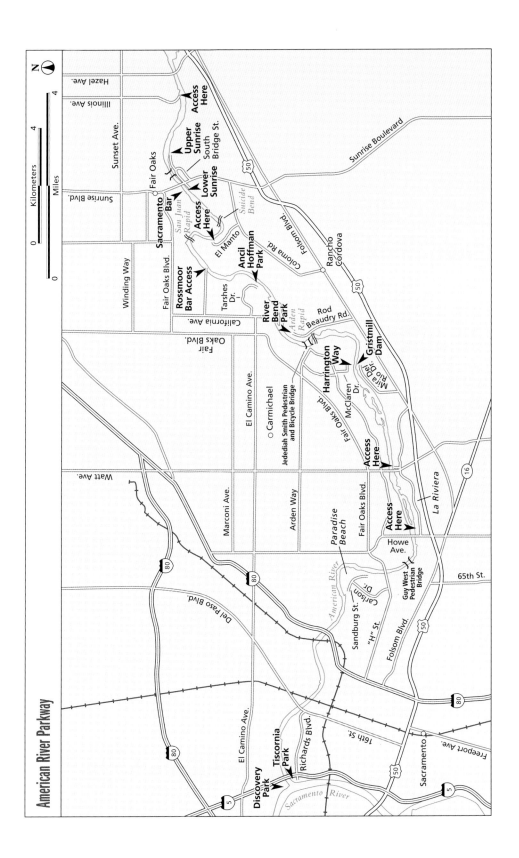

The corridor provides the multiple functions of flood control, wildlife habitat preservation, and a play area for the region's 2.5 million residents. Parks with good facilities line the river. A paved bicycle trail now extends the full length of the parkway. The many access points are for day use, not overnight camping or overnight parking. The parkway charges use fees for parking and boat launching. Boats have a 5 mph speed limit, so the American River is a great place to paddle. Winter stream flows average above 5,000 cfs and are frequently above 15,000 cfs. Summer flows are usually greater than 1,750 cfs. Future flow patterns may change, depending on negotiated agreements for future water supply and preservation of the recreation, fishery, wildlife, and aesthetic values of the river.

The Paddling

Sailor Bar to River Bend (formerly Goethe) Park
Length: 8 miles
Average paddling time: 2 to 4 hours
Difficulty: Riffles and one rapid requiring Class I and II whitewater skills
This section is the most exciting and heavily used portion of the Lower American River. A short distance below Sailor Bar is a long diagonal gravel bar where salmon gather in late summer and autumn. Enjoy the experience of them emerging from the deeper channels, skittering over the shallows, and bouncing against your canoe. On the gravel bars, flocks of seagulls wait for lunch—the next salmon to spawn and expire. It is a sight to remember.

In contrast, think of how high the flows must have been during the spring of 1882. During that flood season, the steamer *Daisy* made trips to Folsom to transport cobblestones and firewood to Sacramento.

From Sailor Bar and Upper Sunrise, the river flows quickly under the old metal Fair Oaks pedestrian bridge toward the large Sunrise Boulevard and Jim Jones bridges. On warm summer days, thousands of rafters float from here to River Bend Park. As you approach the bridges, keep your boats aligned with the current and watch for any snags that may have hung up on the bridge abutments.

Lower Sunrise access and Sacramento Bar access flank the Jim Jones Bridge. Pedestrians and bicyclists use this old gravel hauling structure. The annual triathlon (running, bikes, boats) called the Eppies Great Race ended in 2018 after forty-four years.

Below Sunrise, the wide river runs quickly between gravel bars. At 0.4 mile below Sunrise, the riffle slants right, skirting some brush on the bank. Suicide Bend is encountered 0.6 mile later. At the bend, much of the current starts left before a sharp right turn. On the left, a large strong eddy upsets unwary paddlers. Changes in the riverbed allow paddlers to avoid the eddy when flows are above 3,000 cfs by following the center channel between the gravel bars. From Suicide Bend the river heads northward past the El Manto access. The parking area is visible beyond riverside cobbles. For folks wishing to play in San Juan Rapid without a shuttle, this is a useful put-in. With some effort, you can paddle back upstream from San Juan.

San Juan Rapid (N38 37.823' / W121 17.361') consists of a clay ledge extending from the right across two-thirds of the river. The ledge has runnable slots through it. The best scouting site is the large gravel bar on river left. Most folks prefer the fast channel on the far left, with its long, bouncy wave train directed into the 40-foot-high bank. Immediately left of the wave train is a sharp, fast eddy that exits to river left. On the right side, a much deeper and wider eddy circulates to the far right bank. San Juan Rapid is a favorite play spot for Sacramento-area paddlers on hot summer evenings. The wave train and slots are good surfing spots.

After San Juan Rapid, the paddling is anticlimactic. The wide river slows, and riffles disappear. Overhead power lines and white circular tanks on river left announce the Rossmoor gravel bar access. Downstream 2 miles, picnickers, waders, and anglers enjoy Ancil Hoffman Park. The access is at the upstream end of the park, on the right bank.

After a long turn to the south, riverside homes with wide yards and grouted streambanks announce the approach to River Bend Park. Wide gravel bars line river left. When you can see the long Jedediah Smith bicycle bridge, take out over the left-side gravel bar and up the sandy slope to the parking area and shuttle bus.

River Bend Park to Howe Avenue

Length: 6.1 miles
Average paddling time: 2 to 4 hours
Difficulty: One Class II rapid followed by flatwater for experienced paddlers
At River Bend Park the clear, fast river flows south under the Jedediah Smith bicycle bridge. The bridge provides a good view of the Arden Rapid (N38 35.413' / W121 19.824'), 150 yards downstream. The river here is shallow and 200 yards wide. Each year, winter flood flows shift the gravel bars. Snags ground on the shallow bottom and islands. Often the central channel is deeper, with waves big enough to swamp open canoes. Some rocks produce holes for the open-canoeist to avoid. Immediately downstream of the bicycle bridge, on the extreme right, narrow channels lead to winding backwaters of the William Pond Recreation Area, with good birding opportunities and hiking trails to the river.

A quick mile below the bridge, the river narrows to a fast riffle and bends right. Expensive houses sit above the steep left bank. A surfing wave sometimes forms on the right. Another 0.5 mile downstream, Gristmill access is on the left bank and Harrington Way access provides easy access on the right. Be careful of where you walk on the Harrington side so that you don't disrupt bird-nesting habitats.

From Harrington access you can see several brushy islands and a few snags in the broad river. Downstream 0.7 mile, the river separates into two channels. The left channel is slow, open, and wide. The right channel alternates between ponds and short riffles. Both are good fishing places.

When the salmon or stripers are running, anglers gather at the confluence of the American and Sacramento Rivers, a short distance from downtown Sacramento.

As you approach the Watt Avenue bridge, the current accelerates. At flows less than 3,000 cfs, the river exposes a gravel bar, clay bank, and riffle. The main flow tends to the center and right, but the Watt Avenue takeout is on the left. Upstream of the bridge is a simple gravel bar takeout. Just downstream from the bridge, gravel bars partly enclose a quiet lagoon. Outside the lagoon the current hastens. Beware of the large, circular fish trap sometimes located below the bridge on river right.

The 1.5 miles between Watt and Howe Avenues contain a chain of secluded ponds favored by wildlife. Low levees with sandy banks separate the ponds from the main channel. Sometimes beaver dams block the downstream exits. To enter the ponds, look for breaks in the south bank 75 yards upstream and 50 yards downstream of the power line crossing. Another access to the ponds is 0.25 mile downstream, nearer the Howe Avenue bridge. The water between the ponds is shallow and may require walking at flows less than 3,000 cfs. Howe Avenue access is upstream of the bridge on river left.

Howe Avenue to Sacramento River Confluence

Length: 8 miles
Average paddling time: 3 to 5 hours
Difficulty: Flatwater; beginners

Ten bridges mark your progress down the American between Howe Avenue and the Sacramento River confluence. Most of the adjacent lands were historically subject to flooding. The large structures below Howe Avenue are Sacramento's Fairbairn water intake and treatment plant. Extending from the intake works to H Street is the California State University at Sacramento campus. Guy West pedestrian bridge connects CSUS to the Campus Commons residential district on the right bank.

As the water quickens over shallow riffles below H Street, imagine what this area was like in 1930, when this was the site of a popular beach and giant waterslide. Now levees protect houses on the left and the Campus Commons Golf Course occupies the east bank.

Turning west, the river flows between Cal Expo, with the Bushy Lake Nature Preserve to the north and Paradise Beach to the south. Both flood at high water. The beach's expansive sand and gravel bars make a popular neighborhood play area but lack easy boat access.

The I-80 bridges are near the site of Norris Ferry, a ford and later a cable ferry, which was a popular route to the northern mines of the early gold rush era. Slightly downstream was Sutter's Landing. A now filled-in river channel formerly swept southward and contributed to old Sacramento flooding.

Downstream, the river slows considerably. In the next 2 miles, two railroad bridges, a former railroad bridge—now a bicycle bridge—and the twin concrete bridges of Twelfth and Sixteenth Streets cross the river. Homeless people camp nearby. Below the four bridges, the river is slow and deep. Some summer weekends, dozens of large pleasure boats anchor to worship the sun, fish, or party. The I-5 bridges indicate your approach to Discovery and Tiscornia Parks.

The preferred takeout is Tiscornia Park on river left. Almost under the Jibboom Street bridge is an unpaved ramp for small boats. On weekends the paved Discovery Park ramps to the Sacramento River are very busy with powerboats. Looking down the Sacramento River, you can see Sacramento skyscrapers more than a mile away.

38 Mokelumne River below Camanche

This reach of the Mokelumne is the link between the Mother Lode and the Delta. Paddlers float on releases from Camanche Reservoir for farmers, downstream water users, and anadromous fisheries. The Mokelumne is a great place on a hot summer day, with delightful shade trees, cool water, and fine fishing.

Length: Up to 23 miles
Average paddling time: 2 to 6 hours per segment
Difficulty: Quick water and gravel bar riffles; Class I fast-water experience and skills required
Average gradient: 3 feet per mile
Optimal flow: 400 to 1,500 cfs
Flow gauge: Camanche Reservoir release
Water source: Camanche Reservoir
Best season: Spring, summer, and autumn
Land status: Private
Fees: Required for access
Maps: USGS Clements, Lockeford, Lodi North
Craft: Canoes, kayaks, paddleboards, inflatables, sit-on-tops

Contacts: East Bay Municipal Utility District: (209) 772-8204; ebmud.com/recreation/sierra-foothills/mokelumne-river-day-use-area. Fishing regulations: wildlife.ca.gov/fishing. Heritage Oak Winery: (209) 986-2763; heritageoakwinery.com. Lake Lodi Boathouse: (209) 471-5988. Lodi Paddle Club: meetup.com/Lodi-Paddle-Club. Headwaters Kayak Shop & Boathouse: (209) 224-8367; headwaterskayak.com.
Special considerations: Fast flows near the fish hatchery, an abundance of snags, and low-hanging branches throughout the reach require paddlers to maneuver adroitly to avoid a dunking.

Put-in/Takeout Information

Camanche Fish Hatchery Day Use Area (N38 13.349' / W121 2.040'): From CA 99 in Lodi, follow CA 12 east 11.5 miles to Clements. Stay on CA 12 for another 1.6 miles past the CA 88 junction. Turn north onto McIntire Road at the sign reading "Mokelumne River Fish Installation" and follow it to the EBMUD recreation area. Fee area with toilets.

Stillman L. Magee County Park (N38 12.222' / W121 5.553'): From CA 99 in Lodi, follow CA 12 east 11.5 miles to Clements. The takeout is 1 mile north of Clements on Mackville Road. Fee area with toilets.

Heritage Oak Winery (N38 9.635' / W121 11.558'): From US 99 north of Lodi, exit at Acampo Road and go east approximately 3.5 miles. Turn south onto Buck Road for 1 mile and then turn east onto East Woodbridge Road. Look for the winery on the right at 0.25 mile. Fee access to river by appointment only; toilets available.

Lodi Lake (N38 8.859' / W121 17.679'): From US 99, exit at Turner Road and go west on West Turner Road. Or from I-5, exit at Turner Road and go east toward Lodi. At the stoplight opposite Parkview Avenue and North Loma Drive, turn north into Lodi Lake Park. A road to the right loops around to grassy mid-lake picnic areas with easy put-in and takeout. Kayak lessons and rentals available. Fee area with toilets. **Shuttle:** Fish hatchery to Magee: 6 miles (10 minutes); Magee to Heritage Oak Winery: 8.5 miles (20 minutes via Jahant, Tully, Peltier, Tretheway, and Woodbridge Roads); Heritage Oak to Lodi Lake: 8.5 miles (20 minutes)

Overview

Downstream of Camanche Reservoir, the Mokelumne starts cold and fast. Sometimes numbered blocks mark the many salmon redds. Avoid damaging the redds by not wading near them.

Bring your fishing rod! In summer, trout bite in the main stream and black bass lurk in the backwater dredge ponds. Salmon fishing may be permitted when the adult salmon return. Steelhead runs occur in winter. Check the California regulations for special fishing rules here.

Tall cottonwoods and oaks line most of the riverbanks and contribute to the cool air. Buckeye blossoms scent the air in spring and early summer. Cattle ranches, orchards, and vineyards occupy the adjacent lands. A scattering of homes dot the riparian landscape. Trees and brush hide the gold-dredging tailing mounds, but several dredge ponds still connect to the river, providing bass habitat. The Stillman Magee Park access is the site of the Lone Star Mill, first built in 1855.

Public access to the Mokelumne is scarce. The next downstream public access is Lodi Lake. Lands adjacent to the intervening 19 miles are privately owned, and property rights should be respected.

Heritage Oak Winery offers river access by prearrangement. The winery also provides picnic foods, wines for sale, hiking trails, a beach, and fishing. Their location is about halfway between Magee Park and Lodi Lake.

The Paddling

Comanche to Magee

Length: 4 miles
Average paddling time: 2 to 3 hours
Difficulty: Quick water and gravel bar riffles require Class I fast-water experience and skills.
The large pool near the lower parking area is a good place to practice if the people fishing along the banks are not too close together. The river current is fast, 4 to 5 mph. Beware of trees in the water and hanging over the river at the first real bend in the channel. After 0.5 mile the flow slows.

For landmarks, note that the right bank is low and slopes gently. Several fallen trees are not too difficult to get around. The trees standing on the bank show high-water marks 3 to 5 feet above the summer flow level. Abruptly, the right bank climbs into a low bluff with a deep pool. Nearby is a huge oak. Stay alert where the river turns, and

Mokelumne River below Camanche

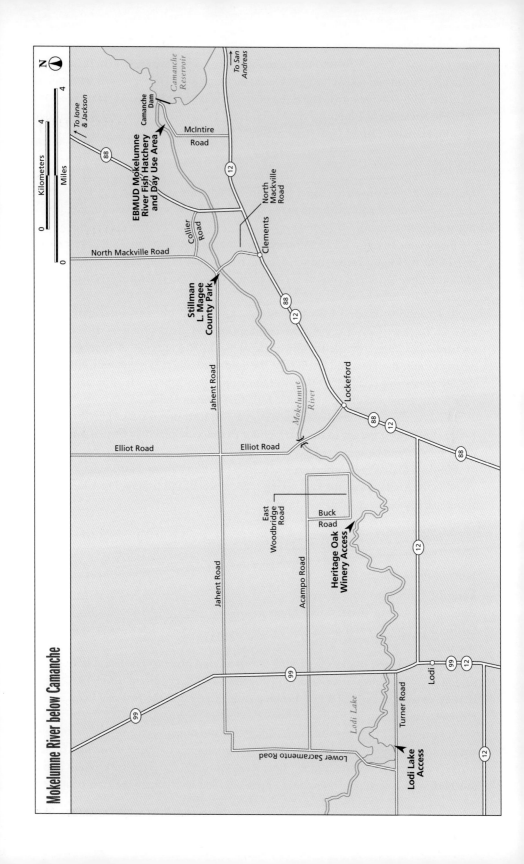

Turtles line up along the Mokelumne River.

then paddle carefully. Downstream 0.5 mile, a skillful paddler might squeeze under a big oak that leans from the left bank. Alternatively, the rest of the channel has ample space to paddle. Behind the oak are piles of gold-dredge tailings.

The first bridge is at CA 88. On the right is a lagoon where we noted a swan. Large houses dot the left bank. An island divides the flow, and the current accelerates. We paddled the left side, although both sides were negotiable. Continue your vigilance for snags in the river.

Soon the river turns abruptly right and then left. Irrigation pumps draw from deep eddies separated by quick-moving water. A few more houses come into view, some with expansive lawns down to the river's edge. Half a mile upstream from the Mackville Road bridge, trees on the left screen dredge tailings. A high bank appears on the right, a warning sign for more snags in the river.

The next bridge (Mackville Road) is the takeout. Land on the left bank, and carry the boats 150 yards along the footpath adjacent to the bridge to the parking area.

Magee Park to Heritage Oak Winery

Length: 9.5 miles
Average paddling time: 4 to 6 hours
Difficulty: Ability to avoid fallen trees in quick water required

Two hundred yards downstream of Magee Park, a large tree toppled during 2011 and blocked most of the river. If it is still there, the right side may be an easier passage. Historically, this reach has many snags and stumps. Still, it is a peaceful setting.

A gravel quarry haul road bridge crosses the river 0.2 mile beyond. Half a mile farther, the channel loops south around piles of old dredge tailings. After the river turns southwest again, the channel narrows into a maze of trees and quick water. Do not be surprised to see many irrigation pumps and levee riprap made from old concrete.

About 3 miles from Magee Park, a sharp left turn to the southeast with an island has a cleared area on river left that may offer a lunch spot.

At 5 miles below Magee, you float under the Elliot Road bridge (N38 10.659' / W121 9.925'). About 2 miles downstream, the river begins a sinuous course with occasional oxbows all the way into Lodi Lake. The river is still narrow, less than 25 yards wide. As you approach Heritage Oak Winery, the river turns abruptly north. Hopefully you have inspected the takeout carefully so that you will recognize the small beach with nearby picnic tables (N38 9.388' / W121 11.665').

Heritage Oak to Lodi Lake

Length: 9.5 miles
Average paddling time: 4 to 6 hours
Difficulty: Skills needed to avoid fallen trees in quick water

From the winery follow the winery's prescribed roads toward the river, across the levee to the beach put-in. Arrange to have your vehicles removed from the riverside. Downstream, the peaceful, pastoral Mokelumne continues its intimate, sinuous path under Bruella Road at 0.7 mile. Occasional pocket beaches offer rest spots. Remember that the lands are private property.

Summer flows are most often 300 to 500 cfs. One trip at 400 cfs encountered quite a few snags and shallows. A different trip at 1,400 cfs made for faster floating but required better maneuvering around fewer obstacles.

When you see spacious lawns and large houses on the south (left) bank, you are approaching US 99.

Lodi Lake

Length: 3.3 miles to US 99
Average paddling time: 1 to 3 hours
Difficulty: Flatwater training stream; beginners
Shuttle: None

Formed by Woodbridge Dam, this lake with its picnic areas and swimming beach is often used by local paddling groups. Their activities include summer evening paddles, learning skills, experiencing different types of boats, touring the Mokelumne River, and ending tours from farther upstream. Headwaters Kayak Shop & Boathouse rents boats at the Lake Lodi Boathouse.

Paddling upstream is winding flatwater with lots of oxbows. Trees line the banks for the first mile between the lake and US 99. Large houses (some with their own docks and powerboats) line the south bank to 0.6 mile beyond US 99. It's a pleasant experience.

39 Stanislaus River–Knights Ferry to McHenry Recreation Area

This reach of the Stanislaus is a quick-flowing stream in a tree-shaded intimate channel that is inviting most of the year. As mitigation for the inundation of the Camp 9 whitewater run by New Melones Reservoir, the US Army Corps of Engineers developed a series of accesses to the river for rafting, canoeing, hiking, and camping. This chapter does not include the extremely difficult (Class IV) whitewater run between Goodwin Dam and Knights Ferry.

Length: 27 miles
Average paddling time: 4 to 9 hours per segment
Difficulty: Generally fast, smooth water with trees and brush; Class I whitewater skills required
Rapids: Russian Rapid, Class II
Average gradient: 5 feet per mile
Optimal flow: 300 to 1,000 cfs
Flow gauge: Orange Blossom
Water source: New Melones Reservoir through Goodwin Dam
Best season: Spring and summer
Land status: Private except at parks

Fees: Required for camping
Maps: USGS Knights Ferry, Oakdale, Escalon, Riverbank, Avena
Craft: Canoes, kayaks, inflatables, including small rafts
Contacts: US Army Corps of Engineers, Stanislaus River Parks: (209) 881-3517; spk.usace.army.mil/Locations/Sacramento-District-Parks/Stanislaus-River-Parks/
Special considerations: Russian Rapid near Knights Ferry has a well-marked portage trail. Otherwise, be alert for occasional fallen trees in the channel.

Put-in/Takeout Information

Knights Ferry Recreation Area (N37 49.159' / W120 39.996'): From Oakdale follow CA 108/120 east for 12 miles. Turn north onto Kennedy Road, then turn left onto Sonora Road. Cross the river and turn right to the paved parking area, put-in, and Stanislaus River Park Information Center.

Horseshoe Road Recreation Area (N37 48.380' / W120 43.205') is off Orange Blossom Road, 3.5 miles east of the Orange Blossom Road bridge toward Knights Ferry. From Knights Ferry take Sonora Road west, through the town. Turn left and follow Orange Blossom Road for about 2.2 miles. The Horseshoe Road Recreation Area access is on the right.

Honolulu Bar (N37 48.016' / W120 43.600') is off Orange Blossom Road, about 2.3 miles east of the Orange Blossom Road bridge toward Knights Ferry. It is 0.6 mile west of the Horseshoe Road access. Paved parking for ten cars.

Orange Blossom Road bridge (N37 47.338' / W120 45.730'): From Oakdale follow CA 108/120 east 3.6 miles, then turn north onto Orange Blossom Road.

Orange Blossom Road crosses the bridge at 1.5 miles. The paved parking area, with permanent restrooms and picnic tables, is immediately downstream of the bridge on the north bank. From the Valley Oak Recreation Area, follow Rodden Road east to Orange Blossom Road and bridge.

Valley Oak Recreation Area (N37 47.110' / W120 48.171'): From the stoplight on CA 120 north of the Oakdale bridge, go 4 miles east on Rodden Road. Turn south at the sign that reads "Valley Oak Recreation Area." The paved road is 50 feet east of the much more visible "Arbini Road" sign and leads to the paved parking area. Follow the unpaved service road 200 level yards to the river. Steps lead down to the water. Large oaks shade most of the area. The environmental campground is several hundred yards downstream, with its own landing place. The Corps requires campers to obtain camping permits from the visitor center in Knights Ferry or at the campground honor vault. Be sure to look closely at the takeout, since the landing is obscure and the sign sometimes absent.

Oakdale Recreation Area and fishing access (N37 46.413' / W120 52.150'): From CA 120 and Rodden Road, go west on River Road 0.5 mile, then turn south onto Liberini Road. Liberini Road is paved and extends 0.7 mile to the parking area, restrooms, and river. A gravel road extends along several ponds and the river channel, offering a choice of easy put-ins. Carefully note takeout landmarks, since the landing is obscure and the sign sometimes absent.

Jacob Meyers Park in Riverbank (N37 44.552' / W120 56.359') is at the north end of the Santa Fe Road bridge, between Santa Fe Road and the railroad bridge. The park is a popular summertime swim area. Downstream 50 feet of the highway bridge, a narrow concrete boat ramp extends to the river. Although there is ample parking, the park is not a good place to leave a vehicle overnight.

McHenry Avenue Recreation Area (N37 45.232' / W121 0.706') joins the River Road 0.8 mile west of the McHenry Avenue intersection, west of the railroad tracks and wastewater treatment plant. Follow the paved entrance road past the kiosk to the day-use areas and steep, unpaved launch ramp beside the riprap banks. The less-steep takeout is downstream at the day-use area, across the sandbar and up the wooden stairs.
Shuttle: Knights Ferry to Valley Oak: 9.5 miles (25 minutes); Valley Oak to Oakdale: 5.4 miles (15 minutes); Valley Oak to Jacob Meyers: 9.5 miles (25 minutes); Valley Oak to McHenry: 17 miles (40 minutes)

Overview

In the 1980s the US Army Corps of Engineers (USACE) created Stanislaus River Parks, with well-developed campgrounds, trails, river access points, and an interpretive center. These amenities are mitigation for inundating the famous Stanislaus River whitewater run under New Melones Reservoir.

Once the Stanislaus county seat, the historic community of Knights Ferry is worth exploring. Originally built in 1864, the 360-foot-long covered bridge, restored mill, and office are within easy walking distance of the put-in.

Boating regulations allow only electric motors between Horseshoe Road and Orange Blossom Road bridge. Ten-horsepower gas motors may operate at 5 mph maximum speed between the Orange Blossom Road bridge and CA 120 in Oakdale.

Remember to bring drinking water, pay for your camping permit, and perhaps reserve a campsite in advance. Ask at the interpretive center about overnight parking.

The Paddling

Knights Ferry to Valley Oak Recreation Area

Length: 10 miles
Average paddling time: 4 to 6 hours
Difficulty: Class I whitewater; one Class II rapid

At the put-in, the clear, cold Stanislaus is only three canoe lengths wide. Paddle upstream 200 yards to enjoy water-level views of the old covered bridge. To sharpen skills at fast-water ferries and turns, continue upstream to the chutes and eddies. This swift-water practice may soon pay off at Russian Rapid.

Returning downstream, the few houses of Knights Ferry are soon left behind. The bank on river left is a brush-covered gravel bar; the right bank climbs upward as the river begins a long, gradual turn to the left. A large sign on the left bank announces the start of the portage trail around Russian Rapid. Use the portage trail if you are new to paddling or uncomfortable with Class II whitewater. Russian Rapid is by far the most difficult rapid below Knights Ferry.

In 150 yards, Russian Rapid contains some rocks, one hole, a midstream tree, and bouncy surfing waves at the bottom. A continuous ledge forms the right side from top to bottom at 450 cfs. The slippery, narrow path on the right bank affords great views for photographing and scouting the rapid, but stay close to the river to respect private property rights. The bottom of the rapid offers good rescue pools, surf waves, and an early lunch site.

Below Russian Rapid, the river is much easier. Wide and narrow sections alternate slow and fast. In autumn, salmon spawn in the riffles. A deep pool forms below Lovers Leap on river left. The mile-long straight section provides distant vistas of the surrounding hills. Look for hawks, vultures, great blue herons, and other wildlife as you enjoy the river. The colder waters of the deeper pools provide trout habitat through the warm summer months.

Past Lovers Leap, 0.75 mile after the river turns southwest, is Horseshoe Road Recreation Area. A sign, if not washed out or stolen, announces this takeout option on river right. Horseshoe also offers boat-in camping. Obtain permits at the campground honor-system kiosk or at the US Army Corps of Engineers Knights Ferry Information Center.

Horseshoe Road Recreation Area exhibits some of the few gold-dredge tailings still clearly visible along the Stanislaus. Quiet ponds invite exploration for wildlife. The Corps' *Birds of the Lower Stanislaus River* lists more than 180 species.

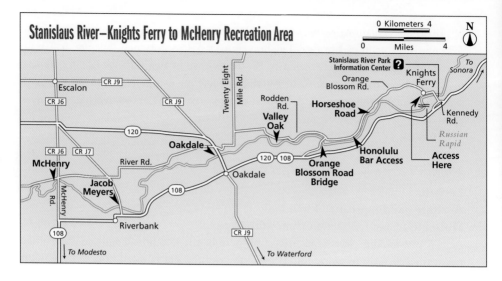

Map: Stanislaus River–Knights Ferry to McHenry Recreation Area

One-half mile below the Horseshoe Road access, the channel splits. The right ends at Honolulu Bar access; the left is the main channel downriver.

An abrupt turn to the north brings the Orange Blossom Road bridge into view, 7 miles from the put-in. Take out under the bridge on river right. Available here are permanent restrooms, drinking water, picnic tables, and paved daytime parking, which is gated at night.

An option is to continue past the Orange Blossom Road bridge to Valley Oak Recreation Area. The current is quick. Tall shade trees lining both banks make this a delightful stretch of river. Several riffles with wave trains provide splash relief from summer heat. Be alert for snags where some tall shade trees have fallen into the river. Some trees show signs of saw cuts where limbs have been cleared from the river.

About 1.4 miles below the Orange Blossom Road bridge, look for a high bluff with houses on the left side. Below the bluff, the Stanislaus turns sharply right and snags periodically block part of the channel.

Valley Oak Recreation Area is about 2.5 miles below the Orange Blossom Road bridge. Look carefully for the wooden railroad-tie steps in the right bank for the takeout. If you miss it, a second set of steps is 100 yards downstream at the boat-in campsite. The picnic tables are visible from the river. Sometimes the recreation area is marked by a sign. When you do the shuttle, check for distinctive landmarks at the takeout, or create one that is environmentally acceptable.

Valley Oak to McHenry Recreation Area

Length: 17 miles
Average paddling time: 6 to 9 hours
Difficulty: Fast water with obstacles; Class I skills required
From the campground the river begins to swing northward and the streamside bluffs begin to drop away, providing a wider horizon. Snags warrant your attention as the

channel bends west. At the top of a bluff, a palatial house dominates the scene 0.5 mile above a small beach on river right.

More snags lie in easy current at the distinct right bend 1 mile from Oakdale. Closer to town, a water tank may be visible 90 feet above the left bank. The old tank sometimes released a waterfall that cascaded onto the left bank and was not usually a hazard to boaters. Houses again line the bluff tops approaching Oakdale. Downstream of CA 120, the river bluffs retreat and the stream character changes. Low banks with wide gravel bars topped with brush form the channel. The current flows intermittently fast and slow.

Where the river zigzags left then right, a sign once hung from a pipeline high above the river. It advised that a research area exists downstream and recommends that boaters stay to river left. Soon wide gravel bars and ponds appear. The access to Oakdale Recreation Area is on river right. The first access point, with its railroad-tie stairs, is at the far side of a pond. The river flows through more ponds to a second takeout. Easier to see than the first, this part of the Oakdale Recreation Area provides a riverside gravel road that ends at a gate, a signpost, and a restroom. Look at the site carefully so that you will recognize it from the river.

The alternate route to these ponds is on the far left, in an obscure channel with many snags. Continuing west across the ponds is easier. Paddle around the gravel bars and through the lazy eddies. The ponds end at a runnable breach in the low levees that form the pond. At low flow, you may scrape some rocks.

Soon the river channel narrows again and the current accelerates. An orchard occupies a low terrace on the right. Then a high bluff slopes steeply to the river. The bluff falls away, and orchards line both sides of the river. The banks are occasionally covered with broken concrete riprap. Approximately 3 miles from Riverbank, the river makes a long S-turn. The current is strong, and the banks are lined with broken concrete to reduce erosion. Tall trees provide shade, and a few fallen trees are in the river.

Upstream of Riverbank 1.5 miles, the river runs due south toward a tall bluff with CA 108 on top. Directly below lie snags that are relatively easy to negotiate. As the channel turns west, the current alternates between gentle riffles and slow pools. Directly under the Santa Fe Avenue bridge, the Jacob Meyers Park concrete ramp on river right is impossible to miss.

Beginning about 1 mile below Riverbank, the bluffs retreat from the water for the next 2 miles. When the river narrows again, you are approaching the McHenry Avenue bridge. This reach is less scenic, with broken concrete riprap, industrial land uses, and the outfall pipe by the bridge. Much of the 1.4 miles along the north bank from McHenry Avenue to the takeout is now managed as part of the McHenry Recreation Area. The water still flows quickly in the narrow channel lined with fallen trees.

Past the golf course, the river turns abruptly northward. The right bank is covered with erosion-control riprap and a boat ramp. Around the bend is a wide beach next to the day-use area. Take your choice of takeout: The ramp is steep, but the beach is a longer carry.

40 Tuolumne River—La Grange to Waterford

The 148-mile Tuolumne River originates at the Sierra Crest in Yosemite National Park. The object of epic river conservation struggles, the clear remnant flows of the Tuolumne River twist through the gold-dredge tailings near historic La Grange. This popular reach is included in the Tuolumne River Parkway, where salmon can be seen during the autumn months.

Length: 19 miles

Average paddling time: 3 to 6 hours per segment

Difficulty: Beginner with whitewater experience

Rapids: Class I whitewater with some brush

Average gradient: 5 feet per mile

Optimal flow: 400 to 700 cfs

Flow gauge: La Grange release to river

Water source: Don Pedro Reservoir through La Grange Dam

Best season: Whenever flows permit, historically during fish flow releases—except during floods

Land status: Mostly private

Fees: Required at most access points

Maps: USGS La Grange, Cooperstown, Paulsell, Waterford; Lower Tuolumne River Parkway and Boating Access

Craft: Canoes, kayaks, small rafts

Contacts: Turlock Lake State Recreation Area: (209) 874-2056; parks.ca.gov; camping: (800) 444-7275; reservecalifornia.com. Turlock Irrigation District for Hickman Spillway discharge: (209) 883-8278. Tuolumne River Trust: (209) 236-0330; tuolumne.org.

Special considerations: When Hickman Spillway discharges heavy flows to the river, it may cause severe turbulence. When winter and spring flows rise to many thousands of cfs, the river is powerful, cold, very fast, and treacherous.

Put-in/Takeout Information

Old La Grange Bridge (N37 39.938' / W120 27.707') is a footbridge. From La Grange look for the short road leading steeply downhill to the old bridge. Or from CA 132, go north on La Grange Road 0.7 mile and turn right onto Old La Grange Road. Unload near the bridge and carry 200 yards. Limited parking.

Basso Bridge (N37 38.820' / W120 29.674') is where CA 132 crosses the Tuolumne River about 30 miles east of Modesto. Exit CA 132 onto Lake Road to the parking area entrance. A designated wildlife viewing area, this access has a large parking area, permanent restrooms, and a concrete boat ramp. The access is on river left, immediately downstream from the CA 132 bridge and upstream of the old steel bridge.

Turlock Lake State Recreation Area Campground (N37 37.883' / W120 35.036'): Exit Basso Bridge onto Lake Road and then go 7.5 miles to the campground entrance. Crowned by tall valley oaks, cottonwoods, walnuts, and sycamores, the sixty-six campsites are open year-round. The launch ramp is screened by vegetation, so visit this takeout before you start downriver. From CA 132 in Waterford, turn right on Hickman Road (CR J9) and drive 1 mile to Lake Road. Turn left on Lake Road and drive 10 miles to Turlock Lake SRA.

Waterford River Park and Trail (N37 38.210' / W120 45.328'): From CA 132, 2 blocks east of CR J9, turn onto North Appling Road toward the river. North Appling Road ends in a driveway into this day-use community park with restrooms and foot access.

Shuttle: Old La Grange to Basso Bridge: 2 miles (5 minutes); Basso to Turlock Lake SRA: 7.5 miles (15 minutes); Turlock Lake SRA to Waterford: 10 miles (20 minutes)

Overview

From granite peaks and the Mount Lyell glacier, the Tuolumne cascades down narrow canyons and slides through lush meadows before O'Shaughnessy Dam captures the river in Hetch Hetchy Canyon. John Muir fought valiantly to save Hetch Hetchy's splendor as equal to Yosemite Canyon. Muir and the fledgling Sierra Club lost that battle, and Congress enacted the Raker Act in 1914. The act authorized the City of San Francisco to dam Hetch Hetchy and divert much of its flow through tunnels, power plants, and aqueducts to San Francisco. The remaining water flows through world-class rapids to huge Don Pedro Reservoir. Modesto and Turlock Irrigation Districts divert water at La Grange Dam. Except during flood periods when La

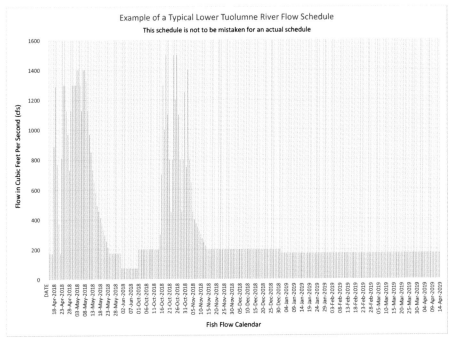

This chart is a sample of how Tuolumne River flows are "pulsed" in spring and autumn to benefit salmon returning to spawn. The increased flows also make paddling more enjoyable.

Turlock Irrigation District

Grange Dam overflows, the little powerhouse below the dam has historically sent the limp remainder of the Tuolumne to the lower river. These flows may change with the Federal Energy Regulatory Commission relicensing of the power projects. Spring and autumn fish flows will be considerably greater than summer flows. (See chart of sample flow schedule.)

Threatened with extinction, salmon spawn again in the Tuolumne due to restored spawning gravels, increased seasonal San Joaquin River flows, and a seasonal ban on all sportfishing.

The Paddling

La Grange to Turlock Lake SRA

Length: 8.7 miles; 6 miles from Basso Bridge to Turlock Lake SRA boat ramp and campground
Average paddling time: 3 to 5 hours
Difficulty: Beginner with whitewater experience
Rapids: Class I; Class II near fallen trees scattered along channel

At La Grange, the Tuolumne emerges from its narrow canyon to sparkle over a wide cobbled bed. The cobblestone bottom provides easy Class I riffles. At 400 cfs the flow is adequate. At 200 cfs, expect some scraping and perhaps walking along the shallows and to avoid snags in the river. At lower summer flows, paddling becomes arduous. Walking in the cool water is a welcome relief from the valley heat.

From La Grange Bridge to Basso Bridge the channel winds with frequent gravel bar riffles. In autumn, salmon make redds in the riffles and skitter between the canoes. Nearing the mouth of Lower Dominici Creek, about 0.5 mile above Basso Bridge, many swallows nest in the low cliffs that line river right. Overhead look for larger birds such as hawks, turkey vultures, lots of ducks, great blue herons, and an occasional osprey. Also look for Native American mortar holes.

On river left is the Basso Bridge boat ramp with its parking area and toilets. Downstream, two 0.5-mile-long pools slow the flow. A few homes are scattered along the left bank. Between the pools is a river-wide riffle with some rebar emerging on river right. The wide stream channel is a remnant of the gold dredging that denuded many of California's river bottoms in the early 1900s. The huge floating dredges gouged the rivers, searching for gold. The remaining rock was dumped in vast piles of cobbles extending hundreds of yards from the river. Ospreys have built a large nest atop an abandoned power pole on river right.

Where picturesque bluffs rise along river left, the channel narrows. Sharp turns with snags and brush test a paddler's abilities. Since the chutes, riffles, and brush change each year, each trip is a new adventure.

Parts of the river channel have been scoured down to bedrock. Long gouges are visible in the sandstone.

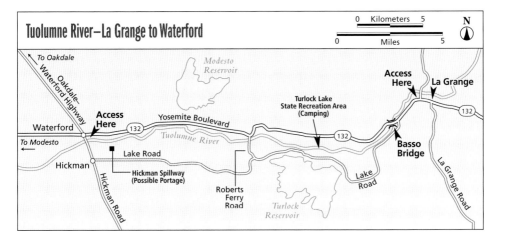

Tuolumne River–La Grange to Waterford

Tall stately oaks line the hillside. Watch the hilltops on river left for a tall chimney. When you see that landmark, you are about 0.25 mile from the takeout. Visit the Turlock Lake SRA takeout before you put in so that you can recognize the boat ramp location. The ramp is tucked into a back eddy on river left, and it is easy to overlook.

Turlock Lake SRA to Waterford

Length: 10.3 miles
Average paddling time: 4 to 6 hours
Difficulty: Beginner with whitewater experience
Rapids: Class I
Downstream of Turlock SRA, the river is mostly flatwater with a few riffles. The oak-studded bluffs and brush-shrouded tailings change sides.

Signs warn that the Hickman Spillway sometimes releases flows to the Tuolumne River. The spillway is 7 miles downstream of Roberts Ferry. Below Roberts Ferry, the geologic flood channel widens as the bluffs retreat from the river. After a few gravel bar riffles, you come to the first of several haul bridges for gravel-mining operations. Gravel miners no longer quarry directly from the river. Habitat restoration has been proposed along this river reach.

About 2 miles below the Roberts Ferry bridge, the landscape varies. Low bluffs on the north side support oaks and grass. The other side is gravel bar covered with willows. Soon a huge quarry structure comes into view. It is actually 1 mile downstream on river right. Before you get there, you will pass under another haul road. An unusual bridge supports a conveyor high across the river.

Downstream from the conveyor, the channel narrows as the river swings north. It becomes more attractive as it parallels CA 132, on the bluff above. Another 1 mile downstream, an obsolete bridge spans the river. Enjoy the blackberries, figs, and grapevines that soon appear. Where the channel approaches the bluffs on the south side of the floodplain, the course turns sharply northeast. Look for a snag in the middle of a riffle. As the river arcs north, there is a good gravel bar for lunch.

Next a power line crosses the river. Then some houses and a picturesque red barn appear on the right bank. These landmarks alert you that the Hickman Spillway is about 0.5 mile ahead. Warning signs may be visible on the banks. The Hickman Spillway is a concrete chute that drops 100 vertical feet from the Turlock Main Canal to the river. The river channel is wide, and the north bank provides a level portage if necessary. For most spillway discharges and river flows, paddlers can avoid the turbulence by staying close to the north bank, opposite the spillway.

To take out at Waterford, the Waterford River Park is 300 yards upstream from the Waterford Riverwalk bridge. Look on river right for a brush-free bank with a path and stairs.

41 Tuolumne River–Waterford to Shiloh Bridge

Bring your fishing pole for some slow paddling through long ponds and a few riffles. The river passes farm fields and impressive gravel-mining operations. Near Modesto, the river flows through Tuolumne River Regional Park.

Length: 30 miles

Average paddling time: 3 to 6 hours per segment

Difficulty: Easy flatwater

Rapids: Class I riffles in the first few miles

Optimal flow: 400 to 2,000 cfs

Flow gauge: Modesto

Water source: La Grange Dam

Best season: Spring through autumn, except during floods

Land status: Mostly private

Fees: Required at some access points

Maps: USGS Denair, Waterford, Ceres, Brush Lake, Westley

Craft: Canoes, kayaks, rafts, dories, small powerboats

Contacts: Tuolumne River Trust: (209) 236-0330; tuolumne.org

Special considerations: Occasional downed trees and bridge construction suggest caution. Slow current and summer heat.

Put-in/Takeout Information

Waterford River Park and Trail (N37 38.210' / W120 45.328'): From CA 132, 2 blocks east of CR J9, turn onto North Appling Road toward the river. North Appling Road ends in a driveway into this day-use community park with restrooms and foot access.

Fox Grove Park (N37 37.134' / W120 50.563'): From Modesto, take CA 132 east 8 miles to Geer Road. Turn south on Geer Road; 0.2 mile past the Tuolumne River bridge, turn east to the Fox Grove access road. Toilet and parking available.

Ceres River Bluff Regional Park (N37 36.962' / W120 55.696') continues to develop as part of Tuolumne River Regional Park. From CA 99 take East Hatch Road 2.6 miles east. Turn north at Eastgate Boulevard into the soccer field complex. Go north, past the parking lot and athletic fields, to a road heading east and downhill to a parking area. Launch sites are planned to shorten a lengthy carry. Open daylight hours, with toilets near the sports fields.

Legion Park, Modesto (N37 37.370' / W120 57.957'): Follow CA 132 (Yosemite Boulevard) east past Gallo Winery. Turn right (south) onto Santa Cruz Avenue and follow it all the way to the river (about 1 mile), where it turns into Legion Park Drive. Follow Legion Park Drive along the river for 0.5 mile to the intersection of Tioga Drive and the paved parking lot adjacent to the river.

Neece Drive boat launch (N37 37.162' / W120 59.939') is proposed for 2020, part of Tuolumne River Regional Park: From CA 99, exit to Tuolumne Boulevard.

Go briefly west, then turn south on Neece Drive. Go 0.3 mile, between the golf course and baseball stadium. Look for the road to the boat launch with parking.

Riverdale Park (N37 36.706' / W121 2.317'): From CA 99, take CA 132 (Maze Boulevard) west about 1.2 miles to Carpenter Road. Go south on Carpenter, cross the river, then turn right (west) onto Hatch Road. Follow Hatch Road 0.25 mile; turn right onto Parkside Drive for about 0.3 mile. Turn right into Riverdale Park. Carry your boat about 100 yards to the river. Flag the site so you can find it later.

Shiloh Bridge (N37 36.146' / W121 7.899'): From CA 99, take CA 132 (Maze Boulevard) west about 6.3 miles to Hart Road. Go south on Hart to Paradise Road, then turn right (west) and go 0.5 mile to Shiloh Road. Turn left and go across the bridge to the Shiloh public access. Carry your boat about 100 yards. No toilets.

Overview

Below Waterford, the river changes to wide, slow reaches with a few riffles and streamside gravel quarries.

Tuolumne River Trust is a participant in the Tuolumne River Coalition, whose goal is to create the Tuolumne River Parkway and improve habitat and recreational opportunities along the lower Tuolumne River. This effort includes Tuolumne River Regional Park, which is being developed along the 7-mile section from the Mitchell Street bridge to the Carpenter Road bridge by the City of Modesto, City of Ceres, and Stanislaus County.

The Paddling

Waterford to Fox Grove Park

Length: 5.7 miles
Average paddling time: 3 to 4 hours
Difficulty: Riffles; Class I whitewater skills required
Rapids: Class I with brush and snags
Shuttle: 7 miles (10 minutes)
Just upstream from the Waterford bridge (called Hickman Road, CR J9, and F Street) are a large gravel bar and snags. Beware of construction, as the bridge is slated for replacement in the next few years. Beyond the bridge, a huge nursery occupies the long river terrace on the left. Broken concrete riprap lines the banks. Soon the channel snakes between gravel bars, brush, and snags. Look carefully to the right and you may see another spillway recessed from the river. Some 2 miles below the bridge are some broken concrete pilings, then the stream velocity increases. Enjoy the faster pace while it lasts.

The next 3 miles are wide, flat, and slow. Waterfowl and fishing boats enjoy the ponds. Some tall cottonwoods mark the north bank. Behind a thin row of trees, a large gravel operation is active beyond the left bank about 1 mile from the takeout. A white house sprawls on river right with sweeping lawns and a picturesque weeping

Tuolumne River—Waterford to Shiloh Bridge

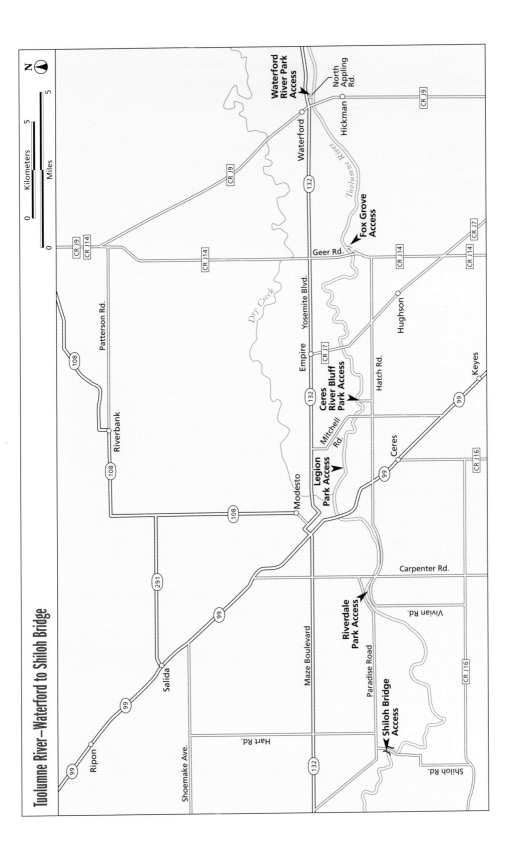

willow. When the Geer Road bridge comes into view, paddle to the cove along the left bank, where the Fox Grove boat ramp provides the takeout.

Fox Grove to Legion Park

Length: 9.7 miles
Average paddling time: 4 to 6 hours
Difficulty: Easy
Shuttle: 7.6 miles (15 minutes)

Downstream of Geer Road, the river narrows. The flow is slow in a winding course with occasional sand and gravel bars. Orchards and riparian trees grow beyond the banks.

Beware of major construction at the Santa Fe Avenue bridge. Approximately 2 miles downstream of the bridge, Ceres River Bluff Regional Park offers a takeout opportunity on the left bank. Look at this takeout (and perhaps flag it) before you start paddling so that you will recognize it.

From River Bluff Park, you may see or hear low-flying aircraft, since you are almost directly under the Modesto Airport flight path.

Mitchell Road is the eastern end of Tuolumne River Regional Park. As proposed, it will stretch along the river for 7 miles as far downstream as Carpenter Road.

Downstream from Mitchell Road, the right bank is lined with trees and the left bank has houses. Look closely for Legion Park Drive and a parking area where there is a takeout on the right bank.

Legion Park to Riverdale Park

Length: 5.1 miles
Average paddling time: 2 to 3 hours
Difficulty: Easy flatwater
Shuttle: 6.5 miles (20 minutes)

As the river swings north, past the buildings of Gallo Winery, and starts to turn west, Dry Creek enters on the right. Modesto calls the right bank lands "the Gateway Parcel"; it's the site of a future river access and recreation development.

Below Dry Creek 0.2 mile is the Ninth Street bridge, former site of Dennett Dam. Its removal in 2018 removed a hazard, allows better passage of fish to the upstream spawning grounds, and provides a free-flowing river from La Grange to the San Joaquin River confluence. The Tuolumne River Trust worked with several agencies to remove the dam.

Within the next 0.5 mile, a railroad bridge and three highway bridges cross the river. Expect some bridge reconstruction in the next few years. A half mile downstream of CA 99, the new Neece Drive boat ramp is planned by 2020 on the right bank. Less than 150 feet wide, the river flows smoothly past tree-lined banks and a wastewater treatment plant, and 0.5 mile below the Carpenter Road bridge you reach the Riverdale Park takeout. If the water is low, a midstream sandbar may be visible at the takeout. Look for your flag and foot trails leading up the left bank.

Riverdale Park to Shiloh Bridge

Length: 9 miles
Average paddling time: 4 to 6 hours
Difficulty: Easy flatwater
Shuttle: 10+ miles (20 minutes)

The San Joaquin River is about 10 miles distant. The Shiloh Road bridge is the only public access for this reach. Slow meanders and smooth flow mark the water's course. Farm fields border the river, and some pumps are apparent.

About 3 miles downstream is a fast riffle; in another 2.5 miles begins an unusual hairpin turn, flowing first south and then north. A lagoon and riparian vegetation are on the south side. This site, known as "Big Bend," was the subject of riparian vegetation plantings completed in 2008 and supported by the Tuolumne River Trust.

Shiloh Road comes into view at a northerly turn of the river. Paddle another 0.25 mile to the bridge and takeout on the sandy left bank.

Sacramento–San Joaquin Delta

The Sacramento and San Joaquin Rivers carry water from the 400-mile-long Central Valley to the 1,100-square-mile marshland known as the Sacramento–San Joaquin Delta before the waters flush into San Francisco Bay. Today more than fifty islands are surrounded by 700 miles of tidal waterways. Some are large channels suitable for seagoing freighters; others are intimate sloughs full of migratory and native wildlife and fish.

Winter days, with the exception of storms or fog, are often mild with light breezes. Those days are a marvelous time for exploring and experiencing this unique place. Summer heat in the Central Valley sucks cool Pacific air through the Delta, producing strong winds and cool temperatures.

This Delta fisherman proudly displays his catch.

42 Suisun Slough

This area is one of two components of the San Francisco Bay National Estuarine Research Reserve. Suisun Marsh is the largest remaining contiguous area of coastal wetland in California. Bisecting the wetland, Suisun Slough connects smaller waterways winding through the wetlands and wildlife areas. These waterways are often protected from the notorious Delta winds.

Length: 6 to 10 miles
Average paddling time: 2 to 5 hours
Difficulty: Open water; beginner to intermediate with self-rescue skills
Marine weather: 162.55 MHz; www.wrh.noaa.gov/sto
Tide reference: Port Chicago: High tides: 36 minutes; low tides: +1 hour, 11 minutes
Best season: Autumn, winter, and early spring to avoid strong summer afternoon winds
Land status: Entirely private
Fees: Required at access points
Maps: USGS Fairfield South, Denverton; NOAA BookletChart 18656, pages 5 & 6; Fish-n-Map Company, The Delta
Craft: Canoes, sea kayaks, motorboats

Contacts: San Francisco Bay National Estuarine Research Reserve: coast.noaa.gov/nerrs. California Department of Fish and Wildlife, Suisun City Office: (707) 425-3828; wildlife.ca.gov. Wildlife of Suisun Marsh: suisunwildlife.org/grizzly.html. Grizzly Waters Kayaking: (707) 341-6141; grizzlywaters.com.
Special considerations: High winds, large fast-moving powerboats, and low tides that can leave you stranded on mud. The dense vegetation and slippery mud banks offer few, if any, places to exit boats to dry land. The surrounding lands are privately owned or disallow boat access. Use a good map, compass, and functioning GPS device.

Put-in/Takeout Information

Suisun City Marina (N38 13.966' / W122 2.284'): Take I-80 to Fairfield and exit onto CA 12 eastbound. At Suisun City, exit to Main Street and turn left (south) onto Main Street. Turn left onto Cordelia Street, go 1 block, and then turn right onto Kellogg Street. Go 0.2 mile; the launch ramp is on the left. Fee area.

Hill Slough bridge (N38 13.589' / W122 1.320'): From Suisun City and CA 12, go 0.6 mile east and exit onto Grizzly Island Road south. Continue 1.25 miles to the wildlife viewing area.

Belden's Landing (N38 11.296' / W121 58.573') on Montezuma Slough: From Suisun City and CA 12, go 0.6 mile east and exit onto Grizzly Island Road south. Continue 5.5 miles to the Montezuma Slough fishing access. Fee area.

Shuttle: Suisun City Marina to Belden's Landing on Montezuma Slough: 7 miles (15 minutes)

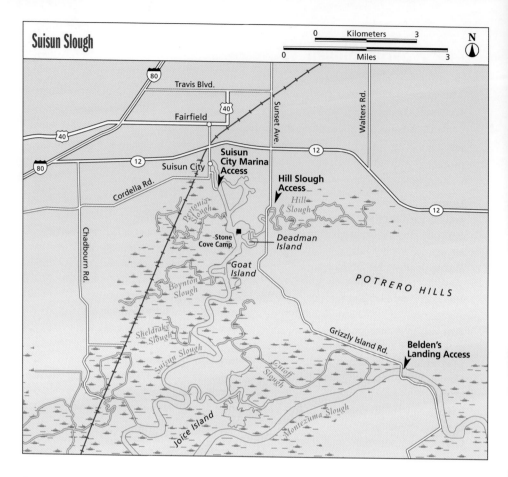

Overview

Sinuous Suisun Slough is located in the northwest part of the Delta. Thirteen miles to the south is broad, windy Grizzly Bay. To the west, several sloughs drain marshlands stretching from I-680. To the east and south is Montezuma Slough, bounding Grizzly Island. Between these waterways lies one of the first wildlife refuges in California, Joice Island.

In winter, the region is an important feeding and resting station for waterfowl traveling the Pacific Flyway and may harbor thousands of ducks and geese. In addition to the migratory population, Suisun Marsh supports a population of resident waterfowl and shorebirds, including heron rookeries and greater egrets. Bring waterproof cameras and binoculars.

The wider sloughs, such as Suisun and Montezuma, are exposed to southwest and northerly winds, but the narrower waterways are more protected.

No camping or campfires are permitted. Grass fires started here can easily spread to the peat soil, where fires are very difficult to control.

The Paddling

There are no road signs in Suisun Marsh, and there are abundant channels to choose. Plot your intended route on a good map (such as NOAA BookletChart 18656) before paddling. Bring the map and a compass, and use them to avoid getting lost. Make sure your GPS device works in that area. Some distinctive landmarks to show general direction include:

- Mount Diablo to the south
- Large military aircraft taking off from Travis Air Force Base to the east of Suisun City
- Large east–west power line towers less than 200 yards south of Suisun launch ramp
- Large wind turbines to the west
- Sprawling hillside wind turbine array 10 miles to the east

Two other considerations: Paddle at higher tides to avoid getting stuck in the mud; and plan to be in your boat for a while—there are almost no places to easily get out of your boat onto dry land.

Suisun Slough is 100-plus yards wide as it winds southward toward Grizzly Bay, Suisun Bay, and eventually San Francisco Bay. From Suisun Slough, several smaller sloughs lead to the west. After the first 1 mile in the slough, the scenery doesn't change much. Distances and approximate paddling times are shown in the table below:

A calm spring day is perfect for peaceful paddling in the Delta.

Slough	Distance from Suisun Launch Ramp to Mouth of Slough	Length of Slough, One-way	Round-trip Distance	Average Round-trip Paddling Time with Favorable Wind and Tide
Peytonia to railroad	0.5 mile	1.7 miles	4.4 miles	2–3 hours
Boynton to railroad	1.6 miles	2.8 miles	8.8 miles	3–4 hours
Sheldrake to pond	3.2 miles	1 mile	8.4 miles	3–4 hours

Suisun City Marsh Island and Peytonia Slough

Length: 5+ miles round-trip
Average paddling time: 2 to 4 hours
Difficulty: Beginner with self-rescue skills
Map: NOAA BookletChart 18656, pages 5 & 6

Directly east of the launch ramp is a 0.5-mile-wide island to paddle around and get a feel for the marsh environment. Go north toward the marina and the Suisun Yacht Club, then go southeast in the wide channel. The width varies as you paddle around the island. This route returns to Suisun Slough, 0.4 mile south of the launch ramp.

As you paddle south another 0.1 mile, Peytonia Slough joins Suisun Slough from the west. A eucalyptus grove shields buildings and docks on Peytonia Slough. On the north shore, the small point of land is one of the few places where it is physically possible to exit a kayak onto unposted land. A trail connects the point to the marina parking lot. Peytonia Slough winds 1.7 miles westward through the Peytonia Slough Ecological Reserve to the railroad crossing.

Suisun Slough—Hill Slough—Boynton Slough

Length: 6 to 8+ miles round-trip
Average paddling time: 2 to 5 hours
Difficulty: Beginner with self-rescue skills
Map: NOAA BookletChart 18656, page 5

Continuing south on Suisun Slough, the channel widens dramatically with several islands. Palm trees, a sign, and a long yellow kayak announce Stone Cove Youth Camp on a small island. The owner lives in a more substantial building with private dock on the east side.

To the east and south, Deadman Island hides the entrance to Hill Slough to the east. A short mile eastward is the Grizzly Island Road crossing with the Hill Slough wildlife viewing area and Rush Ranch. This is a possible access point. You can continue to paddle up Hill Slough if you keep the tides in mind to avoid getting stuck in the mud.

South of Stone Cove camp 0.75 mile, Boynton Slough flows to the west. It winds 2.8 miles to the railroad if you paddle the whole distance. A short distance from the mouth is a large dilapidated building with a fine view of distant Mount Diablo. About 300 yards from the mouth is a small channel circling to the north and back

The Coastal Mountains rise beyond walls of marsh grass.

to Suisun Slough. During an ebbing tide, we saw several fish in the shallows being hungrily watched by a great blue heron.

Across Suisun Slough from Boynton Slough is a low rocky slope at Goat Island that offers some slippery ground if you need to stretch your legs.

Suisun Slough—Cutoff Slough—Montezuma Slough

Length: 8+ miles
Average paddling time: 3 to 5 hours
Difficulty: Beginner to intermediate with self-rescue skills
Map: NOAA BookletChart 18656, pages 5 & 6
This route ventures 3.6 miles down Suisun Slough, passing the mouths of Peytonia, Boynton, and Sheldrake Sloughs. South of Sheldrake Slough, eucalyptus trees mark the confluence with Cutoff Slough, where Suisun Slough's course changes from southeast to southwest.

Four miles long and 100 feet wide, Cutoff Slough separates Joice Island from the wetlands and grazing lands leading up to the 300-foot-high Potrero Hills. After 0.25 mile, at the first confluence, signs on a large mid-channel post indicate a water quality testing station. Take the right (southeastward) channel to go to Montezuma Slough. White-tailed kites, hawks, ducks, and geese were visible here one February day. Floodgates to island channels are built into the low levees. Narrow wildlife trails cut through the tulles and grasses. Curious tall concrete posts, possibly dating from World War II, are scattered along the way.

A narrow bridge to Joice Island crosses the slough. Nearing Montezuma Slough, Cutoff Slough turns south. Diminished wind waves from Montezuma Slough may travel to this part of Cutoff Slough. At the confluence, Montezuma is more than 200 yards wide. The Grizzly Island Road bridge and a large wind farm are visible to the east. During ebb tides, the midstream current may seem fast. Paddle 0.75 mile to the bridge and the adjacent Belden's Landing ramp.

43 Sherman Island Lake

Sherman Island Lake was originally marshland, transformed into dry farmland that flooded when levees failed. Like other Delta-flooded islands, the lake is shallow. Remnants of old levees and small islands are scattered between winding tidal channels. Old maps and satellite images show channels changing direction and islands changing size. Duck hunters have created small docks and boardwalks that are interesting to follow.

Length: 4 to 9 miles

Average paddling time: 2 to 5 hours

Difficulty: Open water; self-rescue skills required

Marine weather: 162.55 MHz; www.wrh.noaa.gov/sto

Tide reference: Port Chicago: High tides: +1 hour, 12 minutes; low tides: +1 hour, 26 minutes at Antioch

Best season: Autumn, winter, and early spring to avoid strong summer afternoon winds

Land status: Private except for put-in

Fees: Required at put-in

Maps: USGS Antioch North; NOAA Chart 18652; NOAA BookletChart 18661, page 16, and BookletChart 18656, page15; Google satellite image

Craft: Canoes, sea kayaks, sailboards, kite boards, motorboats, sit-on-tops

Contacts: Delta Kayak Adventures: (925) 642-5764; deltakayakadventures.com. Sacramento County Sherman Island Park: (916) 875-6961; www.regionalparks.saccounty.net/Parks/SacramentoRiverandDelta/. Brannan Island State Recreation Area: parks.ca.gov. California Department of Fish and Wildlife: wildlife.ca.gov/lands/Planning/Lower-Sherman-Island WA.

Special considerations: High winds, large powerboats in the major river channels, fast sailboarders and kiteboarders, confusing channels—bring a good map, compass, and functioning GPS device.

Put-in/Takeout Information

Sherman Island Sacramento County Park (W38 3.392' / W121 47.179'): From I-5, exit onto CA 12 west. Go 16 miles; within sight of the Sacramento River bridge, turn left onto CA 160. Go 6.5 miles on the levee-top road. Where CA 160 leaves the levee top, turn right onto Sherman Island Road. Follow this narrow levee-top road 3.8 miles to the park at road's end. Fee area.

Antioch Marina, 5 Marina Plaza (N38 1.131' / W121 49.131'): From CA 4 (California Delta Way), turn north onto L Street (aka Connie Loma Boulevard) and go 1.3 miles to Antioch Marina. Site of Delta Kayak Adventures rentals and tours. No-fee kayak launches at public launch ramp and within marina. Kayak storage also available at a low monthly rate. Designated official San Francisco Bay Area Water Trail access site.

Shuttle: None

Overview

Sherman Island sits between the deepwater channels of the Sacramento and San Joaquin Rivers where they merge. This tidal lake was formed when the levees failed in the late 1800s. Now the California Department of Fish and Wildlife manages the resource as Lower Sherman Island Wildlife Area.

Adjacent to the lake's north side, the broad expanse of the Sacramento River is favored by sailboarders and kiteboarders, especially during summer, when Delta winds frequently exceed 25 mph. Paddlers will find the winter more inviting—the winds are gentle, waterfowl are in greater numbers, and the area is less crowded.

Sherman Island County Park provides limited recreational vehicle camping. Nearby Brannan Island State Recreation Area offers camping of all types.

The Paddling

When you arrive, the winds may be different than forecast. As you drive along the levee, look at the Sacramento River. If there is a sea of whitecaps and the car is shaking, it is not a good day for paddle craft. Go elsewhere. If the winds are gentle, get ready for paddling.

This wind vane was sponsored by local windsurfing and kiteboarding enthusiasts.

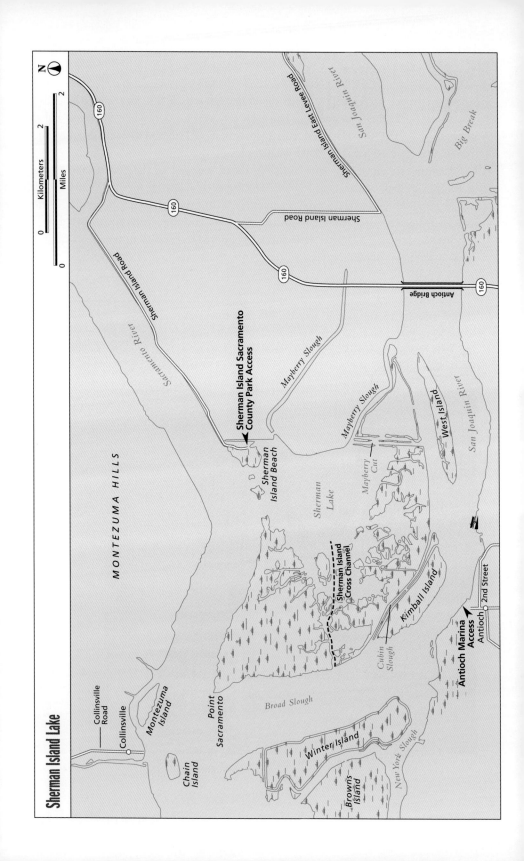

Use a compass and satellite image or map that shows recent channels in the marsh. These can help you to avoid confusion and getting lost. While only a short distance from shore, look around at the landmarks. Note the location and direction of the tall electric tower that spans the Sacramento River—it is only 0.3 mile from the boat ramp. From a distance, that tower (and not the other ten leading to the San Joaquin River) marks your return to the launch ramp. By comparison, the Antioch bridge over the San Joaquin River is 3 miles to the southeast; Mount Diablo is 14 miles to the southwest.

Marsh Islands of Sherman Lake

Length: 3 to 6 miles round-trip
Average paddling time: 2 to 5 hours
Difficulty: Open water; beginner to intermediate with self-rescue skills
Map: NOAA charts and a recent high-resolution satellite image, such as Google Earth

Two small islands lie 0.3 mile west of the ramp. Another 0.3 mile begins an arc of larger islands that form the western and southern boundary of the lake and marsh. Some of the narrow sloughs (more than 0.5 mile from the open lake) have docks and wooden boardwalks (of uncertain repair) that may be used by duck hunters. Enjoy exploring, watching the birdlife, and wondering where you will end up.

Sacramento River to Broad Slough to the Channel back to Sherman Lake

Length: Loop of 8 to 9 miles
Average paddling time: 4 to 5 hours
Difficulty: Open water; beginner to intermediate with self-rescue skills
Map: NOAA charts and a recent high-resolution satellite image, such as Google Earth

This route goes counterclockwise around the north end of Lower Sherman Island.

Start by heading briefly northwest along the 0.5-mile-wide Sacramento River. Stay close to the south bank. At low tides, the several small sandy beaches may be accessible. Approximately 3 miles from the launch ramp, Broad Slough intersects the Sacramento River. Broad Slough, 0.75 mile wide, connects the San Joaquin and Sacramento Rivers. Follow Broad Slough south, staying close to the Sherman Island shore.

About 1.5 miles from the Sacramento River–Broad Slough confluence, a modest slough opens eastward into Sherman Island. Depending on the tide, some current may be flowing through this side slough. Follow the slough approximately 1.25 narrowing miles eastward to Sherman Lake, then head northeast about 1.6 miles back to the put-in.

If you know how to find the slough (approximately N38 2.5' / W121 48.5') connecting Sherman Lake and Broad Slough, you can paddle this route clockwise.

Option: Start or finish at Antioch Marina (N38 1.131' / W121 49.131').

Mayberry Cut—San Joaquin River—Cubin Slough—Broad Slough and Narrow Channel back to Sherman Lake

Length: Loop of 8 to 9 miles

Average paddling time: 4 to 5 hours

Difficulty: Open water; beginner to intermediate with self-rescue skills

Map: NOAA charts and a recent high-resolution satellite image, such as Google Earth

The route goes south about 2.5 miles, exiting the lake through Mayberry Cut into the broad San Joaquin River. Stay close to the north shore and go west. At 1 mile veer northwest into Cubin Slough, between Kimball Island and the remnants of Sherman Island. Houses and wharves dot the Sherman Island side.

Approximately 0.5 mile from the mouth of Cubin Slough, a narrow channel heads due north. If tides and vegetation permit, follow this channel 0.4 mile north (ignore the first side channel at 0.25 mile) and then northeast for about 0.6 mile back into the lake.

If the first slough doesn't work or looks unlikely, continue northwest on Cubin Slough into Broad Slough. Go north about 0.5 mile on Broad Slough past the end of Kimball Island, where a slough opens into Sherman Island. Some current may be flowing (depending on the tide) in this side slough. Follow it approximately 1.25 narrowing miles eastward to Sherman Lake, then head northeast about 1.6 miles back to the put-in.

Option: Start or finish at Antioch Marina (N38 1.131' / W121 49.131').

44 Big Break

"Big Break is a microcosm of the Delta" explains East Bay Regional Park District naturalist Mike Moran in *Bay Nature*'s "Gateway to the Delta" article dated December 31, 2012. You can see water, wetlands, and riparian thickets alive with fish, birds, and mammals. You can also see nearby heavy equipment, rows of houses, and a wind farm across the water. A levee break in 1928 gave Big Break its name when the breach let the San Joaquin River flood an asparagus farm. The below-sea-level lands are now covered by water and marsh.

Length: Up to 8 miles circumnavigating through Dutch Slough

Average paddling time: 2 to 5 hours

Difficulty: Open water; self-rescue skills required

Marine weather: 162.55 MHz; www.wrh.noaa .gov/sto

Tide reference: Port Chicago: High tides: +1 hour, 12 minutes; low tides: +1 hour, 26 minutes

Best season: Autumn through early spring to avoid strong summer afternoon winds

Land status: Mixed private and public

Fees: Required at marinas

Maps: USGS Antioch North, Jersey Island; NOAA BookletChart 18661, pages 17 & 16; Fish-n-Map Company, The Delta

Craft: Canoes, sea kayaks, wind craft, motorboats, sit-on-tops

Contacts: East Bay Regional Parks: (510) 544-3050; ebparks.org/parks/big_break. Big Break Marina: (925) 679-0900; big-break-marina .com. Lauritzen Yacht Harbor: (925) 757-1916; lauritzens.com. Delta Kayak Adventures: (925) 642-5764; deltakayakadventures.com. San Francisco Bay Area Water Trail: sfbaywatertrail .org.

Special considerations: High winds and large powerboats in the major channels. Oceangoing vessels in the San Joaquin River.

Put-in/Takeout Information

Big Break Marina (N38 0.746' / W121 43.981'): From CA 160 in Antioch, exit 18th Street/Main Street and go east 1.1 miles to Big Break Road. Turn north onto Big Break Road to the marina entrance and paved launch ramp. Fee area.

Lauritzen Yacht Harbor (N38 1.008' / W121 44.836'): From CA 160 in Antioch, exit 18th Street/Main Street and go east. Turn left (north) onto Bridgehead Road almost to the water. Turn right onto Lauritzen Lane and into the marina. Fee area.

Big Break Regional Shoreline (N38 0.718' / W121 43.717'): From CA 160 in Antioch, exit East 18th Street/Main Street and go east 1.1 miles to Big Break Road. Turn north onto Big Break Road to the park entrance. Distance from vehicles to water is 0.3 mile.

East Bay Regional Park District Visitor Center (N38 0.685' / W121 43.723'): From CA 160 in Antioch, exit 18th Street/Main Street and go east 1.1 miles to Big Break Road. Turn north onto Big Break Road, then east onto Big Break Regional

Trail. Kayak launch with Mobi-Mat located north of pier. Loaner kayak carts available at visitor center. Designated San Francisco Bay Area Water Trail access site.
Shuttle: None

Overview

Big Break is a pair of shallow oblong bays approximately 2 miles east to west and 1 mile north to south. Marsh habitat forms the long southern and western perimeter. At the north entrance, the 0.75-mile-wide San Joaquin River contributes a mix of salt water from San Francisco Bay and freshwater from the Sierra and Central Valley. The deeper channel and levees of Dutch Slough bound the north and eastern sides. The south and west areas contain a half dozen islands, which may offer narrow beaches at lower tides.

Since the early levees failed, the shape of the islands, levees, and marshlands has continuously changed. These edges are home to sedges, cottonwoods, otters, muskrats, pelicans, herons, hawks, and egrets, as well as migratory wildfowl. The southern marsh edges are included in the Big Break Regional Shoreline.

Visit the East Bay Regional Park District Visitor Center, launch ramp, and huge outdoor three-dimensional map of the Delta.

Expanded paddling and wildlife observation opportunities are being created as part of the Dutch Slough Restoration Project (water.ca.gov/Programs/Integrated-Regional-Water-Management/Delta-Ecosystem-Enhancement-Program/Dutch-Slough-Tidal-Restoration-Project). Between Big Break and Jersey Island Road, Marsh Creek is to be relocated into a winding estuarian stream, Little Dutch Slough deepened, and levees breached to allow tidal wetlands intrusion.

The Paddling

Early mornings and some evenings offer the least-windy conditions. Check the weather forecast—the winds you encounter may be different than those forecast. Whitecaps on the water indicate a tough paddle. Paddle close to the windward shoreline to reduce the fetch of wind on water. If the winds are gentle, enjoy the water and wildlife.

To the southwest, 3,500-foot Mount Diablo provides a great landmark in clear weather. High Antioch Bridge is visible to the west.

Although they are not to be ignored, tides and currents are not strong elements here. Use a map to find your way around the low islands.

Lauritzen Yacht Harbor to Enclosed Marsh
Length: 2-mile loop
Average paddling time: 1+ hours
Difficulty: Open water; beginner with self-rescue skills
Map: NOAA BookletChart 18661, page 16

Big Break & Frank Tracts and Sand Mound Slough

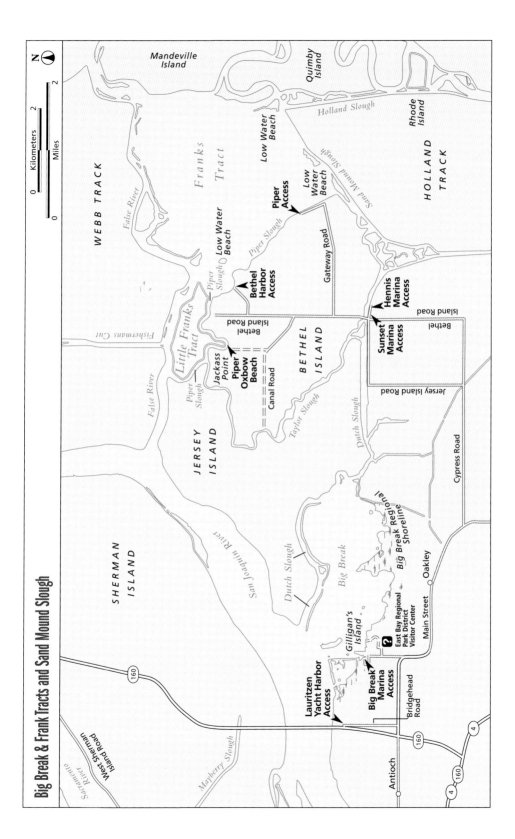

Exit the marina and note the small entrance. Then paddle eastward along the San Joaquin River south shore for 0.3 mile. Turn south into the enclosed marsh, known as Little Break, which is somewhat protected from wind waves. The channel splits to go around an island, and then the open water widens. The views of birdlife should be enjoyable.

Islands along the Western Areas from Big Break Marina

Length: Loop of 3+ miles
Average paddling time: 1 to 2 hours
Difficulty: Beginner with self-rescue skills
Map: NOAA BookletChart 18661, page 17

Three hundred yards from the launch ramp, a channel opens to the east between a peninsula and nearby "Gilligan's Island." Several marshy islands are scattered to the north and south, each with shipwrecks, old pilings, and other forgotten stuff. It is great to explore the nooks and crannies looking for otters, seals, and birds. Beaches may be available at "Gilligan's" and the other islands if the tide is low enough.

Dutch Slough from Big Break Marina

Length: Loop of 8 to 9 miles
Average paddling time: 4 to 5 hours
Difficulty: Intermediate, open water; self-rescue skills required
Map: NOAA BookletChart 18661, page 17

This route explores the north and east perimeters of Big Break and cuts across the open bay. One option is to go clockwise. Heading northeast about 1 mile is the most direct path to Dutch Slough. Entry to the slough is through broad openings in the levee remnants. The far side of the slough is private agricultural Jersey Island. Riprap lines the Jersey Island levees. Dutch Slough is deep enough for large powerboats. The Big Break side of the old levee is shallower and more interesting to explore.

Depending on your enthusiasm and energy, you can follow Dutch Slough southward until it narrows nearing the south side of Jersey Island. Then change course and head west toward the put-in. An alternative, if the wind is freshening, is to take a counterclockwise route so that the wind will be at your back crossing the bay. The Dutch Slough Restoration Project should provide more paddling options in the next few years.

45 Franks Tract and Sand Mound Slough

One of the largest flooded islands in the Delta and accessible only by boat, Franks Tract and Little Franks Tract are part of the Brannan Island and Franks Tract State Recreation Area. Favored for fishing and hunting, the wetlands attract multitudes of waterfowl in winter. Paddlers may best enjoy nature's wildlife by visiting the adjoining sloughs during winter, when the personal watercraft/powerboat crowd is absent.

(See map on page 217.)
Length: 5 to 8 miles
Average paddling time: 2 to 4 hours
Difficulty: Open water; self-rescue skills required
Marine weather: 162.55 MHz; www.wrh.noaa .gov/sto
Tide reference: Port Chicago: High tides: +2 hours, 33 minutes; low tides: +2 hours, 46 minutes
Best season: Autumn, winter, and early spring to avoid strong summer afternoon winds
Land status: Surrounding islands are private
Fees: Required at marinas
Maps: USGS Bouldin Island, Jersey Island; NOAA BookletChart 18661, pages 12 & 18; Fish-n-Map Company, The Delta

Craft: Canoes, sea kayaks, personal watercraft, motorboats, sit-on-tops
Contacts: Brannan Island & Franks Tract State Recreation Area: (916) 777-6671; parks.ca .gov. Sunset Harbor Marina: (925) 453-9471. Hennis Marina: (925) 684-3333. (Jim Rice) Bethel Harbor Marina: (925) 684-2141; bethelharbor.com. Sugar Barge Resort: (800) 799-4100; sugarbarge.com. Delta Kayak Adventures: (925) 642-5764; deltakayak adventures.com.
Special considerations: High winds, personal watercraft, and large powerboats in the major channels

Put-in/Takeout Information

Sunset Marina (N38 0.691' / W121 38.388'): From CA 160 in Oakley, follow Main Street about 4 miles east and then south. Turn east onto East Cypress for 3 miles to the traffic signal, and then go north on Bethel Island Road. As you start up the first bridge (Dutch Slough) turn right, then immediately left to the water and the marina. Launch ramp, toilets. Fee area.

Hennis Marina (N38 0.677' / W121 38.211'): Go to Sunset Marina and continue east 250 yards along the waterfront. Fee area provides an elevator lift for launching several small craft at a time.

Bethel Harbor Marina (N38 2.475' / W121 37.978'): Get to Bethel Island Road as above. Cross the bridge and then go 1.7 miles to Harbor Road. Turn right and go to the road's end at the marina. Toilets, parking, foot ramp to floating dock for launch. Fee area.

Piper Slough (N38 1.515' / W121 36.679') borders the east side of Bethel Island and the west side of Franks Tract. From Bethel Island Road, pass through the village.

Turn right onto Gateway Road, go 1 mile, then turn left onto Piper Road. Go 0.4 mile to Sugar Barge Road, or go to the end of Piper. Both lead to Willow Road, which leads to any of these marinas indicating launch facilities: Beacon Harbor, Russo's Marina, Sugar Barge Resort.

Shuttle: None

Overview

The Delta is home to crawdads and many species of fish, including sturgeon, striped bass, black bass, catfish, bluegill, crappie, shad, and salmon returning to spawn in the Sierra and Sacramento Rivers. Species vary by season, but there's good fishing to be had on the Delta almost year-round. You can fish from shore or by boat.

Little Franks Tract is a smaller submerged farmland, about 1.3 miles east to west and 0.5 mile north to south. Summer winds often blow along the long axis, building wind waves. The levees that used to separate the island from False River and Piper Slough remain partially above water, supporting water grasses, brush, and small trees. The mix of shallow tidal waters and firm ground provides a variety of habitat for birds, fish, and mammals.

Sand Mound Slough offers shelter from the wind by large and small islands along its length. Anglers have good luck there. The slough is also an easy access to the wide-open water of Franks Tract.

Franks Tract is a large submerged peat farm approximately 2.5 miles wide created when levees failed in 1936 and 1938. The only islands are around the periphery, the remains of old levees. The tract is favored by anglers year-round and duck hunters seasonally. The only access is by boat.

The Paddling

Early mornings offer the least-windy conditions but may be foggy. Check the weather forecast—even then the winds may be different than forecast. Whitecaps on the water indicate a tough paddle. Paddle close to the windward shoreline to reduce the fetch of wind on water. If the winds are gentle, enjoy the paddling.

Although they are not to be ignored, tides and currents are not strong elements here. Do bring your map and compass or GPS device. A great landmark in clear weather is 3,500-foot Mount Diablo, 20 miles to the southwest.

Sand Mound Slough and Franks Tract

Length: 8-mile loop
Average paddling time: 3 to 5 hours
Difficulty: Open water; beginner with self-rescue skills

Starting on Dutch Slough provides convenient access to Sand Mound Slough and Franks Tract. Paddle east from the marina. Both shores are lined with marinas or houses with their own private docks. Sand Mound Slough whispers its presence with undeveloped islands of tule marsh. One route is to follow the channel next to Bethel Island to the first or second channel to the right. Either channel takes you to the main Sand Mound Slough channel. The south side of the channel is lined with riprap along Holland Island.

Northeastward 1.5 miles is Franks Tract, separated from the slough by a series of low intermittent islands. Some even have sand beaches at lower tides. Between the islands are entrances to the wide body of Franks Tract. Your paddling can be enlivened by substantial wind waves from the tract's 2.5-mile fetch.

Go another 1 mile. The south levee comes to a sharp point and turns directly south. This is Holland Slough, with privately owned Quimby Island on the east side. This intersection has several small islands with some interesting signs and ruins.

One April day we could see the snow-covered Sierra Nevada, 100 miles distant. Closer at hand were hundreds of coots, ducks and ducklings, a dozen great blue herons, a spy hopping seal, white pelicans, egrets, and two families of river otters playing within 25 yards of us. It was a great reminder to look for the smaller attractions along the banks and in the water.

A Bethel Island yacht berths on northern Piper Slough adjacent to Little Franks Tract.

Little Franks Tract

Length: Loop of approximately 5 miles

Average paddling time: 2 to 4 hours

Difficulty: Beginner with self-rescue skills

Half a dozen breaks allow water and boats to enter the shallow basin inside the levees. From Bethel Harbor you can paddle a circuit of Little Franks Tract both inside the tract and along the deep Piper Slough and False River. Initially, follow Piper Slough north and then west (maybe 0.8 mile) to an opening in the old levee. Inside the tract you can look for otters and birds or show off your fishing skills.

There are a few potential landings spots. At the southernmost curve of the Piper oxbow is a beach at favorable tide. Another is the structure 250 yards south of the False River–Piper Slough confluence. The third is tide dependent—the island at the extreme eastern end of the tract on the inside shore. Keep track of the tide height to ease your return.

If the wind is light, you may wish to visit a small island in Franks Tract, approximately 0.5 mile east of Bethel Harbor. At some tides, it has a sandy shore.

From Bethel Harbor southbound, the Piper Slough Island shoreline is studded with piers and boats. Remnant levees form the east bank of the channel. Several broad levee breaches provide access to the open water of Franks Tract. If the wind is light, these levee openings may be interesting to explore from the open-water side.

46 Delta Meadows

Close to Sacramento and Lodi and adjacent to the historic community of Locke, Delta Meadows contains vestiges of the Delta as it appeared in the 1800s. Explore the peaceful intertwining waterways alive with waterfowl.

Length: 2 to 7 miles

Average paddling time: 2 to 6 hours

Difficulty: Minor tidal currents with flatwater; beginners with self-rescue skills

Tide reference: Port Chicago: New Hope Bridge and Snodgrass Slough (at Twin Cities Road bridge) approximate high tides: +4 hours, 22 minutes; low tides: +5 hours

Best season: Autumn and winter to enjoy migrating birds and avoid powerboats

Land status: Private and public

Fees: Required at marina

Maps: USGS Bruceville, Thornton; Fish-n-Map Company, The Delta

Craft: Open canoes, kayaks, paddleboards, sea kayaks

Contacts: Cosumnes River Preserve: (916) 684-2816; cosumnes.org. BLM Cosumnes River Preserve: blm.gov/visit/cosumnes-river-preserve. Wimpy's Marina and Restaurant: (209) 794-2774; wimpysmarina.com. Lodi Sandhill Crane Festival: cranefestival.com. Headwaters Kayak Shop & Boathouse: (209) 224-8367; headwaterskayak.com.

Special considerations: Check tide tables to go with current. Directions in the sloughs can be confusing, so bring a compass and detailed maps/satellite images. During some summers, dense matts of water hyacinth clog slow-moving waterways, making paddling difficult.

Put-in/Takeout Information

Locke (N38 15.031' / W121 30.401'): From I-5, exit onto Twin Cities Road and go 4.25 miles west to River Road (E-13). Turn south toward Locke and Walnut Grove. Drive 1.7 miles to Locke. Just north of the cross-channel bridge, turn east onto unmarked Levee Road. Go 100 yards to a gated unpaved road. Unload your gear and walk north along the dirt road 0.25 mile into Delta Meadows State Park, where the road comes within a few yards of Railroad Slough. Bring wheelies. No facilities.

Cosumnes River Preserve Visitor Center (N38 15.815' / W121 26.397'): From I-5, exit Twin Cities Road and travel east 1 mile. At Franklin Boulevard, turn south for 1.7 miles to the visitor center. The gated parking lot is open from sunrise to sunset. From the parking lot, follow the concrete path 250 yards across the field to the floating dock just east of the Franklin Boulevard bridge. When winter floods or snowmelt flood the field, put in cautiously.

Wimpy's Marina (N38 13.608' / W121 29.466'): From the preserve go south on Franklin Boulevard to Walnut Grove Road, then turn right. From I-5, exit onto Walnut Grove Road and go 3.2 miles to the bridge at New Hope Landing. Turn right onto the levee top, where Wimpy's Marina and Restaurant is located.

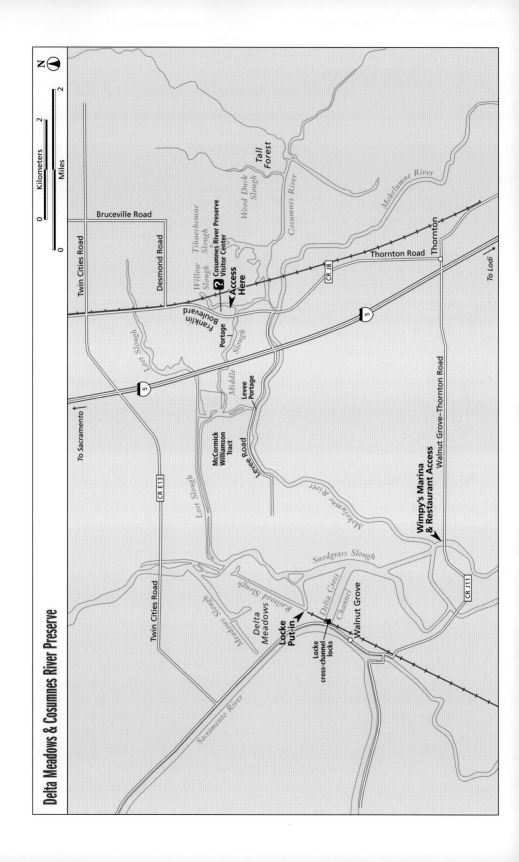

Delta Meadows & Cosumnes River Preserve

Shuttle: Locke to Locke: none; Locke to Wimpy's: 3 miles (5 minutes); Locke to Cosumnes Preserve: 9.5 miles (20 minutes); Cosumnes Preserve to Wimpy's Marina, 6 miles (15 minutes)

Overview

The Mokelumne, Sacramento, and Cosumnes Rivers converge with several sloughs, providing lots of routes to explore. Acquired in 1985, the California State Parks Department describes Delta Meadows as a quiet place to hike and canoe. During summer this is a favorite haunt of houseboats moored for the season. The region is a wintering ground for waterfowl from as far away as Alaska. Otters, beavers, and muskrats inhabit the slough and shores. Along the banks grow oaks, cottonwood, and tule. Trailside blackberries offer a summertime treat. Although the area is owned by California State Parks, there are no facilities and no staff. Day use allows hiking, fishing, and boating. Overnight camping on land is prohibited. The nearby city of Lodi, with its many good restaurants and wineries, annually celebrates the Sandhill Crane Festival in early November. The historic community of Locke was established in 1912 by three Chinese merchants.

The Paddling

Bring maps, a compass, and a GPS device. It is easy to get confused and lost on the sloughs, which repeatedly change directions. There are four 1,000+-foot-tall communication towers nearby. Look at them carefully for reference to directions.

Check the tide times at Snodgrass Slough for easier paddling. Ebbing tides flow from north to south.

Locke and Railroad Slough

Length: 1.2 miles one way
Average paddling time: 1 to 2 hours round–trip
Difficulty: Easy flatwater paddling
Although you have to transport your boat 0.25 mile to the put-in (bring wheelies), this is a short and easy paddle to experience the Delta Meadows. The straight slough heads northeast for 1 mile. Hikers enjoy the gravel road shaded by tall trees along the left (northwest) bank. Paddle as far as you like, then return.

Locke Loop through Snodgrass Slough to Delta Meadows

Length: 3 miles one way
Average paddling time: 2.5 to 4 hours round–trip
Difficulty: Flatwater paddling
Transport your boat 0.25 mile to the put-in (bring wheelies). Head east 0.33 mile from the put-in to Snodgrass Slough. Start north, following a channel that turns east around a marshy island to the main channel of Snodgrass. Again go north. At

Peaceful autumn day near Delta Meadows

about 1.2 miles Snodgrass Slough is joined by Lost Slough from the east. Lost Slough paddles are described under "Locke to Snodgrass, Lost, and Middle Sloughs."

Powerboats may be moored to the banks prior to November, when they are restricted for flood season. Several houseboats broke their moorings during the 2017 winter flood. They got stuck at the Thornton–Walnut Grove Bridge and had to be destroyed to save the bridge.

At 0.4 mile north of the Snodgrass and Lost Slough confluence, Meadow Slough joins from the west. Go west into Meadow Slough. You may see glimpses of vehicle traffic to the north on Twin Cities Road. To the south, the trees and brush retain their thick natural character. Enjoy the birdlife, otters, and maybe beavers. The slough bends sharply south at 0.7 mile from Snodgrass Slough. Look carefully along the banks for brush-free "parks" under tall oaks and cottonwoods. These are good rest spots.

Retrace your path to return to the put-in.

Locke to Snodgrass Slough to Wimpy's Marina

Length: 2.3 miles
Average paddling time: 1.5 to 2.5 hours
Difficulty: Flatwater paddling
Transport your boat 0.25 mile to the put-in (bring wheelies). Head east 0.33 mile from the put-in to Snodgrass Slough. Head south on broad Snodgrass Slough. You may encounter powerboats, so stay away from the channel center.

Downstream 0.7 mile, the Delta Cross Channel links the Sacramento River with Snodgrass Slough and the Mokelumne River system. Water released from upstream reservoirs can flow through the cross channel to Delta diversion facilities near Tracy. In Locke, 0.7 mile to the west, are large flow control gates adjacent to the parking area where you began this paddle. The banks of the cross channel are armored by difficult-to-climb riprap boulders and concrete.

Follow Snodgrass Slough south 0.4 mile, where Dead Horse Island splits the Snodgrass flow. Go left on an almost straight reach for 0.6 mile. The slough around Dead Horse Island joins from the west, the Mokelumne River enters from the east, and the Thornton–Walnut Grove Road bridge is visible downstream.

Take out on river left at Wimpy's launch ramp.

Locke to Snodgrass, Lost, and Middle Sloughs

Length: 8.2 miles round-trip
Average paddling time: 3 to 4 hours round-trip
Difficulty: Flatwater paddling
For this paddle, you really need a recent satellite image or a good map!

Start as though going to Delta Meadows. At the Snodgrass Slough–Lost Slough confluence, go east into Lost Slough. Some seasonal docks line the westerly bank. The first 2 miles of Lost Slough is divided into two channels by a long thin berm with only a couple of places where a shallow-draft boat can change channels. Both

Paddlers drag and carry boats over shallow water between Franklin Boulevard and I-5

channels allow passage into Middle Slough, but the south channel is shorter. Egrets and great blue herons played "follow the leader" with us for miles.

Middle Slough heads south into a backwater divided by two thin islands. The west bank is a high levee bordering the McCormick Williamson Tract. A much lower levee borders the slough's east side. These adjacent lands are managed by agreements with The Nature Conservancy for the Cosumnes River Preserve. When not clogged by water hyacinth, it is a great place for fishing and birding.

The rest of your paddling day has options:

- Return to Locke using the same route used to get here.

- Exit the south end of Middle Slough over a levee and down a brief riprap slope to the Mokelumne, and then go 3.5 miles downstream to Wimpy's. That route will give you a 7.7-mile day and take a total of 3 to 5 hours.

- For an adventure, explore the fork of Middle Slough connecting to the Cosumnes Preserve floating dock. This is better started from the preserve end.

Cosumnes Preserve through Middle, Lost, and Snodgrass Sloughs to Wimpy's

Length: 7 miles
Average paddling time: 4 to 6 hours
Difficulty: A heavy workout but easy paddling

This route is an adventure for explorers. The exercise involves narrow twisty water paths, brief muddy slogs, and good use of higher high tides to minimize dragging boats over shallow clay beds.

From the Cosumnes Preserve floating dock, go directly west to Middle Slough under the Franklin Boulevard bridge. The slough soon narrows. Overhanging trees crowd above the water, while clay beds and mud meet the surface. The next 100 yards may take an hour to negotiate. The sound of I-5 traffic indicates that the slough will soon widen and deepen to allow enjoyable paddling. Vegetation blocks the traffic sounds after passing I-5, and the scene becomes peaceful. As evidenced by small docks and tree swings, local landowners enjoy summer days here. At 1.5 miles from the put-in, you reach the wide north–south reach of Middle Slough, accessible from Lost Slough. From there, the route is the reverse of that described in "Locke to Snodgrass, Lost, and Middle Sloughs."

Cosumnes Preserve along Mokelumne River to Wimpy's

Length: 5.5 miles
Average paddling time: 2.5 to 4 hours
Difficulty: Flatwater paddling

Consult the tide tables for an ebbing tide. From the preserve's floating dock, paddle south 0.5 mile along Middle Slough to the Cosumnes River. At the confluence you should be able to see the railroad bridge to the east. Float south 1.5 miles on the Cosumnes to the larger Mokelumne River. Tree-shrouded levees line the

Paddlers watch egrets and great blue herons along Lost Slough.

Mokelumne, blocking most of the view to preserve lands and farm fields. Farm roads run along the levee tops.

Downstream 1.6 miles from the Cosumnes–Mokelumne confluence, a slim portage track climbs up the slippery riprap and crosses the levee top to a dirt clearing into the south end of Middle Slough. (See "Locke to Snodgrass, Lost, and Middle Sloughs.")

The agricultural acreage of Staten Island is on river right. In an effort to maintain and improve the winter habitat for 15 percent of the Central Valley's sandhill cranes, The Nature Conservancy and local farmers have agreed to agricultural practices that are beneficial to both the farmers and the birds. Staten Island observers have reported more than 10,000 sandhills.

The Mokelumne continues winding south and west another 3.5 miles to meet Snodgrass Slough at Wimpy's. The river is fully exposed to the sun, so bring plenty of drinking water and sunhats on warm sunny days. Wimpy's serves cold drinks and good food.

47 Cosumnes River Preserve

Close to Sacramento and Lodi, this is a rare free-flowing, canoeable waterway. The adjacent lands are being managed and restored by The Nature Conservancy (TNC) and several other organizations to support rich wildlife and riparian oak forests.

(See map on page 224.)
Length: 6 miles
Average paddling time: 2 to 4 hours
Difficulty: Flat moving water; Class I skills required
Tide reference: Port Chicago, corrections for New Hope Bridge: High tides: +4 hours 20 minutes; low tides: +4 hours 56 minutes
Best season: Year-round when the river is not flooding
Land status: Private
Fees: Required at marina
Maps: USGS Bruceville, Thornton; Fish-n-Map Company, The Delta

Craft: Open canoes, kayaks, paddleboards, sea kayaks
Contacts: Cosumnes River Preserve: (916) 684-2816; cosumnes.org. BLM Cosumnes River Preserve: blm.gov/visit/cosumnes-river-preserve. Wimpy's Marina and Restaurant: (209) 794-2774; wimpysmarina.com. Headwaters Kayak Shop & Boathouse: (209) 224-8367; headwaterskayak.com.
Special considerations: Please do not bring pets to the preserve. Spring and winter high flows drown the banks; you have to paddle through brush to reach dry ground.

Put-in/Takeout Information

Cosumnes River Preserve Visitor Center (N38 15.903' / W121 26.447'): From I-5, exit Twin Cities Road and travel east 1 mile. At Franklin Boulevard, turn south for 1.7 miles to the visitor center. The gated parking lot is open from sunrise to sunset. From the parking lot, follow the concrete path 250 yards across the field to the floating dock just east of the Franklin Boulevard bridge. When winter floods or snowmelt flood the field, put in cautiously.
Shuttle: None

Overview

The last free-flowing river within the Central Valley, the Cosumnes River has been designated by TNC as one of the "Last Great Places" and protected as the Cosumnes River Preserve. With a consortium of partners, the 46,000-acre Cosumnes River Preserve works to preserve habitats from conversion to agricultural uses and urbanization while promoting research, educating the public, and providing recreation opportunities.

The river's flood and dry periods foster dynamic hydrologic processes, provide a variety of habitats, and promote abundant biological diversity. Today the Cosumnes River Preserve is one of the few remaining examples of the pristine native habitat and wildlife that once characterized much of the Central Valley. Notable features of the preserve include the "Tall Forest," the annual autumn migration of sandhill cranes, and the winding waterways and wetlands. Scheduled activities usually include birding tours, bird counts, and guided canoe trips. The preserve's location on the Pacific Flyway attracts many resident and migratory wildlife species.

This is where the Cosumnes River meets the tidelands of the Sacramento–San Joaquin Delta. The water depth varies several feet every day, so consult tide tables for higher tide stages. At low tides, the downstream current is stronger.

The Paddling

Cosumnes River to Tall Forest

Length: 5 to 6 miles round-trip
Average paddling time: 2 to 4 hours

From the visitor center parking lot, a concrete path leads 250 yards to a floating dock, which is the launching site. Bring your wheelies, since it is a long carry. The dock is on Middle Slough within sight of the Franklin Boulevard bridge. The bridge is an important landmark when returning to the launch site.

Go south on Middle Slough. The tidal current may be noticeable. In 0.4 mile the slough joins the Cosumnes River. Fishing is allowed from boats in the rivers. Look back and note the power lines in the distance and the tall communications towers to the west. If you miss the Middle Slough turnoff on your return, you will float downstream another 0.25 mile to the Mokelumne River and the Benson's Ferry bridge.

Paddling east upstream on the Cosumnes, you will soon find a busy railroad bridge. The adjacent concrete structure once supported a pipeline. During summer and autumn, the flow here ebbs and floods with the tides. Following winter storms and during spring snowmelt, the river will be much higher, with a strong current.

Explore Tihuechemne Slough, 0.3 mile upstream of the bridges. The slough winds 0.7 mile to the north. The north bank where the slough meets the river, "The Point," is a rest site where you may get out of your boat. Some side channels lead to marshes abundant with life. From the water you can see picturesque valley oaks. The Willow Slough Nature Trail wanders here through the oaks to the river's edge. It is a wonderful place to see many birds, inspect the results of riparian vegetation restoration, and learn about floodplain flora and fauna. When the Michigan Bar stream gauge reads 1,100 cfs, the river overflows some banks in the slough, creating shallow streams through tunnels of willows and oaks. Return down Tihuechemne Slough to the Cosumnes River.

Continuing upstream, the river narrows dramatically and the current increases. Arching trees shade the entire channel. Fallen trees extend into the channel from both banks and require careful maneuvering. At flows above 500 cfs, take special care when paddling downstream to avoid being washed into these strainers. This narrow section is short, and the channel soon widens.

A narrow landing path at the Tall Forest requires that some boats be tied together.

The next 0.7 mile is amazingly straight. Tall cottonwoods and oaks line the south levee. Native grapes hang almost to river level. Just west of Wood Duck Slough is a grassy bank and glade for stretching your legs. You may need to tie boats together. The bank provides an inviting view of the Tall Forest. The sight invites you to reboard your boat and explore Wood Duck Slough, which transports the paddler into the heart of the majestic Tall Forest, with tall valley oaks overhanging the water to provide deep shade. The scene is reminiscent of Bogart and Hepburn on the *African Queen*. Branches reach out from the banks, making this a sinuous passage. Most of the banks are muddy and slippery. Look for the little critters that live in the banks. High water reaches the tops of the banks and moves back and forth from the river to the slough. At summer water levels, a pump structure obstructs the upstream end of Wood Duck Slough. High water submerges parts of the structure, and a careful paddler can continue some distance.

Upstream from Wood Duck Slough, the Cosumnes River turns abruptly north and parallels the slough. This affords another view of the Tall Forest from a channel only a little less mystical and obstructed than Wood Duck Slough.

When returning to your launch site, remember the landmarks. Downstream of the railroad bridge, turn right into Middle Slough, watch for the Franklin Boulevard bridge, and then look for the dock.

Sierra Region

From the Cascade volcanoes of Lassen Peak and Mount Shasta in the north to the 14,500-foot summit of Mount Whitney in the south, the Sierra Nevada is the dominant topographic feature of eastern California. The mountains collect deep winter snows and release them in spring and early summer. The snowmelt feeds the lakes and streams described in the following chapters. Spring is the time to enjoy whitewater. Wonderful summer weather is a great time to enjoy the lakes. Have fun!

Middle Fork Feather River between Sloat and Nelson Point (chapter 54).

48 Ahjumawi Lava Springs State Park

Within sight of Lassen Peak and Mount Shasta in northeastern California, these remote waters are fed by some of the world's largest spring systems. The fine lakeside campsites are only accessible by water.

Size: 4 miles long, 0.1 to 1 mile wide; 13+ miles of shoreline
Elevation: 3,300 feet
Average paddling time: 2 hours to 2+ days
Difficulty: Flatwater lake; suitable for beginners
Water source: Natural spring-fed lake stays at almost constant level.
Best season: Summer and autumn; open year-round
Land status: Private and public
Fees: State park fees required

Maps: USGS Fall River Mills, Timbered Crater; Ahjumawi Lava Springs State Park brochure
Craft: Canoes, kayaks, inflatables, shallow-draft boats
Contacts: Ahjumawi Lava Springs State Park: (530) 335-2777; parks.ca.gov
Special considerations: Because of the remote wilderness location, help is far off and you must be self-sufficient. Hiking the sharp, rugged lava rocks demands sturdy footwear. Remember that rattlesnakes live in the area. Powerboats use the adjacent lakes.

Put-in/Takeout Information

Rat Farm (N41 6.005' / W121 24.720'): From Redding follow CA 299 east to the small town of McArthur. Turn north onto Main Street, past the fairgrounds; cross over to the east side of the canal and follow the unpaved road to the site of the Rat Farm, some 3.7 miles from town. This is the only public launch site on Horr Pond and Big Lake.
Shuttle: None

Overview

Tucked into the far northeast corner of Shasta County, Ahjumawi sounds like paradise revisited. The state park brochure calls Ahjumawi "a place of exceptional, even primeval beauty." Lava beds collect and store snowmelt for summer-long release to many crystalline springs feeding Big Lake, Horr Pond, Ja She Creek, and the Tule and Little Tule Rivers. Ahjumawi is a wonderful place to hike, view wildlife, fish, and explore by paddle and foot.

You can only reach the park by shallow-draft boat. No public roads exist, and the park prohibits private motor vehicles. Outside the park, motorboats ply the lakes and rivers.

Ahjumawi State Park comprises 6,000 acres and includes Horr Pond and the land north of the lakes. Most of the land to the south of Tule River, Little Tule River, and Big Lake is private property, as is the land east of Big Lake.

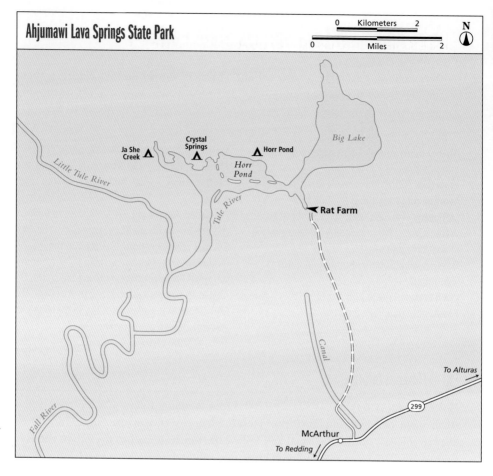

Three primitive campsites are found at each of three campgrounds, with nearby vault toilets. Camp only at these campsites, and keep fires within the fire rings. Water is available from the nearby springs, but you should purify it before using. Soft, silty lake bottoms discourage swimming. Pets should be left at home.

At 3,300 feet in elevation, the summer days are hot and the evenings cool. As in many other areas, the wind will be calm in the morning and strengthen in the afternoon. One advantage of the location is that these lakes are not subject to the Central Valley wind machine that blows up the Sierra canyons much of the summer. On the other hand, the breeze helps keep the mosquitoes away.

The Paddling

Put in at the Rat Farm, a Pacific Gas & Electric site for boat launching. Then paddle 0.5 mile north along a slim finger of water to Big Lake. Big Lake opens to the east and north. The campgrounds are to the west. Horr Pond campsite is closest, a paddle of a little over 1 mile. Along the way are tiny, tree-studded islets with aquamarine bays.

The islets enclose Horr Pond. This is a great place to try fishing for trout and bass. Crystal Springs is a 1.2-mile hike by land or a 1.5-mile paddle from Horr Pond camp. Crystal and Ja She Creek campsites are in the headwater springs of Ja She Creek.

These springs are famous for their rock fish traps used by the Ahjumawi Indians. The rock formations are still there. Fish swim to the uprising water of the springs to spawn. Native Americans built small rock walls that would block the exits, then they could easily spear or grab the fish.

With bald eagles and ospreys gliding overhead, marshy shores stalked by great blue herons, and Mount Shasta shining in the distance, this place "where the waters come together" will make you want to explore every part of it.

49 Eagle Lake

The second-largest natural lake in California is located where the Cascade Mountains and Sierra Nevada meet the high Modoc Plateau. Wildlife and fish abound at this huge remote gem bounded by mountain forest and high desert.

Size: 13 miles long, up to 5 miles wide; 60 miles of shoreline; surface area: 25,000 acres
Elevation: 5,100 feet
Average paddling time: 2 hours to 3 days
Difficulty: Large lake; open-water expertise required
Best season: May to Oct
Land status: BLM, USDA Forest Service, and private
Fees: Required at some sites
Maps: USGS Pike's Point, Gallatin Peak, Troxel Point, Spalding Tract; Lassen National Forest
Craft: Canoes, kayaks, sail craft, powerboats

Contacts: Lassen National Forest, Eagle Lake District: (530) 257-4188; fs.usda.gov/lassen. BLM Eagle Lake Field Office: (530) 257-0456; blm.gov/office/eagle-lake-field-office. Eagle Lake Campgrounds & Marina: (530) 825-3454; eaglelakerecreationarea.com. National Recreation Reservation Service: (877) 444-6777; recreation.gov (camping reservations). Eagle Lake Fishing: eaglelakefishing.net.
Special considerations: Eagle Lake is notorious for gentle morning breezes that blow into afternoon gales pushing 3-foot waves. Other hazards are springtime cold water, occasional summer thunderstorms, and large powerboats.

Put-in/Takeout Information

In recent years, Eagle Lake's surface elevation has changed up and down. Check the Eagle Lake Fishing website (eaglelakefishing.net/gallery/) for recent pictures of launch ramps.

Eagle Lake Marina (N40 33.440' / W120 46.871'): From CA 36, turn north onto Lassen CR A-1 (Eagle Lake Road) about 3 miles west of the CA 139 junction in Susanville. Follow CR A-1 north for 12 miles to the south shore of the lake. Gallatin, Merrill, Christie, and Marina Campgrounds and day-use areas facilitate hand-launch boats. The marina has a concrete launch behind a protective breakwater. All roads are paved.

Spalding Tract (N40 39.855' / W120 46.386'): From the south shore follow Eagle Lake Road (CR A-1) around the west side of the lake to the Spalding Tract turnoff. Go to the lakeshore, then turn north to the marina and launch ramp.

Rocky Point East (N40 40.274' / W120 44.740'): From CA 139 north of Eagle Lake, turn west on Eagle Lake Road (CR A-1) and go approximately 4 miles. Turn onto Lakeside Drive into the Bucks Bay subdivision. Go west on Lakeside Drive to Rocky Point Road. Go south on Rocky Point Road along the shoreline to the BLM Rocky Point unimproved campground. No water, no trash removal, but there is a vault toilet.

Rocky Point West (N40 40.754' / W120 45.431'): From CA 139 north of Eagle Lake, turn west on Eagle Lake Road (CR A-1) and go approximately 6.5 miles. At the bottom of the long hill, near the water tank, turn south on a road that quickly turns to dirt. Go south along the shore for about 0.7 mile to the gravel access. No drinking water, trash pickup, or toilets.

Stones Landing (N40 43.065' / W120 43.334'): From CR A-1 at the northwest corner of the lake, take the side road to the docks at Stones Landing.

Shuttle: Varies from none to 1 hour

Overview

Cascade Mountain forests, Great Basin Desert, and the Modoc Plateau all come together at Eagle Lake. California's second-largest natural lake is a closed basin, meaning a few streams flow in, but no streams flow out. As a result, the lake has accumulated salts that make the water alkaline.

Eagle Lake has had some unusual ups and downs. In the late 1800s the lake rose, flooding ranches and farmlands due to above-average precipitation. In June 1889 strong earthquakes shook the lake. Nearby springs increased their output, but Eagle Lake dropped 2 feet. By 1916 the lake had risen 16 feet (the highest level in 400 years according to tree ring studies). It was like some subterranean outlet had been closed. Bly's Tunnel was constructed to drain lake water to drier eastern valleys. In 1921 the fault shook again. By 1936 the tunnel was abandoned, the lake level having dropped due to the tunnel, drought, and subterranean outflow. Later the lake rose for more than thirty years. During the wet winter of 1983 the lake rose so high that the 1984 Olympic torch route was changed. The tunnel has been intermittently reactivated; dry winters ensued, and the lake level again dropped in 2012. The five-year California drought dropped the levels even more. Some low-water launch ramps were built.

Fisheries biologists believe Eagle Lake trout to be a subspecies adapted to the lake's alkaline waters, where no other trout will survive. The popular trout quickly grow to 18 inches long and weigh 3 to 5 pounds. Two fish per day is the limit.

Diverse habitat supports a wonderful variety of wildlife. Around its shores is located one of the last colonies of nesting ospreys and the largest nesting colony of western and eared grebes in the western United States. You can expect to see ospreys, white pelicans, western grebes, ducks, and bald eagles in summer. Mule deer are common, and pronghorns visit the basin. Summer days are warm, but nights are cool. Spring and autumn days have fewer motorboats and cooler weather. Early-morning breezes often become blustery. The winds may die down toward evening.

Lassen National Forest and the BLM provide many campgrounds around the lake. Forest service campgrounds are on the south shore. BLM offers one developed campground at the north shore and allows shoreline camping for fully self-contained campers at Rocky Point and along CA 139 at least 200 feet from water sources. Most campgrounds open by mid-May. Fees vary with location and season. Campers may use forest service lands along existing roadways as allowed by local ranger districts.

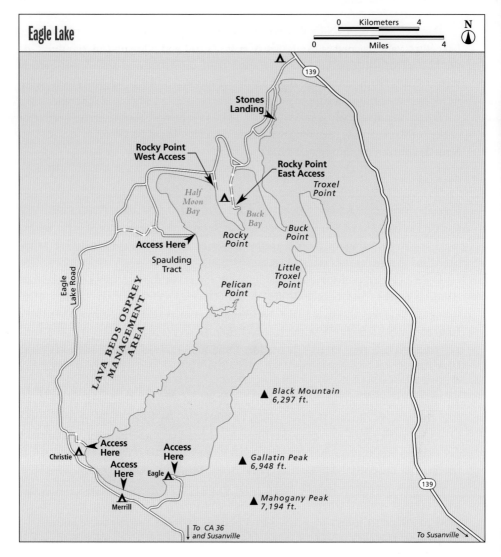

Eagle Lake

Use existing fire rings, fire pans, or stoves. The state, forest service, and BLM require campfire permits for any open burning except in designated campgrounds. Other seasonal fire restrictions may apply.

During summer 2018, the Whaleback Fire burned 18,700 acres above the west shore of the lake.

The Paddling

Early morning and evening are quiet times to view wildlife and enjoy smooth water. Eagle Lake is large, and the winds do not allow paddling most afternoons except in protected areas, so plan your exploration accordingly.

Several long peninsulas divide the lake into large bays that are like separate lakes. The largest and deepest is the southern bay. Merrill and Christie Campgrounds are the nicest developed locations around the lake. Merrill is popular with the fishing motorboat set, since the shore is smooth and the campsites are close by. Christie is more wooded and a better starting point to explore the southwestern shoreline.

The 5.5 miles of rugged shoreline from Christie Beach to Pelican Point offer many small inlets and points to explore. Along the southern third, Brockman Flat Lava Beds come down to the water's edge. An osprey management area contains this shoreline, including Pelican Point. At higher lake levels, Pelican Point becomes an island. North of Pelican Point, the lake is less than 20 feet deep.

Spalding Tract residential development occupies 2 miles of lakeshore in Half Moon Bay. The bay's west and north shorelines are marshy, with aquatic grass growing 100 yards into the shallow lake. In sharp contrast, Rocky Point's west shore is steep lava rock down to the water. A dirt road extends along the northern 0.7 mile.

East of Rocky Point is Buck Bay. A dirt road to the BLM camping area and fishing access leads down the west side. The topography shelters the 0.8-mile-wide bay on three sides, but the mouth is exposed to southwest winds. From the north end to the tip of Buck Point is 2.4 miles. The channel between Buck and Troxel Points is 0.6 mile wide. It leads to the shallow, northernmost lobe of the lake. The shorelines are sandy, with grass growing from the shallows closest to shore. Little of the shoreline is appealing for camping.

The most interesting views are along the eastern sides of the southern basin. Black Mountain rises 1,100 feet above the water, and Gallatin Peak summits at 6,948 feet. Here the lake reaches its deepest point, more than 70 feet. This shoreline is home to the California State University Chico Biological Station and the Lassen County Office of Education Youth Camp.

50 Juniper Lake

In the southeast corner of Lassen Volcanic National Park, this mountain gem sparkles beside the Lassen Wilderness Area.

Size: 1.5 miles long, 0.8 mile wide; 5 miles of shoreline
Elevation: 6,792 feet
Average paddling time: 2 to 4 hours
Difficulty: Easy, small lake
Best season: July to Sept; closed due to snow the rest of the year
Land status: Matrix of private land and national park
Fees: National park fees required

Maps: USGS Mount Harkness; Lassen Volcanic National Park; Lassen National Forest
Craft: Canoes, kayaks, other nonmotorized craft
Contacts: Lassen Volcanic National Park: (530) 595-4480; nps.gov/lavo
Special considerations: Cold mountain water offsets Juniper Lake's charms all summer long. Afternoon winds can make paddling difficult. Avoid being on the lake when summer thunderstorms threaten.

Put-in/Takeout Information

Juniper Lake Campground (N40 27.043' / W121 17.682'): From CA 36 in Chester, turn north onto Feather River Drive. Follow the signs 13 miles to Juniper Lake. The first 6 miles are paved before changing to a steep gravel road. Lassen Volcanic National Park advises against trailers. Carry boats 100 yards to the lake.

This paddler enjoys the high-mountain air and crystal-clear water of Juniper Lake in Lassen Volcanic National Park.

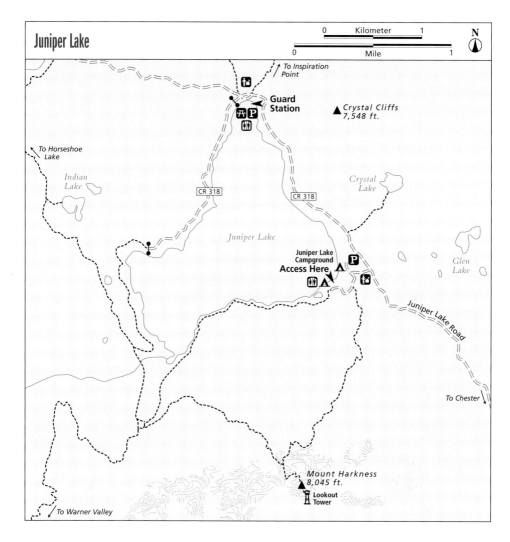

Juniper Lake Guard Station (N40 27.981' / W121 18.495'): The guard station is 1.4 miles farther. The road is right beside the water, with good parking at the adjacent trailhead.

Overview

Juniper Lake lies on a vast lava plateau more than 1 mile above sea level. The lake is accessible after the snow melts. The Tahoe-clear water is fed by snowmelt from the surrounding peaks stretching above 7,500 feet. Lassen's 10,457-foot peak is easily visible 11 miles to the west. About one-third of the shoreline is designated wilderness area. Private cabins blend in with the northwest shore. The nearby trailheads offer attractive hiking trails to other lakes and mountains.

Lassen Volcanic National Park is a fee area. The park requires reservations for group camping at Juniper Lake Campground. Depending on snowmelt, cars may be left some distance from the designated campsites. Bring drinking water, or be prepared to treat local sources. Lakeside camping is prohibited. Use provided metal lockers to protect food from bears.

The Paddling

Paddling on Juniper Lake is like floating above shimmering blue and violet crystals, halfway between the earth and the sky. Streamers of sunlight stab to the depths. Even in shallow areas, the clarity of the water makes the true depth hard to judge.

To the east, the heights of Eagle Cliffs overlook the lake. To the south, snow drapes the slopes of Mount Harkness for much of the summer. Saddle Mountain guards the west. From the eastern half of the lake, Lassen Peak protrudes above the richly forested hills.

With its perimeter of only 5 miles, you can easily paddle around the lake in 3 hours. Early mornings often provide mirror-smooth water that clearly shows the bottom features. As the sky changes hue, the colors of the lake change too. The afternoons offer warm sunshine, which is quickly offset by a dip in the lake. Beware of afternoon breezes that become strong winds. The park service requires that a personal flotation device be worn by everyone floating on the lake.

51 Mountain Meadows Reservoir (Walker Lake)

Hidden in a remote mountain basin east of Lake Almanor, this big lake offers fine fishing under a big sky dominated by Lassen Peak.

Size: 6.5 miles long, 1.5 miles wide; 5,800 acres
Elevation: 5,046 feet
Average paddling time: 1 hour to 1 day
Difficulty: Large lake; open-water skills required
Best season: May to Oct
Land status: Private
Fees: Not at this writing

Maps: USGS Westwood East, Westwood West; Lassen National Forest
Craft: Canoes, kayaks, powerboats, sit-on-tops
Contacts: Lassen National Forest: (530) 257-2151; fs.usda.gov/lassen
Special considerations: Natural hazards are springtime cold water, occasional summer thunderstorms, and winds on a large open lake.

Put-in/Takeout Information

Indian Ole Dam (N40 17.033' / W121 1.473'): From Chester travel 10 miles east on CA 36 to the junction with CA 147. Go south on CA 147 toward Clear Creek; turn east on Lassen CR A21 and continue toward Westwood about 0.8 mile. Turn south on a well-used gravel road. (If you pass the Lassen Power Plant, you have gone too far east.) Follow the forks southeastward, cross railroad tracks, then bear left, staying on the north side of the creek to Indian Ole Dam and a dirt parking area.

East shore access (N40 15.640' / W120 55.589'): From Westwood go east on CA 36, turn south on Lassen CR A21 for 0.3 mile, then turn east onto Old Town Road. After several miles, Old Town Road passes through a big wooden arch, skirts the marshes, and continues past a quarry. Past the quarry 1.6 miles, turn west around a hill to the lake.

Shuttle: Optional, one way about 13 miles (30 minutes)

Overview

Built by the Pacific Gas & Electric Company to supplement water supplies for the North Fork Feather River hydropower projects, Mountain Meadows Reservoir is wide and shallow. Dyer Mountain, an extension of Keddie Ridge, has been proposed as a destination resort and ski area. The only recreational facility is the launch ramp adjacent to the Indian Ole Dam. Private lands surround the lake. Summer days are warm, but nights are cool. Spring and autumn days have fewer motorboats and cooler weather. Bring your fishing rod.

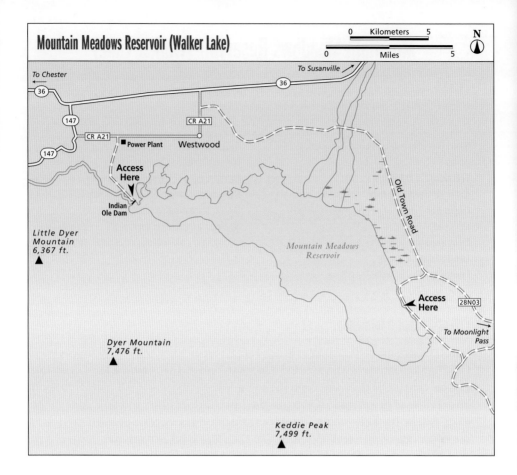

Mountain Meadows Reservoir (Walker Lake)

To Chester

To Susanville

Power Plant   Westwood

Access Here

Indian Ole Dam

Little Dyer Mountain 6,367 ft.

Mountain Meadows Reservoir

Old Town Road

Access Here   28N03

To Moonlight Pass

Dyer Mountain 7,476 ft.

Keddie Peak 7,499 ft.

The Paddling

Paddling this big shallow lake under azure skies is a delight. The western end consists of several deeper bays up to 0.5 mile across. To the east, the lake opens dramatically. Much of the shoreline is shallow, inundated grasslands. Four miles of the northeast shore are marsh. With these conditions, expect to get your feet wet and muddy if you land along the eastern two-thirds of the lake.

In mid-lake the scenery is grand. To the south, pine-covered slopes rise to 7,490-foot Keddie Ridge. To the northwest, 10,457-foot Lassen Peak dominates the scene. The extreme eastern end of the lake is accessible from a gravel road skirting the water. The carry is 100 yards between the cow patties. Early morning and evening are quiet times to view wildlife and enjoy smooth water. Plan your actions in case strong winds pick up with thundershowers.

52 Antelope Lake

Ample camping, boating, and fishing are available in this remote mountain setting where the Sierras meet the interior high Modoc Plateau.

Size: Approximately 3 miles long, irregular shape; surface area: 930 acres
Elevation: 5,025 feet
Average paddling time: 1 to 4 hours
Difficulty: Easy, small lake
Best season: May to Oct
Land status: Plumas National Forest lands
Fees: Yes
Maps: USGS Antelope Lake; Plumas National Forest

Craft: Canoes, kayaks, powerboats
Contacts: Plumas National Forest: (530) 283-2050; fs.usda.gov/main/plumas. National Recreation Reservation Service: (877) 444-6777; recreation.gov (camping reservations).
Special considerations: Powerboats and personal watercraft are the primary hazards. Other hazards include springtime cold water, occasional summer thunderstorms, and visits by bears in the campgrounds.

Put-in/Takeout Information

Launch ramps (N40 11.168' / W120 35.526' and N40 11.085' / W120 34.824'): From CA 89, 6 miles north of the junction of CA 70 and CA 89, take Arlington Road (CR A22) east to Taylorsville. Continue to Genessee and then follow Indian Creek Road to Antelope Lake (27 miles from CA 89). Hand-launch boats can put in at Lone Rock and Long Point Campgrounds, the day-use areas, or the boat ramp on the north shore. All roads are paved.

Overview

Located on Upper Indian Creek, Antelope Lake is the northernmost reservoir of the State Water Project. Its recreational features include four campgrounds, day-use areas, and ramps for trailer and car-top boats. The campgrounds have piped water, flush or vault toilets, stoves or fire rings, tables with benches, and parking spaces. The USDA Forest Service permits camping only at the campsites. Antelope Recreation Area is a fee area.

The California Department of Fish and Wildlife stocks the lake with rainbow and brook trout. Summer days are warm, but nights are cool. Spring and autumn days have fewer motorboats and cooler weather.

Although wildfires have scorched the hills bordering the shore, appealing wildflower displays have emerged and green vegetation remains around the lake.

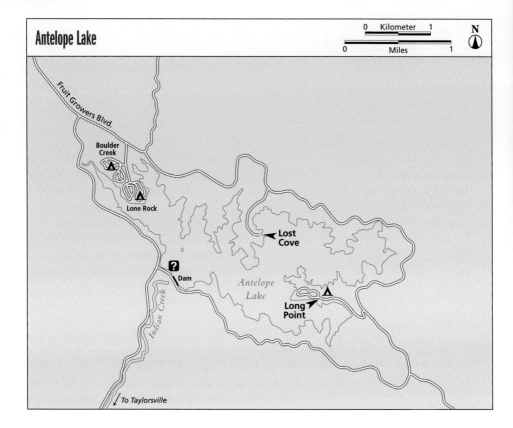

The Paddling

Paddling is a delight along the many bays and peninsulas of Antelope Lake's 15-mile shoreline. Early morning and evening are quiet times to view wildlife, enjoy smooth water, and visit several islands. Later, when the motorboaters emerge, there are many sandy places along the shoreline to fish, picnic, and swim. The irregular shape of the lake makes it easy to paddle from the middle of the water.

53 Round Valley Reservoir

Tucked away in the Plumas National Forest near Greenville is this small, quiet, picturesque high-country lake with good warm-water fishing.

Size: 1.2 miles long, 0.5 mile wide; oval shape
Elevation: 4,470 feet
Average paddling time: 2 to 4 hours
Difficulty: Easy, small lake
Best season: May to Oct, weather permitting.
Land status: Matrix of private and USDA Forest Service
Fees: Forest service fees required
Maps: USGS Crescent Mills; Plumas National Forest

Craft: Canoes, kayaks, other small craft
Contacts: Plumas National Forest: (530) 283-2050: fs.usda.gov/main/plumas
Special considerations: Snowmelt feeds Round Valley Reservoir, so expect cold water in early summer. Afternoon winds can make paddling difficult. Avoid being on the lake when summer thunderstorms threaten.

Put-in/Takeout Information

Round Valley Reservoir Day Use (N40 6.625' / W120 57.292'): From CA 89 south of Greenville, turn west onto Hideaway Road at the Greenville town line. Look for the "Round Valley Lake 3 miles" sign. Follow Hideaway Road parallel to the railroad tracks to Round Valley Road. Turn left and climb along the paved, steep, crooked Round Valley Road to Round Valley Reservoir. Signs advise against trailers. Turn left at the dam.

Overview

Round Valley Reservoir exudes relaxation. Lily pads and algae float on much of the surface; people fish for bass, bluegill, and catfish. The Indian Valley Chamber of Commerce claims that the California record for largemouth black bass was a 14-pounder taken from Round Valley in 1948. Even when we visited on the Fourth of July, it was uncrowded.

The 4,500-foot elevation offers cool evenings. The pine- and fir-covered hillsides reach above 5,500 feet in the lovely Sierra-Cascade setting of the Plumas National Forest.

A USDA Forest Service picnic area is the only public launch site. No overnight camping is allowed. Swimming may be discouraged, since it's a public water supply for the town of Greenville.

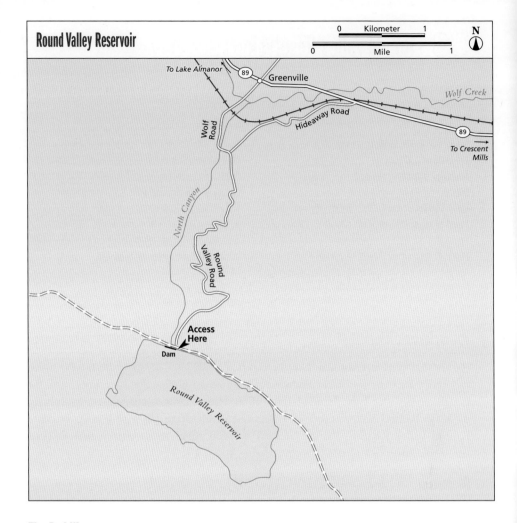

The Paddling

With a perimeter of less than 4 miles, the lake is an easy distance to paddle in 2 hours. One can explore the lily pads of the north and west shores where the bass may lie, or paddle the open water. Early mornings usually offer the quietest water. The afternoons offer warm sunshine. Beware of afternoon breezes that become winds.

54 Feather River, Middle Fork—Sloat to Nelson Point

A National Wild and Scenic River, this moderate whitewater run drops from expansive mountain meadows into a remote, richly forested canyon.

Length: 8 miles

Average paddling time: 3 to 5 hours

Difficulty: Intermediate whitewater skills required

Rapids: Class: II+; one Class III

Average gradient: 30 feet per mile

Optimal flow: 500 to 1,500 cfs

Flow gauge: Estimated "below Sloat"

Water source: Natural runoff

Best season: Apr through June

Land status: Private and USDA Forest Service

Fees: None

Maps: USGS Blue Nose Mountain, Johnsville; Plumas National Forest

Craft: Whitewater canoes, kayaks, inflatables

Contacts: Plumas National Forest: (530) 283-0555; fs.usda.gov/main/plumas. Plumas County Tourism Recreation and Hospitality Council: plumascounty.org.

Special considerations: Since the Middle Fork Feather is runnable during and soon after snowmelt, the water is always cold. Do not miss the takeout; the waterway leads to a remote Class V canyon with few takeouts.

Put-in/Takeout Information

Put-in at Sloat (N39 51.629' / W120 43.651'): From Quincy go east 2.9 miles on CA 70 and CA 89 to the stoplight at the Safeway store. Continue on CA 70/89 another 14.3 miles. Turn south and go 1.2 miles across the railroad tracks and the river. Almost immediately turn left onto FSR 23N08.a. Put in 0.25 mile upstream of the bridge.

Takeout at Red Bridge/Nelson Point (N39 51.570' / W120 51.034'): Go back toward Quincy 11.4 miles and turn south onto FSR 120 toward La Porte. The road leads 7.8 miles beside spacious meadows, over the hills and through the woods to the river crossing at Red Bridge. On the north side of the bridge is a small day-use area with an easy takeout and parking next to the river. Red Bridge Campground has five campsites plus toilets and is perched above the river's south side near the site of Nelson Point.

Shuttle: 20 miles (40 minutes)

Overview

Designated in 1969 as one of the original nine National Wild and Scenic Rivers, the Middle Fork Feather River exhibits spacious meadows, deep, forested canyons, and great trout fisheries. The Union Pacific Railroad follows the right bank but is generally unobtrusive and after 3 miles disappears through the Spring Garden Tunnel. Before the canyon's national designation, engineers studied it for stair-stepped

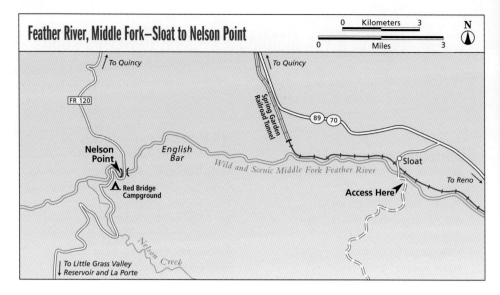

Feather River, Middle Fork–Sloat to Nelson Point

hydroelectric power development like the now concrete-girdled North Fork Feather River.

Unlike many Sierra rivers that originate as steep snowfields on high Sierra ridges, the Middle Fork Feather originates between 4,000 and 5,000 feet. The broad pastures and meadows of the Sierra and Mohawk Valleys soak up copious winter snows and slowly release the moisture to the river all spring and early summer.

I've run this reach as early as April and as late as June. Recent rainfall and snowmelt add to the whitewater challenge. At low summer flows, you bump through the riffles, float the pools, and enjoy the scenery.

Note: Do not confuse this run with the very remote and extremely difficult canyon from Nelson Point to Milsap Bar.

The Paddling

At Sloat, river left provides a convenient gravel bar put-in. The opposite bank is steeply cut cobbles. Shake the kinks out quickly, because the water converges at the first turn to form a chute with bouncy waves and a strong eddy on river right.

The run continues with Class II gravel bar rapids at every turn. It is busy enough that you don't readily notice that the pine-covered terraces are dipping into a steeper canyon. After 1.5 miles, both banks climb into fir-draped slopes. About the place that the railroad seeks a flatter grade through a tunnel, the river steepens to provide some spicy bedrock rapids. With holes and boulders to negotiate, at 600 cfs or more, some of the rapids may rate Class III.

Three miles upstream from the Red Bridge takeout, the river has cut a canyon 1,800 feet deep. Below English Bar the rapids ease a little and the pools lengthen, so enjoy the tranquility. Soon Red Bridge comes into view. *Note:* **This is the takeout; there is no alternative downstream!**

55 Little Grass Valley Reservoir

Rimmed with campgrounds, this isolated reservoir provides boating and fishing in a scenic, forested mountain location.

Size: 3 miles long, 0.5 mile wide at the narrowest point; surface area: 1,930 acres
Elevation: 5,046 feet
Average paddling time: 1 hour to 1 day
Difficulty: Lake for beginners
Best season: June through Oct
Land status: Private and USDA Forest Service
Fees: Forest service fees required
Maps: USGS American House, La Porte; Plumas National Forest
Craft: Canoes, kayaks, powerboats

Contacts: Plumas National Forest: (530) 534-6500; fs.usda.gov/main/plumas. National Recreation Reservation Service: (877) 444-6777; recreation.gov (campground reservations).
Special considerations: Powerboats and personal watercraft are the primary hazards. Natural hazards are springtime cold water, occasional summer thunderstorms, and isolation from communities with hospitals.

Put-in/Takeout Information

Three launch ramps are available: (N39 43.706' / W121 0.738'), (N39 43.338' / W120 59.044'), and (N39 43.512' / W120 58.413'). From Marysville follow CA 20 east 11.5 miles; turn north onto Marysville Road (CR E21) toward Browns Valley and La Porte. Continue 55 winding miles through Browns Valley, Challenge, and Strawberry Valley to La Porte. Follow the signs 2 more miles to Little Grass Valley Reservoir and a paved road around the lake.

From Reno or Quincy, take CA 70 to FSR 120 (La Porte Road), about 3 miles east of Quincy. Take this mountain road 7.8 miles past picturesque meadows, over forested hills, and down into the Middle Fork Feather River Canyon. Cross this National Wild and Scenic River, then ascend steeply for 20 miles. Pass Pilot Peak (7,457 feet) and follow intermittently paved FR 22N60 to Little Grass Valley Reservoir.
Shuttle: None

Overview

In the 1850s, gold miners were snowbound at La Porte. Some Norwegians made long skis steered with a pole. These led to some of the earliest ski races in the US. Today the deep snows around La Porte still attract winter snowshoeing and snowmobiling.

Some private cabins adjoin the road and the lake from La Porte toward the dam. Except for these 2 miles of private property, the Plumas National Forest provides public access to the lake. Running Deer, Red Feather, Little Beaver, Wyandotte, Peninsula Tent, and Black Rock Campgrounds have tables, water, and toilets. They permit camping only at the 320 designated campsites. Little Grass Valley Reservoir is a fee area.

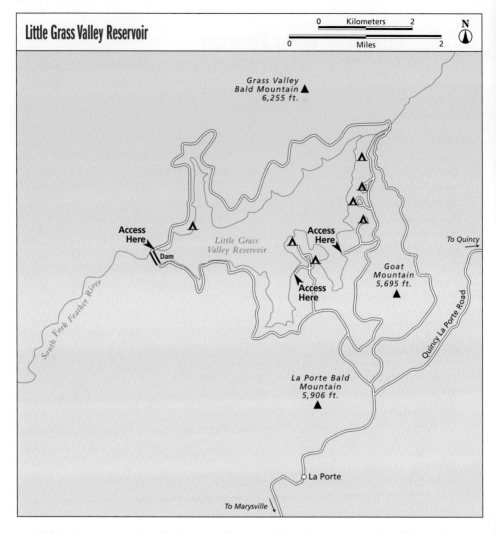

Fishing is very popular for German brown and rainbow trout and catfish. Swimming is pleasant at the day-use beaches. Summer days are warm, but nights are cool. Spring and autumn days have fewer motorboats and cooler weather. Campgrounds are open from June 1 through October 31, snow permitting.

The Paddling

The long arms of this clear lake with 16 miles of shoreline are a delight to paddle. The bare face of Grass Valley Bald Mountain looks down from the north. Ospreys float overhead and maintain a nest in a snag on the high ground above Wyandotte Campground. The red fir growing along the rocky shoreline is a sign of the cold winters.

You can easily paddle the length of the lake and return in a few hours. Plan a full day to carefully explore all the shoreline. Early morning and evening are quiet times to view wildlife, enjoy the smooth surface water, and try your luck fishing.

56 Lake Spaulding

Easily accessible from I-80, this high-mountain reservoir is in a gigantic granite bowl that captures Sierra sunlight, exhilarating air, and liquid snow. Access is usually open mid-May through October.

Size: 2 miles long, 0.5 mile wide; 9 miles of shoreline
Elevation: 5,011 feet
Average paddling time: 2 to 4 hours
Difficulty: Large lake; open-water skills required
Best season: Summer and autumn
Land status: Public
Fees: Yes
Maps: USGS Blue Canyon, Cisco Grove; Tahoe National Forest
Craft: Canoes, kayaks, paddleboards, sit-on-tops, powerboats

Contacts: Pacific Gas & Electric Company: recreation.pge.com
Special considerations: The potential hazards of Lake Spaulding are easily avoidable. Buoys mark the discharge from the Rim Powerhouse. Motorcraft prefer the middle of the lake, so stay close to the shore. Summer afternoons get windy. When snowmelt fills the South Fork of the Yuba River in May and June, the torrent roars down the cataract through the narrow gorge and into the lake. Stay out of the gorge if the current is strong—the turbulence can easily upset a boat.

Put-in/Takeout Information

Lake Spaulding boat ramp (N39 19.357' / W120 38.036'): From I-80, exit at CA 20. Go west on CA 20 for 2 miles, then turn right at the sign marked "Lake Spaulding Recreation Area." For 0.7 mile, follow the narrow paved road past the Pacific Gas & Electric employee houses and the camping area to the large paved parking area above the boat ramp. Fee area.
Shuttle: None

Overview

Lake Spaulding practically shouts for paddlers to visit. The skies are normally deep blue and the water sparkling clear. Mountain ridges soar 2,000 feet above lake level. It is easily accessible in a spectacular setting. Lake Spaulding is a major storage reservoir for PG&E's Drum-Spaulding Hydroelectric Project. Pines and open granite surround the lake.

The coves and inlets on the east side of the lake provide some seclusion, particularly on weekdays. Smooth granite slabs make comfortable spots to soak up the brilliant Sierra sunshine. By midsummer, Castle Peak's crystalline snowmelt warms enough for enjoyable swimming. The high elevation, reflection from the granite and water, and bright sun can quickly cause sunburn.

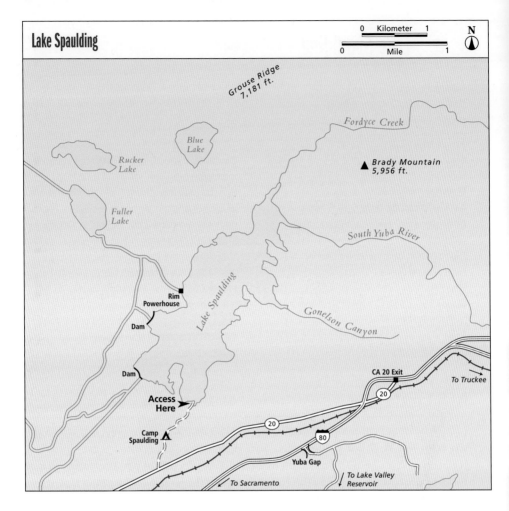

Lake Spaulding

Grouse Ridge
7,181 ft.

Fordyce Creek

Blue
Lake

Rucker
Lake

▲ Brady Mountain
5,956 ft.

Fuller
Lake

South Yuba River

Rim
Powerhouse

Lake Spaulding

Dam

Gonelson Canyon

Dam

CA 20 Exit

To Truckee

Access
Here

20

Camp
Spaulding

20

80

Yuba Gap

To Sacramento

To Lake Valley
Reservoir

The west side of the lake offers great views, particularly the point immediately south of Rim Powerhouse. Grouse Ridge parallels the north side of the lake. Six miles to the east, Old Man Mountain is a steep granite crag that seems to be sheared on the north side. Four miles to the southeast, several antennas identify Cisco Butte. You can find the transcontinental railroad and I-80, but they are not intrusive by either sight or sound.

PG&E operates this fee area with drive-in and walk-in camping areas near the boat-launching area. Shoreline camping is prohibited.

The Paddling

The boat ramp provides an easy put-in. By paddling along the west side, you can easily look into the coves on the east side of the lake. It is a quick way of locating the neighbors.

Three guys and a dog enjoy a fun outing paddling a tree on Lake Spaulding.

Alternatively, following the eastern shoreline is enticing, since new surprises appear around each point and inlet. Some coves are small. Zebra-like stripes coat the granite. The cove near Gonelson Canyon has permanent islands and gentle slopes among the pines at the far end. As you continue northeast toward the head of the lake, Grouse Ridge dominates the northern skyline. A second, long cove invites inspection.

Beyond, ice and water have chiseled a long, narrow cleft in the granite. This is the South Yuba River. Beware during high runoff; the current in the gorge has potentially hazardous turbulence in the recently thawed water. Late in summer, the river dwindles and the lake level drops, so paddling far up this mini-gorge to the cataract is easy. The rock walls magnify the sound of water flowing under great boulders. Further exploration would require a rock scramble up the steep, algae-covered slabs of granite. The pool above is pretty, but the abundant algae hint at pollutants from upstream communities. The most enticing view is looking down the gorge to the lake.

At the north end of the lake is Fordyce Creek. In marked contrast to the South Yuba, Fordyce is broad and boulder-strewn. Even in late summer, Fordyce, Sterling, and Meadow Lakes provide ample flows down Fordyce Creek into Lake Spaulding.

If you follow the west shore back toward the launch ramp, be sure to turn around and enjoy the view of the mountains to the east.

57 Lake Valley Reservoir

Secluded Lake Valley Reservoir is a short 2 miles from I-80. This bowl with forested hills was spared by the wildfires of 2001 and 2018. Such a quiet mountain lake is great family fun.

Size: 1.8 miles long, 0.25 mile wide; 4.5 miles of shoreline
Elevation: 5,786 feet
Average paddling time: A few hours
Difficulty: Small lake; for beginners
Best season: Summer and autumn
Land status: Public and private
Fees: Forest service fees required
Maps: USGS Cisco Grove; Tahoe National Forest

Craft: Canoes, kayaks, paddleboards, sail craft, powerboats
Contacts: Tahoe National Forest: (530) 265-4531, fs.usda.gov/tahoe. Pacific Gas & Electric Company: recreation.pge.com.
Special considerations: The hazards of Lake Valley Reservoir are few. Although motorboats are allowed, signs prohibit waterskiing and personal watercraft. In spring and early summer, the water is liquid snow—very cold.

Put-in/Takeout Information

Silvertip Picnic Area (N39 18.151' / W120 35.878'): From I-80, exit at Yuba Gap. Go south on Lake Valley Road, bearing right at the Y by the big tree. Stay on Lake Valley Road to the junction at 1.4 miles. Go left on the unpaved Mears Meadow Road (FSR 19) to Silvertip Picnic Area and a concrete boat ramp. The total distance from I-80 is 1.8 miles.
Shuttle: None

Overview

Peaceful Lake Valley Reservoir invites family outings. The lakeshore varies from rocky to grassy banks. Dense forests surround the lake below ridgetops rising 500 to 1,000 feet above the water. Lake Valley Reservoir is a component of Pacific Gas & Electric's Drum-Spaulding Hydroelectric Project.

Glacier-polished granite adorns two islands that are great for sunbathing, fishing, and midsummer swimming. Sometimes stinging yellow jackets disturb shoreline visitors. The high elevation, reflection from the granite and water, and bright sun can quickly cause sunburn.

A major feature on the west shore of the lake is Sky Mountain Camp. The camp's summer program offers canoeing and other aquatic activities.

Pacific Gas & Electric operates Lodgepole Campground (fee area) near the end of Lake Valley Road west of the dam. Except at the campground, the shoreline is uncomfortably steep for camping.

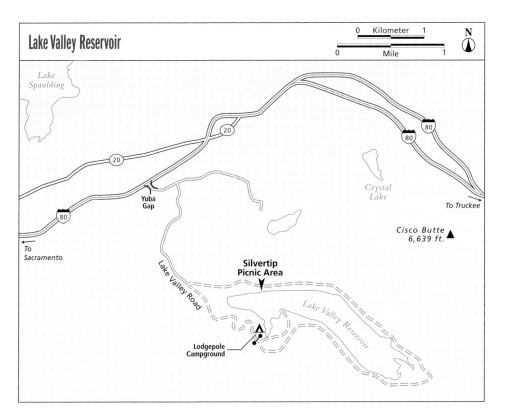

Lake Valley Reservoir

A major wildfire in 2001 spared the views from the lake but destroyed Eagle Mountain Nordic Center and Mountain Bike Park. A 2018 wildfire burned behind the ridge in the north fork of the North Fork American River canyon to the south of the lake. Snowflower Thousand Trails Camp remains.

The Paddling

The boat ramp at Silvertip Picnic Area (fee area) provides an easy put-in and takeout. The adjacent parking has space for a dozen vehicles. Since the shoreline is thickly forested, the best views are from the water. In the distance to the south, cliffs rise 600 feet above the lake. The shoreline at that end of the lake becomes grassy at lower water levels. Closer are two islands that invite exploring.

Immediately west of the put-in is the low dam created in 1911 by Pacific Gas & Electric. The 940-foot-long structure captures water that would otherwise flow into the Wild and Scenic North Fork American River. Instead, Pacific Gas & Electric diverts the water to the Drum-Spaulding Hydroelectric Project on the Bear and South Yuba Rivers. The dam offers the most direct lake access from the Lodgepole Campground.

Sky Mountain campers swarm around the northernmost island and the nearby cove. The camp's permanent buildings are prominent on the west shore. Farther to the south is another island of similar size. Both have lots of bare, polished rock. Close to the second island are a few rocky islets that emerge as fishing and swimming platforms at lower water levels.

Like other mountain lakes, the breeze increases in the late afternoon. Even if the wind becomes too strong, this lake is small, and roads encompass the reservoir as emergency takeouts.

As you return to the put-in, look around and enjoy the view of the mountains.

58 Bear River–Colfax to Dog Bar

The delightful Bear is not often run due to the rarity of adequate flows during warm weather. Enjoy the fun riffles when this intimate stream has high enough releases from Rollins Reservoir. If constructed, the proposed Centennial Dam would inundate this river reach.

Length: 4.6 miles
Average paddling time: 2 to 4 hours
Difficulty: Class II whitewater; intermediate skills required
Rapids: Whitewater gravel bars with brush
Average gradient: 17 feet per mile
Optimal flow: 430 to 1,000 cfs
Flow gauge: At CA 174 bridge
Water source: Rollins Reservoir minus Bear Canal diversions
Best season: Winter and spring
Land status: Mostly private, some public

Fees: Required at parks
Maps: USGS Colfax, Lake Combie; American Automobile Association, California Gold Country
Craft: Whitewater canoes, kayaks, inflatable kayaks, rafts
Contacts: Placer County Bear River Park & Campground: placer.ca.gov
Special considerations: Cold water flows from Rollins Reservoir. Brush grows on a few gravel bars. The last drop above Dog Bar is more demanding than the rest of the reach.

Put-in/Takeout Information

Ben Taylor Road near Colfax (N39 6.585' / W120 58.892'): Exit I-80 at Colfax and follow the signs to Old Colfax. Cross the railroad tracks and go straight onto Grass Valley Road. At the first stop sign turn left onto Rising Sun, which curves around the hill to an intersection with stop signs. Turn right onto Ben Taylor Road, which heads downhill past Colfax High School, bears left, and narrows. Cross the canal. Past the end of the county-maintained road is a flat with small gated roads leading downstream and upstream.

Bear River Park (N39 5.013' / W120 59.345'): From Colfax go west on Tokayana Way; turn right (north) and go downhill onto Milk Farm Road to the park. At the downstream end of the park, Plumtree Road returns uphill to Placer Hills Road. Fee area.

Dog Bar Road bridge (N39 3.757' / W121 0.178'): For the shuttle, follow Ben Taylor Road back to the stop signs. Go west on Tokayana Way, which becomes Placer Hills Road. Follow Placer Hills Road to Dog Bar Road. Go down the winding narrow Dog Bar Road to the bridge. The takeout is downstream on river right. No toilets and extremely limited roadside parking—car pool and shuttle driver recommended.
Shuttle: 8.7 miles (20 minutes)

Overview

Once heavily exploited, the Bear River has made an aesthetic comeback. Ridgetops along the Bear seem nearby, since the canyon is only 300 to 400 feet deep instead of the thousands of feet of other Sierra gold country canyons. Ponderosa pine, black oak, and Douglas fir clothe the slopes.

At Taylor Crossing, the mining equipment and mounds of black and white rock are relics from the gravel quarry days. Homes above the Nevada County riverbanks now enjoy canyon views. Nevada Irrigation District releases water from Rollins Reservoir to supply the Bear River Canal and Lake Combie. The portion going to Lake Combie flows in this river reach. Placer County operates the popular Bear River Park and Campground. Make camping reservations well in advance.

For many years, the River Touring Chapter of the Sierra Club paddled 4 more miles from Dog Bar to Lake Combie. The former takeout has been sold; the lands surrounding the lake are now private property, and a gravel operation gates and posts its roads against trespass. No public access from the Bear River is currently available near Lake Combie.

The Paddling

The delightful Bear is not often run due to the rarity of adequate flows during warm weather. Enjoy the river when the chance occurs.

At the put-in, the Bear runs clear, fast, and shallow. Almost immediately, an easy rapid provides warm-up practice and displays the degree of difficulty for most of this stretch. It is a good place to practice eddy turns and ferries across the wide stream. Downstream 0.25 mile, the Bear turns abruptly south through a brushy gravel bar. Most of the water initially slides to the right and center before it returns to the left. A clear channel starts near the head of the riffle on river left. Such conditions can change with any winter storm. A little farther, the river braids through more brush. The good news is that very little brush exists below here.

For over 1 mile the canyon runs due south. The winding channel provides frequent Class II gravel bar rapids. At 600 cfs you can easily find a channel. Occasional boulders provide fun sport and midstream eddies. Downstream, a hillside house and power lines with orange balls become prominent. They mark another rapid, maybe a little more difficult than the earlier ones.

This is also the upstream end of Placer County's Bear River Park at Plumtree Crossing. The popular campsites and day-use facilities stretch 1.5 miles along the left bank. Inner tubing, sunbathing, and gold panning are common activities. The day-use area is the midpoint of the boating run and an ideal intermediate put-in or takeout.

Past the Plumtree day-use area, the river curves into a long rapid. Downstream, the group campground sits on the left bank and some homes are set back on the right side. At a bouncy rapid, the river abruptly narrows to one-third of its earlier width.

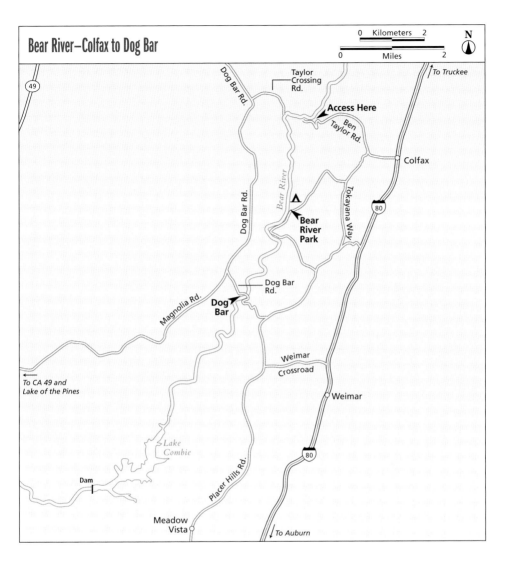

Then the river turns westward and enters a mini-gorge, and the rapids become a challenge to open canoes.

The pièce de résistance of the run is a drop between boulders into a hole only one and one-half boat lengths from a vertical wall at right angles to the channel. A small eddy on the left provides a place to land and inspect the drop. Ledges clutter river right. The center offers a clear channel over a submerged boulder into a hole ready to swamp the unwary. A route tight against the left bank misses the hole. Generous eddies at the bottom provided good picture-taking locations. Fainthearted paddlers can portage on the left. (A 0.25-mile hike upstream from the Dog Bar Bridge provides a good view of this drop.)

Below the drop, smooth water flows through a rock-walled mini-gorge. The locals like it for swimming, fishing, and its proximity to Dog Bar Bridge. The takeout is below the bridge on the right. For those with excess energy, a line of widely spaced boulders offers more play at the bottom of Dog Bar. Take out here unless you have personal acquaintances who own waterfront property on Lake Combie! There is no public access for the next 5 miles of river.

59 American River, North Fork–Colfax to Lake Clementine

From the crest of the Sierras, snowmelt flows freely to this magnificent, challenging whitewater canyon with its emerald water. Wild in every sense, this is a crown jewel of Sierra whitewater.

Length: 14 miles
Average paddling time: 3 to 5 hours per segment
Difficulty: Intermediate to expert whitewater skills required
Rapids: Many Class II, III, and IV rapids
Average gradient: 31 feet per mile
Optimal flow: 500 to 1,500 cfs; rafts up to 3,000 cfs
Flow gauge: North Fork Dam
Water source: Sierra snowmelt
Best season: Spring through early summer
Land status: Public
Fees: Required for access

Maps: USGS Colfax, Greenwood; Auburn State Recreation Area brochure
Craft: Whitewater canoes, kayaks, rafts
Contacts: Auburn State Recreation Area: (530) 823-4162; parks.ca.gov; parks.ca .gov/?page_id=1348 (camping information). Protect the American River Canyon: parc-auburn.org. ReserveAmerica: (800) 444-7275; ReserveAmerica.com (camping reservations).
Special considerations: At high flows the upper run is for experts only. Severe rapids warrant scouting and, at some flows, portaging. Be prepared for turbulent high water and very cold snowmelt in spring.

Put-in/Takeout Information

Colfax–Iowa Hill bridge, also known as Mineral Bar (N39 5.995' / W120 55.489'): Exit I-80 in Colfax and go south 0.3 mile on Canyon Way to Colfax–Iowa Hill Road. Turn east, past the fire station, and continue 3 paved miles to the river. This fee area has a primitive campground with toilets and parking.

Yankee Jim Road bridge (N39 2.412' / W120 54.151'): Go west 1.8 miles from Iowa Hill Road, including 0.7 mile past the next I-80 exit to Yankee Jim Road. Turn south and descend 4.5 "primitive" miles to the river and the old suspension bridge. Fee area with toilet. Limited parking.

Ponderosa Way bridge (N38 59.996' / W120 56.400'): Continue west 2.8 miles on Canyon Way to Weimar, or go west one exit on I-80. Canyon and Ponderosa Ways intersect about 0.2 mile east of the Weimar exit. Go south on Ponderosa Way, cross the railroad tracks, then descend 5.1 rough, sinuous miles to the river. Fee area with toilet.

Upper Lake Clementine Road (N38 58.073' / W120 58.458'): At 5.7 miles from the Foresthill exit, unpaved Upper Lake Clementine Road bounces steeply 1.4 miles down to the lake's east end. This popular day-use area has a large cobble parking area that is closer to the boat-in campsites than the dam. This road is closed to vehicles in

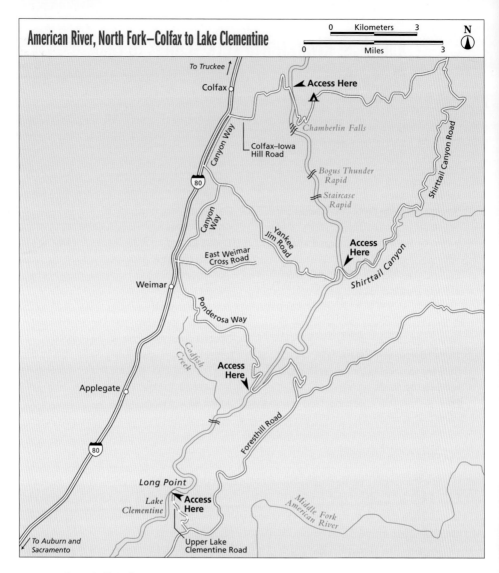

American River, North Fork—Colfax to Lake Clementine

0 Kilometers 3

0 Miles 3

N

To Truckee
Colfax
Access Here
Canyon Way
Chamberlin Falls
Colfax–Iowa Hill Road
Bogus Thunder Rapid
Staircase Rapid
Shirttail Canyon Road
80
Canyon Way
Yankee Jim Road
Access Here
East Weimar Cross Road
Shirttail Canyon
Weimar
Ponderosa Way
Codfish Creek
Access Here
Applegate
Foresthill Road
80
Long Point
Lake Clementine
Access Here
Middle Fork American River
To Auburn and Sacramento
Upper Lake Clementine Road

wet weather. Call Auburn State Recreation Area or check their website before you set out. Fee area with toilet.

Shuttle: Colfax–Iowa Hill to Yankee Jim: 9.3 miles (25 minutes); Yankee Jim to Ponderosa Way: 12.5 miles (35 minutes); Ponderosa Way to Upper Lake Clementine: 22 miles (45 minutes)

Overview

Once scheduled for burial beneath Auburn Reservoir, the North Fork of the American River deserves Wild and Scenic River protection like its upstream reaches. Largely recovered from the gold-mining era of the nineteenth century, the water is marvelously clear, the river canyons dramatic, and the whitewater superb.

Only three roads cross the river, and none follow its shores. Be self-sufficient and prepared to handle your own emergencies. The way out is along the river, not up the 1,400 vertical feet of steep slopes, poison oak, and rattlesnakes.

Mother's Day weekend is often a prime time to be on the North Fork. Fed entirely by Sierra snowmelt, early May flows have yet to reach their peak, and the days are warm. If it is a big snowmelt year, flows will stay above 2,000 cfs for several weeks before and after Memorial Day. When that occurs, desirable flows sometimes last into mid-July.

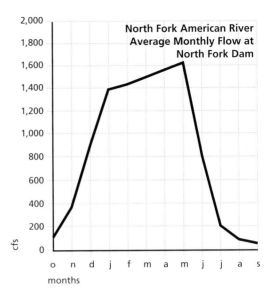

Mineral Bar is a primitive campground at the Colfax–Iowa Hill bridge. Auburn State Recreation Area manages the river from here to Lake Clementine.

A mile upstream of the Yankee Jim Road bridge, the south slopes show scars from the July 2012 Robbers Fire that burned 2,600 acres along Shirttail Canyon.

The Paddling

Colfax–Iowa Hill Bridge to Yankee Jim Road Bridge (Chamberlin Run)

Length: 4.8 miles
Average paddling time: 3 to 5 hours
Difficulty: Class IV whitewater; expert whitewater skills required
Rapids: Steep, continuous, and difficult
Average gradient: 44 feet per mile

Mild riffles at the put-in offer no hint of the demanding whitewater 0.25 mile downstream. The bedrock walls converge, the channel steepens, and boaters need to catch eddies behind every rock. It is definitely a technical big-water challenge of paddle a drop, catch an eddy, and look over your shoulder for the next slot. Then do it all again.

Rafters like higher water than kayakers and whitewater canoeists. The California Department of Boating and Waterways suggests a flow range of 1,500 to 3,000 cfs for rafts. Many kayakers prefer the less-powerful range of 500 to 1,500 cfs.

Chamberlin Falls drops into a two-way reversal. Not only can the hole hold a boat, but the eddy immediately downstream recirculates you back into the hole. At flows between 1,000 and 1,500 cfs, the channel splits around a midstream rock,

Bogus Thunder is a challenging rapid on the North Fork American River.

allowing an alternative route on the right. The slippery rocks on the left provide a precarious place to scout or portage the drop.

The action continues throughout this beautiful bedrock canyon. Bogus Thunder, once named Fen's Folly for early kayaker Fen Salter, is a steep drop over ledges that deserves scouting. Staircase Rapid is a series of three ledges with a huge hole at the bottom. Scout it. Just below Staircase is a little play spot for kayaks on the right. If the water conditions are right, you can find the sousehole, where the kayak bow dives deeply into a nose stand and then is ejected into the air.

Downstream, the rapids continue at a less-frantic, Class III pace. Historically, the rocks near Shirttail Canyon have been used by some well-exposed sunbathers. The Yankee Jim Road bridge is the middle takeout. Upstream of the bridge, a good trail on river left leads to the road.

Between 350 and 500 cfs the river is very technical but lacks the big push of higher flows. Then the emerald pools are especially alluring. Still, it is not a place to take novices or inner tubes. People have drowned in low water when caught by undercut rocks.

Yankee Jim Bridge (Shirttail Canyon Creek) to Ponderosa Way

Length: 4.5 miles
Average paddling time: 3 to 5 hours
Difficulty: Class II+ whitewater; at least intermediate skills required
Average gradient: 24 feet per mile

Put in upstream of the bridge on river left. The bridge yields a tantalizing view of what is to come. The narrow gorge stair-steps into a huge pool favored by local swimmers. By the time the water is warm enough for pleasant swimming, the boating season is nearly over. Still, the pools are luxurious attractions. Check out the fishing for trout and smallmouth bass.

While this run is easier than the upstream action, it is definitely not for new whitewater boaters. Open whitewater canoeists should have some tune-up experience. The whitewater is suitable for inflatable kayaks with experienced paddlers.

The first set of rapids is relatively straightforward, but they soon descend abruptly to Bunch Creek. At low water (less than 600 cfs), they require good route-finding skills to avoid the many rocks. At higher flows (above 1,000 cfs), you will want to eddy hop, watch for the holes, and play the waves. Below Bunch Creek, the mile-long straight section eases up to frequent Class II rapids. Around Sore Finger Point they become more demanding and continue almost to the Ponderosa Way bridge.

Recreational gold mining is popular in this area. (However, Fish and Game Code sections 5653 and 5653.1, and CDFW's definition, prohibit the use of any motorized device to directly vacuum or suction substrate in any river, stream, or lake in California.)

The easiest takeout is downstream of the bridge on river right

Ponderosa Way to Lake Clementine

Length: 4.4 miles
Average paddling time: 2 to 4 hours
Difficulty: Class II whitewater; at least intermediate skills required
Average gradient: 19 feet per mile
The Ponderosa Road bridge put-in is a popular summer swimming hole. A half mile downstream is a challenging rapid. At the end, a ledge extends from the right to produce a sizable hole in higher water. Soon the channel becomes wider. Cobbles and gravel replace boulder and bedrock rapids. Ample gravel bars offer lunch stops.

When the crystal waters of the North Fork are warm enough to swim, the river is too low to float.

The landmark Ponderosa Road bridge crosses the clear, inviting waters of the North Fork American River.

Below 600 cfs, the wide gravel bar rapids reduce the water depth and massage the bottom of your boat. The long diagonal gravel bar at the mouth to Codfish Creek deserves some attention. The top left is shallow, and the flow invites the paddler to go right. This is a trap, as the lower part of the bar runs down the middle of the river and supports a nasty growth of willows straining the flows.

Approaching Long Point, the river turns abruptly eastward. On the right side, a shallow cave lies at water level. About 0.25 mile downstream, before the river turns right, snags await the unwary floater.

On busy summer days, the dust from vehicles on Upper Lake Clementine Road blows upstream around Long Point to advise you that Lake Clementine is near.

The gated steep, unpaved road is closed during winter months and may not be open until the boating season is nearly over. Early-season paddlers must then hike their gear 1.4 miles up the hill to Foresthill Road or paddle 3.8 more miles to the boat ramp at the dam. (See chapter 60 for more about Lake Clementine.)

60 American River, North Fork—Lake Clementine

Easy access and boat-in camping make this narrow lake, located in a deep canyon close to Auburn, a great place to relax and enjoy Sierra foothills wildlife.

Size: 3.8 miles long, 0.1 mile wide; 8.8 miles of shoreline; surface area: 280 acres
Average paddling time: 2 to 4 hours
Difficulty: Deep flatwater lake; OK for beginners
Best season: Year-round
Land status: Public
Fees: State park fees
Maps: USGS Auburn, Greenwood; Auburn State Recreation Area brochure
Craft: Canoes, kayaks, fishing boats, powerboats

Contacts: Auburn State Recreation Area: (530) 823-4162; parks.ca.gov/?page_id=502; parks.ca.gov/?page_id=1348 (camping information). ReserveAmerica: (800) 444-7275; ReserveAmerica.com (camping reservations).
Special considerations: Summer water-skiers share the lake at speeds up to 40 mph. Beware of water spilling over the top of North Fork Dam. The dam access road may be icy in winter.

Put-in/Takeout Information

Both sites can be used for put-ins and takeouts.

Lower Lake Clementine Road to the dam launch ramp and marina (N38 56.154' / W121 1.429'): Exit I-80 at Foresthill Road near Auburn. Go 3.2 miles along Foresthill Road, across the North Fork American River bridge to Lake Clementine Road. Turn left. First go up a hill, and then descend 2.5 miles on a steep, paved lane-and-a-half road to the lake. Unload at the launch ramp, and park in a designated spot up the hill.

Upper Lake Clementine Road (N38 58.073' / W120 58.458'): At 5.7 miles from the Foresthill exit, unpaved Upper Clementine Road curves steeply 1.4 miles down to the lake's east end. This popular day-use area has a large cobble parking area that is closer to the boat-in campsites. The steep road is subject to seasonal closure and is often closed to vehicles in wet weather. Call the Auburn State Recreation Area to check if the road is open. See signs for summer hours.
Shuttle (optional in summer): 6.6 miles (25 minutes)

Overview

In 1939 the US Army Corps of Engineers created Lake Clementine when they built North Fork Dam. They built the dam to stop gold-mining debris from clogging the Lower American River. Later slated for inundation by the never-built Auburn Dam, popular Lake Clementine is now part of the Auburn State Recreation Area.

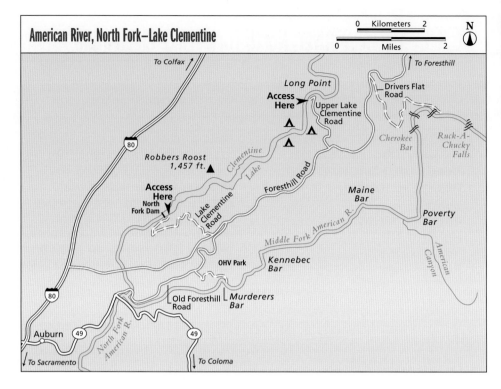

American River, North Fork–Lake Clementine

0   Kilometers   2

0   Miles   2

N

To Colfax

To Foresthill

Long Point

Access Here

Drivers Flat Road

Upper Lake Clementine Road

Cherokee Bar

Ruck-A-Chucky Falls

80

Robbers Roost 1,457 ft.

Clementine Lake

Access Here

North Fork Dam

Lake Clementine Road

Foresthill Road

Maine Bar

Poverty Bar

Middle Fork American R.

American Canyon

OHV Park

Kennebec Bar

80

Old Foresthill Road

Murderers Bar

Auburn   49

North Fork American R.

49

To Sacramento

To Coloma

A boat launch ramp and small marina are near the dam. Several miles upstream, twenty boat-in campsites occupy sandbars. During summer, campsites that are not reserved in advance may be available on a first-come, first-served basis.

Park rules stipulate that waterskiing and boating be done only in a counter-clockwise direction. The maximum speed within buoyed areas is 5 mph. No wakes are allowed at the ramp, marina, and camping areas. No swimming or waterskiing is allowed in the marina area. No powerboats are allowed upstream from the last boat-in camp to Upper Lake Clementine, and no dogs are permitted in boat-in camp and day-use areas. Users must pay boat launch and camping fees.

To avoid the water-skiers, visit Lake Clementine during summer weekdays or in spring or autumn. On summer weekends, launch from the upper end, where power-boats are prohibited. Winter offers a peaceful time; however, the canyon walls block the sun from much of the lake surface.

The Paddling

Only a few minutes from I-80, the deep canyon setting quickly removes you from the hassle and hustle of the workaday world. Limestone cliffs, such as Robbers Roost, look over the narrow, winding waterway. A concrete ramp provides easy launching near the dam. Ten minutes of paddling leaves the launch area and marina behind.

Whether you are enjoying a leisurely daylong float or a brisk evening workout, Lake Clementine is a delight. During the quiet times, you can expect to see deer, waterfowl, and maybe a mountain lion. By midsummer the clear water warms up enough for you to enjoy swimming. Only in the upstreammost mile does the water show any current. Here the water displays its finest emerald green. It may also feel a bit cooler, having just arrived from the distant Sierra snows.

The boat-in campsites are scattered along the upper third of the lake. Most are situated on enticing sandbars with partial shade from the strong Sierra sun. All have nearby floating toilets.

The pools and beaches near the Upper Lake Clementine parking area are popular for swimming and picnicking. This is the takeout for the North Fork American River Ponderosa Way run described in chapter 59. At low water you can

Craggy Robbers Roost dominates the western end of Lake Clementine.

wade across the river to hike the trails along the spine of Long Point. The shady trail offers some views looking upstream. At higher water you can try your skills paddling upstream around Long Point.

61 American River, North Fork—Auburn to Folsom Lake

For almost forty years this river reach was closed to boating while the Auburn Dam diversion tunnel and abutments were constructed. With the dam plans abandoned and closure of the tunnel, Placer County has opened the river to paddling. New access roads are public, and the streambed has been reconstructed for whitewater and an accompanying portage trail.

Length: 5 miles to Oregon Bar; 9.5 miles to Rattlesnake Bar
Average paddling time: 3 to 6 hours
Difficulty: Whitewater in steep-walled canyon; intermediate to advanced skills required
Rapids: Class II and Class III whitewater
Average gradient: 13 feet per mile
Optimal flow: 500 to 2,000 cfs
Flow gauge: North Fork Dam and below Oxbow Powerhouse
Water source: Snowmelt and Oxbow Powerhouse releases. Releases from Oxbow take 8 to 9 hours to reach the confluence.
Best season: Spring and summer
Land status: Public

Fees: State park fees required
Maps: USGS Auburn, Pilot Hill; Auburn State Recreation Area brochure
Craft: Rafts, kayaks, whitewater canoes
Contacts: Auburn State Recreation Area: (530) 823-4162, (530) 885-4527; parks.ca.gov/?page_id=502. Sierra Outdoor Center: (530) 885-1844. Protect the American River Canyon (PARC): parc-auburn.org.
Special considerations: Road gates are usually locked in winter and on summer weekdays. At high flows the run is for experts only. Severe rapids warrant scouting and, at some flows, portaging. Be prepared for turbulent high water and very cold snowmelt in spring.

Put-in/Takeout Information

Auburn Middle Fork and North Fork Confluence at CA 49 (N38 54.923' / W121 2.425'): From eastbound I-80, exit at Elm Avenue. Turn right on Elm and go 0.3 mile to the stoplight at High Street (CA 49). Turn left and follow CA 49 uphill, under a railroad overcrossing, and then down the steep, winding highway into the canyon (2.5 miles). At the bottom, continue straight instead of turning right at the bridge. Roadside parking and a short walk to the gravel bar near the North Fork bridge. Fee area and toilet.

The road to Birdsall, Oregon Bar, and Rattlesnake Bar may be closed during winter, so check with the Auburn State Recreation Area office. The gate at China Bar may be open seasonally on weekends. All sites are accessible on foot when the gates are closed. Fee areas.

Birdsall and Oregon Bar are reached from the same roads. From the confluence, go back up CA 49 to Auburn, follow High Street south, and turn left at the stoplight onto Auburn-Folsom Road. Go up the hill 1.6 miles, turn left onto Maidu Drive, and go 1 mile to the China Bar parking area and gate. Descend down the paved road 1.25 miles to a large parking area and toilet. Watch for road signs, and use low gear.

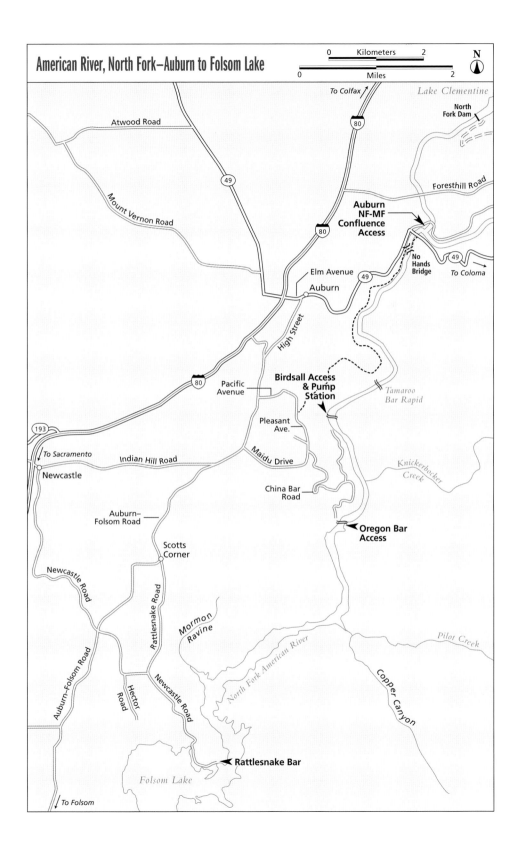

American River, North Fork–Auburn to Folsom Lake

0 Kilometers 2

0 Miles 2

N

To Colfax

Lake Clementine

North Fork Dam

Atwood Road

80

49

Mount Vernon Road

80

Foresthill Road

Auburn NF-MF Confluence Access

No Hands Bridge

49

To Coloma

Elm Avenue

49

Auburn

High Street

80

Pacific Avenue

Birdsall Access & Pump Station

Tamaroo Bar Rapid

Pleasant Ave.

193

To Sacramento

Indian Hill Road

Maidu Drive

Knickerbocker Creek

Newcastle

China Bar Road

Auburn–Folsom Road

Oregon Bar Access

Newcastle Road

Scotts Corner

Rattlesnake Road

Mormon Ravine

North Fork American River

Pilot Creek

Auburn-Folsom Road

Hector Road

Newcastle Road

Copper Canyon

Rattlesnake Bar

Folsom Lake

To Folsom

At the fork, go left 0.8 mile down a steep gravel road to the Birdsall takeout (N38 52.745' / W121 3.645'), with its modest parking lot and toilet. The steep 75-yard segment to water is too narrow for vehicles to turn around.

From the fork, go right to Oregon Bar (N38 51.767' / W121 3.568'), 0.8 mile down a steep gravel road with a small parking area for hikers and bikers.

Rattlesnake Bar (N38 49.081' / W121 5.189'): Exit I-80 at Newcastle and turn immediately south onto Newcastle Road. Follow Newcastle Road, cross Auburn-Folsom Road, and bear right at Rattlesnake Road, following Newcastle Road to the Folsom Lake State Park Rattlesnake Bar entrance. Distance from the I-80 exit to the park gate is 5 miles. After the entrance kiosk, turn left along the paved road and follow it to the boat ramp and a parking area with toilet. Depending on weather and lake level, the park allows off-road access along the lakeshore.

Shuttle: Confluence to Birdsall takeout: 8 miles (25 minutes); confluence to Oregon Bar: 8 miles (25 minutes); confluence to Rattlesnake Bar: 13 miles (30 minutes)

Overview

Long closed to boating through the Auburn Dam construction site, this canyon was opened to paddling in 2008. Then the diversion tunnel was physically blocked, the riverbed adjacent to the pumping station was restored, a portage trail was created next to the pumping station whitewater course, and road access was opened to the public.

These waters offer two very different paddling experiences. The upper 5 miles from Auburn to Oregon Bar offers whitewater in deep canyons. This section includes the Auburn Dam site, with its reconstructed streambed and portage trail. Between Oregon and Rattlesnake Bars, Folsom Lake provides 4 miles of flatwater. To enjoy the whitewater, start at the confluence and do a shuttle. For the flatwater experience, start and return to Rattlesnake Bar as described in chapter 62.

The Paddling

Put in between the bridge over the North Fork and the CA 49 bridge. If the flow is high enough to make the rapid just above the CA 49 bridge uninviting, use the gravel bar to put in below the rapid.

Downstream of the CA 49 bridge are several quiet pools. The remains of former bridges are visible underwater and along the banks. No Hands Bridge passes overhead with a hiking and biking trail. Several riffles and pools with beaches are popular with local residents in warm weather. Steep trails lead from CA 49 to river's edge.

At 2.2 miles the Tamaroo Bar Rapid funnels into a bouncy wave train that exposes rocks at lower flows. There is a long pool at the bottom. The river stays smooth for another mile before you enter the Auburn Dam site, where the Placer County Water Agency pumping station and whitewater rapids are located.

At the pump station the river is split into two channels. The right flows over the metal screens into the pump station. The left channel has been restored to create a

A whitewater channel was created next to a new pump station after Auburn Dam was canceled.

series of five drops of increasing size. Above several thousand cfs, the bottom drop may be intimidating. Along the left bank is a paved walkway. Boaters can easily carry 160 yards back to the top and run the rapid again. This is a good site for whitewater rodeos. Smooth water below the pump station leads to the Birdsall takeout on the right bank.

The most exciting rapids are downstream of Birdsall. Smooth water leaves the dam site. Then the canyon narrows. After 0.4 mile the rapids begin. They are visible if you peer over the edge of the road to Birdsall. At higher water, the rapids come fast and furious to Knickerbocker Creek.

The side canyon of Knickerbocker Creek, with its waterfalls, is an interesting place to explore. The waterfalls may be flowing early in the year. The water comes from the ridge near Cool. There is a good view of the creek from Oregon Bar Road on the opposite side of the canyon.

Another 500 feet downstream is a rapid formed by ledges extending from river left. The clearest path is on the right. Really high water covers most of the rocks.

The canyon widens, and smooth water leads to Oregon Bar. The 0.25-mile-long gravel bar is on river right, but the takeout is at the downstream end. Avoid the shallow rocky water next to the right bank. Follow the deeper channels to the center and left by eddy-hopping around exposed bedrock. At the bottom, head right (upstream), or portage the narrow midstream gravel bar and paddle to the right shore to the takeout trail. The narrow trail goes 25 yards up a steep slope to the wider gravel trail that continues uphill 200-plus yards to the parking area.

Near Auburn, the North Fork American River is peaceful on a low-flow autumn day.

If you choose to continue downstream, there are several Class II rapids followed by 4.5 miles of flatwater to Rattlesnake Bar. Hopefully the entrance gate at Rattlesnake will be open so that your vehicles can get close to the water. (See chapter 62 for a detailed description of this arm of Folsom Lake.)

62 American River, North Fork Arm–Folsom Lake

The hills and narrowing canyon of the North Fork arm of Folsom Lake lure the paddler to explore quiet places, fish, and swim. Cold waters from the North Fork American River submerge under the warmer surface during summer. This reach may be enjoyed by paddling round-trip from Rattlesnake Bar or as an extension of the whitewater paddle from Auburn described in chapter 61.

Length: Depending on lake level, up to 4.4 miles long, 0.2 mile wide; 10 miles of shoreline
Average paddling time: 3 to 5 hours
Difficulty: Flatwater lake; beginners
Best season: Year-round
Land status: Public
Fees: State park fees required
Maps: USGS Pilot Hill
Craft: Canoes, kayaks, paddleboards, powerboats

Contacts: Folsom Lake State Recreation Area: (916) 988-0205; parks.ca.gov/?page_id=500. ReserveAmerica: (800) 444-7275; ReserveAmerica.com (camping reservations).
Special considerations: Summer water-skiers and personal watercraft play in the first mile. Winter storm torrents may fill the canyon. Ticks carrying Lyme disease have been reported in the canyon.

Put-in/Takeout Information

Note: Road gates are often closed during winter.

Rattlesnake Bar (N38 49.081' / W121 5.189'): Exit I-80 at Newcastle and turn immediately south onto Newcastle Road. Follow Newcastle Road, cross Auburn–Folsom Road, and bear right at Rattlesnake Road, following Newcastle Road to the Folsom Lake State Recreation Area Rattlesnake Bar entrance. Distance from the I-80 exit to the park gate is 5 miles. After the entrance kiosk, turn left along the paved road and follow it to the boat ramp and parking area. Depending on weather and lake level, the park allows off-road access along the lakeshore. Fee area.
Shuttle: None

Overview

When the US Army Corps of Engineers completed Folsom Dam in 1954, it created Folsom Lake. The US Bureau of Reclamation owns the lake and surrounding lands and contracts with the California Department of Parks and Recreation for recreation management. With more than 4 million visitors annually, Folsom Lake is one of Northern California's most popular state parks.

The entire shore of the lake and the land for some distance beyond is within the Folsom Lake State Recreation Area and is open to the public. Summer daytime temperatures range from warm to hot, making water temperatures comfortable for

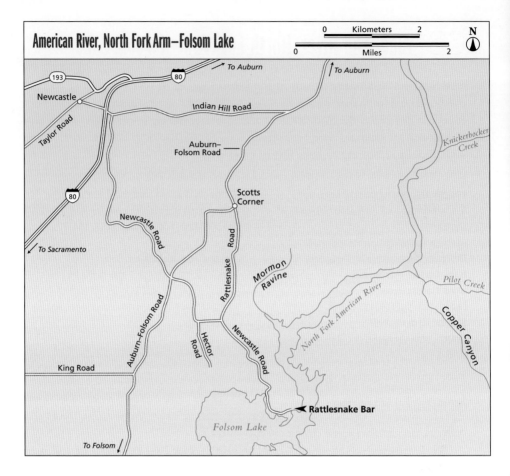

American River, North Fork Arm–Folsom Lake

swimming. Then grasses, brush, and trees become tinder dry, so fires and camping are allowed only in designated picnicking and camping areas. The Peninsula Campground is accessible by boat and car. Beals Point Campground is closer to Folsom, accessible from Auburn-Folsom Road. This is a fee area.

Along the North Fork Arm, the landscape varies. Willow groves emerge from the water to tangle fishing lines. Away from the lake, the warmer slopes host oak and grass savannas mingled with digger pine and chaparral. Be cautious where you walk—rattlesnakes are relatively common, and poison oak is widespread. Where the slope's aspects provide cooler conditions, the vegetation changes to ponderosa pine, Douglas fir, and madrone. You may see black-tailed deer, ground squirrels, raccoons, skunks, opossums, gray foxes, rabbits, bears, or coyotes. In recent years, mountain lions have returned.

As at other large California reservoirs, flood managers partially drain Folsom Lake in winter to increase flood protection for downstream communities. Then the North Fork Arm narrows and behaves more like a river with an obvious current. During and after major storms, the current becomes powerful and loaded with debris.

The Paddling

Early mornings, evenings, and weekdays are the best times to enjoy the lake. Fish for bass, trout, kokanee salmon, and catfish. Watch Canada geese fly from their nightly refuge on the lake to their daily feeding grounds. Bald eagles roost along the east shore during winter and early spring. During those seasons, the water is usually smooth and motorboats are absent.

Rattlesnake Bar access avoids the central portion of the lake frequented by many powerboats that launch at Granite Bay or Beals Point. When the Rattlesnake Bar boat ramp reaches the water, avoid using it on warm weekends; the ramp is often busy with motorboats and personal watercraft. In late summer and fall, the lake level drops below the boat ramp, but you can still launch hand-carried boats here.

Don't misjudge the Delta breeze. It will feel much stronger on the return trip, and if really strong, it will turn your paddling experience into a heavy workout.

Paddle along the shore of the lake to the north and west. Above the rocky cliffs on the west side, the remarkably level artifact that separates the trees from the high-water line is the North Fork Ditch. Constructed in the 1800s, the remains of the channel, abutments, and steel gates are intermittently visible.

An easy 1 mile from the ramp, you will reach the 5 mph zone. Water-skiers and personal watercraft stay behind. Anglers, paddle craft, and a few explorers continue.

At another 0.3 mile, Mormon Ravine joins the west side of the lake amid some low willows. Even during late summer, upstream irrigation canals sustain Mormon Ravine's flow. At high lake levels you can paddle past the powerhouse to see the water cascading down the shaded ravine. At low lake levels, the streambed is a shallow, rocky watercourse. The powerhouse sometimes discharges water without warning. The powerhouse road does not provide lake access; it is private, gated, and closed to the public.

As you paddle beyond Mormon Ravine, the 600-foot-wide lake bends to the northeast. The lower hillside is gentle and affords ample space to picnic. A wide grassy area extends high above the lake's north side. Near the top and plainly visibly, the Pioneer Express Trail, a popular hiking and horseback-riding route, parallels the water and connects Rattlesnake Bar to Auburn.

Approximately 2.6 miles from Rattlesnake Bar, the lake narrows. On the south side, low water levels expose rugged ledges. Some are good for sunbathing. Pilot Creek joins the south shore of the lake at 3.2 miles. Its narrow channel rises after a few yards to a steep, rocky creekbed. It is beautiful in early spring, inviting exploration. Where the canyon turns north again, sand on the west bank makes an attractive beach. Above this point, the river current become apparent and paddling becomes more difficult.

During summer, feel for abrupt water temperature changes from warm to cool to mountain-river cold. The water clarity improves dramatically to reveal the rocky river bottom. This phenomenon occurs where the clear, cold water from the North Fork

Remnants of the century-old North Fork Ditch can be found along the North Fork American River. The canal carried water to parts of Placer and Sacramento Counties. Those areas now draw their water from Folsom Lake.

American River slides under warmer lake water. The exact location of the phenomenon changes throughout the summer, depending upon the water level.

Low water levels present a shallow, rocky Class I river. Higher lake levels flood over the river channels and make for easy upstream paddling. Near the high-water mark, two huge gravel bars limit upstream progress to extensive walking, lining, or portaging. At this point you are about 4.5 miles from Rattlesnake Bar, 0.25 mile downstream of the Oregon Bar takeout described in chapter 61, and 1.5 miles downstream of the canceled Auburn Dam site.

These giant gravel bars were once the contents of the Auburn coffer dam. The 1986 flood destroyed the coffer dam, sending 200,000 acre-feet of water rushing into Folsom Reservoir. This flood entirely filled the reservoir and forced flood managers to release 115,000 cfs down the Lower American River. Tested to their limits, the levees protected the city of Sacramento.

63 Sugar Pine Reservoir

On the west slopes of the Sierra Nevada, this beautiful forested reservoir is 17 miles northeast of Foresthill. Its protected waters and campgrounds invite the entire family.

Size: 1.1 miles long, 0.4 mile wide; 4 miles of shoreline

Elevation: 3,700 feet

Average paddling time: 1 to 4 hours

Difficulty: Small lake; beginners

Best season: Apr through Oct

Land status: Public

Fees: Forest service fees required

Maps: USGS Dutch Flat, Tahoe National Forest

Craft: Canoes, kayaks, paddleboards, sit-on-tops, powerboats

Contacts: Tahoe National Forest, American River Ranger District: (530) 367-2224; fs.usda.gov/main/tahoe. ReserveAmerica: ReserveAmerica.com (camping reservations).

Special considerations: No special hazards

Put-in/Takeout Information

Boat ramp (N39 7.774' / W120 47.555'): Near Auburn, exit I-80 for Foresthill Road. Follow Foresthill Road across the North Fork American River bridge. Continue past the Foresthill Ranger Station for 10 miles. At the "Sugar Pine Reservoir" sign turn north on FSR 10. Go 5.5 miles, past the off-highway vehicle (OHV) staging area to

Paddlers of all abilities can enjoy Sugar Pine Reservoir.

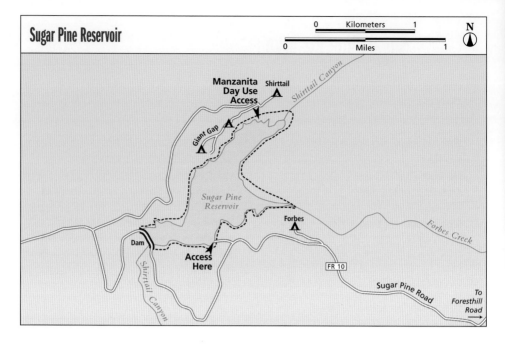

the boat ramp, paved parking, and restrooms. Follow the road across the dam to reach the campgrounds. This is a fee area with toilets and parking.

Shuttle: None

Overview

Scattered around this lake are two family campgrounds, a group campground, Manzanita day-use area, hiking trails, sandy shorelines, and a boat-launching ramp. They are usually open late April to mid-October. The 10 mph boating speed limit attracts canoes. The *Fish Sniffer* reports good fishing for trout and bass. In 1981 the US Bureau of Reclamation completed Sugar Pine Reservoir as a local water supply for the Foresthill Divide. Tahoe National Forest manages this concession-operated fee area.

The Paddling

The launch ramp and nearby ample parking make an attractive put-in. The forested hills are gentle right down to the sandy shores. Comfortable summer weather and excellent camping facilities make this a favorite place for family visits.

With a perimeter of only 4 miles, you can easily paddle around the lake in 2 or 3 hours. Since the lake is only 1 mile long, you are never very far from either camp or the launch ramp. It is really beautiful under a full moon.

64 French Meadows Reservoir

Only 9 miles from the Sierra Crest east of Squaw Valley, camping at this high-mountain reservoir offers lots of stars by night and picturesque fishing by day.

Size: 2.9 miles long, 0.6 mile wide; 7.3 miles of shoreline
Elevation: 5,263 feet
Average paddling time: 2 to 4 hours
Difficulty: Easy, small lake
Best season: May to Oct, weather permitting
Land status: Tahoe National Forest
Fees: Forest service fees required
Maps: USGS Bunker Hill, Royal Gorge; Tahoe National Forest

Craft: Canoes, kayaks, powerboats, sit-on-tops, stand-up paddleboards
Contacts: Tahoe National Forest—American River Ranger District: (530) 367-2224; fs.usda.gov/tahoe. National Recreation Reservation Service: (877) 444-6777; recreation.gov (camping reservations). Placer County Water Agency: pcwa.net/recreation/french-meadows. **Special considerations:** Snowmelt-fed lake is cold water.

Put-in/Takeout Information

Launch ramps are at the south (N39 6.679' / W120 25.713') and north (N39 7.372' / W120 25.537') shores of the lake. From Auburn, take I-80 exit 121 toward Foresthill. Follow the Foresthill Road across the high bridge to Foresthill. Pass the high school

A sit-on-top paddler enjoys French Meadows Reservoir below 9,086-foot Granite Chief.

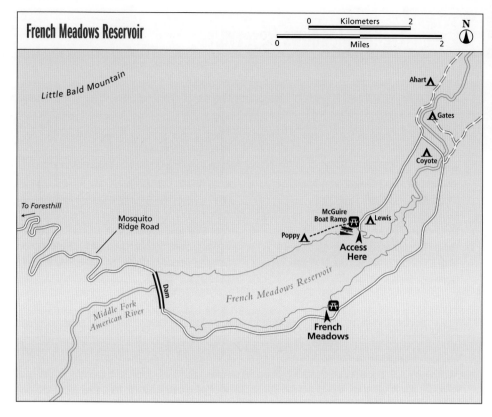

French Meadows Reservoir

Little Bald Mountain

Ahart

Gates

Coyote

To Foresthill

Mosquito
Ridge Road

McGuire
Boat Ramp

Lewis

Poppy

**Access
Here**

Dam

French Meadows Reservoir

*Middle Fork
American River*

**French
Meadows**

0   Kilometers   2

0   Miles   2

N

and turn right onto paved Mosquito Ridge Road. This road provides a 36-mile winding grand tour to the headwaters of the Middle Fork American River. Cross the North Fork of the Middle Fork bridge. Pass the turnoff to Ralston Afterbay, with a great view of Horseshoe Bar, where gold miners diverted the river through a tunnel. Maybe stop at the inspiring sequoias at Placer Big Trees Grove. Continue along the ridgetop road, which skirts the southeast perimeter of the 2013 American Fire to the French Meadows Reservoir dam. Cross the dam and go east 3 miles to the south launch ramp and parking area. Continue around the lake another 4 miles to the north-side launch ramp.

Shuttle: None

Overview

Scattered around the lake are four family campgrounds, two group campgrounds, hiking trails, sandy shorelines, and two boat-launching ramps. Depending on snow conditions, they are usually open from June to October. Since a state game refuge surrounds the entire reservoir, no firearms are permitted. Placer County Water Agency completed French Meadows Reservoir for water supply and power generation. Tahoe National Forest manages this concession-operated fee area, with potable water and vault toilets.

The Paddling

Both the north and south sides of the lake have launch ramps and adjacent parking. Bring your fishing rod—maybe the trout will bite. Look east to enjoy a fine view of Granite Chief and Squaw Peaks, both more than 8,500 feet high. In early summer they will still shimmer with snow that feeds the lake.

With a perimeter of only 7.3 miles, you can paddle around this lake in a morning or an afternoon. Since the lake is only 0.6 mile wide, you are never very far from either side, should the afternoon winds pick up.

The forested hills are gentle right down to the stony shores. Sun-bleached old stumps dot the shores and provide ready-made seats. Thanks to the altitude, summer days are comfortable and the nights are cool.

65 American River, Middle Fork—Greenwood Bridge to Mammoth Bar

This run starts where the Class III and IV "Tunnel Run" whitewater ends. Upstream power projects provide clear water. A short shuttle and fun fishing in the rugged Middle Fork American River's rugged gold mining canyon add to this whitewater run through the Auburn State Recreation Area.

Length: 6.6 miles

Average paddling time: 3 to 4 hours

Difficulty: Fast water, rocks, gravel bars, and trees; intermediate whitewater skills required

Rapids: Many rapids, Class II whitewater

Average gradient: 18 feet per mile

Optimal flow: 600 to 2,000 cfs

Flow gauge: USGS #11433300, below Oxbow Powerhouse

Water source: Snowmelt in spring. Oxbow Powerhouse releases weekday summer flows starting between 8 and 9 a.m. The water takes approximately 6 hours to reach the Greenwood put-in. On summer Saturdays, releases begin at night so that the water reaches Greenwood by midmorning.

Best season: Spring through autumn

Land status: Public

Fees: Required for access

Maps: USGS Auburn, Greenwood; Auburn State Recreation Area brochure

Craft: Whitewater canoes, kayaks, inflatable kayaks, rafts

Contacts: Auburn State Recreation Area: (530) 823-4162; parks.ca.gov; parks.ca.gov/?page_id=1348 (camping information). ReserveAmerica: (800) 444-7275; ReserveAmerica.com (camping reservations).

Special considerations: Summerlong cold water is always a whitewater concern. Pick your poison: Both rattlesnakes and poison oak are present. Do not go past the takeout due to dangerous rapids at Murders Bar. *Note:* Check the lock-up time for the Mammoth Bar OHV Park, and be sure to finish your takeout before they lock the gate.

Put-in/Takeout Information

Greenwood Bridge (N38 57.753' / W120 55.929'): The road gate is closed during wet weather; call ASRA or check their website before you set out. Exit I-80 for Foresthill Road near Auburn. Go 7.5 miles along Foresthill Road and across the high North Fork American River bridge. Turn right at Drivers Flat Road (sign reads "American River 3 miles"). Initially paved, Drivers Flat Road becomes gravel, forking left at a parking lot sign reading "Ruck-A-Chucky." Arrange to leave vehicles at this parking lot—the parking near the put-in is limited and serves both this stretch of river and the upstream whitewater run popular with outfitters. Continue to steeply descend the canyon on a narrow, bumpy dirt road. At the bottom, cross a concrete low-water bridge to a primitive campground with nearby day-use parking. A short distance upstream is the designated raft access and another parking area.

Mammoth Bar OHV Park (N38 55.098' / W121 0.070'): Turn off Foresthill Road opposite Lake Clementine Road and descend Old Foresthill Road for 2 miles. Turn down the canyon to the OHV park. In the park, head upstream past the OHV courses to a rough cobble road that leads to the upstream end of the gravel bar within 100 feet of the takeout. Old Foresthill Road connects with CA 49 by the old North Fork bridge at the canyon bottom.

Shuttle: 9.5 miles (25 minutes)

Overview

Imagine being a visitor to the Middle Fork's gold mines of the 1850s. More than 10,000 men lived and worked at Maine, Kennebec, and Poverty Bars. Machines and men dug deep into the riverbed gravels, obliterating the original streambed. Wood and canvas flumes carried water for mining operations. The miners stripped pines and firs from the canyon slopes. The 150 years since then have healed the Middle Fork Canyon.

French Meadows and Hell Hole Reservoirs capture flows the Middle Fork American River Power Project uses to create electricity to meet peak power demands. The revised Federal Energy Regulatory Commission (FERC) license stipulates recreation flow releases. During summers of normal water years, flows begin in the morning for the upstream whitewater run and reach Greenwood by early afternoon. Only on

Commercial outfitters and their customers load rafts after paddling the Class III and IV Middle Fork "Tunnel Run" upstream of the Greenwood Bridge site.

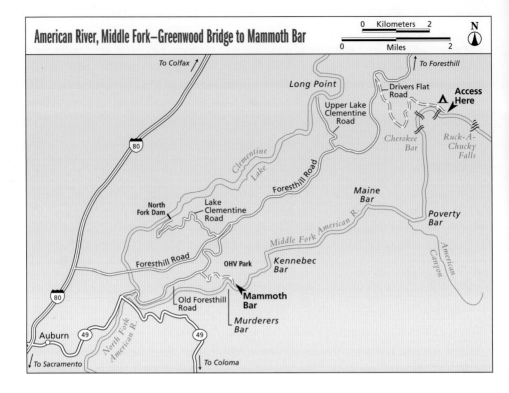

American River, Middle Fork–Greenwood Bridge to Mammoth Bar

Saturdays are flow releases scheduled early enough to reach the Greenwood put-in by midmorning. Check the recent flow patterns on the web at dreamflows.com.

Drivers Flat Road offers good views of the biggest rapids. You can see them close up with a short hike from the put-in. If the first rapid below the campground is too shallow, the river is too low. With time to wait, walk the jeep road 1 mile upstream to see the falls at Ruck-A-Chucky Rapids.

Expect to see mountain bikers, horses, and hikers. Each July the Western States 100-Mile Endurance Run and the Tevis Cup 100-mile horseback ride use trails that cross and parallel this river. Releases from Oxbow Powerhouse are reduced for those events. The Auburn State Recreation Area limits camping to the unimproved areas near the put-in and 1 mile downstream at Cherokee Bar.

The Paddling

The rapids near the put-in are the trickiest of the run. Ledges stretch across the river, with narrow slots and standing waves. These chutes and short pools offer good whitewater practice. If you want to start more gradually, put in downstream at the campground, where there are a long pool and sandy banks.

All the river bends have gravel bar rapids with standing waves that are just large enough to swamp open canoes. The first waves above Cherokee Bar are the biggest. The 1.5-mile straight stretch ends at Poverty Bar with a sand beach on the right.

Slightly downstream on river left is the brush-obscured mouth of American Canyon. The canyon has attractive falls and pools accessible by trail from the next gravel bar downstream. Follow the trail upstream, past the creek crossing and up the hill, where the pools become visible.

Occasional boulders and ledges require enthusiastic maneuvering. The approaches to some rapids can be wide and shallow enough to line a canoe to get to the deeper channel. Watch for brush hanging from the banks. Large sand and gravel bars line most of the river. Broken trees and sand deposits move from year to year.

Even at this low elevation, the north- and east-facing slopes have stands of Douglas fir and black oak. Ponderosa pine is common. Oak woodlands and open grass cover the upper slopes.

Dust from motorcycles may signal your approach to Mammoth Bar takeout at a left bend. The upstream end of the bar (river right) has a fine eddy for a takeout. This has a 100-foot carry over cobbles. A sign on the right bank announces the takeout. Do not float downstream to Murderers Bar—that rapid is as lethal as its name.

66 American River, South Fork–Chili Bar to Folsom Lake

This is one of the most popular whitewater runs in California. Rafting outfitters take thousands of passengers down the rapids every summer. Summerlong flows, exciting pool and drop rapids, and Marshall Gold Discovery State Historic Park are popular attractions.

Length: 20 miles

Difficulty: Class II to IV whitewater skills; intermediate to expert

Rapids: Many rapids throughout the entire reach

Average gradient: 22 feet per mile

Optimal flow: 1,000 to 2,000 cfs. Chili Bar releases take about 2 hours to get to Coloma and an additional 1.5 hours to reach Greenwood.

Flow gauge: Chili Bar

Water source: Chili Bar Reservoir

Best season: Spring through autumn; weekdays best to avoid crowds

Land status: Mix of private, Bureau of Land Management, and public parks

Fees: Required for access

Maps: USGS Garden Valley, Coloma, Pilot Hill; BLM South Fork American River

Craft: Whitewater canoes, kayaks, rafts

Contacts: Coloma area: coloma.com (services, rafting outfitters, lodging, food stores, live webcam of Troublemaker Rapid, and more). American River Conservancy: (530) 621-1224; arconservancy.org. BLM Mother Lode Field Office: (916) 941-3101; blm.gov/office/mother-lode-field-office. Marshall Gold Discovery State Park: (530) 622-3470; parks.ca.gov. Henningsen-Lotus County Park: (530) 621-5300. Camp Lotus: (530) 622-8672; camplotus.com. The River Store: (530) 626-3435; theriverstore.com. El Dorado County Chamber of Commerce: (530) 621-5885; visit-eldorado.com. Coloma Shuttle: (530) 303-2404; colomashuttle.com (shuttle service). Nugget Campground near Chili Bar: (530) 644-6093.

Special considerations: In spring, expert paddlers should be prepared for turbulent high water, very cold snowmelt, and brush hazards. Hydroelectric operations may quickly change flows.

Put-in/Takeout Information

All are fee areas.

Chili Bar (N38 45.970' / W120 49.321'): From US 50 at Placerville, exit north onto CA 49. Follow CA 49 about 0.7 mile to CA 193. Take CA 193 into the steep canyon, cross the bridge, and turn left into the Chili Bar (about 2.4 miles from CA 49) launch area, operated by American River Conservancy.

Coloma Resort (N38 48.067' / W120 53.317') is a private campground that allows boaters who are staying overnight to take out. American River Resort borders Troublemaker (S-Turn) Rapid upstream of Coloma, off CA 49. On the opposite side of the river, Coloma Resort can be reached by crossing the one-lane bridge on Mount Murphy Road and turning upstream.

Marshall State Park North Beach (N38 48.294' / W120 53.606') serves as a put-in for noncommercial craft.

Ponderosa Resort (N38 48.532' / W120 54.154') is a private campground on the right bank between Old Scary and CA 49.

Henningsen-Lotus County Park (N38 48.213' / W120 54.559'): From the CA 49 bridge over the South Fork, go south on Lotus Road about 0.5 mile to the parking area and river access. Gated at night, the park provides toilets, outside shower, paved parking, and an easy launch. Alternatively, from US 50, exit at Shingle Springs. Just north of the freeway bridge, turn east onto North Shingle Road and follow it 4 miles to Rescue. Bear right on Green Valley–Lotus Road for 0.6 mile, then bear left (north) at the Y onto Lotus Road to the park.

Camp Lotus (N38 48.396' / W120 55.210'): From the CA 49 bridge over the South Fork, turn south onto Lotus Road. Go 1 mile and turn west onto Bassi Road. Follow it about 0.8 mile to private Camp Lotus on the right.

Greenwood Creek (N38 49.564' / W120 56.893') is a paved parking lot with toilet on CA 49, 3 miles west of the CA 49 bridge in Coloma. A trail leads 200 yards to the river.

Skunk Hollow (N38 46.375' / W121 2.121'): From the CA 49 bridge over the South Fork, go west and north on CA 49 to Pilot Hill, about 6 miles. Turn south onto Salmon Falls Road, descending the curvy, narrow paved road with scenic views about 6 miles to the river. Skunk Hollow has paved parking on the north side of the bridge. Road-shoulder parking is available on the south side. Downstream of the bridge 0.5 mile is the large parking area for commercial and private boaters.

Alternatively, exit US 50 at El Dorado Hills and go north on El Dorado Hills Boulevard. Continue north across Green Valley Road where El Dorado Boulevard becomes Salmon Falls Road. Follow Salmon Falls Road north to the bridge.

Shuttle: Coloma Shuttle (530-303-2404; colomashuttle.com) provides regularly scheduled shuttle services between Chili Bar, Coloma, Greenwood, and Skunk Hollow. Chili Bar to Henningsen-Lotus County Park: 11.5 miles (40 minutes); Coloma to Camp Lotus: 2.6 miles (15 minutes); Coloma to Greenwood Creek: 5 miles (8 minutes); Greenwood Creek to Skunk Hollow/Salmon Falls bridge: 7 miles (20 minutes); Henningsen-Lotus County Park to Skunk Hollow/Salmon Falls bridge: 12 miles (30 minutes).

Overview

This run is attractive, fun, rich in California history, and has a good section for open whitewater canoeists. Unfortunately, the river is crowded during spring and summer weekends, so try to plan your trip for a weekday.

The South Fork American River has three runs with different character. Chili Bar is the most difficult whitewater, combining greater steepness, strong hydraulics, and

American River, South Fork—Chili Bar to Folsom Lake

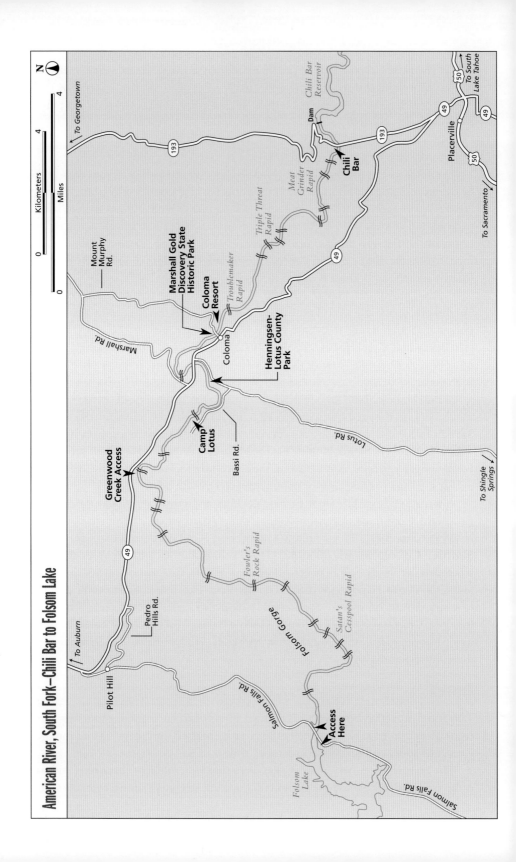

demanding technical paddling. Coloma to Lotus and Coloma to Greenwood Creek are the easiest, but the river is still powerful above 1,000 cfs and suitable for open whitewater canoeists wanting to improve their skills. Folsom Gorge is a big step up from Coloma. The gorge is a fast roller-coaster ride, best attempted by rafters, paddlers in decked boats, or whitewater canoeists with advanced skills.

Its popularity has resulted in large crowds. Paddling out of an eddy during summer weekends is like entering a Los Angeles freeway at rush hour. The best South Fork experience is on weekdays or in autumn. Even then you will have company.

"How much water and when?" is an often-repeated question. Check dreamflows .com for recent flows and schedule. Like other Sierra rivers, the spring snowmelt provides torrents of cold, clear water. The amount and duration vary from year to year. A big-water year can provide flows of more than 3,000 cfs for many weeks into June. During drought years, Pacific Gas & Electric's Chili Bar Powerhouse releases 500 cfs to 1,500 cfs on a limited schedule for some weekdays and weekends. The releases occur at the Chili Bar put-in from midmorning to early afternoon. The same releases may not arrive in Coloma until early afternoon. Check recent release patterns on the internet. At 500 cfs, kayaks can run the river, but that flow is undesirably low for rafts.

Commercial campgrounds, historic attractions, and eating places are plentiful in Coloma and Lotus.

This river is lined with many privately owned homes. Please respect and heed private property rights and rules for quiet zones. El Dorado County details the rules on annual waterproof permits that you should obtain at the put-ins. The permits include free waterproof maps showing public lands for lunch stops, toilets, and access points.

The Paddling

Chili Bar to Coloma

Length: 5.5 miles
Average paddling time: 2 to 4 hours
Difficulty: Intermediate to expert whitewater skills required
Rapids: Many Class III to IV rapids
Average gradient: 33 feet per mile

Put in at the Chili Bar river access below the CA 193 bridge. It is only 0.7 mile downstream of the Chili Bar dam and power station. Upstream from the put-in, near the Nugget Campground, locals have built a slalom course. Just below the bridge, in the center channel, is a hole that has been the site of the Chili Bar Whitewater Rodeo. If it is a summer weekend, many rafts may be around you, some with crews learning how to paddle. If it is spring, the snowmelt will be flowing high and fast down this rollicking, powerful river.

Downstream 0.2 mile, several points of a ledge protrude across the surface. Beyond is Meat Grinder (Quartermile) Rapid. Meat Grinder is long, fast, and rocky; has big hydraulics; and requires your full attention. This is a nasty place to swim.

Troublemaker Rapid provides excitement for boaters and entertainment for onlookers. You can purchase your picture running the rapid from local commercial photographers.

Racehorse Rapid drives into the right rock wall as the river turns left. After that there is a good eddy, the gradient flattens, and during lower flows you get a little rest. The braided area with the brush and grass in the middle is African Queen.

The third mile begins with Triple Threat, a series of three rapids that all have holes and big waves. It is the downstream end of public land managed by the BLM, so it is a good place to have lunch and to watch the whitewater rodeos sometimes held here.

Private lands occupy much of the riverbank from here to below Lotus. Please respect private property rights. Starting at river mile 4.5 (1.5 miles below Triple Threat), the quiet zone begins. Respect homeowners' rural tranquility by not shouting and refraining from water fights. The quiet zone continues to river mile 11.5.

S-Turn, aka Troublemaker, is the finale to this run. Large boulders and ledges block the right two-thirds of the channel. Scout on the left where all the onlookers decorate the rocks. From a rocky entrance, the water funnels left, goes through a hole next to a giant midstream boulder, then swirls into the left-side ledges. The current then surges right to fall over the second drop. In the middle of the second drop, Gunsight Rock forms a wrapping place for rafters undecided between the two slots. Upsets abound, so it is a favorite subject for professional photographers. You can purchase their pictures of you at Coloma.

From here to the takeouts (Coloma Resort, American River Resort, CA 49, Ponderosa Park, or El Dorado County's Henningsen-Lotus County Park), the river is easy compared with the Chili Bar run. A few rapids need some attention.

Coloma to Greenwood

Length: 5.5 miles
Average paddling time: 2 to 3 hours
Difficulty: Beginner whitewater to intermediate whitewater skills required
Rapids: Many Class II rapids
Average gradient: 17 feet per mile

While this run is much easier than Chili Bar, it is definitely not for the first-time canoeist. The North Beach area of Marshall Gold Discovery State Historic Park allows a start on slow-moving Coloma Lake, where you can get a feel for the river. Downstream 0.4 mile is an easy rapid with a hole. Where the river turns south, a rapid called Old Scary awaits. It used to be a turning (over) point for many neophytes. Now the river splits. Be alert for the strong eddies.

After the CA 49 bridge, the Henningsen-Lotus County Park is 0.5 mile downstream on the left. Some ledges and practice spots persist to the pool at Camp Lotus and beyond to the BLM takeout at Greenwood Creek. Take out on river right unless you plan to run The Gorge!

Folsom Gorge—Greenwood to Folsom Lake

Length: 9 miles
Average paddling time: 3 to 5 hours
Difficulty: Intermediate to expert whitewater skills required
Rapids: Many Class III rapids
Average gradient: 19 feet per mile

Put in at Henningsen-Lotus County Park, Camp Lotus, or Greenwood. This run starts easily and increases in difficulty. The rapids are many, and rafters have given most of them names. Barking Dog comes just below Camp Lotus, and then comes a rock island called Current Diver. Two miles below Camp Lotus, wide, rocky Highway Rapid may demand some careful water reading. Afterward, you come closer to CA 49 behind the rafting camps on the right.

A foot access on the right follows Greenwood Creek to BLM parking with a toilet. It is also the downstream end of the Coloma-Lotus quiet zone.

The river narrows into a long, bouncy wave train with good eddies. It is a favorite play spot for whitewater canoes and kayaks. Soon look for a beach and BLM toilet on river right. As the rapids get spicier, watch the distant hilltops for the Lollypop Tree. A round-shaped tree with a bite missing, the tree marks the entrance to the rock walls and rapids of Folsom Gorge. As the channel doglegs right approaching Norton's Ravine (about 0.5 mile above Fowler's Rock), there is a small beach on the right. The toilet there is the last one until the takeout.

The entrance to The Gorge is marked by Fowler's Rock, a house-size boulder with a hole to the left. Much of the current flows between the rock and the left wall. It is a favorite spot for rafts to wrap.

The "River SUP Guy" paddles through rough whitewater.

As the rocky gorge constricts, the water accelerates into big, churning waves. If you swim, you may be in the water a long while if your friends do not help.

Satan's Cesspool is the focal point of the run. Fast water from a smaller drop and a long wave train drive into Satan's. The bedrock rises from the left side, funneling the river into a narrow, nonsymmetrical drop next to a bedrock island. At higher flows, a wide eddy branches to the island's right, leading to a technical chicken chute. You have to be alert to catch it. Most kayakers catch the eddy on the left 25 yards above Satan's, pick their line, then power into the current to run the curling wave in the drop. Smile as you run this rapid—it is a favorite photographer's site.

The Gorge and its whitewater action continue for 2 more miles. Squirrelly water squirms under you below Satan's. Try not to swim—the ledges are hard. At Bouncing Rock Rapid the river bends left but the current drives over a ledge on the right, creating a diagonal wave with a hole on the right. Hospital Bar has a sharp drop with a steep, long wave train. Those waves are a "face wash" to surf. Depending on reservoir level, you may find Surprise Rapid uncovered.

If Folsom Reservoir is high, the last 1.5 miles will be flatwater. Do not be too surprised to see motorboats towing rafts. The Salmon Falls Road bridge marks the takeout. Paddle to the right bank upstream of the bridge. Many people use the loading zone, so try to load your stuff quickly. Commercial outfitters and their shuttle vehicles use the takeout 0.5 mile downstream on river left.

67 Mokelumne River–Electra Run

Designated the Mokelumne River Whitewater Trail, this small, scenic canyon is a cool relief from summer heat and a favorite run for training up-and-coming whitewater boaters. The run is short enough to paddle several times. Enjoy the nearby gold country towns, with their dining and lodging.

Length: 4 to 6 miles

Average paddling time: 2 to 4 hours

Difficulty: Whitewater training stream for paddlers with prior experience

Rapids: Many Class II rapids; one Class III below CA 49

Average gradient: 22 feet per mile, Electra to CA 49

Optimal flow: 500 to 1,200 cfs inflow to Pardee Reservoir

Flow gauge: Electra Powerhouse

Water source: Electra Powerhouse releases.

Best season: Spring through autumn

Land status: Private and public

Fees: Not at this writing

Maps: USGS Mokelumne Hill, Jackson

Craft: Whitewater canoes, kayaks, inflatable kayaks, small rafts

Contacts: Bureau of Land Management: (916) 941-3101; blm.gov/office/mother-lode-field-office. Indian Grinding Rock State Historic Park: (209) 296-7488; parks.ca.gov; camping: reservecalifornia.com.

Special considerations: Spring snowmelt can sustain flows that run through trees and brush, making takeout and rescue extremely difficult. In other seasons, the flows may be highly variable due to fluctuating powerhouse operations. The afterbay dam, between the powerhouse and put-in, has narrow slots that should not be run. Dead trees from a 2015 wildfire may fall into the river, creating hazards that move with time.

Put-in/Takeout Information

Electra Picnic Area (N38 19.712' / W120 40.639'): One hundred yards north of the CA 49 bridge, Electra Road turns uphill and then follows the river 3 narrow miles to the small parking area and beach.

Big Bar at the CA 49 bridge (N38 18.713' / W120 43.236'): Four miles south of Jackson, exit CA 49 immediately south of the bridge. Follow the road under the bridge to the ample parking area.

Middle Bar (N38 17.926' / W120 44.981'): Just south of Jackson, exit CA 49 south onto narrow Middle Bar Road. Follow it 2.8 curvy miles to the paved Middle Bar access area.

Shuttle: CA 49 to put-in: 3 miles (10 minutes); Middle Bar to put-in: 8.3 miles (25 minutes)

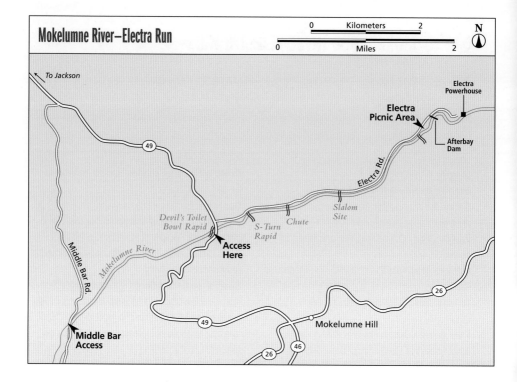

Mokelumne River–Electra Run

0   Kilometers   2

0   Miles   2

N

To Jackson

Electra Powerhouse

Electra Picnic Area

Afterbay Dam

49

Electra Rd.

Slalom Site

Devil's Toilet Bowl Rapid

Chute

S-Turn Rapid

Access Here

Middle Bar Rd.

Mokelumne River

49

Mokelumne Hill

26

Middle Bar Access

26   46

Overview

Below Pacific Gas & Electric's Electra Powerhouse, this narrow, 1,000-foot-deep wooded canyon is a cool retreat from the summer heat. The river is a favorite place to train budding paddlers. This intimate stream is also a favorite of picnickers, inner-tubers, and anglers. The only drawback is that the water stays cold all summer.

With a paved road closely paralleling the river, you can run the short reach several times a day, with time for lunch on the beach. The narrow road is close enough to see many, but not the biggest, rapids.

Parking is limited to a small area near the put-in and a few spots along the road.

Since the Amador County sheriff enforces camping prohibitions, try Indian Grinding Rock State Historic Park for camping, or enjoy the historic landmarks such as the National Hotel in Jackson or the Hotel Leger in Mokelumne Hill.

The Paddling

A sandy beach put-in provides a choice of sun or shade, as well as a beautiful large pool. It is a great spot for novice paddlers to get used to their boats and try a roll or two. Upstream 75 yards, the modest Maytag hole can sharpen your bracing skills.

The run starts with broad, easy rapids. It is good practice for reading water, catching eddies, and fine-tuning communications with your paddling partner. A mile downstream, the river narrows and increases in velocity as it approaches large boulders

Located downstream of the Electra Powerhouse, the purpose of this surge dam is to reduce the rate of flow increases when the powerhouse begins to release water. The slots are less than a paddle-length wide.

A father and child enjoy the annual Mokelumne River races.

with well-defined eddies. The combination of rapids and excellent roadside viewing make this a fun site for the annual Loma Prieta Sierra Club whitewater races. Farther downstream, the channel constricts into a chute filled with steep, exciting haystacks. Some neophyte open-canoeists may want to look it over. A recovery pool waits at the bottom.

The final challenge above CA 49 is the S-Turn. Out of sight from the road, the rocky channel turns left and then increases speed as it careens off ledges and turns right. Your friends can watch from the big eddy on the bottom right. Eddies on both sides of the rapid give you a chance to paddle upstream and try surfing.

Continue downstream, and take out immediately downstream of the CA 49 bridge on river left. Some folks run Electra several times.

Two more rapids can be scouted below the Big Bar launch area via an angler's trail winding between the rocks and blackberries.

The first rapid (a strong Class II) is an S-turn careening off rock on the right bank. Another 100-plus yards downstream, the Devil's Toilet Bowl is a Class III rapid with a 6-foot drop in 15 yards. It has rocks on the right, a hole in the middle, and more rocks on the bottom left. These get markedly more difficult at high water. Both are close enough to the CA 49 access to carry back to your cars.

Alternatively, you can enjoy another 2 miles of easier paddling downstream to Middle Bar, the upstream access to East Bay Municipal Utility District's Pardee Reservoir.

68 Truckee River–Tahoe City to River Ranch

The top 6 feet of Lake Tahoe serve as a reservoir controlled by the small dam at Tahoe City. A federal water-master schedules water releases from Lake Tahoe, Boca Reservoir, and Prosser Reservoir into the Truckee River to provide water to Reno, Nevada, irrigated lands near Fernley, and the Piute Indians at the river's natural destination, Pyramid Lake.

Lake Tahoe's crystal-clear water, a sandy bottom, and spectacular Tahoe scenery combine to make this one of the most popular beginner float runs in Northern California.

Length: 4 miles
Elevation: 6,225 feet
Average paddling time: 2 to 3 hours
Difficulty: Easy beginner float
Rapids: Easy riffles; one Class II rapid at end
Average gradient: 12 feet per mile
Optimal flow: 200 to 800 cfs
Flow gauge: Tahoe City
Water source: Lake Tahoe
Best season: Late spring through autumn
Land status: Private and public
Fees: Required at Tahoe City
Maps: USGS Tahoe City; Tahoe National Forest; USDA Forest Service–Lake Tahoe Basin Management Unit

Craft: Canoes, kayaks, inner tubes, small rafts
Contacts: Tahoe National Forest–Truckee Ranger District: (530) 587-3558; fs.usda.gov/tahoe. Truckee Chamber of Commerce: (530) 587-2757. North Lake Tahoe Chamber of Commerce: gotahoenorth.com.
Special considerations: Placer County ordinance forbids floating or entering the river when flows exceed 1,205 cfs between Tahoe City and River Ranch due to extremely low clearance between the river surface and several bridges.

Put-in/Takeout Information

Tahoe City (N39 9.892' / W120 8.822') has parking areas. They are located 0.1 mile south of the river near CA 89. Two new bridges in Tahoe City are to be built in 2019. Commercial rafters include parking and shuttle bus service when renting their equipment. Toilet available.

Bell's Landing (N39 11.036' / W120 11.744') is 0.1 mile upstream of River Ranch along CA 89. A highway turnout and limited free public parking are beside the bicycle trail. Rafting outfitters operate a larger parking lot on the other side of CA 89. Toilet available.

Shuttle: 4 miles (15 minutes). Shuttle buses are available to Tahoe City parking lots.

Overview

Sparkling clear water pours into the Truckee River from Lake Tahoe, one of the world's clearest lakes. Check out the folks on "Fanny Bridge" watching the fish next to the dam. A very popular recreation resource, the river corridor supports fly fishing, rafting, hiking, and bicycling on the bicycle path. The river is least crowded before Memorial Day and after Labor Day.

From Tahoe City to Alpine Meadows Road, CA 89 and a bicycle path run along the right shore. The road provides an almost continuous view of the adjacent river. You can easily see flow conditions and rafts on the river. Four small bridges cross the river to private land and private cabins.

Several Tahoe City outfitters rent rafts and provide parking and shuttle buses from May through September. Shuttle buses pick up boaters at Bell's Landing or River Ranch and then return to the Tahoe City parking lots.

Paddlers begin their journey at the improved put-in facilities 100 yards below Fanny Bridge in Tahoe City. Folks with their own boats frequently use the "64 Acres" public parking lot near the footbridge. Inner-tubers should be aware that the water stays very cold until midsummer.

Rules are posted to make the river enjoyable for everyone: Wear life jackets. Do not use glass bottles or containers. Use the trash cans and portable toilets strategically located on islands and the riverbanks. Respect private property by not trespassing and keeping noise levels down. Pull out only in designated areas to avoid fragile riverbanks. Do not go beyond River Ranch.

The Paddling

One hundred yards below the downstream traffic bridge, a large pipe crosses the river. This is the lowest of the bridge crossings, clearing the water by 2 or 3 feet at normal flows. At any flow, you should duck to get under it.

As soon as you leave Tahoe City, the first fast-water riffle occurs. Like many others downstream, enjoying the bounce and splash is easy and fun. Interspersed with the riffles are runs of smooth, fast water and slower pools suitable for wading or swimming—if you enjoy cool water.

Several islands make you choose which side to float around. You cannot go wrong. A couple of these have pleasant, sandy beaches. Grasses and alder adorn the banks, and ducks frequently greet floaters, looking for handouts.

Much of this river stretch has a sandy bottom, and summer flows are often shallow. The fir forest on river left grows down to

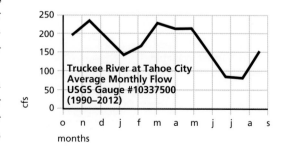

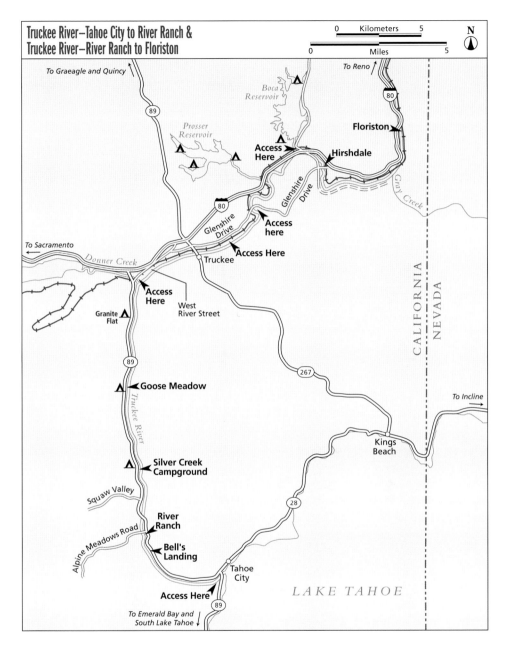

the riverbank. Look right to the canyon cliffs to see the rocky crags of lava flows that once blocked Lake Tahoe. Today these crags bear such names as Ramparts, Thunder Cliffs, Fir Crags, and Twin Crags.

Some of the prettiest scenery is near the end. A bridge with a red beam announces this section. Two channels meander through a long, wide, flooded meadow. This wide, slow section is important because it is the end of the Class I water. On the right, the

Clear waters and warm summer days attract many folks to relax on the Truckee River between Tahoe City and River Ranch.

bicycle path dips almost to river level for an easy takeout at Bell's Landing, immediately up the bank.

Downstream, several fast riffles carry you toward a picturesque house on the sharp U-bend in the river channel. Beyond that house are 100 yards of Class II rapids to River Ranch Lodge. The rapids are shallow and rocky. Rafts often bounce from rock to rock. A long tree lying on the left side of the river is a concern during high water. The rapid pauses at River Ranch pool, where rafting companies have take-out and shuttle facilities. River Ranch Lodge and Restaurant has a great sundeck beside the river, a fun place to eat and drink.

Before condominiums were built opposite River Ranch, the River Touring Section held annual summer whitewater slaloms on the rapids below the pool. We had great fun running the race course, being with friends in the mountains, and partying on the broad deck.

69 Truckee River–River Ranch to Floriston

Flowing from the fir forests near Lake Tahoe to the deep canyons entering Nevada, the Truckee River offers a variety of whitewater play areas. Many access points allow choices of whitewater difficulty. Beginning at Boca, more water is added for the most demanding section of the California Truckee River.

(See map on page 305.)
Length: 27 miles
Elevation: 6,180 feet at Bell's Landing put-in
Average paddling time: 2 to 4 hours per segment
Difficulty: Intermediate to advanced whitewater skills required
Rapids: Many Class II to Class IV rapids
Average gradient: Varies with segment, 30 to 100 feet per mile
Optimum flow: Varies with segment, 300 to 800 cfs
Flow gauges: "Below Lake Tahoe," "Near Truckee," and at "Boca Bridge"
Water source: Lake Tahoe, Boca Reservoir, and several tributaries during snowmelt
Best season: Late spring through autumn, depending on reservoir releases

Land status: Mixed private and public
Fees: Required at some sites
Maps: USGS Tahoe City, Truckee, Martis Peak, Boca; Tahoe National Forest
Craft: Whitewater canoes, kayaks, inflatable kayaks
Contacts: Tahoe National Forest–Truckee Ranger District: (530) 587-3558; fs.usda.gov/tahoe. Truckee Chamber of Commerce: (530) 587-2757; truckee.com. North Lake Tahoe Chamber of Commerce: gotahoenorth.com.
Special considerations: This is a rocky, high-elevation mountain stream. Trees fall and sometimes block the channel. Abutments of small bridges add to the obstacles. Between Gray Creek and Floriston, the channel steepens dramatically to a Class IV rock stairway.

Put-in/Takeout Information

Bell's Landing (N39 11.036' / W120 11.744') is 0.1 mile upstream of River Ranch along CA 89. A highway turnout and limited free public parking are beside the bicycle trail. Rafting outfitters operate a larger parking lot on the other side of CA 89.

Silver Creek Campground (N39 13.392' / W120 12.157') is 7 miles south of I-80 from Truckee on CA 89. The easiest put-in is beside the private bridge near the upstream end of the campground.

Goose Meadow Campground (N39 15.513' / W120 12.697') is 4.5 miles south of I-80 from Truckee on CA 89.

Granite Flat Campground (N39 18.164' / W120 12.298') is 1.5 miles south of I-80 from Truckee on CA 89.

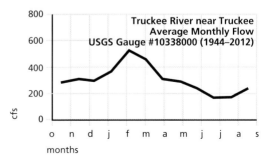

Donner Creek confluence (N39 18.994' / W120 12.021') is 0.5 mile south of I-80 from Truckee on CA 89. Turn east onto West River Street. Look for the riverside turnout at the Donner Creek confluence.

East River Street Bicycle Bridge (N39 19.874' / W120 10.133'): From Donner Pass Road in downtown Truckee, turn south onto Bridge Street, cross the railroad tracks, then turn east on East River Street. Go 0.8 mile to pedestrian/bicycle bridge.

Glenshire Drive bridge (N39 21.233' / W120 7.349'): Continue east another 2.4 miles to the high bridge across the Truckee. A parking area at the east end of the bridge gives easy access.

Boca (N39 23.195' / W120 5.697'): Exit I-80 at the Boca turnoff and go toward Boca Reservoir. Cross the Truckee River and put in by the railroad tracks where the outflow from Boca Reservoir joins the Truckee.

Hirshdale (N39 22.071' / W120 4.582') is a tiny hamlet downstream from Boca. From the I-80 exit at Boca, follow the paved road 1.2 miles on river right. Bear left at the junction with Glenshire Drive (a shortcut over the hill to the Glenshire Drive bridge) to the old bridge across the river. Put in beside the old bridge.

Floriston (N39 23.657' / W120 1.447'): Exit I-80 at Floriston to the secondary road by the bridge. That takeout gives an excellent view of the last steep rapid.

Shuttle: Silver Creek to Donner Creek: 7 miles (10 minutes); Donner Creek to Glenshire Drive bridge: 5.3 miles (15 minutes); Boca to Floriston: 5.5 miles (10 minutes)

Overview

Easy access, steady whitewater, streamside camping, and beautiful surroundings attract paddlers to the Truckee River. From River Ranch to the town of Truckee, CA 89 parallels the river. USDA Forest Service campgrounds alternate with private cabins beside Class II whitewater. Below Donner Creek, the Truckee River turns east through the town of Truckee in a Class III boulder slalom. Then the river cuts through a canyon with easier, well-spaced rocks. The canyon deepens on the way to Gray Creek. Below Gray Creek the channel drops steeply into a Class IV boulder-hopping challenge.

Snowmelt and water deliveries to Nevada affect stream flows in the different reaches. The tributaries between Bear Creek (from Alpine Meadows) and Donner Lake deliver snowmelt that combines with Lake Tahoe releases to dominate the flow as far as Boca. Releases from Boca Reservoir may dominate downstream flows when Tahoe releases and snowmelt are low.

The Paddling

River Ranch to Silver Creek
Length: 3 miles
Average paddling time: 2 hours
Difficulty: Intermediate whitewater skills required

Rapids: Continuous technical Class III rapids
Average gradient: 50 feet per mile
Optimal flow: 300 to 600 cfs
Flow gauge: Truckee River near Truckee

This short run is a rock slalom requiring precise turns on short notice. From River Ranch pool the river drops through the rocky slalom site leading to the Alpine Meadows Road bridge. Although the gradient moderates for 0.5 mile by the old Deer Park Picnic Area, fallen trees have historically obstructed part of the channel.

After the CA 89 bridge, the river drops faster. Steep slopes confine the narrow, rock-strewn riverbed. Be ready to catch an eddy if a tree looms in your path. You can easily inspect a mile of this run from the bicycle path.

CA 89 turns away from the river near Squaw Valley. The wooded right bank rises 1,700 feet to the ridgetop. Several bridge abutments add obstacles and eddies to the river. Downstream of Squaw Creek (river left) the gradient eases and the highway returns to the river. The two separate again 0.3 mile above the takeout. Take out immediately below the next bridge. On river left is Silver Creek Campground. This is the put-in for the next reach.

Silver Creek to Donner Creek

Length: 7 miles
Average paddling time: 3 to 4 hours
Difficulty: Intermediate whitewater skills required
Rapids: Contains many rocky Class II rapids
Average gradient: 30 feet per mile
Optimal flow: 300 to 600 cfs
Flow gauge: Truckee River near Truckee

Put in at Silver Creek Campground for a fun whitewater run that is a major step easier than the previous stretch. Since the river is shallow and CA 89 is never far away, this is a good place to train folks wishing to improve their whitewater skills. The mountain air, many campsites, and brilliant sunshine add to the delights.

During snowmelt season, the tributary streams from Alpine Meadows, Squaw Valley, and the neighboring mountains will add more water than that released from Lake Tahoe; thus the reference gauge is near Granite Flat Campground.

We have successfully run the river at lower flows than appear appropriate from CA 89. At 250 cfs you can reduce scraping by using some careful route finding. At any level, the paddling includes many eddy turns, midstream rocks, shallow riffles, and occasional snags. A few chutes add some bouncy excitement. One challenge involves strong currents trying to erode a house-size boulder located midstream. Another occurs where the river zigs right from the highway and a streamside cabin. The rocky rapid then zags left close to fallen trees.

Children playing, folks fishing, and occasional air-mattress riders are typical of summer days. They are most frequently encountered near Goose Meadow and

Granite Flat Campgrounds, both possible takeout sites. During early summer the meadows are lush green, painted with wildflowers.

West River Street replaces CA 89 at the Donner Creek confluence. Land on river left. A gravel bar and picnic area provide an easy takeout.

Donner Creek to Glenshire Drive Bridge

Length: 5.8 miles
Average paddling time: 2 to 4 hours
Difficulty: Strong intermediate whitewater skills required
Rapids: Continuous intricate Class III boulder slalom
Average gradient: 41 feet per mile
Optimal flow: 400 to 700 cfs
Flow gauge: Truckee River near Truckee

Put in at the Donner Creek confluence. The river heads east into the center of Truckee. Buildings replace trees, and the streambanks run up to houses and businesses. Upstream of Bridge Street, large rocks create long, busy rapids that ease after passing the bridge. You can easily see the rapid from the Bridge Street/Brockway Road bridge.

Leaving town, the gradient steepens. The river turns into a long, steep, technical boulder drop. Floods may wash logs into the mix. At 800 cfs, broadsiding a boat has immediate penalties, and swimming is undesirable. The bicycle bridge and trail along the right bank provide some scouting and portage routes between Bridge Street and Glenshire Drive. The rapid continues where the railroad and river diverge near the Glenshire Drive fishing access.

Toward the regional wastewater treatment plant and Martis Creek, the rapids ease. The river bends to the north as it carves against an exposed canyon slope. The bridge is Glenshire Drive, traditional site of a takeout on river right.

Glenshire Drive Bridge to Boca

Length: 4.4 miles
Average paddling time: 2 to 3 hours
Difficulty: Intermediate Class II whitewater skills required
Rapids: Contains many rocky Class II rapids
Average gradient: 34 feet per mile
Optimal flow: 400 to 800 cfs
Flow gauge: Truckee River near Truckee

Like the last part of the previous run, this reach starts with rapids that are easy in a kayak and more demanding in a canoe. We brought kayakers with limited experience here to hone their skills.

At first, both I-80 and the railroad parallel the river. Sagebrush and scattered Jeffrey pines vegetate the landscape. Below the Glenshire Drive bridge, a fly-fishing club claims private property rights to 2.5 miles of the right bank. Their land extends past

Prosser Creek to the approximate midpoint between the first and second freeway bridges. You paddle past their expansive clubhouse.

After the third freeway crossing, a steeper rapid requires some accurate maneuvering. Soon the discharge from Boca Reservoir enters on the left. This is a good takeout and put-in for the next run.

Boca to Floriston

Length: 6.9 miles
Average paddling time: 3 to 4 hours
Difficulty: Expert whitewater skills required
Rapids: Demanding, steep Class III to Class IV whitewater; Floriston rapid hazardous due to concrete and rebar in the river
Average gradient: Boca to Gray Creek: 20 feet per mile; Gray Creek to Floriston: 60 feet per mile, with the last 0.5 mile almost 100 feet per mile
Optimal flow: 400 to 800 cfs
Flow gauge: Truckee River at Boca Bridge

During summer, several rafting companies operate on this part of the Truckee. Put in at Boca or the fishing access at Hirshdale. Some minor rapids stretch between Boca and the last freeway crossing. Except for a prominent boulder, the river runs 2 fast miles to Hirshdale. Although the railroad stays close to the river, I-80 retreats across the canyon 0.5 mile above the river. An old bridge crossing at Hirshdale has good access for boaters and anglers.

Before the 2001 Martis Creek wildfire, this stretch was the prettiest part of the river below Truckee. The river winds deep in the canyon between sage and pine-covered slopes. Sand and gravel bars invite a relaxing lunch or fishing. The road to Gray Creek from Hirshdale is gated and closed. Look for a sharp Class II rapid at a bend in the river. That rapid broke boats before the era of plastic craft.

The railroad crosses the river at the Gray Creek confluence. Since it collects snowmelt from the 9,600-foot Rose Knob, Gray Creek runs well into the summer. Enjoy the sparkling clear water and the scenery. A large house stands above the creek. As you continue, expect some serious whitewater or a lengthy portage.

To this point, the canyon of the Truckee has provided little warm-up for the rapids ahead. Fortunately they do not start abruptly. Several rapids place increasing demands on the boater. Then the last 1.3 miles drops 62 feet per mile.

At normal summer flows, the rapids are demanding boulder slaloms. Use the eddies to plot your next move. While swimming after missing an eddy here, I saw a piece of steel rebar protruding from underwater concrete. The good news is that the railroad

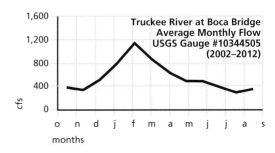

The 0.25-mile, very rocky Class IV Floriston rapid has a portage road along the right bank.

runs along the right bank and affords an excellent means to scout the rapids or portage your boat. Take out by the bridge at Floriston and appreciate your paddling accomplishment.

70 Lake Tahoe

Mark Twain said that the Lake Tahoe Basin "must surely be the fairest picture the whole earth affords." Year-round visitors enjoy the spectacular High Sierra scenery and one of America's clearest and most beautiful lakes. Paddling around the shores is an exhilarating experience.

Size: 21 miles long, 12 miles wide
Elevation: 6,230 feet
Average paddling time: 1 to 6 hours per segment
Difficulty: Very large lake; SCRS III open-water skills and experience required
Best season: Late spring through autumn
Land status: Mixed private and public
Fees: Required at most access sites
Maps: USGS Meeks Bay, Emerald Bay, South Lake Tahoe, Glenbrook, NV, Marlette Lake, NV; USDA Forest Service—Lake Tahoe Basin Management Unit
Craft: Canoes, kayaks, paddleboards, large powerboats
Contacts: Lake Tahoe Basin Management Unit: (530) 543-2600; fs.usda.gov/ltbmu. Camp Richardson: (800) 544-1801; camprichardson.com. D. L. Bliss State Park: (530) 525-7277; parks.ca.gov (campgrounds, day-use beaches, hiking trails). Emerald Bay State Park; parks.ca.gov; (Vikingsholm and boat-in Eagle Point Campgrounds operated seasonally). Ed Z'Berg Sugar Pine Point State Park: (530) 525-7982. Lake Tahoe South Shore Chamber of Commerce: (775) 588-1728; tahoechamber.org. Lake Tahoe Water Trail: (530) 582-4800; laketahoewatertrail.org.

Special considerations: Lake Tahoe's 1,600-foot depth keeps its waters extremely cold. Even in late summer, only the top few feet become warm enough to swim. Afternoon winds typically blow from the west, accelerating down the mountains and across 12 miles of open water to form large waves. The California Department of Boating and Waterways advises that "wind-driven waves can build to a height capable of capsizing or swamping small craft." Powerboats and 500-passenger tour boats observe the 15 mph speed limit in Emerald Bay, but on the open water, fast boats generate choppy waves. Remember that canoes and kayaks are difficult to see from fast-moving speedboats. Open canoes are not recommended when the lake is busy or windy.

Put-in/Takeout Information

D. L. Bliss State Park borders CA 89 on the west shore of Lake Tahoe, 17 miles south of Tahoe City and a couple of miles north of Emerald Bay. From the entrance (N38 58.664' / W120 6.177'), follow the park road down past the campground kiosk, pay the day-use fee, and bear right to Lester Beach (N38 59.942' / W120 5.910').

The access road to Baldwin Beach Picnic Area (N38 56.593' / W120 4.109') is about 4 miles north of the Y junction where CA 89 splits from US 50 in South Lake Tahoe. Turn right after 0.5 mile to the beach, which is a fee area.

Kiva Beach (N38 56.360' / W120 3.208') continues Baldwin's sandy shore. Popular with dog owners (in the picnic area) and paddleboarders, Kiva is 3 miles north of the South Lake Tahoe Y junction with US 50. The entrance to this fee area is 0.7 mile from the parking area. A footpath leads 200 yards to the beach.

Camp Richardson (N38 56.292' / W120 2.349') has a special-use permit from the USDA Forest Service for commercial operations and a marina on Jameson Beach Road. From the South Lake Tahoe Y junction, go north on CA 89 about 2.5 miles. Turn right to the lake. Rental kayaks are available.

Pope Beach (N38 56.213' / W120 1.832') is 2.3 miles north of the US 50 junction. This popular fee area extends 0.75 mile of beach westward toward Tahoe Keys and the Upper Truckee River wetlands.

Privately managed South Lake Tahoe Lakeside Beach (N38 57.595' / W119 57.027') is open to the public, with fees in the summer season. Located just west of the California-Nevada state line, beachside parking is accessible from US 50 by following either Stateline or Park Avenues 0.5 mile west (toward the lake).

Nevada Beach (N38 58.931' / W119 57.211') is a USDA Forest Service day-use and campground fee area. From Stateline, follow US 50 north 2 miles. Turn left (west) onto Elks Point Road and go 0.5 mile to the entrance station. Bring wheelies, as the walk to water is 100-plus yards with soft sand.

Round Hill Pines Beach & Marina (N38 59.304' / W119 56.934') has a special-use permit from the USDA Forest Service for commercial operations and is a fee area with personal watercraft rentals, parasailing, and lots more action. Go north on US 50 2.5 miles from Stateline, turn left (west) down the hill, and then go 0.3 mile to the parking area.

Zephyr Cove Beach (N39 0.394' / W119 56.851') has a special-use permit from the USDA Forest Service for commercial operations. Zephyr is such a popular beach and refreshment destination that parking lots (fee) sometimes fill. It is also the departure point for the *MS Dixie II* paddlewheel tour boat. From Stateline go north 4.2 miles on US 50. The bar and beach are on the left.

Cave Rock Beach (N39 2.539' / W119 56.876') is a State of Nevada fee facility with a small beach and launch ramp. The access fee for one Nevada state park is good at other Nevada state parks the same day. Cave Rock is on US 50 immediately south of the tunnel and requires driving care when exiting onto the park road. The beach is a short walk to the water at the south end of the parking lot. From Zephyr Cove, go 2.6 miles north on US 50. From the other direction, the access is 5.5 winding miles south of the junction of US 50 and NV 28.

Skunk Harbor (N39 7.762' / W119 56.584') is a beautiful small beach on national forest land with only foot access (1.5 miles) down the hill from NV 28. The road head is 2.4 miles north of the junction with US 50.

Secret Harbor (N39 9.314' / W119 55.966') is on national forest land and is accessed on foot via a 0.75-mile fire road from very limited roadside parking along NV 28. Restrooms are on the trails above the cove. The trailhead is about 4.5 miles north of the junction of NV 28 and US 50.

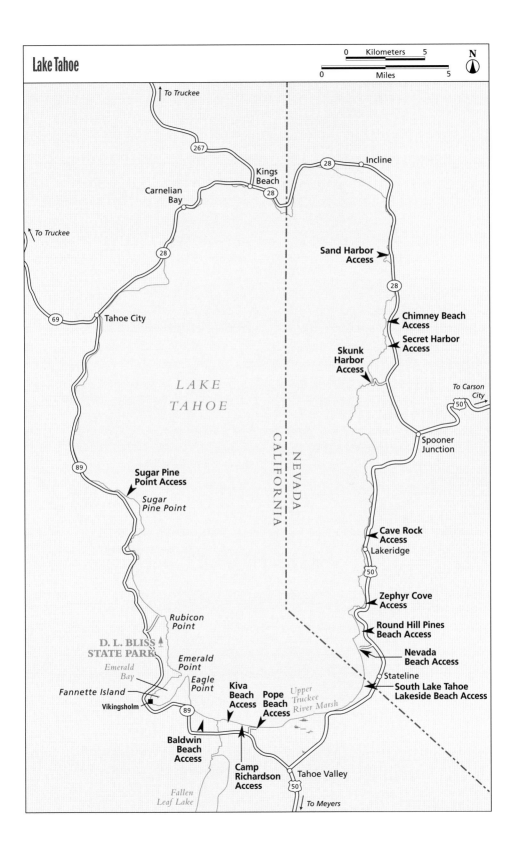

Chimney Beach (N39 9.821' / W119 55.825') is another beautiful pocket beach on national forest land. A toilet is located at the limited roadside parking on NV 28. Access is by foot trail 0.2 mile to beach. The trailhead is about 5 miles north of the junction of NV 28 and US 50.

Sand Harbor (N39 12.021' / W119 55.764'), also known as Lake Tahoe Nevada State Park, is a very popular fee facility with great beaches, big smooth rocks looking into crystal waters, summer theater, and a launch ramp. A small lot is reserved for vehicles with kayaks. Get there early on weekends and holidays! Sand Harbor is the put-in for commercial kayak tours. The location is on NV 28 about 7.7 miles north of the junction of NV 28 and US 50, or about 5.5 miles south of the Incline, Nevada, junction with NV 431.

Overview

Lake Tahoe is world famous for its incredibly clear water, fabulous mountain setting, and recreational playground. Very popular in warm weather, the lake is frequented by anglers, fast motorboats, large tour boats, and sailboats. Fees are charged at most of the many access sites. Campgrounds abound in the Tahoe basin but are so popular in summer that reservations are advised. The least-crowded times on the lake are early morning or early autumn weekdays.

Aquatic invasive species (AIS) are threats to Lake Tahoe. Be sure to clean, drain, and dry your boat and dispose of any debris after paddling in Lake Tahoe or any California water body. Visit the Tahoe Keepers website to learn about inspection programs and how to protect Lake Tahoe.

The Paddling

West Shore—including Emerald Bay

Locations	One-way Paddling Distance	Average Paddling Time
D. L. Bliss Campground–Lester Beach to mouth of Emerald Bay	2.8 miles	1 to 1.5 hours
Emerald Bay mouth to west end	1.6 miles	30 to 45 minutes
Emerald Bay mouth to Baldwin Beach	1.9 miles	45 minutes to 1.5 hours
Baldwin Beach to Kiva Beach	0.5 mile	10 to 15 minutes
Kiva Beach to Camp Richardson	0.7 mile	15 to 20 minutes

Emerald Bay is one of the most popular vistas at Tahoe. Put in at beautiful Lester Beach below the D. L. Bliss State Park campground. Head south past little Calawee Cove Beach, an idyllic anchorage for sailboats. Soon you will round Rubicon Point, where granite cliffs plunge directly into the water. The breathtaking color of the lake changes from emerald green to indigo blue as the depth abruptly increases.

The shoreline to and including Emerald Bay is within state parks. The cliffs give way to steep mountainsides of brush and boulders without good landing spots. Although protected from the worst of the westerly winds, this shore is open to the wakes of hundreds of powerboats. Sea kayaks resist swamping and capsizing better than open canoes, so open boats should stay very close to shore.

From the north, the mouth of Emerald Bay is obscure. The first clues are the lowlands leading to Emerald Point. Look for the two small beaches close to where the ridge drops to the water. Continue to paddle around Emerald Point. Immediately the awesome views of 9,735-foot Mount Tallac jump into sight. Stay close to the shallow north shore to avoid the larger boats.

On warm weekends, many boats parade through the narrow, shallow mouth of Emerald Bay. On the north shore, the beach on Emerald Point is a lovely place to relax and

Paddleboarding is a popular activity on Lake Tahoe.

enjoy the view. The only access is by foot trail or shallow-draft boat. Looking south to Eagle Point, you may spot an osprey nest on a tall snag.

Inside the bay, the mountains pull at your eyes like magnets—Mount Tallac with its snow bowl, the bare slope of the gigantic landslide, and the monumental granite cliffs rising nearly 3,000 feet to Jakes Peak in the Desolation Wilderness Area. Flowing out of the mountains, Eagle Falls punctuates the scene with soaring snowmelt.

The only island in all of Lake Tahoe, little Fannette Island rises 150 feet with an old granite "teahouse" crowning the summit. The southwest corner is rocky but provides the easiest landing site. A partly obscured trail climbs rocky steps to the top.

Vikingsholm presides over the western end of the bay with a delightful beach. Hand-hewn of local granite and timber, the sod-covered house was built to incorporate Scandinavian architecture of ages past. To participate in a tour, you must obtain tickets from the visitor center up the trail toward CA 89.

Cave Rock Beach provides attractive access to Lake Tahoe.

For those boaters wishing to camp away from cars, the north side of Emerald Bay harbors twenty boat-in campsites operated by the state park. The park provides mooring buoys, a dock, and a small beach. A discreet distance up the hill, tent sites have steel containers for bear protection, vault toilets, tables, and freshwater. They allocate campsites on a first-come, first-served fee basis.

If you return to the north from the mouth of Emerald Bay, two distant points protrude into the lake. The farther is Sugar Pine Point. If you aim for it until you reach the cliffs just south of Rubicon Point, the course will save you distance but will take you as much as 0.5 mile from shore.

You can paddle south from Emerald Point to Baldwin Beach, the closest put-in/takeout to Emerald Bay. South of the steep and forested state park lands, chateau-like houses line the shore, many with their own private pier. Baldwin Beach and its southerly neighbor Kiva Beach are flat and covered with pine trees. The marsh area behind the beach is a bald eagle nesting ground. A delightful option is to go south of the mouth of Taylor Creek and follow the foot trails to the marvelous stream profile chamber featuring rainbow trout and kokanee landlocked salmon in Taylor Creek. It is well worth the 0.4 mile (one-way) walk.

South Shore

Locations	One-way Paddling Distance	Average Paddling Time
Camp Richardson to Pope Beach	1 mile	20 to 30 minutes
Pope Beach to Lakeside Beach	4.3 miles	1.5 to 2.5 hours
Lakeside Beach to Nevada Beach	1.5 miles	30 to 45 minutes
Nevada Beach to Round Hill Pines Beach	0.8 mile	15 to 20 minutes
Round Hill Pines Beach to Zephyr Cove	1.7 miles	30 to 45 minutes

In contrast to the steep, rocky, forested shores of the east and west shores of Lake Tahoe, the south shore is largely lined with beaches. Much of the shore is open to public access. The beaches and water are well populated with swimmers, personal watercraft, powerboats, rental kayaks, and paddleboards in warmer months. Fortunately, the waters close to shore have speed restrictions.

The south end of Lake Tahoe is one giant curve, with few peninsulas interrupting the arc. In addition to the plainly visible casinos of Stateline, Heavenly Mountain Resort ski area is a prominent feature to the south. To the west are the peaks of the Desolation Wilderness. Just east of Pope Beach, the Upper Truckee River flows with its wetlands.

Nevada Beach

Locations	One-way Paddling Distance	Average Paddling Time
Sand Harbor to Cave Rock Beach	13 miles	4 to 6 hours
Sand Harbor to Skunk Harbor	5.6 miles	2 to 3 hours
Cave Rock to Zephyr Cove	2.7 miles	1 to 1.5 hours

Sand Harbor and the pocket beaches of the Nevada shore provide delightful opportunities to enjoy Tahoe's crystalline waters and spectacular scenery. Sand Harbor is a very popular Nevada state park offering parking, launch ramps, kayak launching, kayak rental, beaches, and summer theater. Claim your kayak parking spot early, since they rapidly disappear.

Due to the parking situation, most paddlers start at Sand Harbor and go south. Paddling in the opposite direction, with Sand Harbor as a destination, would place wind and waves from the south and west behind you but might pose parking problems.

Heading south in calm weather, you might test your maneuvering skills between big rounded boulders. One and a half miles south is the Thunderbird Lodge National Historic Site with its inviting harbor, lighthouse, stone buildings, and magnificent vistas. Landing and tours are by reservation only.

Less than 1 mile south of Thunderbird, the steep shore opens to a series of attractive pocket beaches. Access to them is by foot or boat. Sometimes the powerboating crowd gets large. More northerly is the aptly named Chimney Beach.

Continuing south, the shoreline is rocky, with few places to land. Approximately 0.75 mile from Chimney is sheltered, sandy Secret Harbor. Then the shoreline turns more southwesterly and rockier. Rounding the point where the shore turns easterly, look for Skunk Harbor. Paddling southwest approximately 2 miles, 1-mile-wide Glenbrook Bay opens to the east and the members-only beaches and piers of Glenbrook come into view. Once you're past Glenbrook and South Point, many large private homes with piers line the lower slopes of Shakespeare Peak.

From South Point your course is almost due south to Cave Rock. You can see the highway tunnel through the cliff above the lake. Cave Rock Beach is south of the tunnel, protected by a small cove.

71 Carson River, East Fork

This Sierra high-country gem offers lots of Class II whitewater, spectacular scenery, great campsites, and hot springs. This is a California-designated Wild and Scenic River from Hangman's Bridge to the Nevada state line.

Length: 20 miles
Elevation: 5,480 feet at put-in
Average paddling time: 4 to 7 hours, often spread over 2 days
Difficulty: Rocky, fast mountain stream; intermediate whitewater skills required
Rapids: Class II whitewater throughout run
Average gradient: 26 feet per mile
Optimal flow: 600 to 2,000 cfs
Flow gauge: Markleeville
Water source: Snowmelt
Best season: Spring and early summer
Land status: Mix of BLM, USDA Forest Service, and private
Fees: Permits required for commercial rafting
Maps: USGS Carters Station, Heenan Lake, Markleeville; Humboldt-Toiyabe National Forest–Carson Ranger District

Craft: Whitewater canoes, kayaks, rafts, inflatables
Contacts: Humboldt-Toiyabe National Forest: (775) 331-6444; fs.usda.gov/detail/htnf/about-forest/offices. Grover Hot Springs State Park: (530) 694-2248; parks.ca.gov. ReserveAmerica: ReserveAmerica.com (camping reservations). BLM Carson City Nevada District Office: (775) 885-6000; blm.gov/nevada. Family Mountain Shuttle Service: (530) 694-2704.
Special considerations: Like other Sierra snowmelt rivers, the water here is cold and swift. No easy access exists between the put-in and takeout. A deadly broken dam awaits the unwary paddler 400 yards below the takeout.

Put-in/Takeout Information

Put-in at CA 89 Hangman's Bridge (N38 41.371' / W119 45.915'): From CA 88 at Woodfords, turn south onto CA 89. Go through Markleeville 1.5 miles to Hangman's Bridge over the East Fork Carson (vault toilet on clifftop), or continue another 0.6 mile to a flat adjacent to the river.

Takeout near Gardnerville above Ruhenstroth Dam (N38 52.107' / W119 41.544'): Return to Woodfords, then follow CA 88 northeast to Minden, Nevada. At Minden, go south about 7 miles through Gardnerville on US 395. Pass the road to the Lahontan Fish Hatchery. Look to the west for the steep-walled river canyon nearing the highway and a tall, skinny tank. Almost immediately turn right (west) onto paved Washoe Road. Instead of going over the bridge, continue straight up the hill on a dirt road. Follow the rough dirt road 0.5 mile along the south side of the river overlooking the breeched dam, then down to the parking areas, loading zone, and toilets. Go down to the river so that you will know what the takeout looks like. **Do not miss the takeout!** *Note:* Due to occasional reported vandalism, you may not want to leave your vehicle at the takeout overnight.

Shuttle: 30 miles (45 minutes); Family Mountain Shuttle Service: (530) 694-2704

Overview

The East Fork of the Carson River is one of my favorite places. Days are delightfully warm, high elevation makes the air feel light, night skies sparkle with stars, hot springs soothe the body, and constant rapids refresh the spirit.

The East Fork Carson well deserves its designation as a California Wild and Scenic River from Hangman's Bridge to the Nevada state line. The Humboldt-Toiyabe National Forest and the Bureau of Land Management administer most of the lands bordering the river. These agencies are studying proposals to include the East Fork Carson in the National Wild and Scenic River System.

Occasional floods change parts of the river, including the put-ins. At high water, little space remains on the beach at Hangman's Bridge for organizing gear. An alternative is to go 0.6 mile upstream to a pebble beach near the East Fork Carson River Resort.

Flows above 600 cfs are suitable for large rafts plus kayaks and canoes. Higher water generates faster currents and bigger waves. Below 600 cfs, the flow is generally unsuitable for rafts, and below 300 to 400 cfs, even small boats encounter more work than fun.

Both California and Nevada require fishing licenses for their respective portions of the river. Wild trout fishing restrictions stipulate use of artificial flies or lures with barbless hooks (no bait) and a two-fish limit with minimum size of 14 inches. The forest service or Alpine County Chamber of Commerce will issue free campfire permits.

The hot pools at Grover Hot Springs State Park in Markleeville are a relaxing way to soothe your body before or after a hike or float trip.

The Paddling

At the put-in, the 50-feet-per-mile gradient makes for some fast boating. Choose carefully which side of Hangman's Bridge to paddle. Just downstream, the channel under the bridge changes with successive floods but always thrusts into a low cliff on river right. The fast current continues to twist and turn into low cliffs and undercut ledges that can easily snare the unwary boater.

Opposite Markleeville Creek is a wide bar suitable for camping, but why stop here when you have just begun? Take advantage of the reduced gradient (30 feet per mile) to catch an eddy and enjoy the spectacular upstream views of 9,000-foot Markleeville and Jeff Davis Peaks. At 1,200 cfs, downstream rapids provide fun-filled, splashy, 2- to 3-foot waves mile after mile.

Progressing downstream, you enter the Humboldt-Toiyabe National Forest where the river has carved a canyon 800 feet below the ridgetops. Steep cliffs alternate with riverside terraces ready-made for camping. The forest service strongly encourages low-impact camping, such as bringing stoves and packing out all trash and human waste.

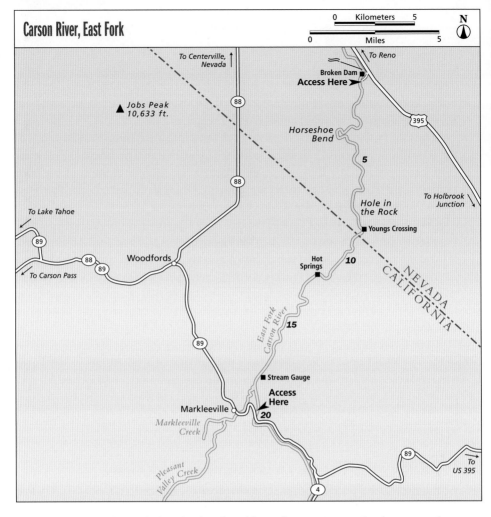

Carson River, East Fork

0 Kilometers 5
0 Miles 5

N

To Centerville, Nevada

To Reno

Broken Dam
Access Here ➤

88

Jobs Peak
10,633 ft.

Horseshoe
Bend

395

5

88

To Holbrook
Junction

Hole in
the Rock

To Lake Tahoe

89

Youngs Crossing

Woodfords

88

89

Hot
Springs

10

NEVADA
CALIFORNIA

To Carson Pass

East Fork Carson River

15

89

Stream Gauge

Access
Here

Markleeville

20

Markleeville
Creek

89

To
US 395

Pleasant
Valley Creek

4

On river left, a high cliff with a bright sulfur-yellow ravine marks the approach to the hot springs (N38 46.176' / W119 42.881') and Sidewinder Rapid. Major floods make major changes to Sidewinder. The 2017 flood re-formed an island near the downstream end of the bluffs. As of this writing, reports indicate that the former left channel now flows into a bedrock wall. A channel to the right of the island has sharp rocks, making passage challenging. Wide terraces on the right provide ample campsites. Beyond another brisk rapid are more campsites on both sides of the river. Volunteer off-road vehicle clubs have helped maintain these campsites.

In recent years, natural hot spring pools of different sizes have been carved from the banks on both sides of the river. Those on river right are large enough for only two or three adults. On river left, the largest is perched on a ledge immediately above the river and gives paddlers below an "in the boat" hot shower.

To preserve this natural area, establish your camp at least 200 feet from the water and do not alter the hot springs. Pack out everything you brought in!

We rescued the passengers from this truck stranded near the hot springs. The cause of their plight was unclear—rising water or poor navigation due to consumption of the red fluid in the big plastic jug! While soaking in the hot springs that night, we could see the yellow glow of the truck's headlights under the water.

Here the canyons open up to reveal vistas of hills swathed in sage and piñon and Jeffrey pines. In 1990 the Humboldt-Toiyabe National Forest planted thousands of Jeffrey pines to replace trees lost to the 1987 wildfire. The gradient slackens to 25 feet per mile in volcanic bedrock that includes imbedded gravel and cobbles. This rough texture encourages "clean" boating. The geology also creates some curious rock pillars with undercut bases.

About 2.5 miles below the hot springs, two fences mark the old Von Schmidt and current state lines. A half mile beyond is Youngs Crossing, one of the largest areas of privately owned land along the river. Look up at the rock outcropping on the left to see "Hole in the Rock." Several pleasant beaches line the nearby shore. Beware of the rapids immediately below—they require some precise maneuvering.

Downstream 3 miles is a delightful boulder slalom. Between turns, enjoy the magnificent views of Jobs Peak (10,633 feet) and Freel Peak (10,881 feet). These mountains are 10 miles from the river and only 7 miles southwest of Lake Tahoe.

A long, straight reach with abruptly rising cliffs on the right marks the beginning of Horseshoe Bend. Dam proponents have proposed building a dam in this canyon. The resultant reservoir would inundate most of the whitewater run. Designating the river as a National Wild and Scenic River would prohibit such a dam. Write your congressional representative to encourage National Wild and Scenic status.

A large sign and a long, willow-shrouded sandbar mark the takeout on river right. **You must stop here!** Four hundred yards downstream, the fast currents drop over the broken 30-foot-high Ruhenstroth Dam. The good news is that cars can be parked only a few yards above the takeout.

72 Mono Lake

Located just a few miles from the east entrance to Yosemite National Park, Mono Lake provides a spectacular experience. To the west, high Sierra peaks are often mantled with snow. Unusual tufa towers emerge from this high-desert saline and alkaline lake. Hundreds of thousands of migratory birds feed on the alkali flies and brine shrimp.

Size: 9 miles north to south; 13 miles east to west

Elevation: 6,383 feet

Average paddling time: 2 to 6 hours

Difficulty: Big lake; open-water skills required

Best season: Spring through autumn; islands closed to visitors Apr 1 through Aug 1

Land status: Private and public

Fees: Not at this writing

Maps: USGS Lee Vining, Sulphur Pond, Mono Mills, Negit Island, Lundy, Mount Dana; Inyo National Forest; Mono Lake Committee; American Automobile Association, Yosemite

Craft: Canoes, kayaks, sit-on-tops

Contacts: Mono Basin Scenic Area Visitor Center (on US 395 just north of Lee Vining): (760) 674-3044 ; fs.usda.gov/detail/inyo/specialplaces/?cid=stelprdb5129903. Mono Lake Committee Information Center & Bookstore (at Third Street and US 395): (760) 647-6595; monolake.org (open year-round).

Special considerations: Calm mornings may rapidly change to high winds and afternoon thunderstorms. Cold seasons may bring snow. Deceptively large distances may cause disorientation.

Put-in/Takeout Information

The only public access is Navy Beach (N37 56.442' / W119 1.195'): From Lee Vining go south on US 395 about 5 miles; turn east on CA 120 and go approximately 5 miles to the "South Tufa" sign. Turn left (north) on unpaved Test Station Road for 100 yards, bearing right at the fork. Follow the straight gravel road about 1 mile to the T; turn left. Go about 0.4 mile on the one-lane dirt road (no turnouts) to the put-in. The launch area has limited parking, interpretive signs, and a port-a-potty. Additional parking is available at the South Tufa parking area, with a 0.5-mile footpath through the brush and along the shore.

Shuttle: None

Overview

Mono Lake is a fascinating ecological wonder in the high desert adjacent to 10,000-plus-foot Sierra Nevada peaks. Fed by several creeks from the mountains, the lake has no outlet. Volcanic rocks and occasional minor earthquakes give evidence to the geologic activity of the region.

Mono Lake is an icon representing resolutions of conflicts between environmental restoration and urban water diversions.

A kayaker enjoys a calm day exploring Mono Lake.

Birds by the millions are warm-weather visitors to Mono Lake. The shorelines are popular for birders and photographers. Their subjects include California gulls, eared grebes, ruddy ducks, killdeer, phalaropes migrating to South America, snowy plovers, avocets, godwits, and a variety of wetland species. Ospreys have built large nests on several tufa towers.

The volcanic islands and rock outcroppings of the lake provide protection from predators; birds lay their eggs and raise their young here. Nesting and migratory birds feed on the alkali flies and brine shrimp endemic to the lake's saline and alkaline waters. Shrimp and insects feed on algae in warm shallow waters. There are no fish. To protect the birds, seasonal restrictions apply to approaching and landing on the islands.

During the past century, the lake level has changed dramatically due to diversion of tributary waters to Los Angeles. The water surface dropped 35 feet, exposing the lake-bottom paths between the shore and the islands. Coyotes and other predators used these land bridges to feed on birds and eggs. The birds stopped nesting on the islands, and their populations declined.

In a decades-long court battle, the Mono Lake Committee, National Audubon Society, California Trout, and other organizations achieved the 1983 landmark Public Trust Doctrine decision by the California Supreme Court. In 1994 the California Water Resources Control Board set a target lake elevation of 6,392 feet and ordered the City of Los Angeles to restore damaged tributaries and wetlands. Today's restrictions on visitor activities are aimed to help the ecosystems of Mono Lake.

Forest service campgrounds and a Lee Vining recreational vehicle park provide camping sites for a fee. Camping is prohibited adjacent to the lake or on the islands, except with a free permit. After the island restrictions are lifted August 1, permits may be obtained at the Mono Basin Scenic Area Visitor Center.

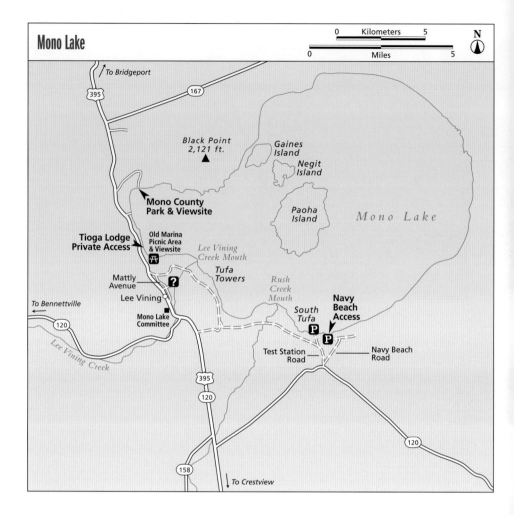

Mono Lake

0 Kilometers 5

0 Miles 5

N

To Bridgeport

395   167

Black Point
2,121 ft.

Gaines
Island

Negit
Island

Mono County
Park & Viewsite

Paoha
Island

Mono Lake

Tioga Lodge
Private Access

Old Marina
Picnic Area
& Viewsite

*Lee Vining
Creek Mouth*

Mattly
Avenue

Tufa
Towers

*Rush
Creek
Mouth*

Lee Vining

To Bennettville

120

Mono Lake
Committee

South
Tufa

Navy
Beach
Access

Lee Vining Creek

Test Station
Road

Navy Beach
Road

395

120

120

158

To Crestview

The Paddling

Before you start out, check the weather forecast. Afternoon starts are not advised, since strong afternoon winds make paddling difficult and may even blow paddlers to the east shore, where there is no water, little shelter, and very difficult vehicle access. Afternoon thunderstorms add to the hazards.

When you begin paddling, go 200 yards from shore and stop. Turn around and note the put-in location, carefully aligning Navy Beach with canyons, trees, and the ridge crests beyond the south shore. Better yet, take a compass bearing. These features will help you return to the put-in when you are miles out on the water and shoreline details are indiscernible.

Between April 1 and August 1, access is restricted to all islands to protect nesting gulls. Between April 1 and September 1, boaters should not approach within 200 yards of osprey nesting sites on offshore tufa towers. Be aware of agitating

The high peaks of Yosemite National Park look down on canoeists exploring the tufa towers along Mono Lake. MONO LAKE COMMITTEE

nesting ospreys—their warning call is a high-pitched shriek that is very hard to hear. Approaching boaters may aggravate parents and fledgling ospreys that are not accustomed to what they see as predators approaching nests.

Two general routes are suggested.

Route 1

Novice paddlers and those in open canoes may feel more confident paddling westward along the shore. South Tufa towers are only 0.5 mile away. Continuing westward another 1.5 miles, the Rush Creek delta hosts flocks of feeding gulls. In September, grebes speckled the water and dove as our boats approached. A great blue heron rested on a tufa tower. From a distance, large osprey nests appeared vacant. Three miles west of Rush Creek are tufa towers similar to South Tufa. Fun to explore, you might imagine a moonlight Halloween scene among these outcroppings.

On the west side of the lake, the interpretive and visitor center is visible on the hillside. Vehicles can be seen traveling on US 395. An unimproved launch ramp, a private road associated with Tioga Lodge, and a private ramp might be used as emergency routes off the lake. The state park picnic site and the county park offer wetlands views from shore but do not provide boating access. On the north side of the lake, the dark slopes of Black Point are a good landmark.

Route 2

From Navy Beach, Paoha Island seems close, but Mono distances are deceiving, so expect several hours of paddling. A circuit of just Paoha Island is about 13 miles.

The 600-foot-high black rocks of Negit Island lie north of Paoha Island with a channel between. If paddling clockwise around the islands, the distant north shore seems to merge with a flat island and Negit. Even with lake levels rising, shallow water abounds, with rocks close to the surface. A small rocky beach on Negit's north shore offers a rest spot. Nearby underwater fence posts penetrate the surface—and potentially your boat. The fence was installed to deter predators from raiding birdlife during lower lake levels.

East of Negit, one rocky outcropping supports the remains of a volcano built for movies *Fair Wind to Java* (1953) and *Krakatoa: East of Java* (1969). The east sides of the islands offer shelter from westerly winds. The sound of large flocks of birds taking off together is like the distant roar of a jet plane.

Paddling Distances from Navy Beach

Location	One-way Miles from Navy Beach	Approximate Round-trip Paddling Time
South Tufa	0.5 mile	30 minutes
Rush Creek mouth	2.25 miles	1.5 hours
Tufa Towers southwest	5 miles	4 hours
Lee Vining Creek mouth	6 miles	3+ hours
Tioga Lodge road	8 miles	6 hours
Paoha Island, south side	3 miles	2 hours
Negit Island, south side	6.3 miles	4 hours
Negit Island, north side	7.4 miles	6 hours

Appendix A: Flows, Tides, Waves, and Storms

National Weather Service Forecasts

Internet

Eureka/Northern California: www.wrh.noaa.gov/eka

Sacramento and Central Valley: www.wrh.noaa.gov/sto

San Francisco Bay Area/Monterey: www.wrh.noaa.gov/mtr

NOAA Weather Radio Frequencies

Especially important for marine forecasts for sea kayakers.

Sacramento to Oroville	162.40 MHz
Sacramento to Modesto	162.55 MHz
Northern Sacramento Valley	162.55 MHz
San Francisco Bay Area	162.40 MHz
East San Francisco Bay	162.425 MHz
North Bay Marine	162.50 MHz
South San Francisco Bay and Monterey Bay Area	162.55 MHz
Monterey Marine	162.45 MHz
Eureka	162.400 MHz
Ukiah and Mendocino	162.525 MHz
Point Arena	162.550 MHz

Tides

NOAA Tide Predictions, California: tidesandcurrents.noaa.gov/tide_predictions .shtml?gid=1393

Winds and Waves

National Weather Service coastal and buoy data, including wind, wave, and temperature conditions

Internet sites worldwide: ndbc.noaa.gov

Northern California: www.wrh.noaa.gov/mtr/buoy.php

Buoys	ID Number (from north to south)
Saint Georges	46027
Eel River	46022
Point Arena	46014
Bodega	46013
San Francisco	46026
Half Moon Bay	46012
Monterey	46042

Trip Planning Maps

Bay Area Sea Kayakers (BASK): bask.org/trip_planner
Google Earth: google.com/earth/index.html
National Oceanic and Atmospheric Administration (NOAA) charts may be downloaded for free from www.charts.noaa.gov/InteractiveCatalog/nrnc.shtml#mapTabs-1.

- 18626: Elk to Fort Bragg
- 18628: Albion to Caspar
- 18643: Bodega and Tomales Bays
- 18647: Drakes Bay
- 18649: Entrance to San Francisco Bay
- 18685: Monterey Bay

San Francisco Bay Area Water Trail: sfbaywatertrail.org
Topographic maps sources:

- MyTopo: mapserver.mytopo.com
- National Geographic: shop.nationalgeographic.com
- US Geological Service (USGS): usgs.gov/products/maps/topo-maps

Stream Flows, Reservoir Inflows, and Releases

Dream Flows—Western states river reports: dreamflows.com
California Data Exchange Center river conditions (uses DWR IDs): cdec.water.ca .gov/riv_flows.html
California Data Exchange Center daily reservoir report: cdec.water.ca.gov/reservoir .html
USGS Water Resources in California (uses USGS gauge numbers): ca.water.usgs .gov/data/waterconditionsmap.html
Placer County Water Agency for North Fork and Middle Fork American Rivers: PCWA.net
Trinity River Flow Schedule from Lewiston Reservoir: trrp.net
Yolo County Flood Control & Water Conservation District Field Office, releases from Indian Valley Reservoir and Clear Lake to Cache Creek: (530) 662-0266

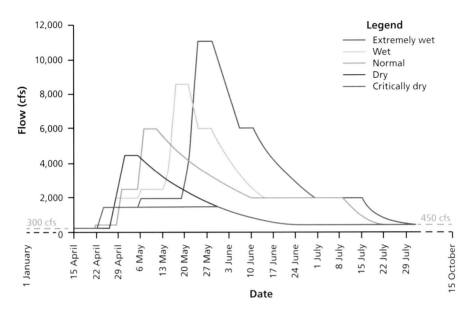

Typical Flow Releases from Lewiston Dam to Trinity River

Legend
— Extremely wet
— Wet
— Normal
— Dry
— Critically dry

The Trinity River Restoration Program, with its many cooperating agencies, has developed this scheme of flow releases to restore fisheries. "Total water allocation" is the volume of water to be released from reservoirs to the river during the year. That volume depends on the amount of precipitation during the previous winter. For each water year type, a flow schedule is applied from the chart. For example: Wet years allow higher spring flows (8,000+ cfs) to manage gravel bar composition and vegetation. Dry years, such as 2013, release only half the cfs (4,000+) during spring. Objectives for summer flows are water temperature and fisheries habitat. TRRP posts the flow schedule for the current year on its website (trrp.net). (Source: Trinity River Restoration Program, Flow Scheduling Process; www.trrp.net/?page_id=150)

Rivers and Gauges

Rivers are listed in alphabetical order and from upstream to downstream.

Gauge Name	USGS Number	DWR ID
American River, Middle Fork near Oxbow Powerhouse	11433300	OXB
American River, North Fork at North Fork Dam	11427000	NFD
American River, South Fork at Chili Bar		CBR
American River, Lake Natoma Release (Nimbus Dam)	NAT	
American River at Fair Oaks	11446500	AFO

Bear River into Lake Combie (Call Nevada Irrigation District Operations at 530-823-2466.)		
Bear River near Wheatland	11424000	BRW
Cache Creek, North Fork releases from Indian Valley Reservoir		INV
Cache Creek at Rumsey		RUM
Cosumnes River at Michigan Bar	11335000	MHB
East Fork Carson River below Markleeville	10308200	
East Fork Carson River at Gardnerville	10309000	GDV
Eel River at Fort Seward	11475000	FSW
Eel River, South Fork at Leggett	11475800	LEG
Eel River, South Fork at Miranda	11476500	MRD
Feather River near Gridley		GRL
Mokelumne River, Pardee Reservoir Inflow		PAR
Mokelumne River, Camanche Reservoir Outflow		CMN
Mokelumne River at Benson's Ferry near Thorton		BEN
Navarro River near Navarro	11468000	NRN
Russian River at Cloverdale	11463000	CLV
Russian River near Healdsburg	11464000	HEA
Russian River near Guerneville	11467000	
Sacramento River, Bend Bridge	11377100	BND
Sacramento River at Ord Ferry		ORD
Sacramento River at Colusa	11389500	COL
Stanislaus River at Orange Blossom		OBB
Stanislaus River at Ripon	11303000	
Trinity River release from Lewiston outflow	11525500	LEW
Trinity River at Douglas City	11525845	DGC
Trinity River at Junction City	11526250	
Trinity River above North Fork near Helena		NFH
Trinity River near Burnt Ranch	11527000	TBR
Trinity River at Hoopa	11530000	HPA
Truckee River at Tahoe City	10337500	TTC
Truckee River near Truckee	10338000	TRK
Truckee River Bocca	10344505	
Tuolumne River at LaGrange		LGN
Tuolumne River (Discharges to river from Hickman Spillway, call 209-883-8222.)		
Tuolumne River at Modesto	11290000	MOD
Yuba River below Englebright Dam		YRS
Yuba River near Marysville	11421000	MRY

Appendix B: For More Information

Adventure's Edge
Arcata, CA 95521
and
Eureka, CA 95501
(707) 445-1711
adventuresedge.com

Albion River Campground and Marina
PO Box 217
Albion, CA 95410
(707) 937-0606
albionrivercampground.com

American River Conservancy
(530) 621-1224
arconservancy.org

American River Conservation
Contacts, and services
theamericanriver.com/rivers/
     conservation

American River Natural History
     Association
facebook.com/American-River
     -Natural-History-Association
     -269555898590

American River Parkway Foundation
5700 Arden Way
Carmichael, CA 95608
(916) 486-2773
arpf.org

American River Parkway Map
regionalparks.saccounty.net; arpf.org/
     pdf_files/map.pdf

American Rivers
1101 14th St. NW, Ste. 1400
Washington, DC 20005
(202) 347-7550
americanrivers.org

Angel Island Conservancy
PO Box 866
Tiburon, CA 94920
(415) 435-3972
angelisland.org

Angel Island Ferry
(415) 435-2131
angelislandferry.com

Bay Area Sea Kayakers (BASK)
bask.org

Beacon Harbor
3861 Willow Rd.
Bethel Island, CA 94511
(925) 684-2174

Benbow Inn
445 Lake Benbow Dr.
Garberville, CA 95542
(707) 923-2124
benbowinn.com

Bethel Harbor Marina
(925) 684-2141
bethelharbor.com

Bidwell Sacramento River State Park
Chico, CA 95926
(530) 342-5185

Big Break Marina
(925) 679-0900
big-break-marina.com

Bigfoot Rafting Co.
PO Box 995
Willow Creek, CA 95573
(530) 629-2263
Fax: (530) 629-1157
bigfootrafting.com

Blue Waters Kayaking
60 Fourth St., #C
Point Reyes Station, CA 94937
(415) 669-2600
bluewaterskayaking.com

Brooks Island
(888) 327-2757
ebparks.org/parks/brooks_island

Bureau of Land Management
Eagle Lake Field Office
2950 Riverside Dr.
Susanville, CA 96130
(530) 257-0456
blm.gov/office/eagle-lake-field-office

Bureau of Land Management
Cosumnes River Preserve
(916) 684-2816
blm.gov/visit/cosumnes-river-preserve

Bureau of Land Management
Mother Lode Field Office
5152 Hillsdale Circle
El Dorado Hills, CA 95762
(916) 941-3101
blm.gov/office/mother-lode-field
 -office

Bureau of Land Management
Nevada District Office
5665 Morgan Mill Rd.
Carson City, NV 89701
(775) 885-6000
blm.gov/office/nevada-state-office

Bureau of Land Management
Redding Field Office
355 Hemsted Dr.
Redding, CA 96002
(530) 224-2100
blm.gov/office/redding-field-office

Bureau of Land Management
Ukiah Field Office
2550 N. State St.
Ukiah, CA 95482
(707) 468-4000
blm.gov/office/ukiah-field-office

Cache Creek Regional Park
Yolo County Parks Division
(530) 406-4880
yolocounty.org

California Department of Fish
 and Wildlife
Region 3
7329 Silverado Trail
PO Box 47
Napa, CA 94558
(707) 944-5500
wildlife.ca.gov/Lands/Planning/
 Lower-Sherman-Island-WA

California Department of Fish
 and Wildlife
Fishing regulations: wildlife.ca.gov/
 Regulations

California Department of Fish
and Wildlife
Suisun City Office
(707) 425-3828
wildlife.ca.gov

California State Parks
parks.ca.gov

Ahjumawi Lava Springs State Park
Burney, CA 96013
(530) 335-2777

Angel Island State Park
PO Box 318
Tiburon, CA 94920
(415) 435-5390

Auburn State Recreation Area
501 El Dorado St.
Auburn, CA 95603
(530) 885-4527
Whitewater recreation: (530) 823-4162

Benbow State Recreation Area
(707) 923-3238

Bidwell Sacramento River State Park
Chico, CA 95926
(530) 342-5185

Brannan Island & Franks Tract State
Recreation Area
(916) 777-6671

China Camp State Park
San Rafael, CA 94901
Ranger office: (415) 456-0766

Colusa–Sacramento River State
Recreation Area
Colusa, CA 95932
(530) 458-4927

D. L. Bliss State Park
Lake Tahoe
(530) 525-7277

Emerald Bay State Park
(530) 541-3030

Folsom Lake State Recreation Area
Folsom, CA 95630-1797
(916) 988-0205

Grover Hot Springs State Park
Markleeville, CA 96120
(530) 694-2248

Hendy Woods State Park
Philo, CA 95466
(707) 937-5804

Humboldt Redwoods State Park
Avenue of the Giants
Weott, CA 95571
(707) 946-2263

Indian Grinding Rock State
Historic Park
Pinegrove, CA 95665
(209) 296-7488
Camping; no reservations—first-come,
first-served

Marshall Gold Discovery State
Historic Park
Coloma, CA 95613
(530) 622-3470

Mendocino Coast State Parks
(707) 937-5804

Monterey District State Parks
(831) 649-2836

Navarro River Redwoods State Park
(707) 937-5804

North Coast Redwoods District
Headquarters
Eureka, CA 95502-2006
(707) 445-6547

Richardson Grove State Park
Garberville, CA 95440-3318
(707) 247-3318

Smithe Redwoods State Reserve
(707) 247-3318

Standish-Hickey State Recreation Area
Leggett, CA 95455
(707) 925-6482

Sugar Pine Point State Park
(530) 525-7982

Tomales Bay State Park
Millerton Park and Heart's Desire
Beach
(415) 669-1140

Turlock Lake State Recreation Area
La Grange, CA 95329
(209) 874-2056

Van Damme State Park
Little River, CA 95456
(707) 937-5804

William B. Ide Adobe State
Historic Park
Red Bluff, CA 96080
(530) 529-8599

Woodson Bridge State Recreation Area
Route 1, Box 325
Corning, CA 96021
(530) 839-2112

Camping Information—State Parks
reserveamerica.com

Camping Reservations—Federal Sites
(877) 444-6777
recreation.gov

Camp Richardson Resort
(800) 544-1801
camprichardson.com

Caspar Beach RV Park & Campground
Mendocino
casparbeachrvpark.com

Catch a Canoe & Bicycles Too
PO Box 487
Mendocino, CA 95460
(707) 937-0273
catchacanoe.com

Coastal Traveler
coastaltraveler.com

Coloma Online
coloma.com

Colusa Levee Scenic Park
425 Webster St.
PO Box 1063
Colusa, CA 95932
(530) 458-5622

Cosumnes River Preserve
13501 Franklin Blvd.
Galt, CA 95632
(916) 684-2816
cosumnes.org

Crown Memorial State Beach
Alameda Island
ebparks.org/parks/crown_beach

Delta Kayak Adventures
deltakayakadventures.com

Dutch Slough Restoration Project
water.ca.gov/Programs/Integrated
  -Regional-Water-Management/
  Delta-Ecosystem-Enhancement
  -Program/Dutch-Slough-Tidal
  -Restoration-Project

Eagle Lake Campgrounds & Marina
PO Box 1771
Susanville, CA 96130
(530) 825-3454; (530) 825-3212
eaglelakerecreationarea.com

EagleLakeFishing.net
eaglelakefishing.net/wp-content/
uploads/2017/11/ELF-Map.pdf

East Bay Municipal Utility District
Lafayette Reservoir
(925) 284-9669
ebmud.com/recreation/lafayette
  -reservoir

East Bay Municipal Utility District
Mokelumne River
(209) 722-8204
ebmud.com/recreation/sierra-foothills/
  mokelumne-river-day-use-area/

East Bay Regional Parks
Big Break
(510) 544-3050
ebparks.org/parks/big_break

Eel River Shuttle
Rick Doty: (707) 926-5444

El Dorado County Visitors Authority
(530) 621-5885
visit-eldorado.com

Elkhorn Slough Foundation
1700 Elkhorn Rd.
Watsonville, CA 95076
(831) 728-5939
elkhornslough.org

Family Mountain Shuttle Service
Markleeville, CA 96120
(530) 694-2704

Fish Sniffer magazine
(800) 748-6599
fishsniffer.com/index.php/maps/

The Fly Shop
4140 Churn Creek Rd.
Redding, CA 96001
(530) 244-1503; (800) 669-3471
theflyshop.com

Fort Baker–Horseshoe Bay–Golden
Gate National Recreation Area
nps.gov/goga/planyourvisit/fort-baker
  .htm

Fort Bragg–Mendocino Coast
    Chamber of Commerce
217 S. Main St.
Fort Bragg, CA 95437
(707) 961-6300
mendocinocoast.com

Friends of the River
1418 20th St., #A
Sacramento, CA 95811
(916) 442-3155
friendsoftheriver.org

Giant Redwoods RV & Camp
Myers Flat, CA
(707) 943-9999
giantredwoodsrv.com

Greater North Tahoe Chamber
    of Commerce
web.gotahoenorth.com/search

Headwaters Kayak Shop & Boathouse
847 N. Cluff Ave., Ste. A-6
Lodi, CA 95240
(209) 224-8367
headwaterskayak.com

Henningsen Lotus Park
El Dorado County Parks & Recreation
950 Lotus Rd.
Lotus, CA 95651
(530) 621-5300
edcgov.us/Government/Parks/pages/
    Henningsen_Lotus_Park.aspx

Hennis Marina
3205 Wells Rd.
Bethel Island, CA 94511
(925) 684-3333

Heritage Oak Winery
(209) 986-2763
heritageoakwinery.com

Historic Camp Richardson Resort
1900 Jameson Beach Rd.
South Lake Tahoe, CA 96158
(530) 541-1801; (800) 544 1801
camprichardson.com

Humboldt County Convention and
    Visitors Bureau
visitredwoods.com

Humboldt Lodging Guide
visithumboldt.com

Humboldt-Toiyabe National Forest
Carson Ranger District
1536 S. Carson St.
Carson City, NV 89701
(775) 331-6444
fs.usda.gov/detail/htnf/about-forest/
    offices

Lafayette Reservoir
EBMUD
(925) 284-9669
ebmud.com/recreation/
lafayette-reservoir

Lake Del Valle
East Bay Regional Park District
(888) 327-2757, option 3, ext. 4524
Rocky Ridge Visitor Center
(925) 373-0432
ebparks.org/parks/del_valle

Lake Lodi Boathouse
(209) 471-5988

Lake Sonoma
(707) 431-7533
US Army Corps of Engineers
    Sacramento District
spn.usace.army.mil/Missions/
    Recreation/Lake-Sonoma

Lake Tahoe Basin Management Unit
USDA Forest Service
35 College Dr.
South Lake Tahoe, CA 96150
(530) 573-2600
fs.usda.gov/ltbmu

South Lake Tahoe Chamber
    of Commerce
(775) 588-1278
tahoechamber.org

Lake Tahoe Water Trail
(530) 582-4800
laketahoewatertrail.org

Lassen National Forest
2550 Riverside Dr.
Susanville, CA 96130
(530) 257-2151
Eagle Lake District
(530) 257-4188
fs.usda.gov/lassen

Lassen Volcanic National Park
Mineral, CA 96063-0100
(530) 595-4480
nps.gov/lavo

Lauritzen Yacht Harbor
(925) 757-1916
lauritzens.com

Lawson's Landing
PO Box 67
Dillon Beach, CA 94929-0067
(707) 878-2443
lawsonslanding.com

Lexington Reservoir County Park
17770 Alma Bridge Rd.
Los Gatos, CA 95032
(408) 356-2729

Loch Lomond Marina
110 Loch Lomond Dr.
San Rafael, CA 94901
(415) 454-7228
lochlomondmarina.com

Marin County Department of Parks
3501 Civic Center Dr.
San Raphael, CA 94903
(415) 499-6387
marincountyparks.org/depts/pk

Marin Islands
(707) 769-4200
fws.gov/refuge/marin_islands

McInnis Park
(415) 473-6405
marincounty.org/depts/pk/divisions/
    parks/mcinnis-park

McLaughlin Eastshore State Park
(888) 327-2757
ebparks.org/parks/eastshore

McNears Beach and Paradise Beach Park
(415) 473-6405
marincounty.org/depts/pk/divisions/
parks/mcnears-beach

Mendocino Camping
mendoparks.org/camping

Mendocino Coast Chamber
of Commerce
217 S. Main St.
Fort Bragg, CA 95437
(707) 961-6300
mendocinocoast.com

Mono Lake Committee
PO Box 29
Lee Vining, CA 93541
(760) 647-6595
monolake.org

Mono Basin Scenic Area
Visitor Center
US 395 just north of Lee Vining
monolake.org/visit/vc

Monterey Bay Aquarium
886 Cannery Row
Monterey, CA 93940
(831) 648-4800
montereybayaquarium.org

Monterey Bay Kayaks
Monterey and Elkhorn Slough
693 Del Monte Ave.
Monterey, CA 93940
2390 Hwy. 1
Moss Landing, CA 95039
(831) 373-5357
montereybaykayaks.com

Monterey Bay National Marine
Sanctuary
99 Pacific St., Bldg. 455A
Monterey, CA 93940
(831) 647-4201
montereybay.noaa.gov

Monterey Harbor Office
250 Figueroa St.
Monterey, CA 93940
(831) 646-3950;

Monterey Visitors and Convention
Bureau
seemonterey.com

National Recreation Reservation
Service
Campsites of USDA Forest Service and
US Army Corps of Engineers
(877) 444-6777
recreation.gov

Navarro-by-the-Sea Center
navarro-by-the-sea-center.org

Navarro River Resource Center
navarroriver.org

Nevada Irrigation District Operations
Center
(530) 273-8571

Ord Bend Park Butte City Launch
Facility
Willows, CA 95988
(530) 934-6546

Oroville Area Chamber of Commerce
1789 Montgomery St.
Oroville, CA 95965
(800) 655-2542
orovillechamber.net

Oroville State Wildlife Area
(530) 538-2236
wildlife.ca.gov/Lands/Places-to-Visit/
Oroville-WA

Pacific Gas & Electric Co. Recreation
(916) 386-5164 (campground
   reservations)
Recreation.pge.com

Placer County Bear River Park
   & Campground
(530) 886-4901

Plumas County Tourism Recreation
   and Hospitality Council
plumascounty.org

Plumas National Forest
Quincy, CA 95971
(530) 283-2050; (530) 534-6500
fs.usda.gov/main/plumas
Camping: (877) 444-6777; recreation
   .gov

Point Reyes National Seashore
Point Reyes Station, CA 94956-9799
(415) 464-5100
nps.gov/pore
Camping: (877) 444-6777

Point Reyes Outdoors
Point Reyes Station, CA 94956
(415) 663-8162
pointreyesoutdoors.com

Protect the American River Canyon
(PARC)
parc-auburn.org

ReserveAmerica
Camping reservations
(800) 444-7275
ReserveAmerica.com

Reserve California
State park camping reservations
ReserveCalifornia.com

River Journey—Rafting on the
   Stanislaus
Oakdale, CA 95361
(800) 292-2938
riverjourney.com

Russo's Marina
3995 Willow Rd.
Bethel Island, CA 94511
(925) 684-2024
russosmarina.com

Sacramento County American
   River Parkway
4040 Bradshaw Rd.
Sacramento, CA 95827
(916) 875-7275
regionalparks.saccounty.net/Parks

Sacramento County Sherman
   Island Park
(916) 875-6961
regionalparks.saccounty.net/Parks

Sacramento River National
   Wildlife Refuge
(530) 934-2801
fws.gov/refuge/sacramento

Sacramento State Aquatic Center
1901 Hazel Ave.
Rancho Cordova, CA 95670
(916) 278-2842
sacstateaquaticcenter.com

San Francisco Bay Area Water Trail
sfbaywatertrail.org

San Francisco Bay National Estuarine
   Research Reserve
sfbaynerr.org

Santa Clara County Lexington
   Reservoir
(408) 356-2729
Boat inspections: (408) 355-2201
sccgov.org/sites/parks/parkfinder/
   Pages/Lexington-Reservoir.aspx

Save the American River Association
4441 Auburn Blvd., Ste. H
Sacramento, CA 95841
(916) 482-2551
sarariverwatch.org

Scotty's Landing
12609 River Rd.
Chico, CA 95973-8911
scottysontheriver.com

Sea Trek Kayak & SUP
Sausalito, CA 94966
(415) 332-8494
seatrek.com

Shasta Cascade Wonderland Association
1699 Hwy. 275
Anderson, CA 96007
(530) 365-7500
shastacascade.com

Shasta-Trinity National Forests
210 Main St.
Weaverville, CA 96093
(530) 623-2121
fs.usda.gov/stnf

Shuttle Services
American River: (530) 303-2404;
   colomashuttle.com
Eel River: Rick Doty: (707) 926-5444
Trinity River: Bigfoot Rafting
   Company: (530) 629-2263; bigfoot
   rafting.com/shuttle.html
Carson River: Family Mountain
   Shuttle Service: (530) 694-2704

Sierra Outdoor Center
440 Lincoln Way
Auburn, CA 95603
(530) 885-1844

Six Rivers National Forest
1330 Bayshore Way
Eureka, CA 95501
(707) 442-1721
fs.usda.gov/srnf

Six Rivers National Forest
Lower Trinity Ranger District
Willow Creek, CA 95573
(503) 628-2118

Skunk Train—California Western
   Railroad
Fort Bragg, CA, and Willits, CA
(707) 964-6371
skunktrain.com

Sonoma Lake, US Army Corps
   of Engineers
3333 Skaggs Springs Rd.
Geyserville, CA 95441-9644
(707) 431-4533 (visitor center)
(707) 433-2200 (marina)
spn.usace.army.mil/Missions/
   Recreation/Lake-Sonoma

South Lake Tahoe Lakeside Beach
Lakeside Park Association
4077 Pine Blvd.
South Lake Tahoe, CA 96150
(530) 542-2314
lakesideparkassociation.org/beach/

South Lake Tahoe Visitor Information
South Lake Tahoe, CA
(530) 541-5255
tahoesbest.com

South Yuba River Citizens League
    (SYRCL)
(530) 265-5961
yubariver.org

State parks camping reservations
(800) 444-7275
ReserveAmerica.com

Sugar Barge Resort & Marina
1440 Sugar Barge Rd.
Bethel Island, CA 94511
(800) 799-4100
sugarbarge.com

Sunset Harbor
Bethel Island Rd.
Oakley, CA 94561
(925) 684-3522

Sunshine Rafting
(209) 848-4800; (800) 829-7238
raftadventure.com

Sycamore Grove Camping at Red Bluff
Diversion Dam
recreation.gov

Sycamore Ranch Park & Campground
(530) 749-5669
parks.yuba.org

Tahoe National Forest
American River Ranger District
(530) 367-2224
Camping: (877) 444-6777; recreation
    .gov

Tahoe National Forest
Truckee Ranger District
(530) 587-3558

Taylor Creek Visitor Center
(530) 543-2694

Tehama Colusa Canal Authority
tccanal.com/fishpassage.htm

Tehama County River Park at
    Woodson Bridge
(530) 528-1111
co.tehama.ca.us/tehama-county-river
-park

Thousand Trails and NACO
    Snowflower Camping Preserve
Emigrant Gap, CA 95715
(530) 389-8241
thousandtrails.com/getaways/
    california/snowflower.asp

Thunderbird Lodge Lake Tahoe
Thunderbird Preservation Society
PO Box 6812
Incline Village, NV 89450
(775) 832-8750
thunderbirdtahoe.org

Tidewater Boating Center and Martin
    Luther King Jr. Regional Shoreline
(510) 562-1373
ebparks.org/parks/martinlking

Tioga Lodge Mono Basin Kayak
    Rental
(760) 937-1934

Tomales Bay Resort
12938 Sir Francis Drake Blvd.
Inverness, CA 94937
(415) 669-1389
tomalesbayresort.com

Trinity County Chamber
    of Commerce
(530) 623-6101; (800) 487-4648
www.trinitycounty.com

Trinity River Restoration Program
    (TRRP)
Weaverville, CA
trrp.net

Truckee Donner Chamber
    of Commerce
(530) 587-8808
truckeechamber.com

Truckee River Raft Company
185 River Rd.
Tahoe City, CA 96145
(530) 583-0123
truckeeriverraft.com
Tuolumne River Trust
(209) 236-0330
tuolumne.org

Turlock Irrigation District for
    Hickman Spillway discharge
(209) 883-8222

US Army Corps of Engineers
Stanislaus River Parks
(209) 881-3517
spk.usace.army.mil/Locations/
    Sacramento-District-Parks/
    Stanislaus-River-Parks

Wild and Scenic Rivers
nps.gov/rivers/information.html

Wildlife of Suisun Marsh
Grizzly Island Wildlife Area
suisunwildlife.org/grizzly.html

Wimpy's Marina and Restaurant
(209) 794-2774
wimpysmarina.com

Yolo County Flood Control & Water
    Conservation District Field Office
Releases from Indian Valley Reservoir
    and Clear Lake to Cache Creek
(530) 662-0266

Yolo County Parks Department
120 W. Main St., Ste. C
Woodland, CA 95695
(530) 406-4880
yolocounty.org

Yuba County Parks
(530) 749-5420
parks.yuba.org

Appendix C: Further Reading

Arnot, Phil. *Point Reyes Secret Places & Magic Moments.* San Carlos, CA: World Wide Publishing/Tetra, 1993.

Ashley, Beth (text), and Hal Lauritzen (photography). *Marin.* San Francisco, CA: Chronicle Books, 1993.

Burch, David. *Fundamentals of Kayak Navigation,* 4th edition. Guilford, CT: Globe Pequot Press, 2008.

California Coastal Commission. *California Coastal Access Guide,* 6th edition. Oakland, CA: University of California Press, 2003.

Clark, Jeanne L. *California Wildlife Viewing Guide.* Helena, MT: Falcon Press, 1996.

Donnelly, Robin. *Biking and Hiking the American River Parkway,* 4th edition. The American River Natural History Association, 1996.

Dowd, John. *Sea Kayaking: A Manual for Long-Distance Touring,* 5th edition. Vancouver, BC: Douglas & McIntyre Division of Greystone Books LTD, 2004.

Gordon, Burton L. *Monterey Bay Area: Natural History and Cultural Imprints,* 3rd edition. Pacific Grove, CA: The Boxwood Press, 1995.

Hayes, Peter J. *The Lower American River: Prehistory to Parkway.* The American River Natural History Association, 2005.

Hutchinson, Derek C. *Expedition Kayaking,* 5th edition. Guilford, CT: Globe Pequot Press, 1999.

———. *The Complete Book of Sea Kayaking,* 5th edition. Guilford, CT, Globe Pequot Press, 2004.

Ingebritsen, S. E., and Marti E. Ikehara. *Sacramento–San Joaquin Delta: The Sinking Heart of the State.* US Geological Survey; pubs.usgs.gov/circ/circ1182/pdf/11Delta.pdf.

Jungers, Craig. "Rules of the Road," *Sea Kayaker* magazine. February 2009.

Least Wanted Aquatic Invaders for Elkhorn Slough and the Monterey Bay Area: A Guide for Recognizing and Reporting Potential Aquatic Invaders to Prevent Their Establishment and Spread. Sponsored by the Elkhorn Slough National Estuarine Research Reserve, Monterey Bay National Marine Sanctuary, California Sea Grant Program; September 2002.

Levene, Bruce, William Bradd, Lana Krasner, Gloria Petrykowski, and Rosalie Zucker. *Mendocino County Remembered—An Oral History.* Mendocino County, CA: The Mendocino County Historical Society, 1976.

Lower Sherman Island Wildlife Area Land Management Plan. Prepared for California Department of Fish and Game by EDAW, Sacramento, April 2007.

Lull, John. *Sea Kayaking Safety & Rescue.* Berkeley, CA: Wilderness Press, 2001.

McClurg, Sue. *Water & the Shaping of California.* Sacramento, CA: Water Education Foundation, 2000.

Meadows, Robin. *Gateway to the Delta.* Long Beach, CA: Bay Nature, 2012.

Schuman, Roger, and Jan Shriner. *Sea Kayaking Rescue: The Definitive Guide to Modern Reentry and Recovery Techniques,* 2nd edition. Guilford, CT: Globe Pequot Press, 2007.

———. *Guide to Sea Kayaking Central & Northern California,* 2nd edition. Guilford, CT: Globe Pequot Press, 2013.

Soares, Eric, and Michael Powers. *Extreme Sea Kayaking.* Camden, ME: Ragged Mountain Press, 1999.

Washburne, Randel. *The Coastal Kayaker's Manual,* 3rd edition. Guilford, CT: Globe Pequot Press, 1998.

Appendix D: California Paddling Organizations

American Canoe Association	americancanoe.org
American Rivers	americanrivers.org
American Whitewater	americanwhitewater.org
Bay Area Sea Kayakers (BASK)	bask.org
California Canoe & Kayak	calkayak.com
California Kayak Friends	ckfkayak.club
Explore North Coast Sea Kayakers Club	explorenorthcoast.net
Friends of the River	friendsoftheriver.org
Gold Country Paddlers	goldcountrypaddlers.org
Headwaters Kayak Shop & Boathouse	headwaterskayak.com
Lodi Paddle Club	meetup.com/Lodi-Paddle-Club
Loma Prieta Paddlers, Sierra Club RTS	lomaprietapaddlers.org
Mono Lake Committee	monolake.org
PaddlingCalifornia.com	paddlingcalifornia.com
POST Canoe Club	postcanoeclub.wordpress.com
River City Whitewater Club	rcwconline.com
Sacramento State Aquatic Center	sacstateaquaticcenter.com
SacYakkers	meetup.com/Sac-Yakkers
San Diego Kayak Club	sdkc.org
Sea Trek	seatrek.com
Sierra Club Angeles Chapter River Touring Section	angeles.sierraclub.org/river_touring
Sierra Club Redwood Chapter	sierraclub.org/redwood
Tuolumne River Trust	tuolumne.org
Sacramento Sea Kayakers	sskpc.org; meetup.com/Sacramento-Sea-Kayakers
Valley Wide Kayak Club	valleywidekayakclub.org
Western Sea Kayakers	westernseakayakers.org

Paddling Index

About the Author

For more than fifty years, **Charlie Pike** has enjoyed paddling wide rivers, lazy float streams, lakes big and small, roaring whitewater, tidal estuaries, and Pacific Coast headlands. While in college, the Appalachian Mountain Club introduced him to whitewater canoeing, starting with sliding canoes over the snow in March. Paddling soon became his passion. Wherever he has lived—upstate New York, New England, Missouri, Arkansas, or the West Coast—he has enjoyed paddling. In each location he has organized training sessions and paddling trips using whitewater kayaks, rafts, canoes, and sea kayaks. His paddling adventures have led him to enjoy waters as diverse as kayaking the Grand Canyon, floating the Allagash River in Maine, and canoeing 160 miles of the Stikine River in Alaska with his two grown sons.

The author stands beside the monument to Sir Francis Drake at Point Reyes National Seashore. A. J. PIKE

Before retiring, Charlie researched and developed water efficiency programs for local, state, and national water organizations. He is still looking for more paddling experiences to enjoy with his grandchildren.